CW00556417

HERTFORDSH
BELLFOUNDERS

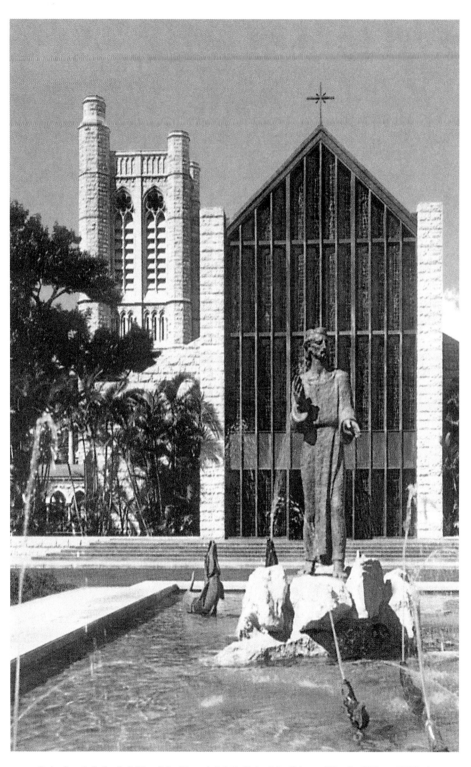

St Andrew's Cathedral, Honolulu. Ring of eight bells by John Briant of Hertford [*George W. Pipe*]

HERTFORDSHIRE
BELLFOUNDERS

JOYCE DODDS

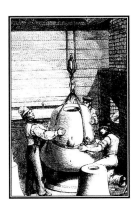

HERTFORDSHIRE PUBLICATIONS
an imprint of
University of Hertfordshire Press

First published in Great Britain in 2003 by
Hertfordshire Publications
an imprint of the
University of Hertfordshire Press
Learning and Information Services
University of Hertfordshire
College Lane
Hatfield
Hertfordshire AL10 9AB

Hertfordshire Publications, an imprint of the University of Hertfordshire Press,
is published on behalf of the Hertfordshire Association of Local History

British Library Cataloguing-in-Publication-Data.
A catalogue record for this book is available from the British Library.

ISBN 0 9542189 1 4

Frontispiece: St Andrew's Cathedral, Honolulu. Ring of eight bells by John Briant of Hertford
(see pp. 263–6) [G. W. Pipe]

Front cover: bell casting past and present at the Whitechapel Bell Foundry.
Photograph by Maxine Trick www.trickphotography.co.uk

Design by Geoff Green, Cambridge CB4 5RA.
Cover design by John Robertshaw, Harpenden AL5 2JB
Printed in Great Britain by Antony Rowe Ltd. Chippenham SN14 6LH

CONTENTS

LIST OF FIGURES

LIST OF MAPS

FOREWORD

T HIS STUDY BEGAN as a spin-off from the research carried out by
Geoffrey Dodds and myself while preparing *Church Bells of Hertfordshire*
between 1988 and 1994. My own interest had been aroused in 1948 when I
began to learn to ring at St Mary's, Hemel Hempstead. From the start I was
more interested in what was on the other end of the rope than in what I
was supposed to be doing with it! It was the ideal place to look at bells,
nothing younger than 1767, the frame of 1759, easy to climb round compared with its 1951 replacement. Two bells in particular caught my eye. Both
were cast by Robert Oldfield, one in 1617 and the other in 1633, but no two
bells could have been more different. That of 1633 was plain, sober and
unadorned; that of 1617 decorated with cresting, ornate lettering and even
a plaited border above the lip. What kind of man could produce two such
dissimilar artefacts? Forty years later came the opportunity to find out. As
Oldfield's geographical range was limited, all of his bells could be examined in detail, and being easily the best-documented of the earlier
founders, he emerges from the shadows as a fully-rounded personality,
warts and all.

Then came a hint – I dare not call it an order! – that it would be a good
idea to take in John Briant as well. Herbert C. Andrews' excellent pioneering
biography, the first ever produced about a bellfounder, was published in
1930 and formed a basis from which to work. After seventy years much had
become out-of-date, so I have gone back to original sources. Also, much
more is now in the public domain in various County Record Offices, but
even so, it is still a wide field.

So the work has expanded to take in all the known Hertfordshire
founders. They were a mixed bag, good, bad and indifferent, a cross-section
of humanity ranging in time from the Dissolution of the Monasteries to the
very dawn of the Railway Age, which could form a sub-title for the whole
work. Some were natives of the county; most came in from outside, but
there is a thread of continuity linking them all together. They either *knew*
each other or knew *of* each other, witness John Briant's reference to Richard
Keene's misfortunes of 150 years earlier, long ago, but still remembered.
One or two were known to the law. There was even a murderer among them!
Several churches have two or even three of their bells: Ardeley with bells by
Dier and Oldfield; Therfield with bells by Dier, Oldfield and Waylett; Offley

with examples from Dier, Oldfield and Briant. In nearly every case, their works have outlasted them.

With the exception of John Briant, their actual words have not come down to us; the evidence of their activities is purely circumstantial but there is sufficient of it to show what must have happened, what they must have done, or must have had to do, in certain situations. Human character has not changed significantly over 400 years so in some cases I have applied the test – what would any reasonable man do now, in the twenty-first century, under the same circumstances? The answer is – exactly what was done in 1557 or 1700 or whenever. They were not some strange species, but normal, and on the whole sensible, *modern* human beings in their own day.

My aim from the beginning has been to tell what is known of the life stories of a varied group of Hertfordshire craftsmen in a way that will be of as much interest to local historians as to bellringers of an archeological turn of mind. The long (and perhaps tedious) cataloguing of bells is necessary because it has not previously been attempted, except in the case of Andrews' life of John Briant. All the lists can be extracted from earlier publications, such as County Bell Histories, but there has been no overall correlation as I have tried to do. Only when *all* the bells by all the founders are added together does a picture begin to emerge of the truly vast number of bells which have emanated from a county which is not famous as being a centre of bellfounding.

What was the criterion for a Hertfordshire bellfounder? Under that definition I have included only those men who are known or can be assumed on good grounds to have both lived and worked within the county for however short a period, but have excluded known itinerants who briefly passed through without settling.

In the lists of bells cast by each founder, bells no longer extant are shown in italics and the numbers on the right are the pattern of moulding wires where known (see Fig.1, p. xiv).

SOURCES

The main sources of information are from the published volumes of County Histories many of which came out in the mid-to-late nineteenth and early twentieth centuries.

Bells

Church Bells of Bedfordshire T. North 1883 (CB Beds.)
Church Bells of Berkshire F. Sharpe, 2nd edition 1939–1970 (CB Berks.)
Church Bells of Buckinghamshire A.H. Cocks 1897 (CB Bucks.)
Church Bells of Cambridgeshire Canon J.J. Raven 1861 1897 (J.J. raven.)
Church Bells of Devon Revd H.T. Ellacombe 1872 (CB Devon)
The Bells and Belfries of Dorset, Part 1 C. Dalton 2000
Church Bells of Essex Revd C. Deedes and H.B. Walters 1909 (CB Essex)
Church Bells of Hertfordshire T. North and J.C.L. Stahlschmidt 1886 (N & S)
Church Bells of Hertfordshire G. Dodds 1994 (Dodds, CB Herts.)
Church Bells of Kent J.C.L. Stahlschmidt 1887 (CB Kent)
Church Bells of Leicestershire T. North 1876 (CB Leics.)
Church Bells of Lincolnshire T North 1882 (CB Lincs.)
Church Bells of Lincolnshire Dr J.R. Ketteringham 2000 (Lincs. K 2000)
Church Bells of Nottinghamshire G.A. Dawson (CB Notts.)
Church Bells of Oxfordshire F. Sharpe 1949–1953 (CB Oxon.)
Church Bells of Shropshire H.B. Walters 1915 (CB Salop)
Surrey Bells and London Bell-Founders J.C.L. Stahlschmidt 1884 (CB Surrey)
Sussex Bells and Belfries G.P. Elphick 1970 (CB Sussex)
Church Bells of Warwickshire Preb H.T. Tilley and H.B. Walters 1910
(CB Warks.)
Peterborough Diocesan Guild of Church Bell Ringers Inventory 1989 (PBG. Dir.)
Dove's Guide for Church Bell Ringers, various editions, 1950–2000
(Dove's Guide)

General information

Hertfordshire Archives and Local Studies, Hertford (HALS)
Hertford Museum
Museum of St Albans

St Albans City Library
North Devon Record Office, Barnstaple   (North Devon RO)
Leicester Record Office
I should like to record my gratitude to the staff of all the above for so much
assistance so readily given.

The Ringing World, Official Journal of the Central Council of
      Church Bell Ringers.   (RW)
The Craft of the Bellfounder George P. Elphick   (Phillimore 1988)
Musical Handbells William Butler   (Phillimore 2000)
The History and Art of Change Ringing Ernest Morris
                                 (Chapman & Hall 1931)
Master of My Art: the Taylor Bellfoundries 1784–1957 Trevor S. Jennings
British and Irish Chime Barrel mechanisms Trevor S. Jennings
International Genealogical Index   (IGI)

Hertfordshire Local History

John Briant Herbert C. Andrews, M.A.
      (East Herts. Archeological Society 1930)   (HCA)
The Inns of Hertford Vol.II, Chap.IV, by A. Baker.
      (Unpublished MS in Hertford Museum)
History of Hertford Dr F.M. Page   (Hertford Town Council 1959)
Hertfordshire's Past No. 32, Spring 1992.
      'Robert Oldfield, Bell Founder of Hertford'   Eileen Lynch
Tudor Churchwardens' Accounts ed. Anthony Palmer
      pub. Hertfordshire Record Society 1985   (Tudor C/W Accts.)

3

ACKNOWLEDGMENTS

M Y SPECIAL THANKS are due to Jean Sanderson of Haslingfield for access to her private library as well as for much useful Cambridgeshire material and to Alan G. Greening of Hertford for allowing the use of his extensive researches into Hertford Corporation Records (HCR) which list many details of the life of Robert Oldfield in his *other* role as an alehouse keeper. Alan Greening's talk on *Law and Disorder in Seventeenth Century Hertford*, given to members of the Hertfordshire Association of Local History Societies was a classic of its kind, informative and amusing and richly deserves publication.

Other kind friends without whose help this study could not have been written are, in alphabetical order:

Ranald W.M. Clouston (died 2002) for his unrivalled collection of material on Suffolk bells (RWMC)

George A. Dawson for information on the origins and early career of Richard Holdfeld and Robert Oldfield and updated information on Leicestershire bells (GAD)

Dr John C. Eisel, Hon. Librarian, Central Council of Church Bell Ringers for information on John Briant

Robin H. Harcourt-Williams, Archivist and Librarian, Hatfield House, for details of Briant tenancies

Alan Hughes of Whitechapel Bell Foundry for foundry photographs.

Roger I. Kendrick for his incredibly detailed photographs and rubbings of the Dier bells at Hulcote, Beds.

Valerie Payne, Hon. Librarian, Middlesex County Association for details of bells by James Butler and William Whitmore

A.J. (Jim) Phillips, Hon. Librarian of the Ancient Society of College Youths for research into John Briant's membership of the Society

Christopher J. Pickford for giving up so much of his time to produce updated and hitherto unpublished information on both John Dier's and John Briant's Bedfordshire bells and the latter's Warwickshire bells (CJP)

George W. Pipe for permission to use his photographs of Honolulu Cathedral and St Alkmund's, Shrewsbury

Richard Sales, Hon. Librarian, the Hertford County Association for allowing so many books to be borrowed at one time and for so long a period; also for his help in examining bells by Oldfield and others   (RS)

David Sloman for information on John Waylett in London

Robert F. Walker for information on Cambridgeshire bells by Dier, Waylett and Briant

Anne Willis of Bradford-on-Avon for the discovery of a St Albans bell-founder

Doreen and Wally Wright of Bishop's Stortford Museum. Also many others who have added snippets of information which, however small, have helped to throw light in obscure places.

Geoffrey Dodds, last but not least, for proof reading, general editing and sorting out occasional nightmarish computer problems with the elderly Acorn Archimedes.

All illustrations are by the author except where individually acknowledged. My grateful thanks to them all.

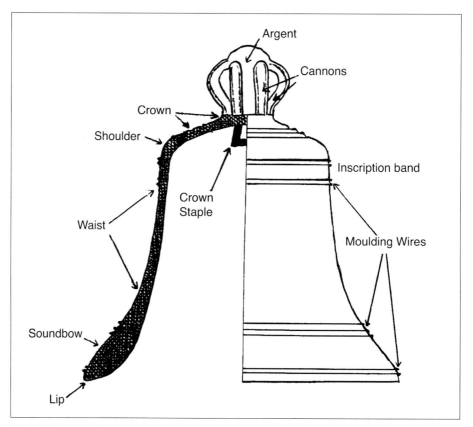

Fig. 1 The parts of a bell

LIST OF SUBSCRIBERS

R. Adam, Stevenage

A. F. Alldrick, Abbots Langley

John D. Allison, Hoddesdon

Michael Allsopp of Grendon, Warwickshire

The Ancient Society of College Youths

ANZAB Library, Australia

Geoff Armitage M.B.H.I., Husbands
  Bosworth

M. A. Atkins, Hunsdon

Richard and Rhiannon Atkins, Barkway

George H. Austin, Hatfield

David and Joan Badger, South Mymms

Dave Bailey, Wheathampstead

John and Beryl Baldwin, Llandaff

Liz Barber, St Albans

Bernard S. Barnaby, Ware

J. H. W. Beardwell, Radlett

George Bennett, Sawbridgeworth

Berry and Co., Malvern

E. Geoffrey Beynon, Welwyn Garden City

R. K. Bickerton, Watford

Bishop's Stortford and District Local History
  Society

Frank and Monica Blagrove, Windsor

J. S. Bonnington, St Albans

Nina Bradley, St Albans

Mrs D. A. Brown, Buntingford

Roger D. R. Brown, St Albans

Rupert Burgess, York

Bushey Bellringers, Bushey

Richard Butler, St Albans

William Butler, Thatcham

Mrs M. and Mr C. J. Carter, Stevenage

C. M. Carter, Harpenden

Cecil, Lord and Lady Charles, Hatfield

Cecil, Lord and Lady Michael, Lawn House,
  Hatfield

The Central Council of Church Bell Ringers
  Library, Ullingswick

Ian Chandler, Ashwell, Herts.

Church Green Books, Witney

Anthony E. H. Clayton, Nottingham

Fraser Clift, Kemsing

Leslie and Amy Coburn, Harpenden

Diane Cox, Bishop's Stortford

Elizabeth J. Cranfield, Hitchin, Herts

Michael and Sara Cranfield, Hitchin

Stephen Crawley, Hemel Hempstead

R. J. Crocker, Kimpton

Adam Crocker, Kimpton

Peter Dalling, North Mymms

Christopher Dalton, Ullingswick

John David, Guernsey

Margaret Davies, St Albans

Owen Davis, Bedford

George A. Dawson, Willoughby on the
  Wolds, Nottinghamshire

Lionel A. Devonish, Potters Bar

Reg Dixon, Tower Captain, Saint Mary the
  Virgin, High Easter

G. A. Duke, St Albans

R. Durrant, Hoddesdon

Peter Dyson, Poynton

John Eisel, Ullingswick

Alan F. Ellis, British Columbia, Canada

Alison and Neil Evans, St Albans

Brian Evans, Norton (Letchworth Garden City)

Chris Forster, Stevenage

Martin Foster, Ewyas Harold

Mike Franklin, Ware

John E. Freeman, Sandridge

H. V. Frost, Milford-on-Sea

Reverend Canon Barry J. Fry, Southampton

D. M. Gambling, Hemel Hempstead

Diana Goodwin, Essendon

Geoffrey Green, Swavesey

Pam Green, Buntingford

David Gregory, Welwyn Garden City

Catherina Griffiths, St Neots

John Haas, Kimbolton, Cambs.

Stuart Hale, Measham

Diana Handley, Kendal

Deryck E. Hannaford, St Albans

Robert E. Hardy, Cardiff

Peter Harper, Codicote

David and Jeanette Harris, Hertford

James and Sarah Hedgcock, Rushden

Neal Henderson, St Albans

D. M. Hibbert, Rickmansworth

Matthew Higby, Chilcompton

Clare Higby, Chilcompton

Christopher Higgins, Godmanchester

Michael C. Homans, Salford Priors, Warks.

Kevin Horan, Sandridge

R. Hornby, Buntingford

Geoff and Margaret Horritt, Royston

Russ Huddleston, Cheltenham

Alan Hughes, Whitechapel Bell Foundry

Nicholas D Hughes, Bishop's Stortford

The Hughes-D'Aeth Family, St Albans

Brian Hullah, Shouldham, Norfolk

Pauline and Paul Hurford, St Albans

A. J. Illingworth, Monks Kirby

Trevor S. Jennings, Loughborough

Ronald Johnston, Salisbury

Martin Jones, St Peter's Church, Colchester,

H. Charles Jordan, Much Hadham

Allan G. Keen

Dave Kelly, Corsham

John Kemp, Hertford

Roger I. Kendrick, Luton

Edmund King, St Albans

David Kingman, Rothwell

David Kingstone, St Albans

David Kirkcaldy, Polegate

Edgar Lake, Hertford

Langleybury Bellringers

Algy Lawrence, St Albans

Keith Lewin, Luton

John P. Loveless, Campton

Alan J. Luxford, Bushey

Alison Macfarlane, St Albans

Barry D. Mack, Welwyn Garden City

Nicholas Maddex, Codicote

Marquess of Salisbury, Hatfield House

The Middlesex County Association and London Diocesan Guild of Church Bell Ringers

R. J. Moore, St Albans

Guy and Sue Morton, Bushey

Museum of St Albans

M. R. Newbold, Hertford

Reverend Dr. Peter Newing, Bromesberrow

C. C. Nicholson, Hatfield

John Nicholson, Hatfield

C. Mark G. Ockelton, Whitby

C. Michael Orme, Congleton

Robert Owen, St Albans

Oxford Diocesan Guild

G. Penning, Barkway

Liz Perry, Broxbourne

Chris Pickford

Julian G Plante, Shoreview, Minnesota, USA

Charles Pocock, Harpenden

David Potter, York

Dick Prime, Bishop's Stortford

Radlett Belfry

John Rank, Hunsdon Church

George Reading, Redbourn

Beverley Reid, Datchworth

David Reidy, Coulsdon

Laith R. Reynolds, Kalamunda, Western Australia

The Richard Hale Association

Bill Ridgman, Cambridge

Christopher Ridley, New Malden

Peter Rivet, Lancaster

Judith Roberts, Watton-at-Stone

Professor Elizabeth Robson, Richmond

K. M. Sanders, Ware

Shane Saunders, Peterborough

R. C. Sayers, Cheshunt

Peter G. Scott, Great Stanmore

Keith W. Scudamore, Bristol

Roger D. Shepherd, St Albans

R. Simmons, Redditch

Neil Skelton, Salisbury

David Sloman, Rochford

Arnold J. Smith, Sheffield

Anthony P. Smith, Winchester

Matthew Smith, Sawley, Long Eaton

Ray Smith, Watford

W. J. Southam, St Albans

John R. Southey, Aldenham

Saint Andrew's Ringing Society, Honolulu, Hawaii, USA

St Albans Cathedral Society of Change Ringers

Andrew and Caroline Stevens, Swavesey, Cambridgeshire

Swan Bells Foundation, Perth, Western Australia

Hugh Thomas, Rickmansworth

Chris and Carol Tough, Carmarthen

The Tower of St. Lawrence the Martyr, Abbots Langley

The Tower of St. Michael's, Bishop's Stortford

Yvonne A. Towler, Inworth

Colin Turner, Milton, Oxon

R. F. Walker, Cambridge

Clarke Walters, Monks Kirby

Brian Watson, Hemel Hempstead

Michael V. White, St Ives, Cambs.

Jenny Whitlock, St Albans

Philip R. Wild, Gedling, Nott's

Anne Willis, Bradford on Avon

Richard Wilsher, Ware

Kay Wood, Luton

Daphne Wright, Therfield

The York Minster Society of Change Ringers

The Yorkshire Association of Change Ringers

PART I

HERTFORDSHIRE
BEFORE
1600

─────────────────────────

AND
THREE ELIZABETHAN BELLFOUNDERS

1

BELLFOUNDING BEFORE 1500

BELLS WERE KNOWN to have existed in pre-Conquest England, although none in Hertfordshire have been identified as coming from such an early period. The earliest documentary evidence of bells in the county records that they were, not surprisingly, cast for the new Benedictine Abbey of St Alban, where there were four bells in the years between 1077 and 1093, augmented to five between 1214 and 1235. Who cast them? Nobody knows; they may have been cast by 'the monks', which is the standard answer, although how many monks had the necessary heavy metalworking skills? It is much more likely that specialist bellfounders existed from very early times, men who moved around from job to job as required, making use of such local labour as could be found and, if the local labourer happened to be a Lay Brother, therein lay the foundation of that hoary tradition!

Early bell-founding techniques differed from those used in, for example, the fifteenth century, in that wax rather than clay (or *loam*, to use the correct founder's term) models were used. In the case of small bells, the core was built up of loam on a turned wooden centre then carefully shaped, either by a pivoted board or a radius rod. For larger bells, the core would have been constructed from brick or tiles covered with a layer of loam, which was carefully profiled. The model bell was then built up on the core in wax, the exact composition of which varied, being a mixture of wax and tallow. After the model had received its finishing touches the cope, or outer section of the mould was built up from loam, reinforced with strips of coarse fabric, probably sacking. The mould was gently heated and the wax was run off. When all the loam was completely dry, a bell-shaped gap between the core and cope was left, ready for the metal to be poured in. The lost wax process was of very great antiquity, being known in Egypt by about 2600 BC. This whole sequence was usually carried out in a pit, thus allowing the mould to be filled by gravity. Charcoal, preferably beechwood, was the fuel used as it could easily produce the required temperature of 1200°C for melting the bell metal which is an alloy of ten parts of copper to three parts of tin.

The remains of a bell-pit at Chichester dating from some time between 1088-1100, were found on excavation to contain microscopic traces of wax. Mass spectrum analysis of these traces showed that the greater part of the wax was hard and of animal origin, probably from a member of the dolphin family, Chichester being, of course, much closer to the sea than St Albans, making the use of marine animal products easier. The provision of bells for both these great churches was almost contemporary. No excavations at St Albans have revealed remains of bell-pits but it is thought that a foundry existed on the north side of the Abbey, close to the Waxhouse Gate, which appears to have had a series of temporary buildings used as the 'Clerk of Works' Department.' However, as the site is partly built-up, it is unlikely to be investigated.

One bell of unquestionably monastic origin was at the Priory of St Mary at Hertford, a cell of St Albans, established at some time between 1086 and 1093, where excavations have uncovered the site of a bell-pit dating from about the fourteenth century. The site (*TL 328129*), excavated between August 1988 and July 1989, had been a timber yard which was sold for residential development. The Priory site also contained traces of the church of St John, which was either the parochial section of the Priory or remains of an earlier building. An excellent account of the investigations on the site by Hester Cooper-Reade are included in *Hertfordshire's Past*, No 29, Autumn 1990. The pit appears to have been close to the west end of St John's, although it is unfortunately not marked on the site map. R.T. Andrews, who carried out limited excavations in 1893, believed that the church had a central tower, whereas Hester Cooper-Reade believes that the siting of the pit suggested a west tower. The actual pit is in the shape of an ovoid, 1 m deep and 2.2 m long, containing a single central flue 0.2 m deep. This furnace was used to cast 'a circular object 0.6 m in diameter, the rim of which had left an impression in the burnt clay on the bottom of the feature' – in other words, a bell of 24 inches diameter. The present writer is not aware of any other bell-pit being found in the county, although an excavation in the churchyard at Ashwell might prove profitable, as a bell was cast there in 1571–2. Whether the Hertford founder was a local man or was called in from elsewhere is not known.

Major foundries sprang up close to large monastic sites such as Bury St Edmunds but this never happened at St Albans, probably because of its proximity to London. Certainly by the fourteenth century, bellfoundries were to be found in the important cities: London, Bristol, Norwich and York, for example. In London, they became organised into a Bellmakers' Guild and established a tradition which lasted for two hundred years, combining the casting of bells, metal pots and, by the sixteenth century, guns; bell-metal and gun-metal being very similar alloys. The vast majority of medieval bells in Hertfordshire are of London origin.

There were small local foundries but they were few in number, compared with their rapid expansion in the sixteenth century. The nearest to Hertfordshire was at Toddington, Beds., where John Rufford worked c.1370 and William, possibly a son, worked c.1390. Five bells from this foundry are still extant in the county, but none was actually cast here. Another comparatively small foundry was at Wokingham, Berks., which sent only one surviving bell to Bushey c.1450.

The old church at Bishop's Stortford was destroyed, probably by fire, in 1440 and there is a blank in the churchwardens' accounts from then until 1479 when the rebuilding was apparently nearing completion. A new ring of five bells had been cast in 1439, by whom is not recorded, and these had presumably been lost. In 1493, the churchwardens visited Reignold Chirche of Bury St Edmunds to order a replacement set of five. This argues that there was either no founder at work locally or that the Bury foundry had the best reputation.

The oldest bell in the county is the blank treble of two at St Mary's, Shephall, Stevenage, dateable by its long-waisted shape to about 1130. It appears to have hung at Shephall ever since. The next oldest, also blank, is the Priest's bell at St Albans Abbey, dating from approximately 1290, followed by an extremely interesting bell at Clothall inscribed + ᙅᙏᒪ I ᙎ : ᙏᙒ I Oᒪ ᙏ ᙏᙒ Whether this is English or Latin is debatable, as the L is inverted and may in fact be a damaged T but it may either be translated as JOHN CAST ME, as thought by Stahlschmidt, or I AM CALLED JOHN. Deedes and Walters in *CB Essex*, p. 6, compare this bell with two at Rawreth, Essex, which they believe were cast by John de Hadham, who worked in London from 1330–39. By his name he could have been of Hertfordshire origin. Certainly the Clothall bell dates from this period, before the change-over between Lombardic and black letter usage in about 1400. One of the most striking differences between the Shephall bell and those at the Abbey and Clothall is in physical shape; Shephall treble is shaped like an elongated flower-pot, very tall in relation to its diameter, whereas the Abbey and Clothall bells are recognisably 'bell-shaped' to modern eyes.

At some uncertain date, founders began to change from using a wax model to one of loam or clay, possibly because it was a cheaper alternative or more readily available. It made little real difference to the basic three-fold process of core, model and cope. Decorations and inscriptions were still made of wax and applied to the model – as they are on the Continent to this day.

During the later fourteenth and early fifteenth centuries, founders became *people*, in the sense that they began to be known by name and identifiable by trademarks. Medieval founders' marks are a study in themselves and there are problems of just who used which mark or shield at any given time as, being portable, they were passed on from one man to another or, even more frustratingly, lost for years and then reused by someone with no connection with the original user. This has led historians to expend much time, effort and ink in trying to explain how the later man obtained the stamp. A more prosaic reason could be that the later man was recasting an earlier bell and simply liked the look of the stamp or design. This will also be encountered later when Robert Oldfield recast an early fifteenth century bell and reused some of the capital letters; when William Whitmore recast the bells of Waltham Abbey and when John Briant, in his turn, recast Whitmore's bells, incorporating the head of King Edward III. Which of these two men was responsible for its use?

Until the religious upheavals of the early sixteenth century, bellfounding went on smoothly; Latin was the usual language for inscriptions which often bore the names of saints, Mary, Anne and John being the most commonly used. Then came the quarrel between Henry VIII and the Pope, the Dissolution of the Monasteries and the overthrow of the Old Faith. Not only the religious life but the political life of the country was changed completely and bellfounders had to change as well. No more Latin; no more saints' names. There were ways round these petty prohibitions; the Watts of Bedford and Leicester inscribed their bells with letters of the alphabet, albeit very elegant Lombardic letters, while one man whose bells are found in Hertfordshire, Buckinghamshire and Oxfordshire solved the problem by putting on what can only be described in modern terms as gobbledegook, a curious mixture of inverted letters, crosses and crowns, thus very carefully disguising his identity. (He may, of course, have been illiterate). Three of his bells are to be found at Clothall, Newnham and Norton. Frederick Sharpe in *CB Oxon.* thought he may have been one of the Appowell family of Buckingham, in which case he was probably not illiterate, but just cautious. John Saunders of Reading, a friend of Appowell, had his ears cropped for using Popish inscriptions; it paid to be careful.

It must not be forgotten that Latin usage in church came naturally to the older generation and during the reign of Mary it surfaced again, to be gradually replaced by English and for the saints' names to be replaced by those of the founders. It is only after the suppression of religious houses that the first unquestionably local founder can be identified. His name was John Clarke and he lived at Datchworth.

2

JOHN CLARKE I
OF DATCHWORTH 1557–62

UNTIL 1910 the 5th bell at Braughing was the oldest dated bell in the county. In that year it became cracked and was recast by Mears & Stainbank. The very interesting inscription was not reproduced, a sadly common feature of early twentieth century bellfoundry practice.

The old inscription read:

(crown)   i c

1 5 62

(inscription band)   deus in adiutrin meu in tende

with the 'uir' reversed, 'r' inverted and 'm's omitted. It was probably meant to read :

deus in adiutorium meum intende – *Haste thee, O God to deliver me*, the first part of the first verse of Psalm 70, as translated by Miles Coverdale in 1535. This plaintive text must have had some deep personal significance either for the donor or the founder; Mary had been dead for about four years and Elizabeth I had succeeded to the throne. Was the donor (or founder) a Recusant? In those turbulent times it was quite possible, but we shall never know.

The knowledge we have of the first named Hertfordshire founder comes in a roundabout way. There was a small Augustinian Priory at Little Wymondley, close to Hitchin, which had been founded between 1203 and 1207 and suppressed in 1536. Four bells were cast, or recast, almost immediately before the Dissolution and were therefore in mint condition. In 1538, James Nedeham, Surveyor of the King's Works, who had cast covetous eyes over this House, appropriated it and modernised it for his own dwelling, leaving intact substantial parts of the original thirteenth century buildings. In anticipation of bountiful harvests to come, he also built a huge barn, still extant, dated by dendrochronology to 1539. As he had no use for the bells, these went to the Augmentation Office (the Government Department responsible for property disposal) at some date between 1536 and 1544, the year Nedeham died, not having had long enjoyment of his ill-gotten gains.

A letter from David Bagley of Malvern Link, Worcs. published in the *Ringing World* 19 July 1985 quoting Public Record Office Ref. SC6/7432 M72, said that the eight bells from Great Malvern Priory had been sold to Watton-at-Stone in 1541. This apparently unrelated fact hints that confiscated bells were held there in what may have been a Government store until such time as use was found for them. This, or somewhere similar, could well have been the destination of the Wymondley bells before they were sold to Graveley in or before 1557.

In that year, the good people of Graveley began to suspect that they had been cheated. They had paid for 24 cwt of bell metal and the feeling grew that the Office had grossly overcharged them. So they took action and consulted a local bellfounder, John Clarke.

Among Land Revenue papers preserved by the County Record Office in Hertford is a certificate, the relevant parts of which read:

> The s'tificat of the weyght of the iiij bells of Graveley sum tyme be longyng to the Priore of Wymū delay pua mad by Edward Brokett & Edward Pult' ye xxvj day of Maii a^o dni m^{l}v^{c}lvij.

> The weyght of the said iiij bells by estimacion of a bell funder woos name is Clarke dwellyng at Thesthewurth in the Count' of Hertf with the hole a sent of the said pishe dowth wey xviij hundryth weyght & that is with the most.

This was signed and attested by the Rector of Graveley, the Churchwardens and all who could write or make their mark. Their suspicion was probably correct and they *had* been overcharged but there is nothing whatever recorded of the result of their petition!

This is the first written information about a genuine Hertfordshire founder. The bare facts only are known; he lived at Thesthewurth, now known as Datchworth and he cast at least one bell which lasted long enough to be recorded by North in 1883–6. His total output of bells is not known; no more have been identified. Whether he was connected in any way with a George (?) Clarke said by Raven to have cast a bell or bells for Duxford, Cambridgeshire, in 1564 is uncertain. He was old enough to be familiar with Latin church texts, is known to have been living in Datchworth as late as 1572–82, was married and a son, John II, was baptised there in 1575. The fact of his being described as a founder in 1557 suggests that he was of adult age, possibly being born in the late 1520s or early 1530s while the birth of a son as late as 1575 gives the impression of a late, or even a second marriage.

This son also became a founder, but it is unlikely that he cast bells in Hertfordshire; most of his bells are in Essex, with the exception of one at Eastwick, right on the Essex border. By the distribution of his bells John Clarke II was itinerant, as they can be found as far afield as Buckinghamshire, Hampshire, Sussex and Suffolk among other places. He was, however, the first Hertfordshire founder whose place and date of birth are recorded; the origins of no other founder except Robert Oldfield and John Briant can be given with any degree of certainty. There is strong circumstantial evidence that he knew John Dier of Hitchin. The Hitchin foundry, which has never been given the recognition it deserved, seems to have been in the hands successively of John Grene and John Dier, although its site has not been identified.

3

JOHN GRENE 1571–75

J OHN GRENE PROBABLY learned his trade with John Clarke as the two were contemporary, his latest surviving bell being cast in the year that Clarke's son was born. Grene's bells are now classed as rare, only three remaining, but these are sufficient to show that he was a very able founder indeed. Where he originated nobody knows and, with so common a surname, it would be like looking for the proverbial needle in a haystack. He must have been semi-itinerant as of his existing bells two are in Huntingdonshire and one is in Essex. (Itinerant is a term which must be used with care; the late nineteenth century bell historians used it as a shorthand way of saying 'we don't know where his foundry was, so he was probably itinerant'!) Other bells known to have been cast by him were at Ashwell, Harpenden and, by implication, Kimbolton (*Map 2. p. 17*). This distribution suggests that his base was at or near Hitchin, the bell at Elsenham being at one extremity about 25 miles, with Kimbolton at 30 miles away at the other.

The writer has seen all three bells by Grene and they are good clean castings, with their inscriptions in a very neat black letter font. These appear to have been cut out of thin parchment or wax sheet and were laid directly on to the inscription band without any pateræ, egg white being the normal adhesive. There is no sign of any use of letters cast in moulds. The sizes vary, not just between different bells, but also within one inscription, showing that each letter was cut as required. This would support the theory that Grene was a part-time bellfounder; a full-timer would be likely to have used ready-made letter moulds. Another idiosyncrasy was that letters with several 'legs' such as m or n were built up from as many units as necessary. Even more striking is the fact that Grene used two varieties of a, one a normal black-letter and the other, a, broader and straight-sided, with only a vestigial cross-bar. This is the same feature which so excited George Elphick when he discovered it on the mid-sixteenth century London-cast bell at Little Hadham, where one a belonged to the Aldgate founders' set and another to the Whitechapel set. The fact that John Dier also used two forms of a implies that it was more common than has hitherto been recognised. Another fact which must be taken into account is that Grene and Dier, who was definitely settled in Hitchin in later life, both used the capital ℑ from the same font, thus strengthening the probability that for some period these two men also worked together. The J was not used in medieval times, in either upper or

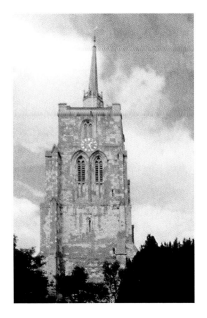

Ashwell St Mary the Virgin. John Greene
cast a bell in the churchyard. Also, bells
were cast by Richard Holdfeld and existing
bells by John Briant.

lower case, the I serving for both sounds, but by the
mid-sixteenth century it had become desirable to
make a distinction and, with no precedent, variety
was inevitable. Grene's version was particularly
fanciful.

In contrast to his neat lettering, Grene's numerals
were very indeterminate in shape, like those of Dier
on his early bells. Although Arabic numerals had
been in use in England since at least 1494, the date
carved on Monken Hadley tower, one is left with the
impression that men still preferred to use the more
familiar Roman figures until about the turn of the
century, when they finally went out of fashion. Fashion is, in fact, the only word to use in this context. It
forms an interesting exercise to compare the dates on
bells with contemporary dates on tomb slabs. The
degree of similarity is very noticeable, from the early
seventeenth to late eighteenth centuries.

The earliest written record of John Grene can be
found in the churchwardens' accounts at Ashwell for
the years 1571–2, during what seems to have been a
never-ending programme of restoration of the
church; the bells were a very small part of these
works.

The relevant entries are :

Item paid for makyng of a obligacion			vi*d*
Item paid for a horse to fetch cley at Hertford			x*d*
Item paid to father Webb for fylling the place where the bell was cast			iiii*d*
Item paid to Grene for castyng of the bell	iii£	vis	iii*d*

All so beautifully clear; 6d for a bond, or guarantee that the bell would
last for a year and a day; clay carted all the way from Hertford, as the local
Gault contained too much chalk, causing it to turn into a milky porridge
when wet; making the mould and 'castyng of' the bell; the old man, probably
the gravedigger, filling in the bell-pit and, last but not least, after a decent
interval, the payment of Grene's charges. This is typical; the founder, however hardup, had to wait for the expiry of the guarantee; he was always paid
last.

Chronological list of bells by John Grene

1. *1571 ASHWELL, Herts. St Mary the Virgin.*
    Recast, by any one of Richard Holdfeld, 1599/1607, Miles Graye I, 1610 or
    Charles Newman, 1694. No physical data known, nor is its position in the ring,
    as all carried out recasting work in the tower at the above dates.

2. *1571 HARPENDEN, Herts. St Nicholas Old 3rd of 5*
    In multis anis Resonat Clampana Johanis 1571
    Diameter 35½"
    This must have been a recast of a bell with a standard medieval inscription
    which could, of course, equally be applied to John Grene himself. It is a remark-
    ably early example of reproducing an inscription.
    Recast by J. Warner & Sons, London 1898.

3. 1571 KIMBOLTON, Cambs. St Andrew   3rd, formerly 2nd of 5
    His tribus hanc formam Grenns dedit arte ioanes 1571
    Diameter 36"   Weight 7¾ cwt   Note A♭
    (TO THESE THREE [BELLS] JOHN GRENE GAVE THIS FORM BY HIS SKILL)
    This was Grene's most ambitious inscription plainly stating that three
    bells were cast. Both forms of a were used, hanc and arte having the
    normal form, while formam and ioanes have the straight-sided variety.
                                      Dodds/ J. Haas

4,5. *1571 KIMBOLTON.*
    These were recast at some date between 1634 and 1713. Their position in the
    ring is not clear (see inscription above).

6. 1572 ELSENHAM, Essex St Mary   Tenor of 4
    Johanes grene me fecit anno dnꞌ ⸍ 2 7
    Diameter 36"   Weight 7¾ cwt
    On this bell also both kinds of a are used, Johanes with the normal and
    anno with the straight-sided version. The numerals are particularly poor
    specimens, the 1 missing, the 5 recognisable only by a slight hump, the
    right side of the 7 non-existent and only the 2 being legible with any
    degree of certainty. This was the result of the thin wax strips falling off
    the model bell due to insufficient egg-white adhesive being used.
                                        G./J. Dodds

7. *1574. HARPENDEN.*   *Old treble of 5*
    Johanes grene me fecit anno dni 1574
    Diameter 29½"
    Recast by J. Warner & Sons, London 1898.   *N & S*

8.   1575 ABBOTSLEY, St Margaret of Antioch, Cambs.   2nd of 5

𝔍ohanes grene fecit anno dm 1575

Diameter 29 ¾"   Weight 5 cwt   Note C#

The bells are, at the time of writing, out of the frame, supported by timbers across the pits.

This is Grene's last known bell, his career having lasted only five years. His successor as a Hertfordshire founder was another John, John Dier of Hitchin, who may also have learned his trade with Clarke, as he followed Clarke and Grene after only a brief interval.

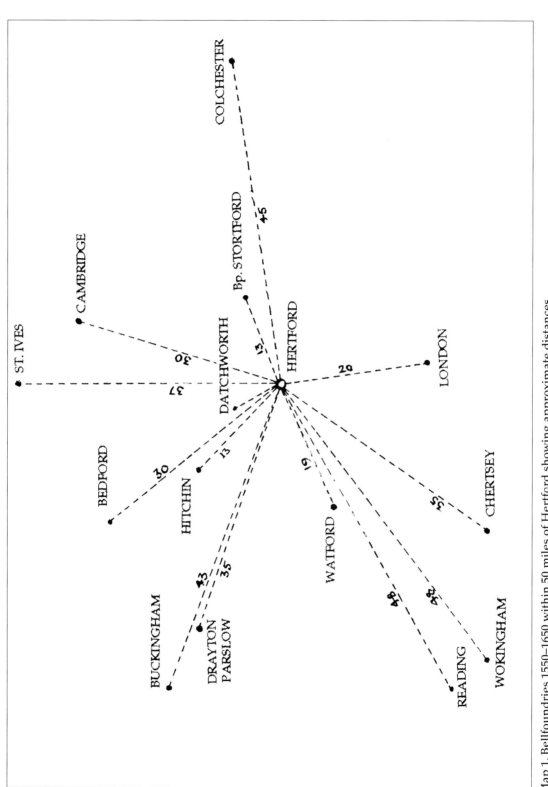

Map 1. Bellfoundries 1550–1650 within 50 miles of Hertford showing approximate distances

4

JOHN DIER OF HITCHIN 1575–1603

I T IS A STRANGE FACT that more is known about this man's death than his life. By his surname he was probably a Hertfordshire man as, in various spellings, it is still fairly common in the north of the county. Dier himself spelled it in at least six different ways, Dier, Diar, Dyer, Dyey, Dir and Dies. This suggests that he could not truthfully be descibed as a scholar. He used Latin on some of his bells, no doubt to impress even less-scholarly churchwardens, but more than once spoiled the effect by inverting a complete word, which could only occur if he was using words made from blocks, as he appears to have done with his Latin inscriptions.

One difficulty in listing Dier's bells is that a surprising number of them are undated, just at a time when more bells were being dated than ever before. John Clarke's lost bell at Braughing was the first in the county to carry a date and all known bells by Grene were dated, so it is unusual for Grene's successor not to continue this. There is documentary evidence that Dier was settled in Hitchin in 1588 but he was more likely to have been there from earlier in his founding career. The distribution of his earliest bells, in Essex with one in Suffolk, dating from 1577 to 1580, gives the impression that he may have had working links in that area but, by late 1580, had moved back into Hertfordshire, as the later list suggests. However, there is evidence that he may on occasion have gone back to Essex as an itinerant for short periods.

He was to be a much more prolific founder than Grene for two reasons: his working life was longer and there was beginning to be an increased demand for new bells due to the introduction of full-circle ringing, for which the long-waisted medieval bells were unsuitable.

In 1588 the churchwardens of All Saints, Shillington, that proud church on its hill which dominates south-east Bedfordshire, sent two or more bells to Hitchin to be recast. The Shillington churchwardens were nothing if not adventurous; over a comparatively short period, they tried every founder within easy (or not so easy) range. In 1575 they tried Bartholomew Atton at Buckingham; in 1579–82 someone un-named; in 1588, Dier at Hitchin; in 1603–4, Watts of Leicester; in 1624, William Haulsey at St Ives and in 1638, Robert Oldfield at Hertford. It reads like part of a survey carried out for *Which?* magazine! One fact which does need consideration is that, had Grene still been founding in 1575, or had there been a successor of his in

Hitchin, they might well have tried him instead of making the two-day journey to Buckingham. It therefore appears that Grene may have either died or retired shortly after casting the bell at Abbotsley in that year and that Clarke, although still alive, was no longer an active founder.

(An irrelevant but interesting item in the 1575 accounts is that the local man who hung the bells was called Robert Greene and that 'grene and his companye when they hung up ye bell for their brekfasts at Deare his howse' were paid xxijd. This shows how common were their surnames, Deare being yet another variation of Dier.)

In 1579–80, there are further entries concerning casting *bells*, definitely in the plural:

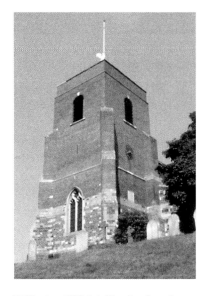

Shillington, All Saints. The churchwardens tried several bellfounders over the years, including John Dier and Robert Oldfield.

Payments :

It^M to the bell founder an earnest		vi*d*.
It^M expence at the castinge of the bells	vi*js*.	ij*d*.
It^M layd out for the belfounder for vi sacks of charcoales and the fetchinge	vs.	vii*jd*.
It^M for the expences at the castinge of the last bell		xi*jd*.

[Charcoal was fuel for the furnace; that the parish bought it confirms that the bells were cast in the churchyard. If it were Dier, he may have been semi-itinerant at this period.]

1580–1

It^M rec. for Bel mettel the xvij daye of Jan. beinge the first paymente	ix *li*.	ij*s*.	
It^M rec. for Bel mettel at one other tyme beinge the last paymente	iiij li.	xvi*js*.	
September the xviijth Paid vnto the belfounder		iiijs.	iiij*d*.

1581–2

It' to the Bellfounder for arnest for casting the Bell			iiij*d*.
It' drynke for the Belfounder			ij*d*.
Payd to the Bellfounder for Casting of the Bell	iiij *li*.	vs.	

[This was probably a bell weighing about 8½ cwt.]

1588

Payd to the Bellfounder for earnest for to cast the Bells			iiij*d*.
Payd for Drynke for the Belfounder			vd.
[A very important item indeed]			
Payd for the Carters dynners and others of the towne when the Bells were caried to Hitchin		viijs.	
Payd to the Bellfounder		xxijs.	
Payd for the Bellfounders dynner the iiijth of october		vijd.	
Payd to the Bellfounder the xth of Octobr		vs.	
Payd to the Bellfounder the xijth of October		xxxi*js*.	
Payd to the Bellfounder	v *li*.	vjs.	viiij*d*.

Adding up the bells recast over these few years, it gives the impression of a very large ring indeed; in fact there were never more than five at any one time, so over the period 1575 to 1638, each bell must have been recast on more than one occasion.

So there, in 1588, is the vital evidence that the foundry was in Hitchin. It was rare to give the name of the founder; they 'took the bells to Hitchin' just as it is now usual to say that 'the bells have gone to Whitechapel or Lough-borough' or wherever. Exactly who was the founder involved in 1579–82 cannot be said for certain, but Dier seems the most likely man as he had cast bells for Houghton Regis, Beds., and Thundridge, Herts., in 1580 and so is known to have been in the area.

Before dealing with Dier's known bells, it is important to consider a bell at St Mary's, Hemel Hempstead, usually said to be by Dier but, in the writer's opinion, equally likely to have been by John Grene. It could even be by John Clarke but without comparison material this is purely theoretical. The inscription is in large, flat and rather coarse sixteenth century black-letter, cut out of parchment in the style of Grene's known work, but much less refined. The unscholarly Latin reads lawd ate :do mini. It is undated but has the colon formed of two lozenges as used by Dier. However, the letter m is formed of three 'units' of the kind used by Grene and Dier, although in this case used the 'wrong way round' and, more importantly, the two a s are of different form, again as used by Grene and Dier. Either man could have cast it but it may have been an early work by Dier while working with Grene or Clarke. The details of this bell are :

HEMEL HEMPSTEAD, Herts. St Mary	5th of 8		3
lawd ate :do mini			2 / 3
			3
Diameter 36"	Weight 7cwt 3 qr 2 lb	Note A	3

All except one of Dier's other bells bear his name in a coarse late six-teenth century black letter. Dier used words constructed from individual let-ters mounted on word-sized paterae with large hand-cut capitals, the 𝔞 of which is identical to that used by Grene. Two other fancy capitals regularly used are 𝔇 and 𝔐 , the latter obviously cut out of parchment as it shows where a straight cut was made then pulled apart, leaving a clearly visible wrinkle in the letter. In most cases, the capitals were cut as required and differ from one example to another. That Dier eventually had a complete set of capitals is proved by his bells at Hulcote, Beds. (*See Fig. 3*)

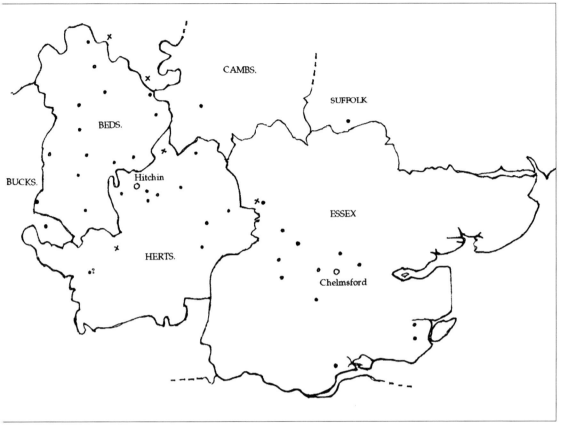

Map 2. John Grene and John Dier distribution of bells. Grene shown as X Dier shown as +

Chronological List of Bells by John Dier

1.   1577 STOCK, Essex All Saints   Tenor of 3
        IOHN dIAR AND RObERT WICKES MAdE THIS bELL I577
        Diameter 36"   Weight 9 cwt
        Robert Wickes is unknown, but 'John Diar' may be the founder later of
        Hitchin, although the use of mixed roman and black letter is not char-
        acteristic of his later work. The inscription is incised. This entry is
        included for the sake of completeness.   *CB Essex*

2.   1579 CLARE, Suffolk SS Peter and Paul   6th of 8   *3*
        ℑohn: :dier: made: :me: I5 79 ○   *3 / 3*
        Diameter 32⅛"   Weight 15 cwt   Note F#   *3*
        ○ – *Fig.* 2. This consists of a ring of six fleurs-de-lys and   *3*
        probably was on the medieval bell which Dier was recasting.
        The word John is inverted.   *RWMC*

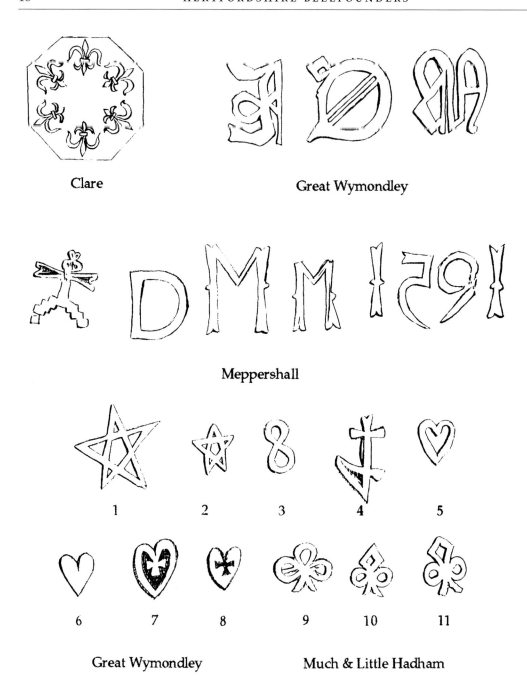

Clare

Great Wymondley

Meppershall

1   2   3   4   5

6   7   8   9   10   11

Great Wymondley   Much & Little Hadham

Fig. 2 John Dier lettering and decorations

3.   *1580 BROOMFIELD, Essex St Mary*   *Old treble of 2*
      𝕵ohn: :dier: made : :me : |5 80
      Diameter 33"
      Recast by John Warner & Sons, 1874/5.   *CB Essex*

4.   1580 CORRINGHAM, Essex St Mary   *Treble of 3*
      𝕵ohn : : dier : made : : me : |5 80
      (on waist incised) RICHARD CHAMPION ESQVIER
      Diameter 33"
      Richard Champion was owner of the manor of Hassingbrook, 1568–99.
                                                       CB Essex

5.   *1580 HOUGHTON REGIS, Beds. All Saints*   5th of 6
      𝕵ohn : dier : made : me : |5 80
      Diameter 40"   *Weight 10 cwt*   *Note G*
      Recast by J. Taylor & Co. 1899 with inscription excellently reproduced in
      facsimile.   *R.I. Kendrick*

6.   1580 THUNDRIDGE, Herts. St Mary   Tenor of 4   3
      𝕵ohn : dier : made : me : |5 80   3 / 3
      Diameter 34⅜"   Weight 7½ cwt   Note B ♭   3
                                                                  3

      Transferred from the old church, of which only the tower remains, in
      1853. Hung 'dead' in a weak softwood frame and derelict now for many
      years.   *Dodds, CB Herts.*

7.   1581 LITTLE WYMONDLEY, Herts. St Mary the Virgin   2nd of 3
                                                                  3
      𝕵ohn : dier : made : me : |5 8| 2 / 2
      Diameter 23⅛"   Weight 2¾ cwt Note F + 22 cents   3
      Each word is on a patera and the colons are solid lozenges.   3
      This bell and the tenor are on ancient headstocks, which may date from
      work done by Eayre of St Neots in 1760. In 1821, there were 4 bells, the 3rd
      of which cracked and was sold in 1866. This was therefore the 2nd of 4.
                                                       Dodds, CB Herts.

8,9. *1581/2 SHILLINGTON, Beds. All Saints*
      Known from churchwardens' accounts only. At least two bells were cast.
                                                       CB Beds.

10.   1583 ARRINGTON, Cambs. St Nicholas   Single
      𝕵ohn : : dier : made : : me : |5 8 3
      Diameter 33½"   Weight 6¼ cwt
      Formerly treble of 3.   *R. Walker, Histon*

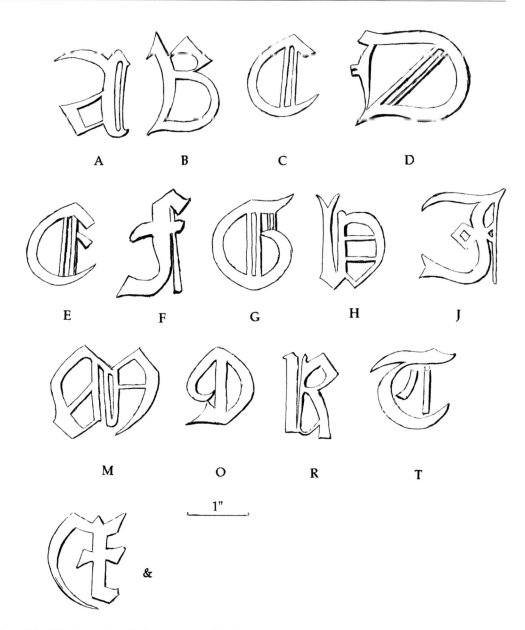

Fig. 3 John Dier's capitals Hulcote 2nd and 3rd

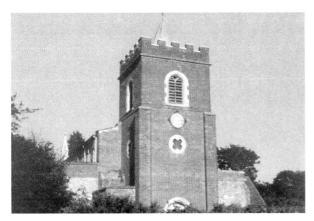

Offley, St Mary Magdelene.
John Dier added a treble to make
four bells, Robert Oldfield made
five bells into six and John Briant
recast the tenor. All were then
transfered to the rebuilt tower
in 1815.

11. 1583 OFFLEY, Herts. St Mary Magdalene   3rd of 6

                                                                  3

John : dier : made : me : 1583 ,   3 / 3
Diam. 34¾"   Weight 7 cwt 3 qr 20 lb   Note B♭   3

                                                                  3

This bell augmented the ring of three listed in the Edwardian Inventory of 1552. Tuned, weighed by Eayre & Smith 2000.

                                                     Dodds, CB Herts.

12. 1587 ARDELEY, Herts. St Lawrence   4th of 6

                                                                   3

John : dier : made :aw : 1587   3 / 3
Diameter 28⅞   Weight 5½ cwt   Note C   3
The word 'me' is inverted, showing the use of word blocks.   2

                                                       Dodds, CB Herts.

13. 1587 BOLNHURST, Beds. St Dunstan   2nd of 4
    John : dier : made : me : 1587
    Diameter 29½"   Weight 4½ cwt

14. 1587 BOLNHURST   3rd of 4
    John : dier : made : me : 1587
    Diameter 32½ "   Weight 6 cwt   *CB Beds.*

15. *1588 HIGH EASTER, Essex St Mary*   *2nd of 6*
    John : : dier : made : : me : 1588
    Diameter 32"   Weight 5½ cwt   *Note B*

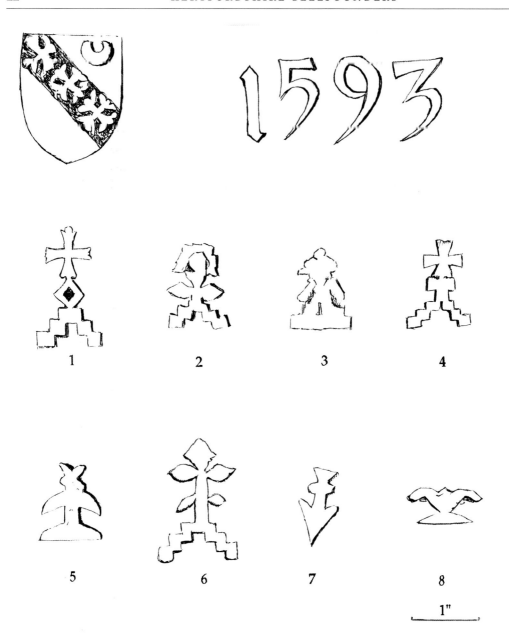

Fig. 4 John Dier Hulcote 2nd

16.   *1588 HIGH EASTER*   *3rd of 6*
      John : dier : made : me : 15 88
      Diameter 32 ½ "   Weight 6 cwt   *Note A*
      Both recast by John Warner 1910.   *D Sloman / CB Essex*

17,   *1588 SHILLINGTON, Beds.*   *Known from churchwardens' accounts*
18.   *only. At least two bells cast. Recast at some date up to or including 1638.*

19.   1589 GRAVELEY, Herts. St Mary   5th of 6, formerly 3rd of 4
      Johannis dier hanc campanam fecit : 15 89
      Diameter 33 ¾ "   Weight 7 cwt   Note B♭
      (JOHN DIER MADE THIS BELL) The words or pairs of words are on paterae
      and the colons are solid lozenges. This was a recast of one of the bells
      from Little Wymondley Priory.   *Dodds, CB Herts.*

20.   1591 MEPPERSHALL, Beds. St Mary the Virgin   2nd of 6
      John " DYer " Made " Me : I?91✝
      Diameter 28 ¹⁄₁₆ "   Weight 4 cwt   Note D#
      V- triangle randomly applied; positions vary. ✝ – *Fig. 2*, cross with
      triangular base and small head, not known to have been used else-
      where. The 5 is reversed.
      This was originally the treble of five. Tuned by Whitechapel and
      augmented to six in 1986.   *CB Beds./ CJP*

21.   *1591 WILLINGTON, Beds. St Lawrence*   *Old 4th of 5*
      JOHN: DYEY: MADE: ME: 1591.
      Diameter 35 "
      As recorded by North, the inscription was in Roman capitals and completely
      reversed, except for the date, which was partly inverted. Roman capitals sound
      most unlikely and can probably be explained by the fact that even Victorian
      printers did not have a reversed black letter font. Recast by Mears & Stainbank
      1898
      CB Beds./ CJP

22.   *1593 HULCOTE, Beds. St Nicholas*   *Old treble*
      This bell, the treble of a complete ring of four by Dier, was recast by Chandler of
      Drayton Parslow in 1683.
      The inscription was presumably as on 2 and 3.

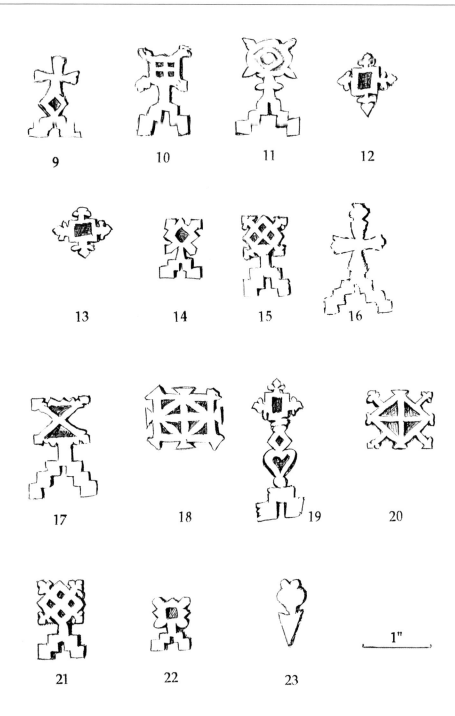

Fig 5. John Dier Hulcote 3rd

23. 1593 HULCOTE   2nd of 4

(shoulder) (1) ☐ ℞𝒴 chard (2) 𝕮harnock (3) 𝕰rqueir   3

✯ 𝕵ohannes : 𝕯ir : 𝕸e : 𝕱elet : a : 𝕝𝟝𝟡𝟛   3 / 3

(below i.b.) (4) 𝕺nl𝒴 (5) 𝕿o (6) 𝕲od:𝕭e (5) all : 𝕳onor (7) 𝕷t (8) 𝕲lorie   3

Diameter 29¾ "   Weight 5½ cwt   3

The bell is untuned and retains its moulded cannons.

24. 1593 HULCOTE   3rd of 4

(shoulder) (9) ☐℞𝒴chard (10) 𝕮harnock (11) 𝕰rqueir   3

✯   𝕵ohannes (12) 𝕯ir (13) 𝕸e (14) 𝕱elet (15) a : 𝕕𝕝𝟝𝟡𝟛,   3 / 3

(below i.b.) (16) 𝕺nl𝒴 (17) 𝕿o (18) 𝕲od: (19) 𝕭e (20) all : (21) 𝕳onor (22)

𝕷t (23) 𝕲lori   3

Diameter 32⅛ "   Weight 6½ cwt   3

Chip-tuned on the sound-bow and cannons retained.

These two bells are very different from any others known to have been cast by Dier and may in some degree reflect his status as a founder at this period. They are high quality works and show that Dier, while no great innovator, was a thoroughly competent founder, a fact which is sometimes overlooked. To have obtained this particular commission speaks well for his reputation. The decorations appear to have been specially cut for each bell, as was the case at Great Wymondley, Much and Little Hadham in 1595, and with the exception of the pentacle, are not found on the other bells. Note the spelling of Dier.   *R.I. Kendrick*

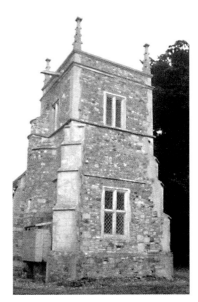

25. 1593 *HULCOTE*   *Old tenor*
This bell was recast by Richard Chandler of Drayton Parslow in 1723. The inscription was probably as on Nos. 2 and 3.

Hulcote is a most remarkable church, a building of great beauty 're- edified' in 1590/3 by the same Richard Charnock, or Chernocke, who gave the bells. He is commemorated on a monument which states that he also 'newe bvilt his mansion Howse, Thrice bare office of Highe Shrife in this Shire'. He died at the age of 84 on

Hulcote, St Nicholas. The whole church was rebulit in 1590/93 by Richard Charnock and richly furnished, including four bells. Remarkably, almost all of it is still intact.

14 August 1615. His arms, which appear on the surviving Dier bells are '(arg.) on a bend (sa.) three cross crosslets of the first with a crescent in chief for difference'. His initials, in nail-heads, appear on the church door.   *CB Beds.*

26.   *1593 MAULDEN, Beds. St Mary*   3rd of old 5
      Ijohannes dier hanc campanam fecit i 5 95
      Diameter 32½ "   Weight 6 cwt   *Note A#*
      Recast by Mears & Stainbank 1912.   CJP/CB Beds.

27.   *1593 or 95 WOOTTON, Beds. St Mary*   Old 4th of 5
      Recast by J. Taylor 1874.
      C.J. Pickford quotes the date as 1593, North as 1595.

28.   1594 BERNERS RODING, Essex   Dedication unknown   Single
      Ijohn + Ø Yer + Made x me i594 *
      Diameter 21½ " Weight 2 cwt
      The lettering and decorations on this bell are unusual, in that the let-
      ters are much smaller than on his earlier bells. The decorations are
      reminiscent of those at Therfield, 1597, where the words are separated
      by small quatrefoils. (*See No. 33*).   CB Essex

29.   1595 GREAT WYMONDLEY, Herts. St Mary the Virgin   5th of 6
                                                                                     3
      Ijohn ♡ Ø Yer 8 Made : me i595 *   1a1 / 3
      Diameter 34¾" Weight 7 cwt 3 qr 18 lb   Note B♭   3
      :– outline lozenges. * – pentacle. ♡ – heart.   2
      8 – Eternity sign; all *Fig. 2.*   1a1 = moulding wires separated by a
      filet moulding.   *Dodds, CB Herts.*

30.   1595 LITTLE HADHAM, Herts. St Cecilia   3rd of 6
      * Ijohn ♣ Ø Yer ♣ Made ♣ me ♣i595   3
      Diameter 30¹¹⁄₁₆" Weight 5 cwt 3 qr 17 lb   Note D♭   1a1 / 3
      *–Fig.2. ♣ – a variant *Fig.2 .*   3
      This bell may have augmented the ring to four, and remained   2
      as treble until a further bell was added in 1855. A new treble
      of six was added in 1980.   *Dodds, CB Herts.*

31.   1595 MUCH HADHAM, Herts. St Andrew   5th of 8
      * Ijohn ⚶ ØYer ⊛ made ♡ me: i595   3
      Diameter 30¼ "   Weight 5 cwt 0 qr 27 lb   Note C   1a1 / 3
      * – *Fig. 2.* ⚶ – *Fig. 2*   3
      The cannons have been removed.

32.   1595 MUCH HADHAM   6th of 8
      * Ijohn ⊛ Ø Yer: made : me: i595   3
      Diameter 31½" Weight 6 cwt 1 qr 14 lb   Note B   1a1 / 3
      : – outline lozenges. * – pentacle. ⚶ – cross. ♥ ⊛ ♥ – hearts,   3
      all *Fig. 2.*   1

This bell retains its cannons, which are of great interest, being
of a fine cable design and rather lop-sided.   *C. Jordan / Dodds*

33. 1597 THERFIELD, Herts. St Mary the Virgin   4th of 6

𝕵ohn ˣ dier ˣ made ˣ me ˣ i 5 97   3

Diameter 35"   Weight 7½ cwt   Note B   3 / 3

This bell formed one of the six which came from the old   3

church, demolished in 1873. As the new building did not have   2

a tower, all but one of the bells were stored until a new tower

was erected in 1911, when they were rehung on deadstocks, without

wheels, but in a ringing frame. The stops are small quatrefoils, proba-

bly similar to those at Berners Roding (*No. 28*).   *Dodds, CB Herts.*

34. *1597 WRITTLE, Essex All Saints*   'Great bell'
Known from churchwardens' accounts only.
1597
It^m payd John Dyer the bell founder for casting of
       the great bell   *x26jli*   *vj^s*   *viij^d*
for caraying of the great bell to Chelmsford &
       bryngyng her hom agayne   *vj^s*   *viij^d*
for Goodman Dyer's dynner and his mens when he dyd
       take down the bell   *iij^s*   *viij^d*
John Dyer and Goodman Dyer were one and the same person. The reference to
Chelmsford shows that Dier had set up a temporary furnace there. The bell was
recast in or before 1811, when the tower fell.   *CB Essex*

35. *1598 PAGLESHAM, Essex St Peter*   *Former treble of 3*

𝕵ohannes dier hanc wᴏwᴏdᴍᴏ I 5 98

Diameter 30"   Weight 4½ cwt
The word 'campanam' is inverted, showing once again his use of word blocks for
Latin as well as English inscriptions. Possibly cast at Chelmsford. Only the
inscription band survives.   *D Sloman/ CB Essex*

36. 1600 ELSENHAM, Essex St Mary   2nd of 4

𝕵ohn : dier : made : this bell: I6OO

Diameter 30"   Weight 4½ cwt
This is Dier's last surviving bell. The most striking change from his
usual practice is that the date numerals are exceedingly neat and of a
pattern previously unused by him, as though he had a new set of figures for the new century. This would, of course, be necessary. It is also
interesting to see how like these numerals are to the earliest ones used
by Robert Oldfield, only five years later. This was obviously the latest
fashion! Another innovation is the use of the English translation of his
stock Latin inscription.
The bells were hung dead on beams for hammer chiming only in 1903,

the cost being borne by Sir Walter Gilbey of gin fame. The cannons
have been removed.   *Dodds*

37.   *1602 WRITTLE, Essex*   *Old 3rd*
      Known from churchwardens' accounts only. Dier is not named but he seems to
      have worked in Essex in his later years and it is not unreasonable to suggest
      that it was he who recast the 3rd bell, five years after the recasting by him of the
      'great bell'. If so, this was one of his last products.
      1602.

      to the Bell founder for casting of the thyrd bell and for two houndereth
      and fyve pownd of mettall xi^{li} $xii^{i}s$ ij^{d}
                                                                      CB Essex

38.   *1602 SUTTON, Beds. All Saints*   *Old treble of 4*
      Recast by C. & G. Mears 1856.   *CJP*

Undated Bells (Listed alphabetically)

39.   *BARLING, Essex All Saints*   *Treble of 2*
      𝔍𝔬𝔥𝔫 ⠂ ⠂ 𝔡𝔦𝔢𝔯 ⠂ 𝔪𝔞𝔡𝔢 ⠂ ⠂ 𝔪𝔢 ⠂
      Diameter 33"   Weight 5 cwt
      In 1552 there were 4 bells. These were reduced to 3 and now to 2.
      Recast by John Warner 1902.   *D Sloman/CB Essex*

40.   CHEDDINGTON, Bucks. St Giles   3rd of 6
      𝔍𝔬𝔥𝔞𝔫𝔫𝔢𝔰 𝔮𝔯𝔯𝔱. 𝔥𝔞𝔫𝔠 𝔠𝔞𝔪𝔭𝔞𝔫𝔞𝔪 𝔣𝔢𝔠𝔦𝔱
      Diameter 34¾"   Weight 7 cwt   Note B
      The name 'dier' is inverted.   *CB Bucks.*

41.   CLAPHAM, Beds. St Thomas à Becket   4th of 6
      𝔍𝔬𝔥𝔫 ⠂ ⠂ 𝔡𝔦𝔢𝔯 ⠂ 𝔪𝔞𝔡𝔢 ⠂ 𝔪𝔢 ⠂
      Diameter 27½"   Weight 4 cwt   Note D
      This was the 3rd of 5 when recorded by North. The bells hang in a fine
      late-Saxon tower.   *CB Beds.*

42.   CHICAGO, Ill., USA Our Saviour at 530 West Fullerton Parkway
      Single (*Formerly 4th of 5 at EVERTON cum TETWORTH, Cambs.*)
      𝔍𝔬𝔥𝔞𝔫𝔫𝔢𝔰 𝔡𝔦𝔢𝔯 𝔥𝔞𝔫𝔠 𝔠𝔞𝔪𝔭𝔞𝔫𝔞𝔪 𝔣𝔢𝔠𝔦𝔱
      Diameter 31¼"   Weight 5 cwt 2 qr 11 lb   Note C
      This church and parkland to its north formed a detached part of
      Huntingdonshire, while the village was in Bedfordshire, an anomaly
      which ended when the boundaries were redrawn in 1964, although the
      church was and remains in the Diocese of Ely.
      On 16 June 1974 the tower was struck by lightning and half-demolished.

As the bells had been silent for about ten years, (the writer rang on them in 1964) there was neither the money nor the incentive both to rebuild the tower and rehang the bells. It was therefore decided to remove the top stage of the tower and construct a new roof at about the level of the old bell-chamber floor.

   One bell only, by Richard Holdfeld, was retained. One was sold as scrap and was recast to augment the John Briant five at Rushden, Herts. Two more were recast to form two trebles for the Briant six at Newbold on Avon, Warwicks, while the Dier bell was retuned at Whitechapel and sent to Chicago. This information comes from a most interesting article by C.J. Pickford, which appeared under the title 'Silence at Christmas' in the *Ringing World* of December 21/28 1984.

43. FYFIELD, *Essex St Nicholas*   *Former 2nd of old 4*
     𝔍ohn ⦂ ⦂ dier ⦂ made ⦂ ⦂ me ⦂
     No details recorded. Recast by John Warner & Sons, London 1862.   CB Essex

44. LITTLE BADDOW, *Essex St Mary the Virgin 7th of 8, formerly 3rd of 4*
     𝔍ohn ⦂ ⦂ dier ⦂ made ⦂ ⦂ me ⦂
     Diameter 36"   Weight 7½ cwt   Note B♭
     Preserved in the tower but no longer as part of the ring
                                                            D Sloman/ CB Essex

45. OLD LINSLADE, *Bucks. St Mary*   *Treble of old 3*
     The inscription as recorded by Lipscombe read:
     𝔍ohes 𝔇ies hanc ℭampanam fecit
     (John Dies made this bell) *which sounds unlikely. (Lipscombe was a slap-dash copyist of Browne Willis, the bell historian. He also produced a garbled version of an Oldfield inscription at Ivinghoe.) The most probable explanation is that the final 'r' of Dier can be fairly easily mistaken for a black letter 's' at a cursory glance.*
     The five old bells were recast by William Chapman of Whitechapel in 1781 and transferred from St Mary's to St Barnabas, Linslade in about 1849.   CB Bucks.

46. SWINESHEAD, *Beds., formerly Hunts. St Nicholas*   *4th of 5*
     𝔍ohannes dier hanc campanam fecit
     Diameter 25"   Weight 2 cwt 0 qr 21 lb   Note E
     This bell was the fourth of a very light ring of five which were taken down from the tower in the summer of 1969 to enable restoration work be carried out. On the actual day of their removal they were stolen from the churchyard and never recovered; nobody was ever charged with the theft so they were probably sold by the theives for scrap. A new ring of Dutch bells was provided in 1989/90.
     The above weight is as given in **CB Hunts.** *by Revd T.M.N. Owen; the inscription is from the note books of C.W. Izzard.*
                                 Article in **Ringing World** *26/1/1990 by Ann M. Fletcher.*

47.   TINGRITH, Beds. St Nicholas   Treble of 3
       𝔍𝔬𝔥𝔫 ː 𝔡𝔦𝔢𝔯 ː 𝔪𝔞𝔡𝔢 ː 𝔱𝔥𝔦𝔰 𝔟𝔢𝔩𝔩 ː
       Diameter 27 ¼ "   Weight 4 ½ cwt
       This inscription is the same as that of the 1600 bell at Elsenham and
       may, therefore, be equally late, as it does not occur on any other exist-
       ing bell.   *CB Beds.*

48.   GREAT CANFIELD, Essex St Mary   2nd of 3
       ✠ 𝔏𝔞𝔲𝔡𝔞𝔱𝔢 𝔡𝔬𝔪𝔦𝔫𝔲𝔪 𝔡𝔢 𝔠𝔢𝔩𝔦𝔰 𝔏𝔞𝔲𝔡𝔞𝔱𝔢 𝔢𝔲𝔫 𝔦𝔫 𝔢𝔵𝔠𝔞𝔢𝔩𝔰𝔦𝔰
       Diameter 33"
       In *CB Essex* Deedes and Walters tentatively ascribe this bell to Dier on
       the grounds that the L comes from the same font as Dier's set. As none
       of the bells listed above bear a capital L it is not possible to compare it
       with anything still extant. The bell bears the cross of John Tonne
       (1522–42) so it may have been a recast by Dier of a bell by Tonne, repro-
       ducing the inscription in his own font. There is nothing improbable in
       this as, on his early bell at Clare (*No. 2 above*), he reproduced a
       medieval stop of six fleurs-de-lys. The Latin inscription (Psalm 148) is
       certainly in Tonne's somewhat florid style.   *CB Essex*

Reading the above list suggests that there was very little variation in his
inscriptions. In fact, after careful study a pattern begins to emerge which can
be used to give an approximate date to the undated bells.
    Discounting the 1577 bell by Diar and Wickes at Stock, which is totally
out of character with Dier's other products, it is noticeable that all the earlier bells, i.e. prior to 1589, bear the same basic inscription 𝔍𝔬𝔥𝔫ː 𝔡𝔦𝔢𝔯ː 𝔪𝔞𝔡𝔢ː
ː𝔪𝔢ː made up of standard blocks, each word being on its own patera. (This
is especially clear when a complete word is inverted.) Any variations may
possibly be the result of different observers not all seeing the same thing in
the same way! The undated bells at Barling, Fyfield and Little Baddow,
Essex, and that at Clapham, Beds., all have these blocks and it is not unreasonable to assign them to sometime between the the years 1580–8.
    𝔍𝔬𝔥𝔞𝔫𝔫𝔢𝔰 𝔡𝔦𝔢𝔯 makes his first appearance at Graveley in 1589, by which time
he was known to be working in Hitchin. The lettering on these Latin blocks
is quite different in character from the earlier set and the solid lozenge
colons are not used between words. These features are shared by the
undated bells at Cheddington and Old Linslade, Bucks., (assuming that that
was what the inscription *really* said, and not as quoted by Lipscombe) as well
as by those cast for Swineshead and Everton, so they may be tentatively
assigned to 1589–97.
    A very interesting group of bells made its first appearance at Mepper-
shall in 1591. Here Dier used capitals for each word, his normal 𝔍, roman D
and M and also minute triangles between the words for the first (known)
time, as well as a curious initial cross. (*Fig. 2*, p. 18) On others of this 'special'

group he varied the number of capitals, obviously designing some as he went along, culminating in the tortured forms found at Hulcote. The C, G, H and T were Lombardic in origin but the rest are undeniably original, the O bearing no resemblence to the real thing: its nearest equivalent being an inverted G. Furthermore, there are variations from bell to bell (*Fig.* 3, p. 20). Also, instead of just colons between words, he began to use a series of small, exquisite cut-out symbols: crosses of increasing complexity at Hulcote; hearts, including a sacred heart at Graveley; small quatrefoils, variants of clubs from playing cards; an Eternity sign and what looks like a mason's mark. (See *Fig.* 2, p. 18) Just what lay behind these signs can only be guessed at – was he a secret adherent of the Old Faith or was he dabbling in the occult? Or just enjoying himself?

Dier was not the only founder who used playing card symbols at this period. With the publication of Christopher Dalton's masterly *The Bells and Belfries of Dorset*, it becomes clear that at least one other contemporary founder was doing likewise. William Warre of Leigh, Dorset, was using hearts, clubs, diamonds and spades on bells at Lillington in 1590, Batcombe in 1592 and Maiden Newton in 1593, all in Dorset. As there was almost certainly no connection between the two men, this feature can only be ascribed to a passing fashion.

Whatever the reason, the image of Dier as a second-rate founder has to be revised. These bells provide plenty of material for thought in more ways than one. They are splendid castings but show that Dier, like Grene, was looking backward to the early part of the century rather than forward to the 1600s. At Much Hadham the sixth has retained not only its beautiful cable moulded cannons, but also the broad fillet moulding above the inscription band, stated by the late George Elphick to have become disused by about 1530, is still evident; it is also used at Great Wymondley and Little Hadham, all cast the same year. This is the work of an old-fashioned craftsman rather than an innovator.

The distribution of his bells shows that he lived a semi-itinerant life, with frequent visits to Essex interspersed with periods during which he appears to have been working in or around Hitchin. Even an itinerant founder had to have a base where he lived between jobs and where he kept a wife and family, if any. (*cf.* John Waylett).

The death of John Dier is the most surprising thing known of him. He was at the height of his powers as a craftsman, with work enough to bring in a steady income and with the prospect of several more productive years before him. But the documentary evidence of what happened is to be found in the *CALENDAR OF ASSIZE JAMES I, Hertfordshire Indictments*, published by HMSO.

HERTFORD ASSIZES

23 September 1603

Before Francis Gawdy, J., and Sergeant John Heale.

¶7.   Gaol Prisoners. In a list of twenty-five names of every conceivable
      variety of malefactor, including thieves and witches, the thirteenth is
      that of **John Dyer**.

¶9.   Dyer, John, of Hitchin, bellfounder, indicted for murder.

> By an inquisition held at Hitchin, 9 Aug. 1603, before Denis Hind, coroner,
> on the body of John Bonce, a jury – William Maynerde, Simon Leeper,
> Thomas Saunders, Edward Jeve, John Baker, William Mitten, Edmund
> Baker, Robert Warde, Thomas Cooke, John Esam, Francis Huckle, William
> White alias Vyncent, found that on 3 Aug, at Hitchin [Dyer assaulted Bonce
> and] did wringe and breake his neck.

Guilty: to hang

What happened is not in doubt; why it happened is less clear but it was
probably an alehouse brawl which ended in tragedy. To have broken a man's
neck implies a considerable degree of strength but years of heavy work as a
founder would have given Dier strong muscles. He may also have been a
touchy character, quick to take offence and to react violently. Whatever the
explanation, Dier is the only bellfounder known to have been hanged for
murder, not an enviable reputation. For the historian, the value of this
record is that it enables Dier to be firmly placed at Hitchin, a fact long sus-
pected but finally confirmed.

John Dellow
The fourth North Hertfordshire founder of the period, as yet known only
from the Assize Calendar, was *John Dellow*, also, by his surname, a local man.

BISHOP'S STORTFORD ASSIZES

9 March 1604

Before Francis Gawdy, J., and William Daniel, J.

¶44. Gaol Prisoners – out of fifteen names the third is **John Dellow**.

¶47. Dellow, John, of Hitchin, bell-founder, indicted for petty larceny.
      On 25 (*sic*) Dec. 1603, he stole a kettle (11d) from John Pearle (Church)
      On 21 (*sic*) Dec. 1603 before Ralph Ratcliffe, J.P., John Pearles, butcher,
      and William Terrill, brazier, of Hitchin, entered recognizances [to give evi-
      dence against Dellow, and on] 21 Dec.1603 before William Cock, J.P.,
      Richard Dellow, collarmaker and James Dent, tilemaker, of Hitchin,
      [entered recognizances for his appearance].
      (Note the inconsistency of the dates quoted)

      Not Guilty.

That is all. No bells can be ascribed to him: it seems likely that he had
worked as assistant to Dier and may have been one of 'Goodman Dyer's'
men mentioned at Writtle in 1597 and that he was either trying to carry on

the foundry in a small way, casting mortars, pots and kettles, or having to dispose of Dier's effects, but this can only be conjecture. The poor man was probably still in a state of semi-shock following Dier's execution and then had to face the charge of theft although, mercifully, the kettle was valued at less than one shilling. Over that value, he could have faced whipping or even death if found guilty. The charge may have been trumped up by a pro-Bonce faction in an attempt to get possession of Dier's assets by way of revenge, as there is a faint whiff of conspiracy about the affair, especially as William Terrill is described as 'Brazier' and could easily have been a business rival of Dier's. (Medieval founders were sometimes described as braziers). The murder must have caused more than a nine days' wonder in such a small town and feelings would run high for months. John Dellow deserves sympathy, even to this day. What Judge Gawdy privately thought of having to try *two* Hitchin bellfounders within six months will also have to remain in the realms of conjecture!

It is an intriguing thought that, at the very time of Dier's trial and execution, Robert Oldfield may have been in the process of setting up his foundry in Hertford. That he knew of Dier is certain – all the founders knew each other, being members of a small specialist trade. He may even have watched the execution. It is also likely that he was aware of Dellow's brush with the law, as it occurred only about six weeks before his own wedding when he was already working in the county.

The fact is that, with Dier dead, the small north Hertfordshire bell-foundries which had existed since 1550 came to an end, thus leaving a vacuum waiting to be filled. As a footnote to the careers of Dier and Dellow, these surnames are still common in north and east Hertfordshire.

5

JOHN CLARKE II

B ORN IN 1575, he cast his first bell in 1599 at the age of twenty-four. He appears from circumstantial evidence to have learned his trade with Dier as he used the ℥ from the same font as both Grene and Dier. It is clear that he did not carry on the Datchworth foundry, probably because his father was dead and also because he would have been a rival to Dier had he remained in Hertfordshire. His earliest bell was cast for Wimbish, Essex, where he used Dier's pentacle instead of an initial cross. Another early bell was the tenor at Eastwick, Herts., of 1601, where the date appears to have been formed of crudely cut-out parchment and is almost illegible.

He was itinerant in the true sense of the word. In 1607, he cast a bell for Cold Brayfield, Bucks. and the same year one for Rumboldswyke, near Chichester, Sussex. These bells still exist, the Rumboldswyke example now being the Sanctus at St Nicholas, Brighton. In 1608, he was back in his home area, casting a bell for Flitwick, Beds., using Dier's capitals, Latin word blocks hanc campanam fecit and pentacle. So close indeed is the resemblence that apart from the name, the bell is almost indistinguishable from one by Dier, so much so that it seems that Clarke must have returned to Hitchin and taken over much of Dier's equipment, forestalling Terrill's attempt to gain possession. Then he was off on his travels again. A dozen of his bells are known and are included mainly for completeness.

List of Bells

1599	WIMBISH, Essex	Treble
1601	EASTWICK, Herts.	Tenor
1607	COLD BRAYFIELD, Bucks.	Treble
1607	RUMBOLDSWYKE, Sussex	Now at Brighton, St Nicholas
1608	FLITWICK, Beds.	Third
1613	WELNEY, Norfolk	Single
?	NORTHINGTON, Hants.	
?	WRENTHAM, Suffolk	
1620	LITTLE BURSTEAD, Essex	Treble
1621	ROXWELL, Essex	Third
1621	*CHIGNAL St. James*	*Single. Recast 1868*
Undated	TILTY, Essex	Single

PART II

HERTFORDSHIRE
1600–1660

ROBERT OLDFIELD OF HERTFORD
JAMES BUTLER OF BISHOP'S STORTFORD
AND WILLIAM WHITMORE OF WATFORD

6

SEVENTEENTH CENTURY
BELLFOUNDING

C ASTING A BELL PROBABLY involved about three weeks' work. After settling the exact dimensions of the bell, both external and internal, the founder built a brick core over a hearth in a pit. (See *Fig. 23*, p. 306) On this core, clay, and sand mixed with animal hair and horse dung, known in the trade as 'loam', was built up in stages to the approximate thickness required and then smoothed to the final profile with a strickle board. This, still used today, is a pivoted template shaped to the form of the inside of the bell. A fire was then lit in the hearth and the core carefully dried. (A carelessly dried mould could be lethal, as in the case of Matthew Bagley and his son, when in in 1716, a damp mould burst during casting at the Royal Foundry, Moorfields, killing both men).

A 'false' bell of finer grade loam was then built up over the core, being shaped to the external profile of the bell with another strickle board. This board may have included notches for forming the moulding wires, as at the present day, or, alternatively, the wires may have been formed from 'worms' of clay and laid on by hand. The iron crown staple (for hanging the clapper) was then inserted and the argent and cannons (*see Fig. 1. p. xiv*) built up from either wax or wooden patterns. A high degree of finish was necessary at this stage as this represented the final appearance of the bell. A striking feature of all Oldfield's bells is the smoothness of the surface, both external and internal; of all the bells examined, only one showed a tiny casting fault showing that he was a careful workman. The model on the core was then dried.

At this stage the inscription was added. The inscription band was brushed with horizontal strokes to provide a key for the letters. The 5th bell at Therfield shows these brush marks very clearly. Letters, cut either from parchment or sheet beeswax, mounted on word-sized paterae, formed from thinner sheet wax (as at Stanstead Abbots 1605), or on individual paterae (Therfield 1608), were placed the right way round on the inscription band, together with crosses, shield, stops, date and any other decorations. Another method was to use cast wax letters made in wooden or low-fired earthenware moulds. This was Oldfield's later technique. If the clay model was still slightly warm, bubbling and distortion of the letters could occur, but this did not occur on any of Robert's bells, further proof of his high standards. The model was then coated with grease or tallow to facilitate the separation of model and outer cope. The next stage was to build the cope. Using the same clay/hair/dung mixture as the core and probably reinforcing it with strips of sacking – an anonymous 1664 clock bell at Sawbridgeworth shows clear evidence of this – or other fibrous material, the cope was moulded over the model bell. Lifting points had to be incorporated, so that after the whole mass was completely dry, the cope could be lifted off, the false bell broken up and the cope replaced accurately over the core, leaving a bell-shaped gap between. It was this sequence of moulding and drying that occupied so much time but, space permitting, more that one bell could be worked on simultaneously.

Casting was carried out in a pit to allow the metal to flow by gravity from a charcoal-burning furnace at ground level. Draught was supplied by bellows, hand- or foot-operated.

Although the founder had taken precise measurements of the size and note for the new bell, the actual pitch was sometimes a matter of chance so, after it was hung, the bellhanger would tune it in the tower. This process was carried out with a double-ended hammer, rather like an ice-pick, and involved chipping out grooves either horizontally or vertically, until the correct pitch and harmonics were attained. The Ashwell churchwarden's accounts make it quite plain that this was done after their tenor was recast and that the process was lengthy.

It will be apparent to the reader that the techniques described above were almost identical to those of the fourteenth and fifteenth centuries decribed in Chapter 1 and, except for the chip-tuning, they are similar to those used on the Continent to this day. Little change, apart from the development of stamped letters in the eighteenth century, was to occur until the mid 1850's. Bellfounding was not a particularly innovative trade.

Much of the technical information in this section has been gathered from

> *Suffolk Bells and Belfries* R.W.M. Clouston and
> *The Craft of the Bell Founder* G.P. Elphick,

which latter is a very detailed study of the subject and a useful booklet is Shire Album no 212 *Bellfounding* by Trevor S. Jennings

7

ROBERT OLDFIELD OF HERTFORD
1604–1640

HIS FAMILY AND FOUNDRY

Background

ROBERT OLDFIELD WAS NOT a Hertfordshire man. He has always been regarded as a slightly mysterious figure of unknown origin, so before embarking on a study of him, he must be placed in context. The four Hertfordshire founders who preceded him have been examined in some detail, so it is therefore necessary to consider the situation among bell-founders in the late sixteenth century (*Map 1*, p. 13). Before doing this it is profitable to look at London and Cambridge, the latter in particular

1. London Competitors, Whitechapel

In London, the Whitechapel bellfoundry, with links back to c.1420, was not doing too well. **Robert Mot**, who had been in business since 1570, died in 1604 and the future was uncertain. Only two of his bells are definitely known to have reached Hertfordshire, both at Elstree on the county boundary. Neither survives, having been recast in 1880. The bellfoundry was bought by **Joseph Carter** of the Reading bellfoundry and he supplied a clock bell to Hatfield House in 1608, but nominally cast by Mot in 1604. He installed his son, **William**, to run the London foundry. The tenor at Ridge is the only bell in the county from the Carter years. It is dated 1613 and bears William's name. He was succeded by his foreman, **Thomas Bartlet**, one of whose earliest bells, dated 1616, remains at Shenley. Three more, dated 1618/9, are at Offley. Thomas Bartlet died in 1632 on a business journey to Durham to recast the cathedral bells and is buried there in the church of St Mary-le-Bow. His widow Ellinor carried on the foundry with the help of a 'works manager', John Clifton. It appears that village churchwardens were somewhat averse to dealing with a mere woman, as both at Offley in 1632 and at Shenley in 1633, they went to Hertford for additional bells. No further bells from London entered the county until 1652, thus they posed no threat to a local man. Conversely, no bells appear to have gone in the opposite direction but, at the time of writing, no information on Middlesex bells has been published, although the Middlesex County Association and London Diocesan Guild of Change Ringers is compiling an inventory to be published in due course. It is therefore necessary to look in other directions.

If both Hertfordshire and London contributed little to the background understanding of Robert Oldfield, the Cambridge position was entirely different.

2. Richard Holdfeld

In 1599, a founder cast two bells for Bedfordshire churches, one at Shelton in the extreme north of the county and the other at Studham, in the extreme south. His name was **Richard Holdfeld** and his foundry was in Cambridge. Before settling there, he had been itinerating for several years as there is documentary evidence that he was casting brasses for St Margaret's, Kings Lynn in 1595, payment being made to 'Rychard Howlfeld, a belfounder' (*C.W. Accts.*) and the present sixth bell for Terrington St Clement, Norfolk, of 1595 is usually ascribed to him, although it bears a roundel with the initials RO and MN. MN was **Matthew Norris**, who probably originated from Leicester and learned his trade there with the Newcombe family. Norris and Holdfeld seem to have been in temporary partnership at this date and the Terrington bell was therefore a joint product. From there they moved to Swaton and Newton in Lincolnshire, both near Sleaford, where there are bells dated 1596, neither bearing the RO/MN roundel. The lettering on the Swaton and Newton bells is a widely distributed late medieval type, remarkably similar to that also used by **Richard Bowler** of Colchester (1587–1603).

Both these examples have sections of cresting in the inscription, very similar to some of the Oldfield of Nottingham bellfoundry designs. This, and his use of a version of the Nottingham cross, points to some link with the Nottingham founders and, according to recent research in Nottingham Record Office by George Dawson, Holdfeld was indeed a Nottingham man. He was the son of Reginald Oldfield, described as a 'Potter' and was born at some date between 1545 and 1550. (Oldfield and Holdfeld were varieties of the same name). He is mentioned in the will of Reginald, dated 12 January 1576/7. Reginald was buried at St Peter's, Nottingham on 4 February 1576/7. In or about 1570, Richard married; the name of his wife may have been Margaret. A son, Robert, was baptised on 1 February 1572/3 at St Peter's, Nottingham, and other children followed until 1585. It is likely that Richard worked with Henry Oldfield I until the latter's death in 1589–90 and then with Henry Oldfield II until 1593-4. He then broke away from his settled life for some unknown reason and worked as an itinerant until 1599, taking his eldest son and possibly a younger son, Richard, with him to learn the trade. In 1597 Holdfeld cast one bell for Seaton, Rutland, and Norris cast another, using a plain roman font. At this point the parnership came to an end and Norris moved to Stamford where he set up his own foundry. Richard senior and Robert then headed south and settled in Cambridge in 1599. From a map, it can be seen that they had moved westwards and then southwards in a very large semicircle. Robert must have gained a great deal of experience from his travels and it was a good way of picking up news of possible trade openings and this is what seems to have occurred. The younger Richard appears to have left the group and moved into the west Midlands.

3. Cambridge

There had been a bellfoundry in Cambridge from 1590, when the treble at Great Shelford was cast, bearing the inscription *Cast in Cambridge 1590* so Holdfeld may have taken over the lease of an existing site on the retirement or death of the previous owner.

   The Studham bell mentioned above was recast in 1909, but the inscription was reproduced in facsimile and reads + PRIES THE LORD; the cross used is a cross crosslet. That same year, the Ashwell churchwardens decided to have their 'great' bell, i.e. the tenor, recast. The slow progress of the work can be followed from the year ending 24 March 1600 through to October 1602. It began well enough as the accounts show:

Item given to the bell-founder in earneste		vi d
Item payde to the Custome of the towne of Cambridge		iiii d
Item given to the bell-founder's men		xiiii d
Item for my chardges at Cambridge	ii s	
Item payde to the bell-founder	xxxiii s	iiii d

   All this is perfectly clear; the deposit had been paid, a visit had been made to the foundry and a further, larger, payment made. It is also very specific about people – the bellfounder and his men are plainly differentiated. What is not said is the exact site of the foundry. A parcel of land at 13 St Bene't Street was known as the Bell Ground but, as it was at that time, 1599/1600, a garden and had been so for many years, it could not have been the site of Holdfeld's foundry. A paper entitled *A Cambridge Bell-Foundry* by the Revd Canon Stokes, read to the Cambridge Antiquarian Society on 8 February 1926, explored the ownership of 13 St Bene't Street but reached no firm conclusions as to the date of its use as a foundry.

   It is now necessary to look at the situation in Colchester.

4. Colchester

Richard Bowler was founding in Colchester from 1587-1604. Documentary evidence shows that he was there in 1598, when he was in trouble with the law for allowing his cattle to stray on to the land of one Reginald Oldfield (the name may, or may not, be significant). The outcome of the case is not known. (*Ref. CB Essex.* p. 86). In 1600, he was assaulted and seriously injured by one Ambrose Gilbert, 'soe as it is thought the said Richard is in great daunger of Dethe'. (*Ibid*)

He did in fact recover but, during the period of his incapacity, his outstanding orders were completed by Richard Holdfeld, who must have been known to Bowler, if only by repute. Holdfeld duly put Bowler's name on the bells in question but added a roundel with an arrow and the initials RH as on the 3rd and 4th at Witham, Essex, in 1601 and the RH shield at Prittlewell in 1603 (*Fig. 16 a,b, p. 72*). The situation is further complicated by the fact that Holdfeld cast a bell for Barton, Cambs., in the same year and put Bowler's name on it but his own mark.

The interaction between Bowler and Holdfeld has never been fully explored. Deedes and Walters, in *CB Essex*, treated the two men separately whereas, from the late months of 1600 until early 1603, Holdfeld was casting for Bowler at Colchester, presumably as a 'works manager'. At the same time, the Cambridge side of the business appears to have been working as normal, which suggests that Holdfeld had left someone with the necessary experience in charge.

Among Bowler's apprentices in 1600 was **Miles Graye**, not yet having completed his indentures and therefore not legally competent to run the foundry, hence the need to install a qualified manager. Graye later became the leading East Anglian founder of his day and carried on the business from 1604 until its destruction in the siege of Colchester in 1648 and his own death in 1649. He was also a persistent rival to Robert Oldfield.

Who was in charge at Cambridge during these upheavals is not mentioned by name, but it is fairly obvious. Firstly, the use of the cross crosslet and PRIES THE LORD by Holdfeld at Studham. They later became a standard part of Robert's inscriptions. Secondly, the Ashwell accounts show that work was proceeding on the hanging of their tenor.

> 1601/2
> Payd unto the bell hanger the last day of February
>   in part of payment   iii £
> 1602
> Payd unto the bell hanger 25 March more   xxvi s
> Payd unto the bell hanger the 5 of Apprill for
> his last payment for chipping the great bell   xii s
> 4th Oct.
> For drinck for bell hanger fyrst day   iii d

The 'bell hanger' (not bellfounder) was obviously a skilled man in that he was also able to chip-tune the bell in the tower without supervision. (*see Chapter 6, Seventeenth century bellfounding techniques, p. 38*). This would fit Robert Oldfield who was in fact nearly thirty years old.

After Bowler's recovery, Holdfeld returned to Cambridge, where he was to remain until 1612. Neither Holdfeld's set of beautiful late-Gothic sprigged capitals nor the Nottingham cross were ever used by Miles Graye, but both were to be used at Hertford in later years. The roundel and the RH shield (*Fig. 16, p. 72*) show evidence that they were made by the same hand as

Robert Oldfield's shield, thus adding another link to the chain which bound the two men.

During the Cambridge years, Holdfeld sent only one bell into Hertford-shire, the beautiful third at Great Hormead, inscribed + SONORA ✤ SONO ✤ MEO ✤ SONO ✤ DEO 1606, with cresting above and a plaited border on the lip which is identical to that on the 7th at Hemel Hempstead and fleurs-de-lys with sprouting buds. It has been locally attrib-uted to Robert, but the Nottingham cross, the spelling of 'Sonora' instead of 'Sonoro' and the lettering are conclusive.

When Holdfeld finally returned to Cambridge it was time for the younger man to strike out for himself. There is a gap from October 1602 to the execution of Dier in September 1603 and Oldfield's marriage in April 1604. That he did some work at Watton-at-Stone, thus meeting his future wife, is probable. Two or three months can be accounted for in this way. Dier's execution had left a vacuum in Hertfordshire so by late 1603 or early 1604, a new bellfounder had moved to Hertford. Why Hertford? The Ashwell churchwardens' accounts of 1571/2 show that suitable foundry clay was available there. Also, it was customary, if not actually obligatory, for an apprentice out of his time or a junior partner to move away from his master's area, to avoid unfair competition; in many cases the distance was specified. The sketch map showing the location of bellfoundries, (*Map 1.* p. 13) shows that Hertford was the requisite distance from both Colchester and Cambridge.

Robert Oldfield in Hertford

It is important to remember that Oldfield was the first *settled*, as opposed to semi-itinerant, founder to have worked in the county, i.e. all his bells appear to have been cast in Hertford and not as a result of itinerating. Obviously he had to travel to inspect bells in situ before they were sent to the foundry but all quoted churchwardens' accounts speak of bells being carried to Hertford and not of the purchase of supplies of bricks and charcoal which would be required for casting in the local churchyard.

The first document which mentions Robert Oldfield by name is the Parish Register of Watton-at-Stone for 1604. It reads :

1604 Aprille 29   Roberte Olffeelde and
                                    Sara Cranne married

Sara, (or Sarah or Zara) Cranne, (or Crane) had been christened at Watton-at-Stone on 10 November 1587 so that at the time of her marriage she was sixteen, while Robert was thirty-two. Exactly what work he had been doing at Watton is not known. The churchwardens' accounts for 1603 and 1604 give no help, the latter year being illegible. So much later work has been done on the church bells, culminating in their disposal and replacement in 1977, that all clues have been eradicated. Thus, whether he was casting a bell for the church or a clock bell for Watton Woodhall, the local manor, cannot now be verified; the old Woodhall was destroyed by fire in 1771. Likewise, the later clock and its bell installed in the rebuilt house were removed in the 1950s. What can be stated with some certainty is that he was at Watton to work and not just to eye the local girls!

Sara may have been either a maid at Woodhall or a servant at a local inn frequented by a thirsty founder, but wherever and however they met, Old-field made a good choice for his future wife. She became a helpmeet in the truest sense of the word.

At or before the time of his marriage, he became the tenant of 38 St Andrew's Street, Hertford, and he and Sara were to remain there for over forty years. No. 38 is situated on the north side of St Andrew's Street, opposite the east end of the churchyard, (Maps 3 & 4). It seems to have been a fairly large house, probably a medieval rabbit-warren of small rooms, comprising a hall, a great parlour, a little parlour, a kitchen, a little buttery, a great buttery, cellars and chambers over the hall and the parlour, as well as a brewhouse, which may have been converted to that use after 1624. All these are listed in the Inventory of goods in 1650 (see p. 57). There would also have been enough space at the rear of the premies for setting up his foundry, a process which would take a month or two, at the end of the long croft, stretching down to the River Beane.

It has been pointed out to the writer that, unless Oldfield became 'free' of the Borough, he would be unable to carry on his trade, and that he was not listed as a Freemen until 1636. He must have in fact 'paid his shilling' to the Borough as there is incontrovertible evidence that he cast a bell in Hertford in 1604. This comes from outside the county, at Roydon, Essex, and is quoted at length in CB Essex, p. 377. The relevant extracts are :

1604/5

laid out for bread & beere at the takeing down and loadinge of the bell		ij s	
for mending the bellofte & boards & nailes		iij s	iiij d
or makening a bonde at Hartford & to give the Carters drincke			xiiij d
for castinge the bell	iiij li	vj s	
for fetching the bell from Hartford		iij s	iiij d

The 'bonde' referred to was a guarantee that the bell would last for a year and a day. The usual cost of a bond was sixpence, so 'drincke' for the carters was the more expensive item. The item for timber and nails for mending the 'bellofte', i.e. the belfry, implies that some damage had occurred to the floor, possibly caused by the bell falling and becoming broken.

This commission, so soon after moving into Hertford, suggests that the months prior to his marriage had been occupied with building up business connections in the neighbourhood. The following year, trade was good.

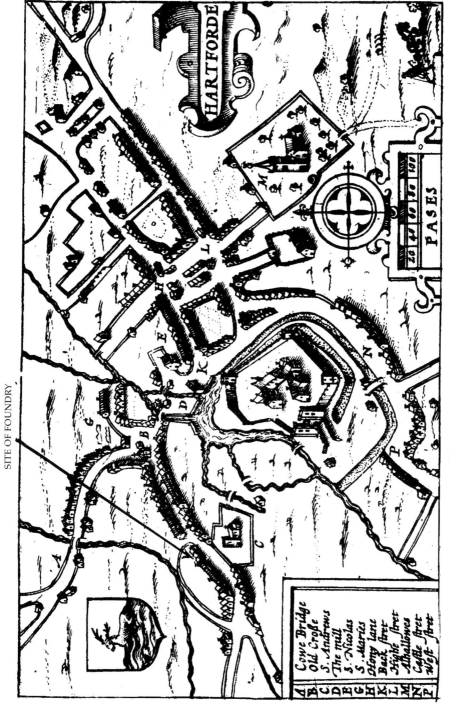

SITE OF FOUNDRY

Map 2. Speed's Map of Hertfordshire 1610

HARTFORDE

PASES

A	Cowe Bridge
B	Old Croſſe
C	S. Andrews
D	The mill
E	S. Nicolas
G	S. Maris
H	Stony lane
K	Back ſtret
L	Highe ſtret
M	Althallowes
N	Caſtle ſtret
P	Weſt ſtret

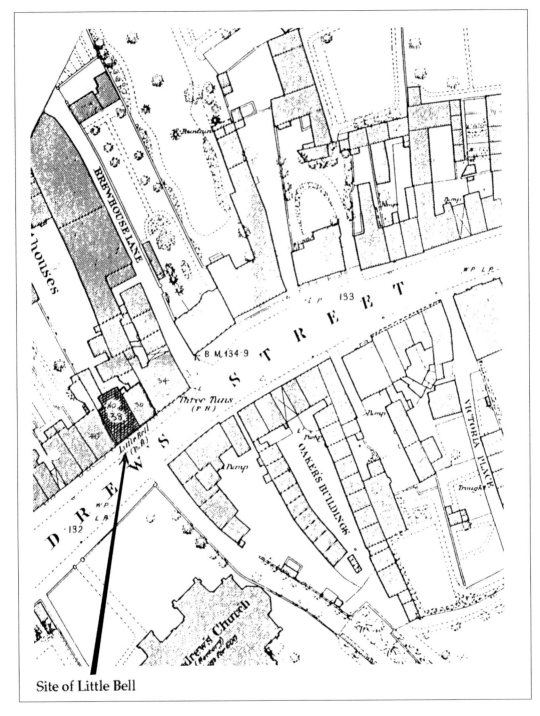

Site of Little Bell

Map 4. St. Andrew's Street, before 1860

A bell was cast for St James, Stanstead Abbots, one for Graveley and three for St John's, Digswell. Of these early products, three remain, the Stanstead Abbots tenor, which bears his name, and two of the Digswell three, which carry his trademark, a shield with an arrow rebus. This rebus was similar to his 'mark' with which he signed documents, suggesting that he was only partly literate. There were three degrees of literacy: those who could read and write; those who could read but not write and those who could do neither. Oldfield probably fell into the second category.

A son, **William**, was born in January, 1605/6, his baptism being entered in the St Andrew's register on the fifteenth of that month. No bells have survived from 1606 but that does not mean that none were cast. As with so many other bells by Oldfield, they may have been replaced in later years by something more 'modern'. The next reference to his family came with the birth of **Denis** (*sic*), a daughter baptised at Watton-at-Stone on the 16 January, 1608/9. The spelling of names in those days depended on the literacy of clergy and parish clerks.

The following year, Robert's name appears, for the first time in official records, the Calendar of Assize Records. Under –

HERTFORDSHIRE INDICTMENTS , James I, Published by HMSO,

¶370 p. 76 Robert Dulefeild, Bell-founder and
          John Ireland, Yeoman, of Hertford –
          Discharge of their Recognisances for
          the appearance of Richard Buttone
          of Edmonton, Cook
          30th March 1610.

Despite the eccentric spelling of his name by the Clerk to the Court, who may have been baffled by a Midlands accent, there is no difficulty in identifying Robert.

The baptisms at St Andrew's continued with **Ann** (spelled An in the Register) on 6 January 1610/11 and **Sarye**, on 6 February 1612/13.

After two years, 1609 and 1610, from when no bells survive, trade picked up again in 1611. He was now known over a wider area than Hertfordshire, with bells going to mid-Essex. By this time, the Colchester foundry under Miles Graye I was a formidable rival, being a much larger concern and it is fascinating to see the 'poaching' which each carried out in the other's territory.

The most outstanding example of this 'poaching' occurred over the recasting of an early fifteenth century bell at Great Dunmow in 1613. This fine bell, cast between 1400–10, by Robert Burford of Aldgate, had become cracked and had to be recast. (Gabriel, the Clock Tower bell in St Albans is a splendid specimen of Burford's work). With hindsight, it would seem more sensible to have gone to Miles Graye at Colchester, whose reputation as a founder was well known, rather than travel the greater distance to Hertford.

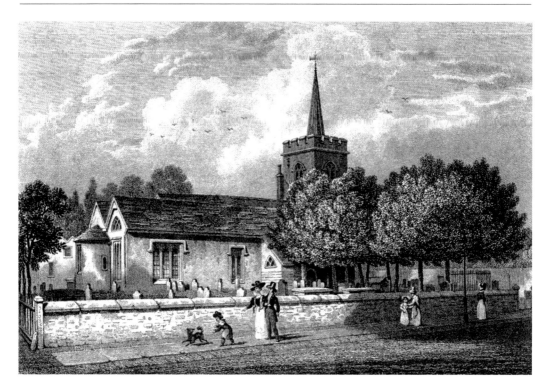

Hertford, Old St Andrew's where Robert Oldfield's children were christened. Later, John Briant recast the bells into a ring of eight. [*HALS*]

Both Graye and Oldfield must have tendered for the job, for which money seems to have been no object. Graye, master craftsman though he was, was very limited in his range of inscriptions and would have been in difficulties with that particular one, which involved re-using some of Burford's 3 inch high capitals, (*Fig. 14*, p. 69). However, Holdfeld, now at Hertford, had been for some time in charge at Colchester and Graye would not care to offend his old boss.

Oldfield's production of bells (Fig. 6) shows a sharp rise in 1612/13 which may be accounted for by the fact that Richard Holdfeld's foundry in Cambridge closed down in the former year, due either to Holdfeld's advancing years or because of the expiry of a lease. Whether he had outstanding orders that Robert fulfilled, which may explain the odd situation at Berden, Essex, where two bells were cast in the same year by two different founders, or whether Holdfeld moved to his son's house at Hertford and assisted in the foundry cannot be certain after so many years. Such evidence as there is points to the latter explanation, as the identical alphabet used by Holdfeld at Eaton Socon in 1607 (*Fig. 10*, p.65) made an appearance on a bell at Broxbourne in 1615, bearing a unique version of his 'Nottingham' cross and Robert's shield. (*Fig. 17d*, p. 75) The bell was cast at Hertford and may have formed part of a complete ring of five, of which three still remain.

On 2 April 1614, a Margaret Oldfield was buried at St Andrew's. Her

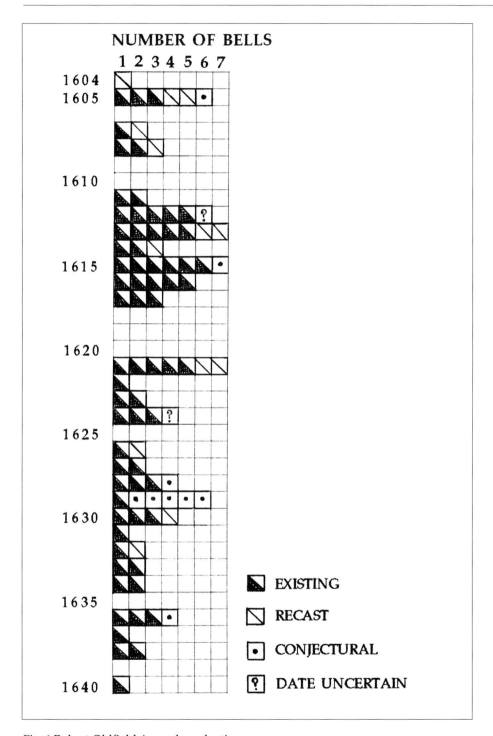

Fig. 6 Robert Oldfield Annual production

exact identity is unknown, but she may have been the wife of Richard Hold-feld and therefore Robert's mother.

The next baptism at St Andrew's was that of **Robert** on 21 May 1615 and he was followed by **John** on 20 November 1617. Sadly, neither of these boys outlived their childhood, young Robert dying before his eighth birthday, being buried at St Andrew's on 3 March 1622/3 and John, aged eleven, buried on 2 December 1628.

In 1617 another masterpiece, the present 7th at St Mary's, Hemel Hemp-stead was cast. Like Holdfeld's 1606 bell for Great Hormead, this fine bell has everything: plaited border on the lip, 'Nottingham'-type cresting above the inscription band, special cross and a highly decorative alphabet (*Fig. 12*, p. 67). As at Great Dunmow, money seems to have been no object. The cresting was that previously used by Holdfeld and, as at Broxbourne, it was prob-ably a joint product.

The 'Little Bell' Alehouse

A major change occurred in the life of the Oldfield family in 1625. Robert had been listed in the Corporation Records of 1624 as 'tenant' of 38 St Andrew's Street. Bellfounding had fallen off after a peak year of 1621 and times were hard. In the seventeenth century, bellfounding was carried out at small local foundries, whose products rarely occur outside a radius of about thirty miles, due to the state of the roads, therefore any problems within the catchment area, such as outbreaks of disease, would cause demand to fluc-tuate. These economic woes were not confined to town-dwellers. A poor harvest meant that village churchwardens had more trouble in collecting their dues and bells had to wait. At that period, most bellfounders had a second string to their bow, as must have been the case with John Grene (p. 9). A regular part of a founder's output came from other metal castings such as bronze mortars for domestic use and brass bearings for rural bell-hangers and similar assorted small items. Richard Bowler of Colchester kept cattle and probably doubled as a farmer. The Chandler family of founders from Drayton Parslow, Bucks., began as village blacksmiths and carried on both trades. Only the large concerns, such as the Oldfields of Nottingham carried enough capital to see them through lean times. For Robert Oldfield a different solution suggested itself. His house was sufficiently commodious to allow him to turn part of it into an alehouse. In 1625 his house was known as the Bell and he was listed as licensee (*HCR*).

The year 1625 was not a good one for Hertford. The accession of Charles I was to be a future disaster, but a more present one was an outbreak of pestilence, probably plague, which brought great suffering and hardship to much of Hertfordshire. Certainly bellfounding was at a low ebb, no extant bells being known for that year (*Fig. 6*). The alehouse, therefore, became a vital source of income. Whose idea it was is hard to say. Sara, like most

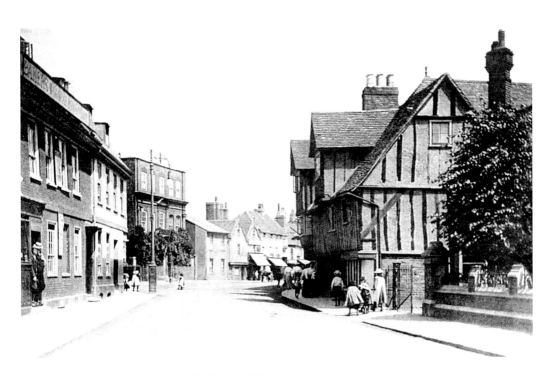

countrywomen of that period, would have been brought up to bake and brew and it was obvious that most of the work involved would fall on her shoulders. It was quite common for women to be the licensees of alehouses and in this case it would represent a fair division of labour: Robert would carry on with the bellfoundry and Sara would run the alehouse although Robert would be named as the licensee. The name of the house presented no problem. It was absolutely logical for the bellfounder/alehouse-keeper to call his house the Bell. Nothing could be simpler than for him to cast a small bell as a trade sign and hang it outside.

Hertford, St Andrew's Street. The building on the far left was 'The Little Bell', the successor to 'The Bell Mould'. [Hertford Museum]

There was, however, a major snag which should have been foreseen. Occasional lack of foresight was one of Robert's weaknesses. The licensee of an inn of respectable antiquity, first recorded in 1431 (Ref. *Hertfordshire Inns & Public Houses* by Graham Jolliffe & Arthur Jones), called the Bell, which stood in High Street (now Fore Street) not unnaturally took exception to an upstart alehouse calling itself by the same name. The Bell derived its name from the old Market bell which hung outside. This fine bell was possibly cast by John Walgrave of Aldgate (1418–40) and is now in Hertford Museum. Its bracket was still on the inn as late as 1800 and can be seen in Rowlandson's print of Hertford Market in that year, although the bell is not visible. The licensee of the Bell Inn, William Hill, died of the plague in 1625 and by 1626, probably in order to avoid further offence, Robert backed down and renamed his house the Golden Bell. This was not so far-fetched when one considers that a recently-cast bell would still retain its original bright appearance, before weathering occurred.

On 17 January, 1625/6, a Richard Oldfield was buried at St Andrew's. It is impossible to be absolutely certain, but he was most probably Robert's father. If so, his age would be close to eighty. He was a founder of considerable artistic feeling, characterised by his use of the beautiful late-medieval alphabet and his own exquisite fleurs-de-lys. Only the third at Great Hormead survives within the county; there were more, at least two being cast for Ashwell in 1607.

The foundry had a major commission in 1626. In that year the fourth bell (possibly the tenor) of Waltham Abbey was brought to Hertford to be recast. (*CB Essex* p. 429). The extracts from the churchwardens' accounts read:

Item for casting of the fourth bell and for new metal added and put to her	x l^i	xix s	ij^d
Item to Wm Wandleing for carrieage of the fourth bell to Hertfort to be cast and for his charges		xvj s	x d

£10 19s 2d represented a large sum for a bell and it is possible to calculate the size of the bell from the cost. Oldfield's recasting charges in 1638 (*CB Beds.* p. 190) were 11/- per cwt so the Waltham Abbey bell weighed in the region of 21 cwt or more, allowing for inflation. It is amusing to note that the bell was feminine. To the ringing fraternity, bells still are. It was a welcome addition to the household's income as commissions of that size were comparatively rare for small founders. Oldfield would have a workforce probably consisting of at least an apprentice or two and labourers to assist with the heavier jobs, such as moving large bells like this one. By this date it is a fair assumption that William, the eldest son, would be a part of the workforce, although there is no record of him carrying on the trade.

In 1627, exact date not specified, the next document to name Oldfield concerns a 'bastard begotten of Jane Greene of St. Andrew's parish' in respect of whom he entered into a bastardy bond. (*HCR 78 : 215*). This he signed with his 'mark', the arrow rebus, (*Fig.16c*, p. 72). It appears that he entered into this on behalf of one of his workman and *not* on his own account. The fact that Jane Greene lived in the parish inevitably raises the question of whether she was a local lady of easy virtue or a living-in servant at the Golden Bell. Six beds are listed in the inventory of 1650, which suggests that at least double that number of people, family, servants and workmen, were squashed in together, a very common situation leading to a very common result.

Also in the same year a bell was cast for St Mary's, Studham, Beds. There is no indication that it was cast by Oldfield and it is rightly ascribed to the founder whose initials it bears, **James Keene** of Bedford. There are, however, several oddities which call for an explanation. The cross, initials 'I K' and the date are in Keene's normal characters. The inscription, ᏩOD ✢ SAVE ✢ OVR

✠ KING is in Oldfield's thin alphabet, complete with the Gothic 'G' and a small version of the 1605 Stanstead Abbots fleur-de-lys. The 'K' is unmistakably part of the same alphabet used by Oldfield at Hemel Hempstead, although it did not form part of that inscription. This could imply that the bell may have been cast by Keene at Hertford, making use of Oldfield's foundry facilities, not an unheard-of situation or, equally possible, that Keene had spent some time at Hertford as a journeyman. There is another indication that the two men were well-acquainted; Keene used and developed Oldfield's acorn stops (see p. 75).

For the next five years it is possible to follow much of Oldfield's everyday life from Hertford Corporation Records, St Andrew's registers and, most importantly, from his bells. Each bell is a document in itself. The HCR lists him as 'occupier' in 1628. The parish registers record the death of his youngest child, John, on 2 December the same year. Also in 1628, bells were cast for Gilston, Thorley and Great Wymondley, suggesting that trade was picking up again.

There is an interesting entry in *CB Bucks*, p. 435, which appears to misquote Browne Willis, the historian, concerning the bells at Ivinghoe. The tenor inscription was given as 'SACRA MANET CHRISTI PLEBISQUE RELIGIO VANA' and the date as 1628. George Lipscombe (c.f. the John Dier bell at Linslade, No. 45), who noted this, was a careless copyist and the first word should surely have been 'Sana'. This was an inscription used by Oldfield on his larger bells and which was only used by one other founder in the country, Thomas Hancox of Walsall, who was unlikely to have been working in central Buckinghamshire. This was a very big bell, the weight being quoted as '2900' (lb). There is nothing inherently difficult about ascribing it to Oldfield, as he cast bells for Tring in 1622/4 and for Aldbury in 1634, so it was well within his normal range. He may, of course, have travelled to Ivinghoe to cast it on the spot but there is no evidence, written or otherwise that he moved around in this way. It seems to have been his biggest casting and may indeed have been the tenor of a complete ring of five, all of which were recast in 1875.

The sheer problems of moving a bell of this size were considerable. It had first to be craned on to the wagon, then manoeuvred round the back of the foundry and out into Brewhouse Lane. Then came the turn into St Andrew's Street, which would be no wider then than it is now, followed by the slow uphill plod towards Hertingfordbury. As far as St Albans, it would travel over the Assize road, so called because it was the route travelled by the Justices between Hertford and Reading; beyond there, the road through Berkhamsted was tolerable, but the final stretch along the foot of the Chilterns must have called for a huge amount of effort. The effect in Hertford of the passage of this great bell must have been a nine days' wonder with the whole town turning out to watch. Probably most of his casting days had their quota of onlookers, idlers and nosey-parkers.

Recognisances crop up again in 1629, when the name of the house was still the 'Golden Bell'. The following two years find him listed as 'bell-founder' (1630) and as 'occupier' (1631) in Borough Records. However, in 1634, the name of the house is given as the 'Bell Mould'. This unattractive title was nevertheless an accurate description. Once again, licensee's recognisances were recorded. Founding went on, although at a reduced level, with orders coming in chiefly from Hertfordshire churches, including the local one at Bengeo. There is no firm evidence that he did, or did not, carry out work in any of the Hertford churches. In the 1552 Inventory, there were three bells at St Andrew's and five at All Saints. In 1610, an inventory records four bells and a clock at the former and still five at the latter. Sir Henry Chauncy, Recorder of Hertford and himself a keen bellringer, noted 'four small bells' at St Andrew's in 1700 and a 'Good ring of eight bells' at All Saints, which had been augmented in 1674 and which were the earliest octave in the county. It is therefore clear that a bell was cast for St Andrew's in or before 1610 and it was almost certainly by Oldfield. With a bellfounder living practically on the doorstep, the churchwardens of both churches would make use of him. If, as is suggested by the Ashwell accounts, he was also a skilled hanger, any rehanging or repairs would also come his way.

The great Priory church of St John's, which had fallen into disrepair after its Dissolution in 1535, from which year there is a gap in the records until 1622, was rebuilt by Sir Thomas Wilys of Balls Park, utilising the south wall of the original building, in 1629. If any bell were supplied, it would have been a local one, but again, concrete evidence is lacking. St John's parish was amalgamated with All Saints in 1640 and was demolished by order of the Bishop of Lincoln about 1680 so a bell would not have survived.

It is not until 1637 that there is any indication of Oldfield's financial status. This makes him unique among Hertfordshire founders as none of the others, apart from Briant, was settled within the Borough, which has very comprehensive records. On 26 February 1637 a sum of £55 was levied as Ship Money. This hated tax had long outlived the original purpose of its name and was being levied throughout the kingdom and not, as formerly, in coastal towns only. Oldfield was one of fifty-three names on the St Andrew's parish list, amounts ranging from £2 to 2/6d; his assessment was 4/- (*HCR* Vol. 46. p. 907).

On 8 May in the same year, a Pest House rate was levied. Oldfield was assessed at 2/-. He was one of forty names on the St Andrew's list and amounts ranged from 20/- to 1/- (*HCR* pp. 909–11). He was obviously in a position to pay taxes, but not in any high tax bracket. Frequent recognisances suggest that he was willing to stand surety for friends, or customers, in trouble with the law, so he was solvent rather than wealthy.

The following year, 1638, saw the recasting of Kimpton tenor, the last of four bells cast for that church between 1636 and the later date. Oldfield had run into a minor snag with one bell in 1636 because he did not have the necessary letters 'C' and 'W' in his late alphabet. He overcame this by unearthing his early letters which fortunately had not been thrown away. When he came to the tenor, however, the 'H ' of the early set had become broken, so a new crossbar was grafted on to the uprights, giving a unique letter used nowhere else and also neatly solving the difficulty. In the writer's opinion it shows that Oldfield was sufficiently literate to cope with such unexpected problems.

In the same year, on 9 June, a party was held at the Bell Mould, at which Robert was the host. A group of Sir John Boteler's servants from Watton Woodhall walked into Hertford and called at the alehouse, which was in fact the first public house on the road in from Watton. Now unless Sir John and his lady were away from home, these servants would not have had the leisure to indulge in an outing, but when the cat's away… ! Bearing in mind that Sara was a Watton girl, some at least of these men must have been relatives of hers, possibly nephews and the outing and meal were part of a family occasion or celebration of some kind. Following a meal and 'throwing the barre', which may have been a primitive form of skittles (or tossing the caber), they proceeded to the Bell Inn, taking Robert with them. By this time they were probably well and truly drunk and disorderly and fighting broke out. The Constable was called and the unruly rabble had to be bailed out by Sir John's steward and gamekeeper. Robert seems to have had the common sense to take no part in the affray, as no deposition of his survives. After all, he was getting on in years (he was 66) and, as a licensee, he had to observe certain standards of behaviour(!) (HCR 17: 251, 252 & 257) Such goings-on were not, however, unknown in seventeenth century Hertford.

Another bell cast in 1638 still survives; the present second at Shillington, Beds. The churchwardens' accounts are very detailed (c.f. John Dier, p. 15) and were quoted in C.B. Beds, p. 190. Curiously, North transcribed the prices into a more modern form for nineteenth century readers.

		£	s	d
Ite'	spent at Hartf' when we went with the bell		8	8
Ite'	to John Baxter for hanging the bell		14	0
Ite'	at going out of our bell and at coming in for bread and beare		1	4
Ite'	to John Crouch for drawing our bell to Hartford		13	0
Ite'	to Robert Oldfeild for casting our bell at eleaven shilling the hundred	4	10	6
Ite'	spent at the payment of the money			9
Ite'	paid for two Bonds about casting of the bell		1	6

This bell is the second of the heavy ring of five, not the treble as stated in CB Beds., weighing about 8¼ cwt. Previous churchwardens' accounts dealing with bells cast at Hertford failed to link the name of the founder with his place of work and this is therefore the earliest to do so.

No bells have survived from 1639 and what appears to have been Oldfield's last one was cast in 1640, the tenor for Matching, Essex, (see No. 84) a very good-toned bell. Strangely enough, it is inscribed ᏧOᎧ SAVE THE KINᎧ. In view of the fact that Hertford was Parliamentarian, this can almost be read as God Help the King. This inscription had not been used on any (surviving) bells for ten years, the previous ones being at Hunsdon and Stapleford Tawney in 1630. Perhaps Matching retained some lingering sense of loyalty to the Crown.

After this, the bellfounding business closed, with a possible small-scale production of mortars and other domestic utensils for a short while afterwards. An inventory of his goods in 1650 records only a very small amount of bell metal remaining. The tenancy was still in Oldfield's name and the name of the Bell Mould was kept until at least 1646. William Whitmore was founding in Hertfordshire from about 1647 and may have bought most of Oldfield's stock of metal.

A Poll Tax assessment of 1646 sheds more light on Oldfield's financial status. This list may have been used on more that one occasion as there is a change in the writing. There were five major categories:

Those able to expend £100 per annum	(7 in the list)
" " " " £50 " " "	(10 " " ")
" " " " £20 " " "	(24 " " ")
" " " " £10 " " "	(25 " " ")
" " " " £5 " " "	(41 " " ")

Oldfield came within the list of those able to pay £10 per annum and was asked to pay 2/-. All this proves that, although able to pay his way, he had not exactly made his fortune out of either bellfounding or keeping an alehouse. The interesting point is that his financial status was almost exactly the same as it had been in 1637, for the Ship Money and the Pest House rate.

Two separate reasons must have prompted his retirement. The first was that he was getting on in years, being nearly seventy; the second was that the political situation was deteriorating rapidly. There was no market for luxuries like bells when the country was dividing itself into two armed camps. Some founders did carry on their trade during the later stages of the Civil War, e.g. William Whitmore of 'Wolford', usually thought to be Watford, who was working his way around that area in 1647. The majority just seemed to have given up for the duration. It is an odd fact that, during the Commonwealth, there was no ban on bells and bellfounding. This was because bellringing had become a secular activity, divorced from the original purpose of calling the faithful to worship. Several founders worked in Hertfordshire in the 1650s. Perhaps the most plaintive of all bell inscriptions can be found at Northchurch in 1651, O LORD HAVE MERCI OF MAN. This was cast by Anthony Chandler of Drayton Parslow and sums up the whole tragic situation.

Within Hertford itself, the Corporation was trying to work as normal. However, in 1642, a stock of gunpowder was moved into the Town House, thus turning Hertford into a garrison town, with all that that implied. The quartering of Roundhead troops, without payment, on the local populace caused considerable hardship and resentment. The main tide of war passed by the area, but Cromwell and Fairfax spent one night in the town in 1647, presumably at The Bell Inn, when Cromwell went to quell a mutiny among Roundhead troops at Cockbush Field on the road to Ware. No doubt the whole town turned out to see the great man!

Notwithstanding all this upheaval, Borough records continued to be kept, although the Borough itself was to all intents and purposes bankrupt. A list of Freemen in 1646 contains Oldfield's name but there is no further mention of him.

In April 1649 a Court of the Market was convened and a list of jurors given. Their function was to list all weights and measures held by various tradespeople in the Borough. Among the names recorded was Widow Old-feild, who held 'Pottes' measuring one quart and one pint. The same year, Sara was listed as licensee of the Bell Mould. Clearly, Robert had died aged between seventy-four and seventy-seven at some date between 1646 and before April 1649, when is not known. Neither is his place of burial known, but it is the writer's opinion that he was most likely buried at St Andrew's. It was a period of turmoil, both locally and nationally, St Andrew's parish being no different from any other in having a rapid turnover of ministers. It is not surprising that the death of one elderly man should have gone unrecorded. All that can be certain is that his death must have been unexpected as he died intestate.

Sara continued as licensee and she appears in respect of recognisances the same year: they may have originally been entered into by Robert. As there had been no will, it was necessary for an inventory of goods to be made before his estate could be administered. This was done on 29 April 1650, a year or more after Robert's death. The inventory is held in the Hertfordshire Archives and Local Studies (*AAH 23/ 1795*). This lists the rooms in order and their more significant contents.

Inventory of the goods of Robert Oldfeild

In the chamber over the parlour (?)
Item table and fowre
chairs cubbards one bason
and ewer (- - - - -)
one paire of andirons one paire
of bellowes one window (- - - - -)
one standing bedsted one tumble(?) bed
one feather bed one floc bed two
bedsteds two pillowes one (- - - - -)
one rugg three blankets - - - one paire
of sheets a dozen pillow (- - - -) half
dozen of napkins a dozen of toweles with
some other similar Lumber

} xviij l

In the kitchin (*sic*)
  Item one dresser bord three (- - -) turn
  spitts fowre quart pottes (- - - -) pottes
  fowre pewter flagons (- - - - -)
  (- - - -) of pewter one dozen of   } iiij l
  (- - - -) half a dozen porringers two brasse
  pottes fowere brasse kettles one frying pann
  with some other similar Lumber

In the brewhouse
  Item one copper one masshinge
  butt one maltquarter and (- - -)   } L s
  brewing vessells with some other
  Lumber

The contents of the Little Buttery were valued at xij s, those of the Great
Parlour at vij l, the Little Parlour at xv s, the Chamber over the Buttery at xls.
In the Great Buttery were listed the remnants of the bellfounding business:
  Item one old cubbard (- - - - -) weights
  (- - - -) piece of bell mittle   } xx s

  with some other similar Lumber
  (*Probably no more than a hundredweight of metal*)

In the yard :
  Wood in yard   xx ^s
  (*This was a considerable amount and inevitably raises the question of whether it
  was intended for bellhanging rather than domestic or brewing purposes. It was not
  described as kindling*)
  Item his wearing apparrell   5 l

The total found came to 55l. 17 s (£55 17s) and the inventory was signed by

Hugh Northe
Oliver North

This pathetic document, written on tattered sheets apparently torn out of a
pocket-book, with its illegibilities and crossings-out seems, by the writing, to
have been written by Oliver North, as it is in the same hand as his signature.
It is a standard secretary hand typical of its time. Hugh Northe signed in a
firm italic hand, which suggests that he was a lawyer. It was sent to the
Court of the Archdeanconry of Huntingdon and was returned in very
prompt time with the Administration lond, dated 18 May 1650, probate
being granted to **Sara Oldfeild, widdowe.**

There is a discrepency concerning the date of the Administration Bond
which arises from a reference in *CB Bucks.*, p.163. A.H. Cocks, the author, in
the course of his researches, had discovered Oldfield's Administration Bond
in Somerset House, dated 7 May 1650. He tried to communicate with J.C.L.
Stahlschmidt, co-author of *CB Herts.* 1886, but Stahlschmidt died before the
letter reached him. Presumably there were two copies of the bond. (See also
Victoria County History of Hertfordshire Vol 4, p. 269).

There was no stable government in England until about 1654 and a major problem of those years was the huge number of travellers on the roads, discharged soldiers, petitioners going to and from London, all the leftovers of war. In the words of Dr Frances M. Page in her *History of Hertford* – 'this motley collection of travellers had but one thing in common – they drank'. Sara must have indeed needed strength of character to cope with some of those wayfarers.

At first the local inns would do a roaring trade, but the Puritans frowned on such practices and there was increasing regulation of licensed premises, culminating in Draconian measures in July 1656, against tippling (spending more than an hour over a drink) and other such sins. For Sara, who was then in her sixty-eighth year, enough must have been enough. She gave up the tenancy and retired. However, she stayed within St Andrew's parish, probably going to live with one of her daughters. This redoubtable old lady lived in retirement until 1673, when she was in her eighty-fifth year. The item in St Andrew's register reads :

> 1673 May 16th Old Widow Oldfeild buryed.

The reference to 'Old Widow Oldfeild' implies that there was another, 'Young', Widow Oldfeild. As the only son who did not die in childhood was William, the first-born, this seems to indicate that he too was dead by this date.

In 1660 the licence was held by Robert Churchman. The alehouse became known variously as the Bell and Shears, the Bell and Punchbowl, the One Bell and finally as the Little Bell, under which name it closed in 1958. It had proved nearly as durable as some of its licensee's bells. The premises were partially rebuilt in about 1760, with a plain Georgian frontage, but the cellars and back may belong to the earlier building. At a later date the house next door, No 36, was added to the alehouse, but the arrangement was comparatively short-lived and the premises are once again under separate occupation. At the time of writing (June 2001) No. 38 is in the process of conversion to another use, having been for a number of years a high-class furnishings store, trading as Peter and Susan Brown, to whom the writer is indebted for being shown the cellars on an earlier visit.

To the rear of the plot, leading to the River Beane, on the site where the foundry stood, the tradition of small-scale industry, going back to the Middle Ages, was still being carried on by a motor engineering business as late as 1998. Now (2001) all traces of the old industry have gone. In their place stands a housing development, so sensitively designed that in years to come it will be an integral part of the old town, although in the process, the original settlement pattern has been obliterated.

8

ROBERT OLDFIELD'S WORKS

ANALYSIS OF OLDFIELD'S LETTERING

AND DECORATIONS

Alphabets

M OST BELLFOUNDERS HAVE tended to use only one or two alphabets over a long period. Not so Oldfield. He was constantly experimenting with his type faces. Up to 1616 he used a neat, flat roman type in
two sizes, (*Figs. 7, 8, 9*), with minor differences between the 'R's of the two
sets. Following so closely on the coarse black letter of John Dier and John
Clarke II, this type comes as a clear symbol of the start of a new era. In 1615
he used Bowler's beautiful sprigged Gothic capitals on the present 4th bell
at Broxbourne, (*Fig. 10*). These almost certainly came from Colchester or Lincoln via Cambridge (Holdfeld). By this time the set, notably the 'P', was
showing signs of wear and no other existing bell has these letters. The worn
'P' also appears on the preserved inscription band of the old 4th bell at
Eaton Socon, Cambs., known to have been cast by Holdfeld in 1607, supplying further evidence that the same set was used by both men. If there is any
truth in the writer's theory that the Richard Oldfield buried at St Andrew's
in 1625/6 was the Cambridge founder, then he would have brought the tools
of his trade, including the letter-moulds, at some time post-1612, when he
moved to Hertford. The Broxbourne bell, which correctly bears Robert's
shield, may therefore have been actually cast or at least moulded by
Richard.

In 1616, came a change to a thin, elegant, roman type, cast in earthenware
moulds, (*Fig. 11*), used individually at first but later grouped into word
blocks. The first 'S' was doubled and ornate, similar to Holdfeld's, but
changed to a simple form after 1621. Then came the introduction of the
archaic 'ð' (D) and 'ꝺ' (G), the latter being derived from his early letters.
Still experimenting, he then produced another short-lived version of these
two letters, sprouting tiny leaves.

At that period, all twenty-six letters of the modern alphabet were not
used – 'I' for 'J' and 'V' for 'U' were normal usage. In this later set neither 'Q',
'C' nor 'W' appear. The 1621 bell at Little Berkhamsted has the largest alphabetical variety of any of his later bells and on that the 'W' was constructed
from two 'V's. The lack of these letters was to have an interesting sequel.

In 1617 at Hemel Hempstead, a large 1.4"/35mm version of the thin
alphabet appears, highly decorated with a sprigged background of flowers

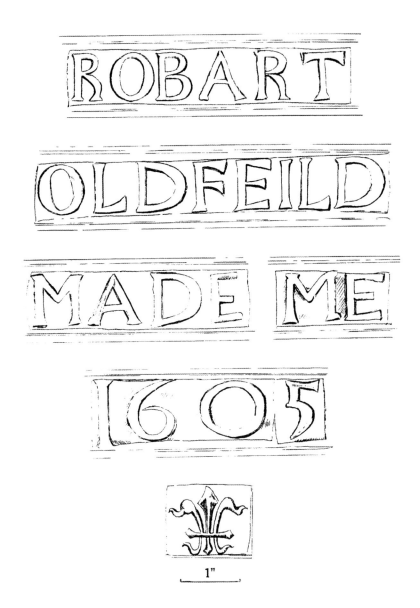

Fig. 7 Stanstead Abbots (St James) tenor

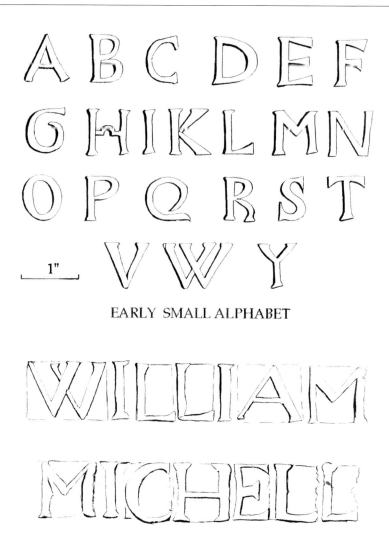

EARLY SMALL ALPHABET

Fig. 8 Intermediate Alphabet Kimpson 8th, 1638

and fleurs-de-lys, (*Fig. 12 p 67*). At first sight this could be mistaken for the work of James Keene of Woodstock who ornamented his inscriptions in a similar way, but there are significant differences. The H of 'CHRISTI' is formed from two 'E's with upper and lower bars cut away and then roughly placed face to face. Keene would have found a more elegant solution! Again the bell bears Robert's shield, but on the evidence of the cresting, could have been by Richard.

Richard Oldfield the younger, working in Warwickshire and Shropshire, followed a similar evolutionary path with his alphabets and he too used a large, heavily-sprigged version at Claines, Worcs. This is yet another fruitful field for future research.

Robert Oldfield's penultimate variation appeared in 1623 at Thundridge. Here and at Gilston 1628, Hunsdon 1630 and Offley 1632, he used 'IESVS BE OVR SPEDE' made up as blocks, with small raised rings which give the impression of having been made by the end of a thick straw pushed into damp clay, which would then be fired to earthenware temperature (Fig. 13 p 68). The inscriptions on these four bells are identical as comparative casts have shown.

The 'PRAISE THE LORD' blocks were apparently first used at Little Hadham, also in 1623; all examples show a slight fault between the 'R' and 'D', which looks like a scratch on the clay.

'GOO SAVE THE KING' seems not to have been made into blocks, as so many versions exist and Oldfield was content to mount the letters either on word-sized or individual paterae. In his later years he rarely used this inscription, possibly for political reasons, although it is on his last-known bell, Matching tenor 1640 (see No. 84).

The lack of 'C' and 'W' in his thin alphabet caused problems at Kimpton in 1636/8, where he cast or recast at least four bells, of which three remain. 'THOMAS HOO' (Lord of the Manor of Hoo in the parish) gave no trouble, as all the necessary letters existed. However, ''WILLIAM MICHELL' needed two of the missing ones, so Oldfield utilised a variant of his early large set for 'W M CW' on the present 5th, with his late cross and (bungled) late thin numerals. For the tenor, 1638, he not only employed a similar but slightly smaller type allied with his early cross crosslet, last used in 1616 – doubtless to confuse bell archeologists! The 'H' however seems to have been a special replacement. The uprights are original but the cross bar is a later alteration, being much cleaner in appearance, besides being straight instead of curved. Presumably the original had been broken. (*Fig. 8*)

At the present it is becoming customary, for English founders at least, to reproduce in facsimile the inscriptions on old bells which must unavoidably be recast. This, despite its lapse during the eighteenth and nineteenth centuries, is not a new phenomenon; over the years, founders have seen decorations which took their fancy and therefore reproduced them, to the bewilderment of historians trying to account for the reappearance of a stop or cross after the passage of two hundred years.

Richard Holdfeld recast a medieval bell at Eaton Socon in 1607, reproducing the beautiful inscription, not in facsimile, but using his own Gothic capitals. However, one of the best-known examples of early facsimile reproduction is the 'Gabriel' bell at Gloucester Cathedral, originally cast c.1400 by Robert Burford and recast in 1626 by John Pennington at Monmouth. (Ref. *Ringing World* 1977 p. 774. Article by Dr John Eisel). Unfortunately, Pennington was confused and applied the wax 'squeezes', rather than the letters

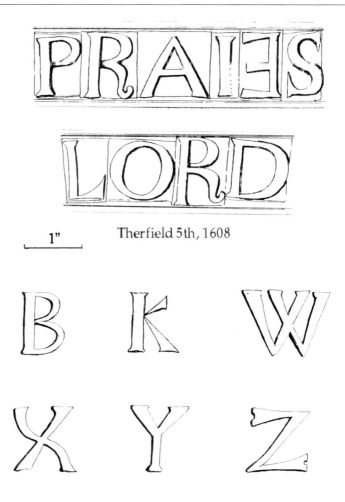

Therfield 5th, 1608

1"

Fig. 9 Early Alphabet

produced from them, to the false bell so that the inscription is recessed as well as reversed.

By coincidence, one of Oldfield's 1613 commissions was the recasting of another Robert Burford bell, the present 7th at Great Dunmow. Here the pompous Latin couplet states that the bell, being discordant (i.e. cracked) was re-made (*refecta*) to the order of Andrew and Chrysogona Jenoure, who paid for it. Burford's large (3"/76 mm) capitals and cross were skilfully re-used, although the juxtaposition of these with Oldfield's ¾"/20mm type and cross crosslet is mildly incongruous. It is however, a sensitive and remarkably successful attempt and represents what must be one of the earliest facsimile reproductions, coming as it does thirteen years before Pennington's work at Gloucester. While Burford's large capitals can hardly

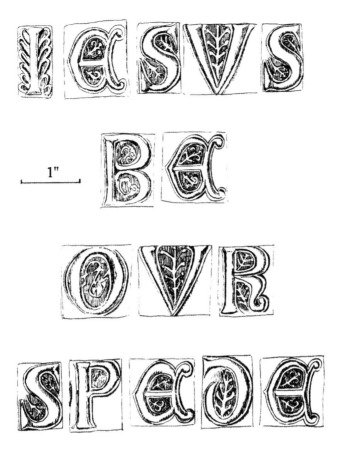

Fig. 10 Broxbourne 4th Holdfield's Sprigged Capitals

be described as an Oldfield alphabet it is yet another letter-form used by this most innovative craftsman (*Fig. 14* p 69).

One puzzle remains. What could possibly have been the original inscription on Burford's bell, using capitals Q, S, A, C and I?

Numerals and Dates

Oldfield's numerals follow roughly the sequence of development as his alphabets – early thick numbers matching early thick letters; late thin with late thin. This is logical enough but there was a time-lag of about a year before letters and numbers matched completely. The first existing bell to have the full late/late combination was either the 2nd at Stanstead Abbots

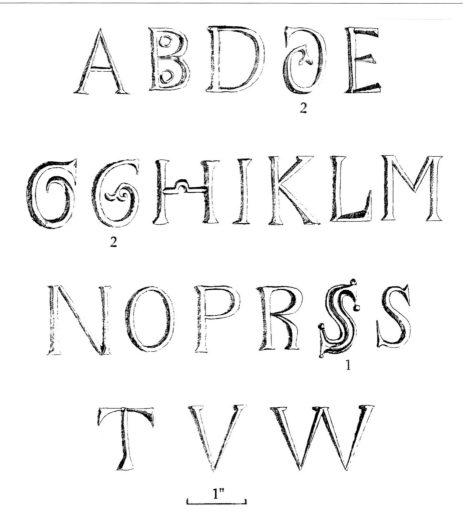

Fig. 11 Late Alphabet 1616–40
1. S early form used 1616–21
2. D & G used 1626–28

or the 2nd at Little Canfield, both dated 1617. The 7th at Hemel Hempstead, also 1617, bears the early thick numbers, so must precede the others. One minor idiosyncracy was that he never altered his 7, the small thick figure duly making its appearance in 1617, 1627 and 1637.

The point must be made here that Robert's early numerals bear no resemblance to those used by Richard Holdfeld, which are smaller and completely different in form. They do, however, resemble those used by Richard Oldfield, so much so that it is hard to believe that they are the work of different men (cf. Albury, Herts. 1607 and Sandon, Staffs. 1609). Another striking

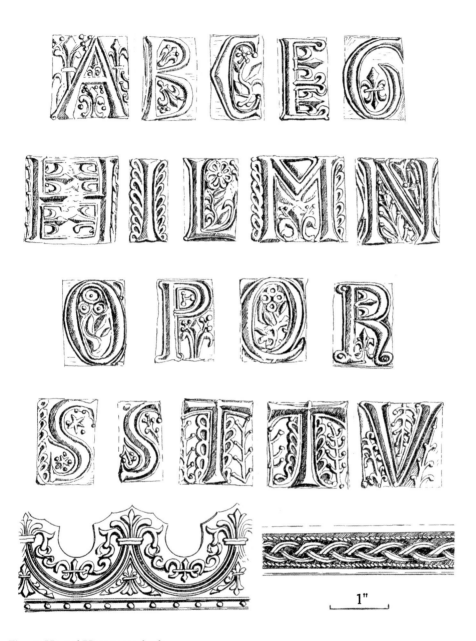

Fig. 12 Hemel Hempstead 7th

parallel is that Richard Oldfield also introduced a later, thin version very similar to Robert's. There is great scope here also for a future researcher in the West Midlands.

Another point worth reiterating is that lettering and numerals used by bellfounders followed current fashions very closely, as they do to this day.

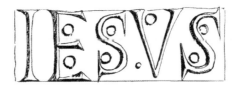

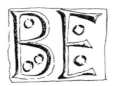 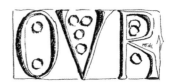

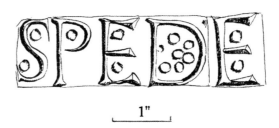

1"

Fig. 13 Standard Blocks Used at
  Thundridge 1623
  Gilston 1623
  Hunsdon 1630
  Offley 1632

Inscriptions

The ability to reproduce a complicated Latin couplet such as appears at Great Dunmow certainly suggests that Robert was capable of reading a written order.

   N & S, 1886, and Deedes and Walters (*CB Essex*) imply criticism of his limited range of inscriptions. This can more justly be ascribed to common prudence than illiteracy. The late sixteenth and early seventeenth centuries were times of upheaval, religious and political and, more than fifty years earlier, the fate of John Saunders of Reading, whose ears were cropped during the reign of Edward VI for using 'Popish' inscriptions, would not have been forgotten by the bellfounding fraternity. It still paid to be careful in Oldfield's day, with the rise of Puritanism. Likewise, Miles Graye played

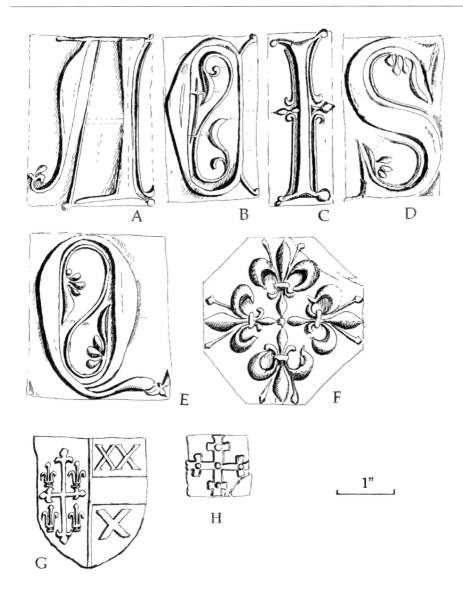

Fig. 14 Great Dunmow 7th, 1613
A–I Capitals and cross, probably by Robert Burford, re-used in facsimile
G   Arms of jenoure on shoulder
H   Crosslet with broken palera

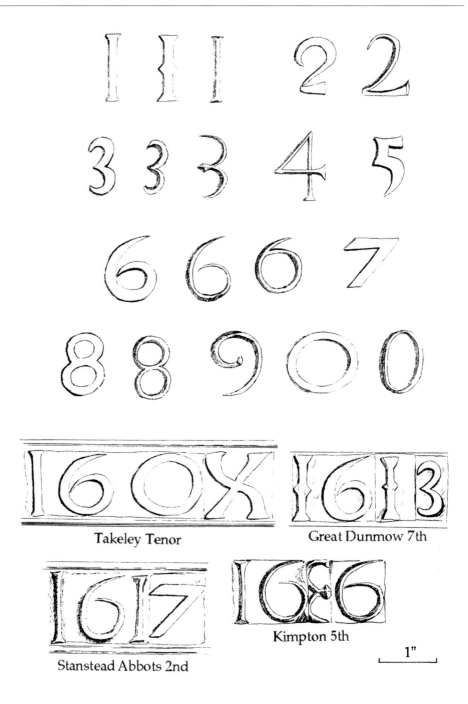

Fig. 15 Numerals and specimen dates

safe; he ran to little more than MILES GRAYE MADE ME and the date.

So far as is known, Robert placed his name on only one bell, his oldest surviving, the tenor at St James, Stanstead Abbots, inscribed ROBART OLD-FEILD MADE ME 1605 (*Fig. 7*).

Basically he had three stock inscriptions. PRAISE THE LORD was a good Protestant sentiment and could offend nobody. In the reign of James I, after over half a century of petticoat government, GOD SAVE THE KING passed from being a novelty to a decently patriotic prayer, whereas by the later years of Charles I these words could have sardonic overtones. Oldfield in fact used this sparingly in the 1630s but, surprisingly, as mentioned above, it is on his last-known bell, the tenor at Matching, Essex. IESVS BE OVR SPEDE was an old and popular inscription much used by the major bell-foundry of Oldfield of Nottingham, in a rich variety of spelling, and also by Richard Bowler. It was pious and uncontroversial. GOD SAVE HIS CHVRCH, another Nottingham inscription, was used once only, on the tenor at Albury in 1607.

Latin appears on occasion, chiefly on the larger bells in an important ring. SONORO SONO MEO SONO DEO – WITH MY RESOUNDING SOUND I SOUND TO GOD – was also used (spelled 'SONORA' by Holdfeld at Great Hormead and Ashwell, since recast, in 1606). SANA MANET CHRISTI PLEBISQUE RELIGIO VANA – THE RELIGION OF CHRIST IS SANE AND THAT OF THE PEOPLE VAIN – at Hemel Hempstead and Great Munden (tenor, recast) was also used by Thomas Hancox of Walsall at Aston Cantlow, Warks., in 1626 and, so far as is known, by no other founder.

Vicars' and churchwardens' names appear rarely. The earliest example is at Takeley, Essex, where initials are used. On the shoulder of Harpenden old tenor, 1613, there are four initials, probably churchwardens'. At White Roding, Essex, tenor, 1614, churchwardens' initials are recorded – one gentleman's Christian name began with Z, doubtless of Biblical origin. Names of churchwardens also appear at Great Munden and Kimpton.

A rhyming couplet at Little Berkhamsted, THOMAS STENO TRVTH TO TEL GAVE TVVENTE POVND TOARD THIS BELL 1621, is not only unique but a masterpiece of tight spacing, as is the early medieval treble. The complex Latin sentence on the 7th at Great Dunmow was self-aggrandisement by the wealthy donors, who must have paid through the nose for the privilege of having their names so immortalised.

Occasionally the ghost of a long-since-gone bell can be seen, e.g. the old treble at Redbourn with PRAYSE THE LORD, an inscription never used by John Waylett of Bishops Stortford, who reproduced it when recasting in 1716 and also by J. Taylor of Loughborough who again recast in 1950. SANA MANET from the old tenor at Great Munden, quoted amid a welter of verbiage by J. Warner; the same recorded by Browne Willis (*MSS xxxviii,* 2) at Ivinghoe and Bletchley; PRAISE YE THE LORD at Tewin, recast 1673 by Anthony Chandler, who rarely stepped beyond CHANDLER MADE ME .

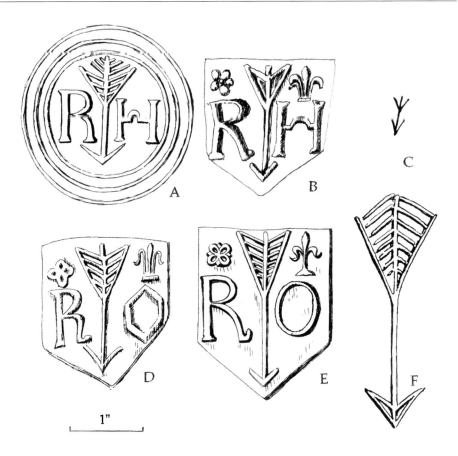

Fig, 16 Shields and Marks
A/B Richard Holdfield
C   Robert Oldfield's Mark
D   Robert Oldfield (early)
E   Robert Oldfield (late)
F   Mark (Much Hadham sanctus)

Had a wider variety of inscriptions been used, these tantalising clues would be less obvious.

Inscription Errors

All bellfounders, even modern ones, make mistakes on occasion. From the earlier section on seventeenth century foundry techniques (p. 37), it will be remembered that the inscriptions were laid on the outside of the false bell where, in theory if not in fact, they were plainly visible to the moulder, affording no excuse for a literate founder, or his foreman, to make errors.

However, working in a pit, lit by rushlights or candles, while applying a translucent material like wax, was not conducive to exactitude, so mistakes did occur. The great surprise is that, out of Oldfield's total of about 80 or 90 bells, of which 68 still exist, the errors are so few. In some cases, these little lapses are invaluable in elucidating his techniques.

The letter N was a source of much trouble to seventeenth century founders; the Chandler family of Drayton Parslow, Bucks., never quite mastered this small problem, while the Norris family of Stamford, Lincs., had difficulty with S as well. Now there is no way of reversing an N or S made in a clay or wooden mould except by making the mould incorrectly in the first place. With a single letter, however, it must have been all too easy to pick it up the wrong way round or upside down. On several occasions, Oldfield slipped up with his И, but always whilst using his early alphabet, e.g. at Great Munden 4th, 1621.

At Therfield, 1608, the S and E of PRAISE appear as ƎS (the E being reversed) showing that he was laying on two letters at once and that the pair became inverted. At Ugley, Essex, 1612, and Widford, 1624, letters were merely placed in the wrong order. At Aldbury, 1634, the complete word block of LORD was inverted – most sacrilegious!

All of these errors give an insight into some aspect of his working methods, but none more so than the 1636 date on the 5th at Kimpton (*Fig. 15 p 70*). Sensibly, many founders of that period made up a block for the century, adding tens and units as appropriate. Oldfield did likewise but at Kimpton he applied his date from right to left as may have been his routine. The final 6 was correctly placed; 3, on its thin patera was placed to the left of it, upside down, then the 16 block, again to the left, but much too close, so that its very thin patera overlaps the 3, but leaves the figure visible underneath.

At Little Canfield, 1627, he used the 162 on a single patera, which he accidentally inverted, adding the undersized 7 correctly. There are other similar examples, but perhaps his finest howler is on the tenor at Takeley, dated 16OX, when the 8 must have been mislaid. It turned up in time for him to cast the bell for Therfield in the same year.

Shields

Unless a bellfounder put his name on a bell, there was no certain way of identifying his work. It is of course possible to make an inspired guess, using details such as the style of lettering or, if no words are used, the shape of numerals. However, most founders wanted their work to be easily identifiable, hence the use of name or trademark. In the medieval period founders used shields or roundels; modern English founders still use roundels for the same purpose.

Many writers have remarked on the number of founders whose surname, in a rich variety of spelling, was Oldfield. The fact that three of these men, roughly contemporary, have similar shields cannot be solely ascribed to coincidence, (*Fig. 16b, d, e*). Richard Holdfeld of Cambridge, Richard Oldfield (or Oldfeild) of Walsall and elsewhere, and Robert Oldfeild, as he wrote it, all shared a common initial and the arrow as a rebus for R O is a perfectly logical idea. That Richard Holdfeld also used an arrow while plainly marking his shields with R H seems conclusive proof that, however he spelled his name, he pronounced it as Oldfield. It is not too far-fetched to conclude that the shield/rebus was in the nature of a family joke. As their common ancestor, Reginald, shared the same initials, it may even be that he also had used the same device.

This would explain the very close similarity between the later shield (as opposed to roundel) of Holdfeld and the early (1605-8) shield of Robert. Misled by this similarity, H.B. Walters in *Church Bells of England* (1912) clearly mixed up the R H shield with the early R O shield (with the hexagonal O), implying that Holdfeld was using two versions of his name, rather than being the work of two different men. In a later edition, Walters corrected this error and in *CB Essex* he dealt with the two men separately. It is even possible that the same hand and tool cut both shields, as the depth of cut is the same for both. The childish drawing of the flower and the fleur-de-lys seem also to be the work of one person. If Robert was working for Holdfeld until 1603/4, the likeness is easily explained.

Robert's early shield (*Fig. 16d*) had the 'O' drawn as a hexagon, similar to that of the Richard of Walsall. After an apparent break of two years (1609–10) from when no bells survive, he resumed in 1611 with a new shield (*Fig. 16e*) with the oval 'O' and a subtle variation of the flower in the top left-hand corner.

His earliest remaining bell at Stanstead Abbots has his name in full, but no shield. The now recast bell, also of 1605, at Graveley had no shield recorded in *N & S*. so that the oldest examples are at Digswell, where the clarity and freshness of the shields is very striking. By 1608, at Therfield, signs of damage are apparent, which would explain the cutting of a new, improved design at some time after that date.

Normally, the shield is placed below the inscription band, immediately under the cross. Where the cross is missing, as on Gilston 2nd, 1628, the shield is placed beneath the word I E S V S.

Initial Crosses

The purpose of the initial cross on bell inscriptions was not purely decorative but served to mark the beginning of the phrase or sentence. Pre-Reformation founders frequently spaced their letters evenly around the inscription band so some form of punctuation mark was necessary. Early crosses tended to be simple but, as so often, became more complex as time

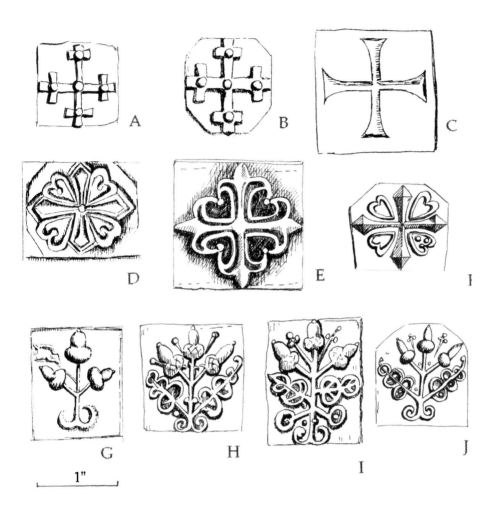

Fig. 17 Crosses and Stops
A/B Cross crosslet
C   Cross palée
D   Cross, Broxbourne
F   Cross, Hemel Hempstead
G   Acorn stop, Broxbourne
H   Acorn stop, Radwinter
I   Acorn stop, Hemel Hempstead
J   Acorn stop, Tring

went on. In the same way 'stops' were used to separate words. Oldfield, at least in his standard inscriptions, spaced his words evenly round the bell so, in a sense, the cross was fulfilling its original function.

In *N & S, 1886*, North illustrated three crosses (*Figs. 39, 40, 41*) attributed to Robert Oldfield. *Fig. 40* is shown as a plain cross crosslet on a square patera, without raised circular knobs at the intersections. At the time of writing no example of this cross, as drawn, has yet been found, although this is not to deny its possible existance. All recorded examples have raised knobs (*Fig. 17a,b*) and experiments carried out by the writer with clay and a sculptor's square-ended wire tool show that those knobs were there for a purpose – to neaten any irregularities at the joins!

The paterae surrounding the crosslet vary; square, octagonal or with two lower corners cropped, giving rise, in *CB Essex*, to the fallacy that the crosslets at White Roding, 1614, were on shields. Occasionally, e.g. Therfield 1608 and Ardeley 1613, the crosslet on an octagon is set diagonally, probably due to the narrowness of the inscription band, making it technically a St Julian's Cross. On Great Dunmow 7th, the lower right-hand corner of the patera broke off while being laid on the bell and was firmly pressed back into place, leaving a thumbprint. After a lapse of twenty-two years, the crosslet reappears on one of Oldfield's last bells, Kimpton tenor, 1638.

The thin cross patée (*N & S. Fig. 41*) was introduced in 1616 at much the same time as the late thin alphabet, being first used at Anstey and Radwinter, Essex, probably as part of a general design modernisation. There are no variants of this cross (*Fig. 17c*) which is always mounted on a square patera.

An ornate cross (*Fig. 17d*), not illustrated by *N & S*, is that on the present 4th at Broxbourne, dated 1615. It is Oldfield's first use of a cross akin to the ancient 'Nottingham' type which was used by Holdfeld. This bell has other highly idiosyncratic features which suggest that Holdfeld had a hand in its casting, such as the use of his capitals and the first, tentative form of the acorn stop (*Fig. 17g*). The cross is small and enclosed within ridges forming a lozenge. No other examples are known to survive.

In 1617 on the 7th at Hemel Hempstead a beautiful, slightly asymetrical version of the Nottingham cross was used, so far as is known, for the only time. (*Fig. 17e*)

The final cross, (*Fig. 17f*), not illustrated in *N & S*, made its debut in 1622 at Tring. This is smaller than the cross at Great Hormead 1606 (see below) and is a variation of the popular cross cercelée, widely employed from the fourteenth century onwards and much in evidence on bells from both the Nottingham and Stamford foundries. This was almost certainly picked up by Holdfeld during his early years. If he was a Nottingham man, the likeness is self-explanatory.

N & S. Fig. 39, as drawn appears only once, on a 1606 bell at Great Hormead. An examination of this bell and a comparison with the remaining inscription band of the 1607 bell at Eaton Socon, Cambs., proves conclusively that the cross and numerals 160- are identical. As the Eaton Socon bell was known to be by Richard Holdfeld, the only conclusion must be that the Great Hormead bell is by Richard, not Robert, and that N & S, Fig. 39, as drawn, does not apply to the latter.

A chronological list of bells showing their initial crosses proves that they were not used at random. In this respect Oldfield was surprisingly methodical and the cross, in conjunction with the lettering, is a powerful tool for dating doubtful bells.

The present 4th bell at Widford has an incomplete date reading 162- (or 16–2), with a cross crosslet and thick letters. This strongly suggests 1612 as the correct date, rather than the 1624 as given by N & S. Again, the tenor at Little Canfield has the late cross cercelée and thin letters, so the date, which is cast as 乙917 is undoubtedly 1627, partly inverted, rather than the 1617 postulated by Deedes and Walters in CB Essex.

The Acorn Stops

The earliest of these decorations appeared at Broxbourne in 1615, where a simple branched stem bears three acorns, with a faint outline of an oak leaf in the left background (Fig. 17g). This basic idea, (charmingly described by North in late-Victorian English on p. 39 of CB Herts. as 'a stop of floral device') was developed in the following year on the (present) 7th bell at Radwinter, Essex, (Fig. 17h) with the addition of further leaves, thus filling the square patera more effectively. In 1624, Oldfield used a version of this pretty design on the (present) 7th bell at Tring, (Fig. 17j).

A photograph of this stop appears in CB Essex and it is also drawn in both CB Beds. and CB Northants., where it is attributed by North to James Keene of Bedford and Woodstock. A copy of CB Northants. in the private collection of Miss Jean Sanderson of Haslingfield, annotated by H.B. Walters, states that 'this stop used by Oldfield at Radwinter'. Keene first used this stop in 1619 at Ecton, Northants., i.e. three years after the Radwinter bell, so Oldfield clearly takes precedence in this small detail. It must be noted that the oakleaf stops were used only after Holdfeld ceased founding at Cambridge in 1612 and did not appear later than 1626 at which date the 'Richard Oldfield' was buried at St Andrew's.

The third and final development of the acorns can be found on what is undoubtedly Oldfield's masterpiece, the 7th bell at Hemel Hempstead, (Fig. 17i), where the design is taller and shows detailed differences. At Broxbourne, Radwinter and Hemel Hempstead the stops are mounted on square or rectangular paterae, whereas the examples at Tring have the top corners cropped. An extra feature at Tring is that the design is very shallow and it is therefore very difficult to make either a satisfactory rubbing or plaster cast.

Plaited Border

This (*Fig. 12*, p. 67) was placed between two moulding wires above the lip. It takes the form of a central double hair-plait made from some smooth material, probably very thin 'worms' of wax, impressed into fine-grained moulding clay. On either side, a coarse 2-ply Z-twist yarn was then pressed into the clay to form a neat edging. Each section was 15"/39cm long. This would then be dried or low-fired to make a mould for wax replicas.

It was a common design, widely employed by founders of the period, e.g. Newcombe of Leicester at Bulkington, Warks., 1605 and Haselor, also Warks., 1610, although his outer cord was coarser. Other men who used it were Godwin Baker of Worcester 1615–25 and Thomas Hancox of Walsall 1622–31. On occasion, it appears as a decoration on the cannons of a bell. The first Hertfordshire bell on which it appears is the 3rd at Great Hormead by Holdfeld in 1606. Oldfield used it at Great Dunmow in 1613 and Hemel Hempstead in 1617.

Nottingham-type Cresting

There were several varities of this highly decorative cresting, widely used by the Oldfield family of Nottingham from c.1595, on the present 11th bell at St Mary's, Nottingham, and by other founders, ranging from the Oldfield branch foundry at Congleton to Hancox of Walsall, 1628, and as late as 1640 by Finch of Hereford and 1660 by John Martin of Worcester, to whom it may have been handed down from Richard Oldfield.

It was used as early as 1596 at both Swaton and Newton, Lincs., by Richard Holdfeld and its appearance at Hemel Hempstead can only be explained by the theory it must have reached there by his agency. No other bell in the south-east carries this crest. (*Fig. 12*, p. 67). Each section of the cresting on this bell is 9"/23 cm long.

The Stanstead Abbots Fleur-de-Lys.

The fleur-de-lys is an ancient Christian symbol, being a highly stylised lily bud, traditionally associated with the Annunciation. During the medieval period it was one of the most popular of all decorations. Many bellfounders used it and it ranged from the extremely elegant to the extremely clumsy. Being so widespread, it is surprising that Oldfield apparently used it once only, on Stanstead Abbots tenor bell, 1605. His version is thin, slightly wider than it is high, with a comparatively long cross-bar, bearing little real resemblance to a lily but with a definite look of the version later used by the Stamford founders (*Fig. 7*, p. 61). Its original source was probably Nottingham, again via Richard Holdfeld.

At Great Hormead, 1606, there is another fleur-de-lys, this time by Holdfeld. There is a strong likeness between the two versions, as in the case of the shields, although an extra feature is present. The lily bud is beginning to open, with sprigs emerging on either side of the centre lobe. This lovely idea was carried to its logical conclusion at Eaton Socon, formerly in Bedfordshire, where small, exquisite fleurs-de-lys are fully opened to reveal the mature flower.

A small version of Oldfield's 1605 fleur-de-lys appears on the 1627 tenor at Studham, Beds., by James Keene, in conjunction with lettering that is practically indistinguishable from Oldfield's.

Transferred Bells

At least six of Oldfield's bells have at some time been transferred from their original tower to some other church, usually within the same parish.

The ancient ring of four, including Oldfield bells of 1623 and 1631, was moved from the remote and inconvenient medieval St Mary and All Saints, Thundridge, to the new St Mary's in 1854, the old church being demolished, apart from the sturdy tower which is now ruinous. These bells have apparently never been rung in their new home due to a combination of tower instability on a clay slope (its walls are cracking), a weak frame and the almost unbelievable fact that many of the worn-out fittings were re-used. Ellacombe chimes were fitted in 1900 but the medieval treble is the only bell in use, the back three being derelict and held up by timber battens across their pits. A classic case of parochial parsimony!

At Chingford, Essex, the church of All Saints was superseded in 1844 by SS Peter and Paul. The 1626 Oldfield bell, with its two companions, the treble by Anthony Bartlet, 1657, and tenor by Thomas Mears, 1835, were moved to the new church, remaining there until 1930. All Saints had been allowed to decay, but was slowly restored over a period of twenty years, up to 1929. The three bells returned to their old home in 1930, being succeeded at SS Peter and Paul by a chime of six.

The 1621 bell at Loughton, Essex, with its partner of 1655 by Anthony Bartlet, may have come from the old church of St Nicholas to the new church of St John the Baptist when that church was built in 1844. The two bells remained until 1867, when a new ring of eight was installed by John Warner & Sons. They were nominally 'combined' into the present fifth. St Nicholas was completely rebuilt on a new site in 1877.

The bells of Shenley have had a very chequered history. The second, by Thomas Bartlet of Whitechapel, 1616, (the earliest remaining bell bearing his name), the tenor by Oldfield, 1633, and the treble by Richard Phelps, also Whitechapel, 1730, originally hung in the west tower of St Botolph's, Shenleybury. This, the medieval parish church, standing a mile north of the present village centre, was severely damaged by fire in 1753. The tower, south aisle and chancel were demolished and, according to Cussans (*History of*

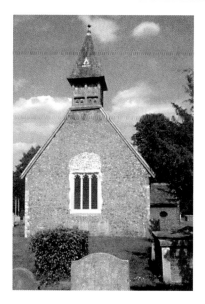

Bengeo, St Leonard

Hertfordshire, 1879) the bells were hung in a small wooden campanile on the site of the old south porch. In 1841, the Chapel-of-Ease of St Martin was built in the centre of the village. This building has only a brick bell-turret, now unsafe. At some later date, probably 1891, the bells were moved to St Martin's and augmented to six by the addition of a new 2nd, 5th and tenor. As there was no tower, the bells languished close to ground level in a chiming frame housed in a bicycle-shed-like structure; they were used for target practice by the children in the adjacent primary school. Their survival can only be described as a miracle. Finally, in 1979/80 they were hung 'dead' on two beams in a 'tower' over the entrance to the new church room where they are at least protected from the elements but still vulnerable to theft, being unenclosed from below.

On the outskirts of Hertford, the delightful twelfth century church of St Leonard, Bengeo, had three bells. In 1855 they were transferred to the new, more centrally-placed church of Holy Trinity. When, in 1883, a new ring of six bells was installed at Holy Trinity, the Oldfield bell of 1630 was returned to St Leonard's; its two companions were sold for scrap.

Perhaps the most widely-travelled Oldfield bell is the 1637 former priest's bell from St Mary's, Luton. In *CB Beds.* p. 169, North stated that 'the Priests' bell was missing, but was eventually found in an outhouse at the Rectory. It had been lent for use at a temporary district church and had not then been restored to its proper place'. It was returned to St Mary's, but in about 1966 it was transferred to its third and, hopefully, final home at St Augustine's, Limbury, Luton.

Narrow Escapes

The Shenley bell is not the only Oldfield bell to have survived a fire. At Stapleford Tawney, Essex, traces of fire damage are visible in the timber tower and a painted date of 1969 with names from Danbury suggests that the well-known firm of Baker's of Danbury carried out repairs in that year. The 1630 Oldfield bell and the rare 1611 bell by William Carter escaped damage.

Two more of Oldfield's bells also were unscathed when their respective towers collapsed. At Shillington, Beds., the tower fell in 1701 but the five bells were undamaged. In the next parish, Pirton, Herts., part of the tower fell during restoration in 1874 but the bells had been taken down and thus escaped intact.

Chronological List of Bells by Robert Oldfield

Bell examined by RS (Richard Sales), Dodds, CB Herts. (Geoffrey Dodds). Added date is that of inscription.

1. *1604/5 ROYDON, Essex.*
   Churchwardens' accounts concerning the casting of a bell.

      for casting the bell   *iiiil*   *vjs*
       for fetching the bell from Hartford   *ljs*   *llljd*
   Known only from this source. Probable weight c.8 cwt.
   Recast 1625 by Miles Graye.   CB Essex

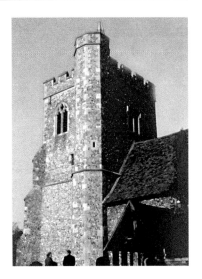

2. 1605 STANSTEAD ABBOTS, Herts. St James
                 Tenor of 3

   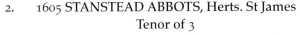

   I6O5   3

   Diam 36″   Wt 8cwt 1 qr 0 lb   Note A   3 / 3
   No shield. Cross crosslet (*Fig. 17a*)   5
   Fleur-de-lys between words (*Fig. 7*)   2
   Small thick letters on word-sized paterae.
   Cast-in crown staple; cannons retained.
   *Scheduled for preservation.
   Church now in Churches Conservation Trust. This is Oldfield's earliest surviving bell.   *RS / Dodds, CB Herts.*

   Stanstead Abbots, St James, has Oldfield's oldest surviving bell, the only one bearing his name

3. *1605 GRAVELEY, Herts. St Mary*   *Old treble of 4? or 2nd of 4?*
   + IESVS BE OVR SPEDE I6O5
   Diameter given variously as 30½″ or 33¼″; weight 5¼ – 6¾ cwt.
   The different estimates can be explained by doubts as to whether this bell was the treble or second of the old ring of 4, if the frame were anticlockwise. No shield was recorded in **CB Herts** *(N & S) which suggests that this bell predated the three at Digswell. The inverted 5 in the date was as Digswell 3rd. Recast by Mears & Stainbank 1894. Inscription not reproduced.*
   N & S

4. *1605 DIGSWELL, Herts. St John the Evangelist*   *Treble of 3*
   Recast 1829 by Thomas Mears of Whitechapel.   3
   By inference, the inscription could have been: 2 / 2
      IESVS BE OVR SPEDE I6O5   3
   Diameter 24–25″   2
   This is entirely consistent with Oldfield's inscriptions and moulding wire pattern. If so, this was Oldfield's earliest complete ring.

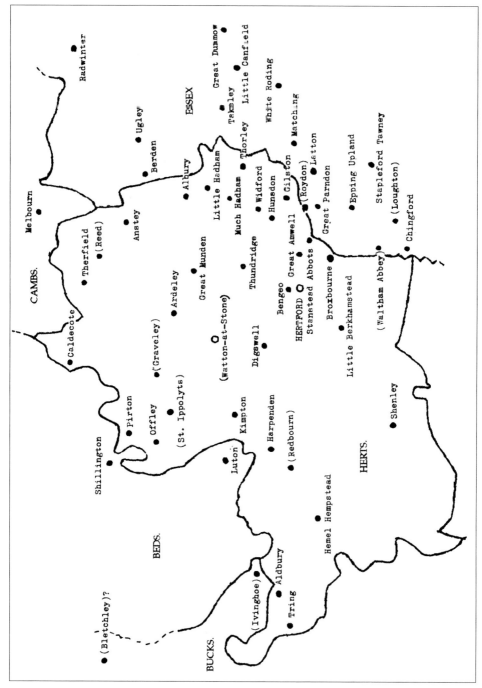

Map 5 Robert Oldfield Distribution of bells

5. 1605 DIGSWELL, Herts.   2nd of 3
    + PRAISE THE LORD |6O5   3
                            ⎕   2 / 3
    Diameter 27¼" Weight c.4 cwt   Note E
    + Crosslet. Shield (*Fig.16d*) with   3
    hexagonal 'O' in unusual position below   2
    date, in pristine condition.
    Hung dead by Whitechapel Foundry 1962, the
    tower being structurally unsound.
                                Dodds, CB Herts.

6. 1605 DIGSWELL, Herts.   Tenor of 3
    ⚓ GOD SAVE THE KING |6O5   3
    Diameter 29½" Weight c.5 cwt   Note D
    Crosslet. Shield placed under the   3 / 3
    cross, which became the   3
    normal position.   2
    Stated in *N & S* to be cracked. This was
    incorrect. Hung dead 1962.
                                Dodds, CB Herts.

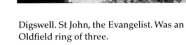

Digswell. St John, the Evangelist. Was an
Oldfield ring of three.

7. 1607 ALBURY, Herts. St Mary the Virgin   Tenor of 6
    ⚓ GOD SAVE HIS CHVRCH |6O7   3
    Diameter 43"   Weight 13 cwt 2 qr 25 lb   Note F   3 / 3
    Crosslet (*Fig. 17a*)   3
                                                                 2

    Cannons removed, either by Gillett & Johnston, who rehung the old 3
    bells in 1920, or by J. Taylor & Co. who augmented the bells to 5 in
    1965, using two bells from Wyddial. This inscription is unique in Herts.
    but was frequently used by both the Oldfields of Nottingham and by
    Norris of Stamford.   *Dodds / F.W. Ellis*

8. *1607 TAKELEY, Essex Holy Trinity*   *Old 3rd of 4*
    + GOD SAVE THE KING I6O7
    Diameter 38"   Weight c.9 cwt
    Stated in CB Essex to have a piece broken out of shoulder. Shield not
    recorded. Recast by J. Warner & Sons 1896. Inscription reproduced in Warner's
    lettering. Cross and shield not reproduced. By analogy with existing tenor, let-
    tering was probably early thick type and cross crosslet used.   *CB Essex*

9.   *1608 ST. IPPOLYTTS, Herts. St Ippolyts*   *Old tenor of 3*
     ⚓ *GOD SAVE THE KING 1608*
     Diameter 40 ⅛"   Weight 11 cwt 2 qr 24 lb
     **Broken, with piece out of lip, due to being sounded with a hammer, as nobody
     in the village knew how to ring or chime properly.*   *N & S*
     *Recast by J. Taylor & Co. 1893. Cross and inscription not reproduced in facsim-
     ile. The present inscription reads :*
                    + GOD SAVE THE KING 1608
                              R. O.
                         RECAST 1893 (on waist)
                              J. T.
     * Present weight 12 cwt 3 qr 6 lb in G. (Weights supplied by J. Taylor &. Co)
                                        Dodds, CB Herts.

10.   1608 TAKELEY Essex   Tenor of 4

                           B   Ꙩ
                         VICⱯR

     ⚓ ꙨOD SAVE THE KINꙨ 16OX   3
                         M C W M   3 / 3
                    CHVRCH   WARDENS   3

     Diameter 41"   Weight c.12–12½ cwt   Note G   2
     Inscription in large letters; initials and names in small type.
     Date 'X' (*Fig. 15*) apparently stands for 8. (*CB Essex*)
     Cannons retained. Quarter-turned by J. Warner & Sons London 1896.
     'B G' was Benjamin Gonnel or Gunnel, Vicar 1598–1629. RS

11.   1608 THERFIELD, Herts. St Mary the Virgin   5th of chime of 6
     x PRAIꓱS THE LORD 16O8   3
     Ʊ   3 / 3
     Diameter 39¼"   Weight c.10 cwt   Note A   3
     Early shield with hexagonal 'O' damaged.   2
     Cross crosslet set diagonally. S E of PRAISE inverted. (*Fig. 9, p. 64*)
     Large alphabet on separate paterae, about 1" high. Very narrow
     inscription band with clear brush-strokes.
     Cannons removed by J. Taylor, 1911. Crown staple not drilled out. This
     bell was not noted by *N & S* as being by Oldfield, but a rubbing of the
     shield and inscription is in the C.H. Hawkins Collection at Burlington
     House. (*Soc. of Antiquaries*).
     A comparison of casts of the shields at Takeley and Therfield shows
     subtle differences of detail and that the 'O' at Therfield is incomplete.
     It is very difficult to say which bell is the earlier but as the Takeley
     shield is in better condition, it may come first. The tower of this church
     was not built until 1911, the old church having been demolished in

1878. One of the bells was hung in a walnut tree, the ringer being protected from the weather by a wooden 'sentry box', the rest being stored
in a shed.   *RS / Dodds, CB Herts.*

12.   1611 EPPING UPLAND, Essex All Saints   Tenor of 6
       ⚓ PRAYSE THE LORD ¡6II   3
       Diameter 40"   Weight c.11 cwt   Note G   3 / 3
       Thick letters. Note the different 1s in date (*Fig. 15*, p. 70,   3
       top line) and the use of the late version of the shield   2
       (*Fig. 16e*, p. 72) with the normal 'O'. Cannons removed. Cast-in crown
       staple plus 19th century false staple.   *RS / CB Essex*

13.   1611 LATTON, Harlow, Essex St Mary the Virgin   Third of 4
       ⚓ GOD SAVE THE KINGE ¡6II   3
       Diameter 32½" Weight c.6½ cwt   3 / 3
       Small alphabet (*Fig. 8*, p. 45)   3
       Cannons retained; quarter turned. Crown staple broken.   2
       Date identical to Epping Upland tenor.   *RS / CB Essex*

14.   1612 LATTON   Treble of 4
       ⚓ GOD SAVE THE KING ¡6¡2   3
       Diameter 27⅜" Weight c.4¼ cwt   3 / 3
       Small alphabet, as on the 3rd of 1611. Numerals large.   3
       Crown staple broken, cannons retained, bell quarter turned.   2
       These bells are now hung dead in the original 17th century king-post
       frame.   *RS / CB Essex*

15.   1612 HARPENDEN, Herts. St Nicholas   Old 5th of 8
                                                           now Service bell

       ⚓ PRAYSE THE LORD ¡6¡2   3
       Diameter 32½" Weight 6 cwt 3 qr 18 lb   Note B   3 / 3
       Large alphabet (*Fig. 9*, p. 64)   3
       Cannons removed, crown staple drilled out,   2
       bell quarter turned. Hung dead in September 1990.
       Last rung for service 24 June 1990 by Mary A. Coburn. *Dodds, CB Herts.*

16.   1612 WIDFORD, Herts. St John the Baptist 4th of 6, formerly treble of 4
       ⚓ GOD SAVE THE KING ¡62   3
       Diameter 30"   Weight 5 cwt 0 qr 23 lb   Note C   2 / 3
       Small alphabet (*Fig. 8*, p. 62)   3
       The date is incomplete, but the combination of early alphabet   2
       and the cross crosslet points to this being a 1612 bell. *N & S* listed it as
       a 1624 bell (See tenor No. 55 dated 1624). Cannons retained, tuned by
       Whitechapel 1985.

This was originally the treble of the old ring of 4, later augmented to 6, thus becoming the 3rd. However, the old tenor was scrapped in 1985, the 1624 5th becoming the new tenor and this bell the 4th, a treble having been added (!)   *RS / F.W. Ellis*

17. 1612 GREAT AMWELL, Herts. St John the Baptist   4th of
                                                          6, formerly 2nd of 3

    ⊕ PRAISE THE LORD |6|2   3
    Diameter 28½"   Weight 4 cwt 3 qr 4 lb   Note D   3 / 3
    Small alphabet. Date numerals large.   3
    H of THE inverted.   2
    Rehung, tuned by Gillett & Johnston during augmentation to 6 in 1953.
    Cannons retained; staples cut flush.   *RS / Dodds, CB*
    Herts.

18. 1612 UGLEY, Essex St Peter   Tenor of 3
    ⊕ PRAIES THE LORD |6|2   3
    Diameter 32"   Weight c.6¾ cwt   2 / 2
    Crown staple in situ, cannons retained.   3
    17th century clapper, probably original.   2
    The lowest moulding wire is actually on the edge of the lip.
                                                              RS / CB Essex

19. 1613 ARDELEY, Herts. St Lawrence   5th of 6.
    x PRAISE THE LORD |6|3   3
    ⛉   2 / 3
    Diameter 36½"   Weight c.6½ cwt   Note B♭   3
    Large alphabet. Diagonal crosslet on octagon. Cannons   2
    retained. Crown staple probably drilled out (uncertain).
                                                             Dodds, 11/7/90

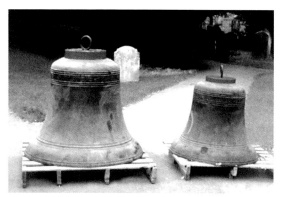

The old 5th and tenor of Harpenden. Two Oldfield bells now hung dead.

20. 1613 HARPENDEN, Herts. Old tenor of 8, now clock bell

T C ⊖ C

⊕ PRAISE THE LORD |6|3   3
Diameter 41½" Weight 12 cwt 3 qr 7 lb
Note F#   3 / 3
Large alphabet. Churchwardens' initials on shoulder.   3
Two small casting faults on shoulder.
The middle oulding wire on the   2
soundbow is slightly enlarged, probably copied from the medieval bell which he was recasting.
Cannons removed, crown staple drilled out; quarter

turned. Now hung dead beside the old 5th (1612) as clock bell.

Last rung 24/6/1990, by L.G. Coburn.   *Dodds, CB Herts.*

21.   *1613 GREAT PARNDON, Essex St Mary*   *Old treble of 4*

   ✠ *IESVS BE OVR SPEDE 1613*

   Diameter 28½"   Weight c.4¾ cwt

22.   *1613 GREAT PARNDON*   *Old 3rd of 4*

   ✠ *GOD SAVE THE KING 1613*

   Diameter 34"   Weight c.7½ cwt

   Both bells recast by Mears & Stainbank 1902.

   Inscriptions not reproduced.   *CB Essex*

23.   1613 GREAT PARNDON   Old 4th of 4, now tenor of 6

   ✠ PRAISE THE LORD 1613   3

       I B   W B   3 / 3

        CHVRC WARDENS *(on waist)*   3

   Diameter 35¼" Weight 9 cwt 1 qr 0 lb   Note G   2

   Inscription and date large. Small initials, etc. on waist.

   Cannons retained. Tuned and weighed by Whitechapel.

                                             RS / CB Essex

24.   1613 BERDEN, Essex St Nicholas 3rd of 4, formerly 4th of 5

   ✠ PRAISE THE LORD 1613   3

   Diameter 35¼" Weight c.8 cwt   2 / 3

   Large alphabet; note the use of numeral 'I' as 'I' in PRAISE.   3

   Cannons retained, quarter turned and lip skirted.   2

   Staple broken; new central hole for clapper.

   Hung dead on beams; no floor underneath. The 5th bell was stolen in

   about 1840.   *RS / CB Essex*

There is an unusual item concerning this tower. The 2nd bell,
unascribed in *CB Essex*, later identified by H.B. Walters and F.C. Eeles
(*unpublished MS on Church Bells of Middlesex, in the Library of the Society of
Antiquaries*), as being by James Butler, was recast in the same year (*See
Butler, No. 2*). A possible explanation could be that Oldfield, who was
extremely busy in 1612-13, sub-contracted this job to Butler.

25. 1613 GREAT DUNMOW, Essex St Mary   7th of 8

   ∪ *(on crown, Arms of Jenoure)*

   + QVESONITV DISCORS PVLSAT CAMPANA REFECTA

   ∪

   + SVMPTIBVS ANDREE EST CHRYSOGVNES QVE IENOVR

   1613 *(one line)*

Diameter 44⁷⁄₁₆" Weight 14 cwt 0 qr 14 lb   Note F   3
Cannons removed, tuned and weighed by J. Taylor, 1926.   2 / 2
All letters on separate paterae.   RS   3
Arms of Jenour :   2
Az. a cross patonce between 4 fleurs de lys or, impaling Smith
sa. a fess between 3 saltires coupled or. (*Fig. 14 g*, p. 69)
This shield is cut in very low relief and appears to be by the same hand
that made the Oldfield shield and the acorn stops of 1615, 1616 and
1617. Around the soundbow is a plaited decoration, identical to that at
Hemel Hempstead. (*Fig. 12*, p. 67)
Small alphabet, with 3" high capitals and cross as used by Robert Bur-
ford of Aldgate 1392–1418. (*Fig. 14a–f*)   RS
Note 1. Translation – THAT (BELL) WHICH SOUNDED DISCORDANT WAS RE-
MADE (*i.e. recast*) AT THE EXPENSE OF ANDREW AND CHRYSOGONA JENOURE.
This, as the inscription states, was an old bell which became cracked
and was recast by Oldfield, who reproduced the large cross and re-
used the appropriate capitals.
Note 2. Andrew Jenoure died in December 1622, aged 84 years. He
married Chrysogona Smith of Campden, Gloucs. Their son, Kenelm,
was created Baronet in 1628.
Note 3. The peculiar design of moulding wires on the soundbow, with a
very pronounced central hump was of 14th/15th century provenance
and was no doubt on the original bell.
A similar feature, in lower relief, was reproduced at White Roding the
following year.
Note 4. The lower right-hand corner of the crosslet patera broke off and
was stuck on again; the break is clearly visible. (*Fig. 14h*)

26. 1614 WHITE RODING, Essex St Martin   4th of 5
     ✠ GOD SAVE THE KIИG 1614   3
     Diameter 35¾" Weight c.7½ cwt   Note A   2 / 3
     Large alphabet, with N reversed.   3
     Centre moulding wire on soundbow enlarged.   2
     Cannons retained. Old clapper twisted 90° on staple.
     Richard Sales states that this bell is the 4th, not the 3rd as given in
     CB Essex. The kingpost frame of 1722 is anticlockwise.   RS

27. 1614 WHITE RODING   Tenor of 5
     ✠ PRAYSE THE LORD 1614   3
         CHVRCH WARDENS   3 / 3
            W B   Z   B   3
     Diameter 39¼" Weight c.10½ cwt   Note G   2
     Two sizes of letters; 'churchwardens' being small, the rest large.
     Cross crosslet not on shield, as stated in *CB Essex*, but has upper

corners clipped. Cannons retained; quarter turned, likewise clapper
turned 90° on staple. Centre moulding wire on soundbow enlarged.*RS*

28. *1614 REED, Herts. St Mary*   *Old tenor of 3*

  ⚮ *GOD SAVE THE KING 1614*

Diameter 32 ½ "   Weight c.7 cwt

*Three bells in 1552 and also in 1972. 1 and 2 were uninscribed and may have
been cast by Richard Keene at Royston.*   *N & S*

*R.W.M. Clouston reported on these bells in 1972. Two were not hung, awaiting
sale. They were offered to Cottered for possible augmentation, but proved
unsuitable. In his report to the Diocesan Advisory Committee, dated 9/9/1972,
he   suggested that the parish should keep the best-toned bell, the 2nd, and further, that the crown, inscription band and shield of the Oldfield bell should be
cut out and preserved, either in the church or on permanent loan to a local
museum. A further letter dated 5/6/1973 implies that this had not been done.
This bell was therefore sold for scrap (not to a bellfoundry) at some date after
1972. Recent enquiries of the churchwardens as to its fate by Richard Sales and
Geoffrey Dodds (1989) were inconclusive.*

29. 1615 BROXBOURNE, Herts. St Augustine   4th of 8,
                                                     formerly treble of 5

  ⚮ IEℝ SVS □BEℝ □ OVℝ □ SPEℯℰ □ |6|5   3

Diameter 34"   Weight 7 cwt   Note B   2 / 3

Special cross (*Fig.* 17d, p. 75).   Acorn stops (*Fig.* 17g).   3

Cannons removed.   2

Alphabet (*Fig.* 10, p. 65); sprigged capitals on separate paterae, previously used by both Richard Bowler of Colchester and Richard Holdfeld
of Cambridge.   *RS*

The cross appears to be unique; it has not been found elsewhere.
Simple acorn stops between words. It is possible that the bell was cast
by Holdfeld and Oldfield working together.

30. 1615 BROXBOURNE   5th of 8, formerly 2nd of 5

  ⚮ ᏀOD SAVE THE KIℕᏀ |6|5   3
                                                                2 / 3

Diameter 36"   Weight c.8 ¼ cwt   Note A   3

Large alphabet, with N reversed. Date as on 4th.   2
                                                               RS

31. *1615 BROXBOURNE*   *Old 3rd of 5*

*In 1863, the old 3rd (present 6th), being cracked, was recast by John Warner
& Sons.*   *(N & S)*

*No details of the old bell have been found and the inscription was not repro-
duced. It may well have been the 3rd of a complete ring of 5 by Oldfield. Logic,
and a thorough knowledge of his inscriptions, suggests to both Richard Sales*

and the writer that it was inscribed SONORO SONO MEO SONO DEO.
The bell was again recast by J. Taylor & Co. in 1903.

32.　1615 BROXBOURNE　　　　　　　　　　7th of 8, formerly 4th of 5
　　🔔 PRAIES THE LORD |6|5　　　　　　　　　　　　　　3
　　　　　　　　　　　　　　　　　　　　　　　　　　　3 / 3
　　Diameter 43 ½ "　Weight c.14 cwt　　　　Note F#　　　3
　　Large alphabet. Date numerals as on 4th and 5th above.　　2
　　　　　　　　　　　　　　　　　　　　　　　　　　　RS

33.　1615 MATCHING, Essex St Mary the Virgin　　　　4th of 6
　　🔔 GOD SAVE THE KING |6|5　　　　　　　　　　　3
　　Diameter 31 ¼ "　Weight 5 cwt 2 qr 13 lb　　Note B　　2 / 3
　　Large alphabet, date as above.　　　　　　　　　　　3
　　Eighth – turned, tuned and rehung with new fittings by　　2
　　Whitechapel Foundry 1990. Cannons retained.　　　RS / CB
　　Essex

34.　1615 MELBOURN, Cambs. All Saints　　　　　　4th of 8
　　🔔 IESVS BE OVR SPEDE |6|5　　　　　　　　　　3
　　Diameter 33"　　6 cwt 2 qr 12 lb　　　Note B　　2 / 3
　　Large alphabet, date as at Matching.　　　　　　　3
　　Cannons removed, tuned by Bowell of Ipswich 1913.　　2

35.　1615 MELBOURN　　　　　　　　　5th of 8
　　🔔 ᏩOD SAVE THE KIИᏩ |6|5　　　　　　　　　3
　　Diameter 35 ½ "　Weight 7 cwt 1 qr 17 lb　　Note A　　2 / 3
　　Large alphabet. Date as above.　　　　　　　　　3
　　Cannons removed, tuned by Bowell, 1913.　　　　　2
　　These two bells were probably cast at the very end of 1615/16 as, on
　　stylistic grounds, they are obviously part of the same order as the 6th.

36.　1616 MELBOURN　　　　　　　　　6th of 8
　　🔔 PRAISE THE LORD |6|6　　　　　　　　　　　3
　　　　　　　　　　　　　　　　　　　　　　　　　3 / 3
　　Diameter c.38"　Weight 9 cwt 1 qr 15 lb　　Note G#　　3
　　Large alphabet. The date consists of two 16 blocks –　　1
　　an economical use of figures.
　　Formerly two wires on the lip, but tuning by skirting in 1913 by Bowell
　　has removed the lower of the two. Cannons also removed.
　　This bell, while cast as part of the same order as the other two, must
　　have been cast just after New Year, i.e. April 1616.　　*Dodds 16/2/1992*

37.   1616 ANSTEY, Herts. St George   3rd of 6
   ⚜ SONORO SONO MEO SONO DEO ⎮6⎮6   3
Diameter 30½" Weight c.5 cwt Note B approx.   2 / 3
Quarter turned, cannons retained.   3
None of the six bells appears to have been tuned, giving a   2
peculiar scale. Plain thin cross patée (*Fig. 17c*, p. 75) and late thin
alphabet (*Fig. 11*, p.66) probably used for the first time here.
The S is ornate (*Fig. 11₁*). Date as on Melbourn 6th.

38.   1616 ANSTEY   4th of 6
   ⚜ ᴳOD SAVE OVR KINᴳ ⎮6⎮6   3
Diameter 33½" Weight c.6½ cwt   Note A# approx.   2 / 3
Quarter turned, cannons retained. Late thin alphabet.   3
No other example of this inscription has been found in   2
Oldfield's work, but it was fairly common among the Nottingham
founders. However, the tenor at Studham, Beds., by James Keene, 1627,
has this inscription and the lettering bears some resemblance to Oldfield's.   *Dodds / F.W. Ellis 28/7/1990*

39.   1616 RADWINTER, Essex   St Mary the Virgin   4th of 8
   ⚜ ᴳOD □ SAVE □ THE □ KINᴳ ⎮6⎮6   3
Diameter 30"   Weight 4 cwt 3 qr 26 lb   Note C   2 / 3
Cannons retained. Tuned, rehung by J. Taylor 1972.   3
Thin alphabet; date as Melbourn.   2
Acorn stop between words.(*Fig. 17h*) A photograph of this stop appears
in *CB Essex*; it is also drawn in *CB Beds.* and *CB Northants.*, where it is
ascribed to James Keene.   *RS / CB Essex*

40.   1616 RADWINTER   7th of 8
   ⚜ SONORO SONO MEO SONO DEO ⎮6⎮6   3
Diameter 38½" Weight 12 cwt 1 qr 26 lb   Note G   3 / 3
Thin letters on word-sized paterae. Cannons retained.   3
Tuned, rehung by J. Taylor 1972.   2
(*CB Essex* omits the shield, but R. Sales confirms its presence.) *RS*

41.   1617 HEMEL HEMPSTEAD, Herts.   7th of 8
   ⚜ SANA □ MANET □ CHRISTI □ PLEBISQVE □ RELIGIO □ VANA
   □ ⎮6⎮7   (one line)   3
Diameter 41³⁄₁₆" Weight 12 cwt 0 qr 3 lb   Note F#   1 / 4
                                                              3
Special cross, (*Fig. 17e*)   2
Cannons retained; crown staple drilled out. Tuned by Gillett &
Johnston 1951.
Very large special lettering, similar, but not identical to that used by

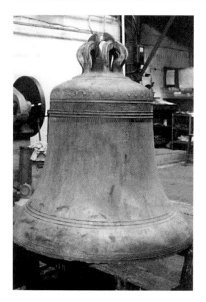

Hemel Hempstead, St Mary, 7th bell
*[Photograph taken by Gillett & Johnston,
Bellfounders in 1951*

James Keene. 'Nottingham'- type cresting above the inscription band. Plaited border between the two wires on the lip (*Fig. 12*, p. 49). Complex acorn stop between words (*Fig. 17i*). Date; 1 and 6 large, with bars on 'I'; 7 small and flat from early set.

J. Dodds /RS /D. Gambling

Note 1. This is a fairly long-waisted bell and rather thin. From the 1552 Inventory, it is clear that Oldfield was recasting the 4th of the medieval five. The lavish decoration implies that, as at Great Dunmow, money was no object in this job.

Note 2. When Hemel Hempstead bells were being rehung by Gillett & Johnston of Croydon in 1951, the foundry staff were sufficiently impressed by the beauty of this casting as to photograph it standing apart from the other seven. This photograph was given to the writer in 1951 and is now a treasured possession. It has been reproduced on p.31 of *Ringing in Hertfordshire* by Mrs. L. G. Goodman, and also as Plate 8 in *Church Bells of Hertfordshire* by G. Dodds, 1994.

Note 3. This is now the only surviving Hertford bell with this combination of inscription, alphabet and cresting and may have been cast jointly by Oldfield and Holdfeld.

It is the writer's opinion that it ought to be included in the list of bells scheduled for preservation

42.	1617 STANSTEAD ABBOTS St James		2nd of 3
	✠ GOD SAVE THE KING |6|7		3
	Diameter 32" Weight c.6 cwt	Note B	2 / 3
	Thin alphabet (*Fig. 11*, p. 66)		3
	Date in thin numerals (*Fig. 15*, p. 70)		2

This bell marks the change to later style numbers and therefore is possibly later than Hemel Hempstead 7th.   *RS / Dodds, CB Herts.*

43.	1617 LITTLE CANFIELD, Essex All Saints		2nd of 4
	✠ GOD SAVE THE KING |6|7		3
	Diameter 25⅝ " Weight c.3 cwt		2 / 2
	Thin alphabet; date with small 7 as above.		3
	Cannons removed, quarter turned.		2

These bells are hung 'dead' as a chime. They sound 2, 4, 5, 6 of a 6.

RS 13/3/1990.

44. *1621 LOUGHTON, Essex St. John the Baptist*   Old tenor of 2

✠ *SONORO SONO MEO SONO DEO 1621*

Diameter 37"   Weight c. 8 cwt

The two old bells were transferred from the Old Church of St Nicholas in c.1844. In 1867 these were recast during the installation of the present octave by J. Warner & Sons. The inscription, not in facsimile, is now on the 5th.

          CAST BY JOHN WARNER & SONS LONDON 1867$_x$ (inscription band)

(waist)   ST. NICHOLAS$_x$

     RECAST 1867 FROM 2 BELLS A.D. 1621–1655

          SONORO SONO MEO SONO DEO$_x$ CB Essex

45. 1621   LITTLE BERKHAMSTEAD, Herts. St Andrew
                                      Tenor of 3

✠ THOMAS STENO TRVTH TO TEL GAVE TVVENTE POVND
TOARD THIS BELL |62| (one line)   3

Diameter 31"   Weight c.6 cwt   2 / 3

W = VV on separate paterae. The S (*Fig. 11i, p. 66*)   3

is the ornate type first used at Anstey, 1616.   2

The whole inscription is a masterpiece of tight spacing; the left-hand serif of the T of Thomas actually overlaps on to the patera of the cross. Oldfield must have been influenced by the early 14th century 2nd bell, which bears a long quotation from the Ave Maria, taking up the whole inscription band. (*See also J. Waylett, bell No. 105*). All letters on the tenor are on separate paterae.

Quarter turned; cannons and crown staple retained. Untuned. Used as clock bell. The three bells were formerly hung for ringing, then swing-chimed only. They were hung dead by Whitechapel in the 1960s, as the turret is now unsafe even for swing-chiming.

£20 was a very large sum for a 6 cwt bell, and must have also covered the cost of a complete rehanging of all three bells.

          RS / Dodds, CB Herts.

Great Munden, St Nicholas has the most Robert Oldfield bells in any tower.

46. 1621 GREAT MUNDEN, Herts. St Nicholas   2nd of 6,
                                      formerly treble of 5

✠ IESVS BE OVR SPEDE |62| 3

Diam. 26"   Wt. 4 cwt 0 qr 17 lb   Note C#   2 / 3

This was the treble of a complete ring of   3

five by Oldfield.   2

47. 1621 GREAT MUNDEN   3rd of 6,
                      formerly 2nd of 5

  ⚓ PRAISE THE LORD 1621   3

                       2 / 3

  Diam. 28" Wt. 4 cwt 2 qr 15 lb Note B   3
  Thin letters on separate paterae.   2

48. 1621 GREAT MUNDEN   4th of 6,
                      formerly 3rd of 5

  ⚓ GOD SAVE THE KING 1621   3

                       2 / 3

  Diameter 31 ½"   Weight 6 cwt 0 qr 26 lb Note A# 3
  Early large thick alphabet, on separate paterae. 2

49. 1621 GREAT MUNDEN   5th of 6,
                      formerly 4th of 5

  ⚓ SONORO SONO MEO SONO DEO 1621   3
  Diameter 35 ½"   Weight 7 ¾ cwt   Note G# 2 / 3
  Lettering on word-sized paterae. Date and alphabet as on 3
  2nd and 3rd.   2
  Cannons retained on all four bells. The clock strikes on this bell.
  This is the only certain ring of five cast by Oldfield, although others,
  including Tring and Broxbourne may have existed. Contrary to his
  usual practice, he kept the same pattern of moulding wires on all the
  bells in the ring.   *RS / Dodds, CB Herts.*

50. *1621 GREAT MUNDEN*   *Old tenor*
  ⚓ *SANA MANET CHRISTI PLEBISQVE RELIGIO VANA 1621*
  (waist)   *RICHARD BAKER JOHN GARNER C.WARDENS.*
  This bell was recast by John Warner & Sons in 1881; they also added a treble to
  make six. The full inscription now reads :
  RECAST BY JOHN WARNER & SONS, 1881 (inscription band)
  (waist) SANA MANCT CRISTI PLEBISQUE RELIGIO VANA 1881ₓ
      RICHARD BAKER⎫
            ⎬ *C. WARDENSₓ*
      JOHN GARNER⎭

     THE REVᴰ C.W.MAUDE – RECTOR.
      Wᴹ COOPER _____ C.WARDEN.
    I TO THE CHURCH THE LIVING CALL
    AND TO THE GRAVE DO SUMMON ALLₓ

  The exact layout of the original inscription is unknown, but Warner's probably
  reproduced it fairly closely. Note the error in MANET, mis-spelled as MANCT

and also CRISTI instead of CHRISTI. Whether or not the original spelling was
correct is now impossible to verify.

Sir Roger du Boulay / RS / Dodds / F.W. Ellis

51. 1622 TRING, Herts., SS Peter and Paul   5th of 8
☖ ☊○☊ SAVE THE KIN☊ |62☖   3
Diameter 39⅝"   Weight 9 cwt 1 qr 20 lb   Note F#   3 / 3
Cross (*Fig. 17f*, p. 75) This is the earliest bell on which   3
this cross appears. The date is made up of a 162 block;   2
the final 2 is inverted. Note the archaic letter ☊ (*Fig. 11₂*, p. 66).
Cannons removed, crown staple drilled out by Whitechapel 1932.
Tuned and weighed 1988, Whitechapel.   *Dodds, CB*
Herts.

52. 1623 LITTLE HADHAM, Herts., St Cecilia   5th of 6,
formerly 4th of 5
☖ PRAISE THE LORD |623   3
Diameter 36"   Weight 8 cwt 2 qr 20 lb   Note A   2 / 3
This is the earliest example of the standard   3
PRAISE THE LORD block which was in use for the remainder   2
of Oldfield's working career.
Cannons retained, tuned, quarter turned and crown staple drilled out
by J. Taylor 1960. Collar type headstock.   *Dodds,*
16/8/1990

53. 1623 THUNDRIDGE, Herts., St Mary (New Church)   2nd of 4
☖ IESVS BE OVR SPEDE |623   3
Diameter 29¹/₁₆"   Weight c.5 cwt   Note D♭   2 / 1
Note D♭ –.43 semitones / 082, 780, 660, 530, 265 Hz. (RWMC)   3
This bell is seriously cracked across the shoulder; a 17" crack   2
is visible. Crown staple still in situ – the cause of the crack.
The bell could be saved by welding. Cannons retained. Untuned. Note
the 2 / 1 moulding wires in inscription band.
This is the earliest use of the IESVS BE OVR SPEDE block.
(*Fig. 13*, p. 68)   *Report by RWMC, 15/4/1993*
The transfer of this ring from the old church is described on p. 60.

54. 1624 TRING   6th of 8
☖ PRAISE THE LORD |624   3
Diameter 41¾"   Weight 11 cwt 1 qr 22 lb   Note E#   2 / 3
Cannons removed by Whitechapel 1936.   3
Tuned, weighed by Whitechapel 1988.   2
Dodds, CB Herts.

55. 1624 TRING   7th of 8

    ⛫ SONORO □ SONO □ MEO □ SONO □ DEO   3
                  |624   3 / 3

Diameter 45¾"   Weight 14 cwt 0 qr 27 lb   Note D#   3

The date seems to have been added as an afterthought   2

Its exact position is as shown. Cannons removed by
Whitechapel 1936. Tuned and weighed 1988.

Note acorn stops (*Fig. 17j*, p. 75) between words, as at Radwinter and
Hemel Hempstead. The central wire on the soundbow is thickened
and was no doubt copied from the previous medieval bell.

Note. These bells were possibly part of a complete five recast from a
medieval five in 1622–4. (Ref. Article in *Ringing World* 17/3/1989 by
H. Collings)   *Dodds, CB Herts.*

56. 1624 WIDFORD   Tenor of 6, formerly 3rd of 4

    ⛫ PRAIES THE LORD |624   3

Diameter 35"   Weight 7 cwt 0 qr 25 lb   Note A♭   3 / 3

Cannons retained. Note the mis-spelling of PRAIES.   3

The standard block was obviously not used here.   2

This bell was the 3rd of the old four, becoming, after augmentation, the
5th of the new six in 1890. The tenor of that new ring was recast in 1912
and to the writer's memory, was a poor bell. In 1985, the 1912 tenor was
scrapped and a new treble added, thus making the Oldfield 5th into
the present tenor. This of course resulted in the ring, which had been
in the key of G♭/F#, going up a tone into the key of A♭.

This work was carried out by Whitechapel Foundry (*See also No. 16*).

                                                F.W. Ellis, 1990

57. *1626 WALTHAM ABBEY, Essex*   *Old tenor of 4*

*In 1626 Waltham Abbey had a heavy medieval ring of four bells. In that year
'the great bell'(the tenor) was brought to Hertfort (sic) to be recast. Oldfield's
name is not mentioned, but there was no other bellfounder working there. (See
section on 'The Little Bell'). The charge of £10: 19s: 2d (£10. 96) shows that this
was a large bell. Later, in 1638, Oldfield charged 11s (55p) per cwt for recasting.
Allowing for inflation, this puts the bell at 19–22 cwt, assuming that he
charged about 10s–10s 6d per cwt in 1626.*

*This bell had a short life. In 1656, all four bells were recast into six by William
Whitmore of Watford. In 1806 Whitmore's six were recast and augmented to
eight by John Briant of Hertford, who was thus the third Hertfordshire founder
to work on these bells that were finally augmented and partly superseded by the
present Taylor twelve in 1914.*

*It is possible that the bell was carried to and from Hertford via the River Lea,
although the churchwardens' accounts do not make this clear, merely referring
to 'carriage' by William Wandleing, which accounted for another 26s 10d.*

                                            CB Essex p. 429

58. 1626 CHINGFORD, Essex All Saints   2nd of 3
    ⚲ ᏮΟᎧ SAVE THE KINᏮ |626   3
    Diameter 34½" Weight 7 cwt 1 qr 3 lb   Note A   2 / 3
    Cannons retained; lip chip-tuned; no modern tuning.   3
    Hung dead in non-ringing frame.   2
    Quarter turned, crown staple cut off, but roots left in. Safely clocked by
    new central clapper with eye on end of flight. Tonally very good. The
    story of its travels is told on p. 79.   *RS 20/2/1991*

59. 1627   LATTON   2nd of 4
    ⚲ ᏮΟᎧ SAVE THE KINᏮ |627   3
    Diameter 29½" Weight c.4¾ cwt   2 / 3
    Note the use of the Gothic Ᏼ and Ꭷ with small leaves   3
    (*Fig. 11₂*, p. 66). Date has 162 on a block, with small 7   2
    from the early set. Cannons retained; quarter turned; staple broken;
    new centre bolt and two side bolts. Lip slightly skirted. Hung dead in
    17th century kingpost frame.   *RS / CB Essex*

60. 1627 LITTLE CANFIELD   Tenor of 4
    ⚲ PRAISE THE LORD ᘔ9|7   3
    Diameter 30"   Weight c. 5 cwt   2 / 3
    Cannons retained; crown staple broken but retained.   3
    Supported by bolts. Tuning by skirting has removed   1
    the lower wire on the lip. The partially inverted date caused Deedes
    and Walters in *CB Essex* to assign this bell to 1617, although the cross
    points to a 1627 date. Close inspection shows that the 162 block was
    accidentally put on upside down and that 1627 is correct. (see p. 73)
    As usual, the 7 belongs to the early set of numerals.   *RS 13/3/1990*

61. 1628   GILSTON, Herts. St Mary   2nd of 2, formerly tenor of 3
    IESVS BE OVR SPEDE |628   3
    Ꝺ   2 / 2
    Diameter 29¾" Weight c.5 cwt   Note C   3
    Cannons retained; untuned; not quarter turned.   2
    No cross. Lettering consists of decorated standard blocks as at Thun-
    dridge. Hung in a tall, very fine medieval or 16th century truss frame.
    N & S noted 'the bell to be rehung in 1883'. The gudgeons and wheel
    date from about that year.   *Dodds, 7/8/1990*

62. 1628 THORLEY, Herts., St James the Great   Tenor of 6
    ⚲ ᏮΟᎧ SAVE THE KINᏮ |628   3
    Diameter 36⅞" Weight 8 cwt 2 qr 1 lb   Note A   3 / 3
    Cannons retained; quarter turned, tuned by J. Taylor 1936.   3
    Words on single paterae. Ᏼ and Ꭷ with leaves   2
    (*Fig. 11₂*, p. 66).   *Dodds, 1990*

63.   *1628 IVINGHOE, Bucks.*   *Tenor of 5*
      Ref. **CB Bucks**, *p. 435. Known from documentary sources only.*
      The old five bells, were described by Geo. Lipscombe* and Sheahan[†] (p. 696) as
      'five large and excellent bells'. In **Records of Bucks II** *46, 1859, the tenor is*
      quoted as dating from 1629 and inscribed SACRA (sic) MANET CHRISTI
      PLEBISQVE RELIGIO VANA. Browne Willis, the antiquarian (MSS xxxviii,
      2) gave the weight as '2900'. (lb)
      In 1875 the Vicar, Revd H.J. Rawlinson, considered the bells to be too heavy for
      the tower and, further, informed A.H. Cocks, author of **CB Bucks.**, *that the*
      churchwardens had bought a second-hand clapper which was too heavy for the
      tenor and which had at once cracked it.
      The five bells were recast in 1875 by John Warner & Sons of London, into six
      with a 15 cwt tenor, which are still rather too weighty for the frail central tower.
      There is no written evidence that the tenor or any other of the bells was cast by
      Oldfield, but the rarity of the inscription suggests that it is his work. Ivinghoe is
      only four miles from Aldbury, where there is one of his bells, and is therefore
      within his range. If so this could have been his biggest bell, weighing '2900' lb,
      not 29 cwt. In the 17th century 1 cwt weighed 100 lb.
      * George Lipscombe M.D. **The History and Antiquities of the County of**
      Buckingham 1847. *He used to copy Browne Willis MSS, often inaccurately.*
      † Sheahan was also a careless copyist.
      Further references can be found in an article on St Barnabas, Linslade, in **The**
      Ringing World *dated 21/2/1992.*

64.   *1628 GREAT WYMONDLEY, Herts., St Mary the Virgin*   *Old treble of 4*
      ⊕ *PRAISE THE LORD 1628*
      Diameter 26¾ "   Weight c.4 cwt   Probably standard word blocks.
      Recast by Mears & Stainbank 1903. Inscription not reproduced.

                                                                       N & S

65.   1629 RADWINTER, Essex   5th of 8
      ⊕ PRAISE   THE   LORD ▎629   3
      Diameter 26½" Weight 5 cwt 3 qr 6 lb   Note B♭   2 / 3
      Standard word blocks. Date: the 9 is an inverted 6,   3
      with a knob. Cannons retained. Tuned, weighed by   2
      J. Taylor 1972. CB *Essex* omits the shield but Richard Sales, who
      inspected this bell, states that the shield is present and in its normal
      place.   RS

66.   1630 HUNSDON, Herts., St Dunstan   4th of 8, formerly treble of 5
      ⊕ IESVS   BE   OVR   SPEDE   3
                      ▎630   2 / 2
      Diameter 31"   Weight 6 cwt 0 qr 19 lb   Note C   3
      Note the placing of the date. Standard word blocks.   2

Cannons retained, tuned by skirting by Mears & Stainbank 1883.
The bells hang in a two-tier wooden frame by J.R. Gray of Little
Munden.   *Dodds, 7/8/1990*

67. *1630 HUNSDON*   *Old 2nd of 5*
     + GOD SAVE THE KING 1630
     Diameter 33 ½ "   Weight c.7 cwt
     This bell was stated by North & Stahlschmidt in N & S, 1886 to be cracked.
     Their information was gathered before 1883, as the bell was recast by Mears &
     Stainbank in that year. The inscription now reads:
     1630,   GOD SAVE THE KING   *(not in facsimile)*
     (on waist)   MEARS AND STAINBANK, LONDON
                           RECAST ME 1883
                      GOD SAVE THE QUEEN, V. R.   *Dodds, 7/8/1990*

68. 1630 CALDECOTE, Herts., St Mary Magdelene   Single,
                                                      formerly tenor of 3

     + PRAISE THE (LORD) *lost*
                 |63O   3
     Diameter 32⅝"   2 / 3
     Weight c.6 ½ cwt   3
     Cannons retained, also   2
     crown staple.
     Standard word blocks.
     The bell became badly cracked and
     had to be welded by Barimar of
     Fulham in 1959, with the loss of the
     shield and part of the inscription.
     The disused bell hangs in a
     medieval three-bell frame. The
     church is closed and redundant
     with only one service annually.
              C. Dalton / CJP, 1990

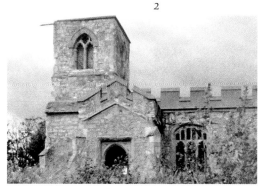

The redundant Caldecote, St Mary
Magdelen

69. 1630 STAPLEFORD TAWNEY, Essex, St Mary   Treble of 2
     ⚓ GOꝺ SAVE THE KINꝺ |63O   3
     Diameter 27 ½ "   Weight c.4 cwt   2 / 2
     Cannons retained, quarter turned. Untuned.   3
     Staple cut off flush; new central clapper.   2
     Hung on ball bearings in steel frame for two. Lever chimed
     with wooden levers and headstocks.
     The timber tower appears to have suffered fire damage. A painted
     date, 1969, plus a name from Danbury suggests that the fire and subse-
     quent rehanging occurred about that year.   *RS 7/1991*

70.   1631 THUNDRIDGE   3rd of 4
      ⊕ PRAISE   THE   LORD |63| 3
      Diameter 31 ⅛"   Weight c.4 ¾ cwt   Note C   2 / 3
      Standard word block. Chip-tuning on the lip reduced   3
      diameter from 31 ¼". The bell is disused, being supported by   2
      battens underneath. (See p. 79 for the history of these bells)
                                                            Report by RWMC / RS

71.   1632 OFFLEY, Herts. St Mary Magdelene   Treble of 6
      ⊕ IESVS BE OVR SPEDE |632   3
      Diameter 30 ¼" Weight 5 cwt 3 qr 7 lb   Note D   2 / 3
      Standard decorated word blocks.   3
      Cannons retained; false staple inserted. Tuned by skirting,   1
      removing the lowest moulding wire on the lip.
      Rehung, quarter turned and probably tuned by Bowell of Ipswich,
      1927, and rehung, in a new frame and retuned by Eayre & Smith of
      Derby in 2000.   *Dodds, 7/9/1991 / RW 25/8/2000, p. 834*

72.   *1632 ST. IPPOLYTS*   *Old treble of 3, present 4th*
      ⊕ *PRAISE THE LORD 1632*
      Diameter 32 ½ "   Weight 5 cwt 2 qr as received by J. Taylor & Co.
      Cracked in crown (N & S). Recast by J. Taylor, 1893.
      Inscription and cross (not shield) reproduced, but not in facsimile.
      The present inscription reads :
                        + PRAISE THE LORD 1632
      (on waist)   *R. O./RECAST 1893/ J. T.*
      Present weight 6 cwt 3 qr 4 lb Note B   *K. Waples / Dodds, 1993*

73.   1633 SHENLEY, Herts., St Martin 4th of 6, formerly 2nd of 3
      ⊕ PRAISE THE LORD |633   3
      Diameter 32"   Weight c.6 cwt   Note B   2 / 3
      Note B – .17 semitones. 978, 760, 592, 476, 257 cycles/sec.   3
      Both cast-in and false crown staples.   2
                                                  Report by RWMC, 14/5/1973
      The story of its travels is told on p. 79 and the six bells were hung by
      A.S. Kent of Albury, Herts. The crown staples were drilled out by R.
      Hayden, engineer and bellringer of Bishop's Stortford. All the bells are
      hung dead on beams. They were rededicated by the Archdeacon of St
      Albans, the Ven. D.J. Farmborough, on 21/12/80.   *Dodds, CB*
      Herts.

74. 1633 HEMEL HEMPSTEAD   4th of 8
    ⊕ PRAISE THE LORD ⌶633   3
    Diameter 34"   Weight 7 cwt 0 qr 13 lb   Note B   3 / 3
    Standard word blocks.   3
    Cannons retained, crown staple drilled out, tuned and   2
    weighed by Gillett & Johnston, Croydon, 1951.   *Dodds, CB Herts.*

75. 1634 ALDBURY, Herts. St John the Baptist   4th of 6,
                                                     formerly treble of 3
    ⊕ PRAISE THE ꓶЯOꓶ ⌶634   3
    Diameter 27½" Weight 4 cwt 0 qr 4 lb   Note D   2 / 2
    Standard word blocks, with LORD inverted.   3
    Cannons retained, crown staple drilled out.   2
    Tuned and weighed by J. Taylor & Co. 1984.   *RS / Dodds*

76. 1634 PIRTON, Herts. St Mary the Virgin   Tenor of 5
    ⊕ PRAISE THE LORD ⌶634   3
    Diameter 39½" Weight c.10 cwt   Note G approx.   3 / 3
    Standard word blocks.   Good toned bell.   3
    Cannons retained, crown staple drilled, false staple.   1
    Tuned by skirting, which has removed the lower moulding wire on the
    lip, probably by Mears & Stainbank, 1899. Frame anticlockwise.
    The tower partly collapsed in 1874 but the bells were undamaged.
                                                  Dodds, 7/9/1991

77. 1636 BENGEO, Herts. St Leonard   Single, formerly 2nd of 3
    ⊕ PRAISE THE LORD ⌶636   3
    Diameter 29"   Weight c.4¾ cwt   Note D   2 / 2
    Maiden casting; six cannons and argent. Crown staple intact.   3
    Not quarter turned. Hung dead on headstock of c.1855.   2
                                                                 RS
    The story of the transfer of bells between the old and new churches is
    told on p. 80.

78. 1636 KIMPTON, Herts. SS Peter and Paul   3rd of 8,
                                                     formerly treble of 6
    ⊕ THOMAS   HOO ⌶636   3
    Diameter 28" Weight 4 cwt 1 qr 5 lb   Note E   2 / 2
    Thin letters, assembled singly as at Little Berkhamstead 1621.   3
    Cannons retained; rehung and tuned Whitechapel 1959.   2
    'New' frame 1981. Thomas Hoo was Lord of the Manor of Hoo in this
    parish.   *Dodds, CB Herts.*

79. *1636 KIMPTON*   *Old 2nd of 6*
     Details uncertain. Estimated 29" diameter. Weight c.4–5 cwt.
     Recast by John Waylett 1728. (see waylett No. 181)
     There were four bells in 1552; four augmented to six by R. Oldfield 1636, with
     treble of four recast, giving three bells of 1636.   *Dodds, CB Herts.*

80. 1636 KIMPTON   5th of 8
     ☦ W M   CW   ]6Ɛ6   3
     Diameter 31 ½ " Weight 5 cwt 1qr 18 lb   Note C   2 / 3
     Early thick alphabet, medium size. Date in late numerals.   3
     Cannons retained. Retuned, weighed Whitechapel 1959.   2
     Note. Early letters had to be used, as Oldfield's late set did not include
     C or W. The date was put on from right to left, beginning with 6; 3 was
     then accidentally inverted and 1 6 partly superimposed. (*Fig. 15*, p. 70)
     W M was William Michell, Churchwarden. See also tenor, 1638.
                                                              Dodds, CB Herts.

81. 1637 LUTON, Beds., St Augustine, Limbury   Single
     Inscription band blank. (On waist)   I637   2
                                       ☐   2 / 2
     Diameter 18 ⅞ " Weight c.1 ½ cwt   Height 17"   Note A.   3
     Cannons retained.   2
     This was the Priests' bell at St Mary's Luton; transferred to Limbury
     c.1966. The story is on p. 80. This much-travelled bell is therefore now
     in its third home. Hung for lever chiming in (ritual) W gable.   CJP

82. 1638 KIMPTON   Tenor of 8
     ☦   WILLIAM   MICHELL   ]638   3
     Diameter 40"   Weight 10 cwt 2 qr 15 lb   Note G   3 / 3
     Cross crosslet used. Early thick alphabet. Date in late numerals. 3
     Cannons retained; tuned and rehung by Whitechapel 1959.   2
     The bells were rehung in the 17th century frame in 1959, but in
     1981, the old frame was removed and the bells hung in a second-hand,
     Warner, steel frame from St Lawrence, Brentford, by voluntary labour.
     Oldfield probably used the early alphabet in order to save making the
     two letters, C and W. The H of that set appears to have been damaged
     and a new, straight cross-bar was substituted for the normal form (*Fig.
     8*, p. 62). The early cross crosslet matched the early lettering.
                                                             Dodds, CB Herts.

83.   1638 SHILLINGTON, Beds. All Saints   2nd of 5
      ⚑ PRAISE THE LORD 1638   3
                                                                   3 / 3
      Diameter c.38"   Weight 8 cwt 0 qr 25 lb   Note A   3
      Cannons retained; quarter turned.   2
                                                                     RS

The casting of this bell is comprehensively documented in the churchwardens' accounts. (See Section on 'The Little Bell' p. 50).
The tower of this church 'fell' in 1701; the collapse, however, must have
been only partial as none of the bells was damaged. The rebuilt tower
is so strongly constructed that further collapse is very unlikely. CB
Beds. wrongly listed this bell as the treble, whereas Richard Sales states
that it is in fact the 2nd and C.J. Pickford confirms this. It appears to be
another case like White Roding, Essex, and Graveley, Herts., where the
researcher was confused by an anticlockwise frame.

84.   1640 MATCHING, Essex, St Mary the Virgin   Tenor of 6
      ⚑ GOƉ SAVE THE KING 1640   3
      Diameter 37 ¼ "   Weight 7 cwt 3 qr 5 lb   Note G   3 / 3
      Late thin alphabet, with archaic G and Ɖ (Fig. 11. p. 66)   3
      Cannons retained; tuned and rehung by Whitechapel, July 1990.2
This is Oldfield's last known bell and has been described as 'a good
bell' by Nigel Taylor, Whitechapel Foundry's present tuner.
                                                              RS / CB Essex

Bells which can possibly be ascribed to Robert Oldfield

1.   Undated. MUCH HADHAM, Herts. St Andrew   Priest's bell
      Diameter 10 ⅛ "   Height 9 ¾ "   Weight c.30 lb   2
      Described as blank by N & S. However an arrow rebus,   3
      (Fig. 15f, p. 70) scratched on the cope bears a strong likeness   3
      to the arrow which Oldfield used as his 'mark' (Fig. 15c) on   2
      documents, making it reasonable to ascribe it to him.
      Hung for lever chiming on a vertical extension of the bellframe.
      The cannons are moulded and the lip is, unfortunately, badly chipped.
                                                           Dodds, CB Herts.
This is very small for a church bell. It is the right size to have been
used as an inn sign and the rather battered condition of the lip would
seem to bear this out. (Small boys throwing stones to sound the bell –
just like Shenley! See No. 73). When it came to Much Hadham is
uncertain, but William Whitmore cast a bell for there in 1654 and two
bells for Hertingfordbury in 1656, so he may have been the link in the
chain.

2.   REDBOURN, Herts., St Mary   *Old treble*
      The treble was inscribed PRAYSE THE LORD 1716 H. KNIGHT.
                                                           Ref. N & S p. 209

      This bell was cast by John Waylett of Bishop's Stortford, sub-contracting for
      Samuel Knight, (not H. Knight, which was an error by Waylett). On several
      occasions, Waylett did reproduce the inscription when he was recasting an ear-
      lier bell, e.g. Baldock tenor 1711 and St Ippolyts fifth, 1721, so there is good
      reason to think that he was doing the same in this case. If so, it must have been a
      pre-1616 bell because of the antique form of PRAYSE.
      The likeliest date would be between 1612 and 1614, as Redbourn is three miles
      from Harpenden, where the old fifth of 1612, now the service bell, bears the
      same spelling.
      The Redbourn bell was again recast by J. Taylor in 1953.

3.   1616 LUTON, St. Mary   *Old 3rd of 5*
      Old ring of 5 prior to 1761/75. 3rd dated 1616 – possibly by Oldfield.
                                                           CB Beds. p. 169

4–   1629 BLETCHLEY, Bucks.
8.   *Browne Willis MSS in the Bodleian C 1X, 30, quotes the inscription of one of*
      the
      bells previous to the Rudhall ring of 1712–17 as :
      SANA MANET CHRISTI PLEBISQVE RELIGIO VANA (no date given)
      Bletchley is well outside Oldfield's normal range, but, as at Ivinghoe, the rarity
      of the inscription suggests his work or at least, his influence. It is possible that
      there was some co-operation between him and James Keene of Bedford.
      In 1760 Revd W. Cole recorded that in 1712, the five bells, cast in 1629 from
      four old bells, being 'untunable', were recast by Rudhall of Gloucester.
                              Ringing World *20/8/1971; article by Roger Cadamy*

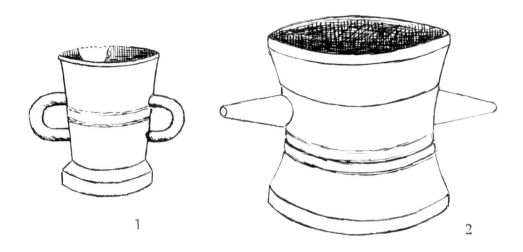

1   2

Fig. 18 Bronze Mortars in Hertford Museum

Bronze Mortars

Hertford Museum (Annexe).

Two bell-metal mortars, uninscribed, but said by the Curator, Mrs Rosemary Bennett, to be seventeenth century work of local origin:

1. Diameter 6", with loop handles in the form of bell cannons, slightly moulded. Section broken from lip.

2. Diameter 11 ¾", with peg handles.

Both mortars have gently-rounded ridges as a decorative feature, as though formed by finger pressure in a sand mould. Similar small articles formed a regular part of a founder's output, as did assorted pots and pans as well as bearing brasses for use by local carpenters who also acted as bellhangers. Both look like typical bellfounder's work.

9

JAMES BUTLER 1604–1633

A CONTEMPORARY OF ROBERT OLDFIELD'S was James Butler, about whom practically nothing is known. Their paths crossed at Berden, Essex, where each man cast a bell in the same year, 1613, an uncommon occurrence. Deedes and Walters in *CB Essex* admitted being unable to name the founder of the bell at Berden or three bells, cast in 1632, then at East Thurrock, which they described as a very early work by John Clifton, who had just taken over the running of the Whitechapel foundry after the death of Thomas Bartlet. In 1920 H.B. Walters and F.C. Eeles were, however, able to identify the founder as James Butler on the strength of his initial cross (*Fig. 19*) which appeared on a bronze mortar, at that date in the ownership of Mr. G. Hemming of Horley, Surrey, inscribed

IEAMES BVTLER MADE ME

with a border of ++++++++++ identical to those on the Berden bell and also to those on four out of five bells which the same founder had cast for St Bartholomew's, Layston, Buntingford in 1633. There is also a bell by the same man at old St Andrew's, Kingsbury, Middx, dated 1604, making a total of nine which can be ascribed to him.

Neither his dates of birth nor death are recorded, but casting a bell in 1604 suggests about 1580 for the former and he would therefore be in his fifties at the time of the Layston and Thurrock bells.

It seems likely, judging by the distribution of the bells, that after 1613 he was based either in or near Bishop's Stortford. This is a reasonable assumption as, like Hitchin and later Hertford, foundries tended to be set up in the same towns (*c.f. John Waylett*). Another reason for placing Butler there is that, when he recast the old four at Layston, the vicar was the Revd Alex Strange, who also held the living of Bishop's Stortford and would probably have preferred to employ a local man.

Butler may have learned his trade at Whitechapel under Robert Mot, assuming that the second at Kingbury was cast in London. Support for this comes from the fact that a shield on the Kingsbury bell is one used by Richard Hille, a member of the Bellmakers' Guild between 1420–40 and which may have been on the bell being recast. In view of the continuity of the foundry from the Aldgate founders however, this shield could just as easily have been found in the bottom of a drawer or the back of a shelf,

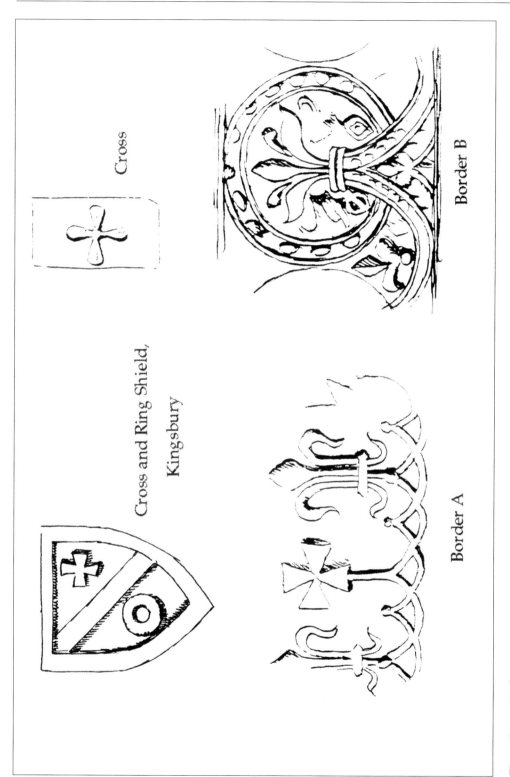

Cross

Cross and Ring Shield,
Kingsbury

Border B

Border A

Fig 19. James Butler

exactly as several other Aldgate crosses and shields surfaced in 1608 when
Joseph Carter, the new owner, supplied a bell for Hatfield House, ostensibly
in the name of Robert Mot, giving it a date of 1604. Further support for
Butler's origins comes from the earlier attribution of the West Thurrock bells
to John Clifton, not only because of the lettering but also because of a decorative border of alternate crosses and fleur-de-lys, clearly related to that
used by Thomas Bartlet at, e.g. Offley, Herts. After Joseph Carter bought the
Whitechapel Foundry in 1604, Butler may have found any avenue to promo-
tion blocked and decided it was time to move on.

Chronological List of Bells

1. 1604 KINGSBURY, Middx.   Old St Andrew   2nd of 3
    ANNO DOMINI 1604 *(Border)* GOD ☊ SAVE ✠ KYNGE ☊ IAMES
    (upper waist)   F + H + I + B
    Diameter 28 ½ "   Weight 4 ½ cwt Note C#– ½ semitone
    ☊ – *Fig. 19.*   Every letter is on a separate patera. The cast-in
    crown staple remains and the bell has been flattened by chip-tuning.
    The fittings were in very poor condition at the time of Father Cawley's
    visit but it now appears to have been bolted on to a new timber beam
    or deadstock.   *R.B. Meadows 1950/Revd D. L. Cawley 1988*

2. 1613 BERDEN, Essex,   St. Nicholas   2nd of 4
    + I + AM + THE + GIFT + OF + CHRISTOFHER + PARRISH + 1613
    Diameter 30"   Weight 4 ½ cwt
    + – *Fig. 19.*
    The spelling is as noted by Richard Sales and not as given in *CB Essex*.
    This was the second of five until about 1840, when the third was stolen.
                                                              RS/CB Essex

3. 1632 GRAYS, Essex,   SS Peter and Paul
    JOHN PETCHY *(border A)* RICHARD HARVELL 16Ɛ2 *(border A)*
    Diameter 35"   Weight 7 cwt

4. 1632 GRAYS
    JOHN PETCHY *(border A)* RICHARD HARVELL 16Ɛ2 *(border A)*
    Diameter 37"   Weight 8 cwt

5. 1632 GRAYS
    JOHN PETCHY RICHARD HARVELL *(border B)* 16Ɛ2
    Diameter 40"   Weight 10 ¾ cwt
    Border A – *Fig. 19.*   Border B – *Fig. 19.*   *CB Essex*
    These bells were formerly the ring of three at St Clement's, West
    Thurrock, which, after tuning at Whitechapel, were transferred to

Grays in 1984 to augment the existing Warner three. Two more bells were also acquired from another source to make eight. As the present tenor weight is given as 10-3-16 these form nos. 6, 7 and 8 of the octave.

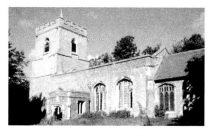

The redundant church of St Bartholemew's, Layston

6. 1633 *LAYSTON, Buntingford, Herts.,*
    St Bartholomew   Old treble
    +ALEX+STRAYNG+VICAR+FRA+
    SENNOCKE+ANTHO+ GARRETT
    CHV+WAR MARCH+20+1633   *(one line)*
    Diameter 29"
    Stolen c.1964.   N & S/Dodds, CB Herts

7. 1633 *LAYSTON*   Old 2nd
    +ALEX+STRAYNG+VICAR+FRA+SENNOCKE+ANTHO+GARRETT
    CHV+WAR MARCH+20+1633   *(one line)*
    Diameter 31"
    Stolen c.1964.   N & S/Dodds, CB Herts

8. 1633 LAYSTON   Treble of 3
    +ALEX+STRAYNG+VICAR+FRA+SENNOCKE+ANTHO+   3
    GARRE$_T^+$ MARCH+20+|6 3 3   *(one line)*   3 / 2
              ^{T} CHV+WAR   3
    Diameter 34"   Weight 7 cwt   Note B   2

9. 1633 LAYSTON   2nd of 3
    +ALEX+STRAYNG+VICAR+FRA+   SENNOCKE+ANTHO+ 3
    GARRETT+MARCH+20+|6 3 3   3 / 2
              CHV+WAR   3
    Diameter 36"   Weight 8 ½ cwt   Note B♭–   1
    + – *Fig. 19.* It is extremely rare for a founder to give the date as well as the year. The layout of the above inscriptions is exactly as on the bells.

10. 1633 *LAYSTON*   Old tenor
    The Edwardian Inventory of 1552 listed four bells. Chauncy recorded five bells in 1700, so Butler may have recast the four into five. The tenor could therefore been part of a complete five by Butler. It was recast by Pack & Chapman in 1776.
    The church stands on a hill away from the village, so making it an easy target for thieves. Since the theft of the bells, the tower has been made secure. The nave is unroofed and ruinous and the churchyard overgrown. Occasional services are held in the chancel.
                                        Dodds, CB Herts.

Miles Graye III c.1650

During the civil war very few bells were cast but by 1650, Miles Gray III, grandson of Miles Gray I, the contemporary and rival of Robert Oldfield, was moving around Essex, North Hertfordshire, Huntingdonshire and Bedfordshire. He seems to have been itinerant in the true sense of the word, setting up his furnace wherever he found work and then moving on. Bells were cast for Baldock, Cottered and Ickleford in 1650, and for Hinxworth and Cottered in 1651, probably at Baldock, but the site of his temporary foundry is not known.

10

WILLIAM WHITMORE 1647–1657

W HITMORE WAS ANOTHER example of the founder from outside moving into the county, staying for a few years and then moving on, leaving nothing but his bells to show that he ever passed this way. What makes Whitmore exceptionally interesting is that he arrived in the middle of the Civil War, at a time when all bellfounding was supposed to have ceased for the duration.

His origins appear to have been in the south-west Midlands. A 'WW' who may have been his father, cast a bell for Tal-y Llyn, Gwynedd in 1589 (*CB Breconshire p. 105*). Bells were cast in 1624 for Bredon, Worcestershire, by **William Witmore**. The name then recurs in 1639 when **William Whetmore** cast at least three bells for Frocester, Gloucestershire. H.B. Walters (*CB Essex p. 112*) first assumed that they were one and the same, but on analysis of their lettering, he came to the conclusion that two different men were involved and that 'William Whetmore' rather than 'Witmore', was the man who moved to Hertfordshire. Walters reasonably assumed them to have been father and son. There is, however, the vital question of his age; he is described by the churchwardens of Waltham Abbey as 'Ould Whitmore' in 1659-60. Assuming that anyone over the age of fifty-five or sixty was old, as they really were in those days, he could have been born about 1600 and would have therefore been of an age to cast the Bredon bells in 1624, possibly as a journeyman.

Why did a middle-aged man with an established career suddenly set off into the unknown in the middle of a war? Was he in the militia or trained bands and under marching orders? Had he made enemies on one side or another or was he in trouble with the law? Was he unable to expand because of two established founders, John Finch of Hereford and John Martin of Worcester? Or did he just want to carry on his trade in peace in an area where he was not known? Any of these reasons. If not in the militia, as a skilled founder he could pick up a living as he went along, casting pots, mortars or brassware wherever there was a need and resting his horse at the same time; in other words, leading the life of a travelling tinker. There was no great hurry and, provided he kept clear of any passing soldiery, he would be left alone. How long his journey took is not known, weeks, months or even a year.

When his journey took place is uncertain, but a possible answer can be found in the fluid political situation in Gloucester between 1642 and 1644. In the earlier year, Gloucester was a Parliamentarian garrison which put up a strong resistance to Royalist forces. It was gained for the King in December 1643. Judging by his use of Psalm quotation on the Hertingfordbury bell, Whitmore was more Puritan than Royalist and it may have been expedient for him to move to a Parliamentarian area, such as the eastern Association, which included the whole of Hertfordshire.

Eventually, he arrived in 'Wollford', Hertfordshire, generally thought to have been Watford. If a seventeenth century scribe, writing in the normal secretary hand forgot to cross the 't', the confusion could be explained. That Watford *was* the correct place is borne out by the fact that several of his bells are, or were, to be found around that area. As with so many other foundries of that period, the exact site is unidentified and, with all the demolition and massive redevelopment of the town in recent years which has wiped out so much of the medieval centre, unidentifiable.

He was settled in by 1647, as the priest's bell at Aldenham dates from that year. No bells survive from 1648 but in 1649 he cast three for Langley Marish, Bucks., and in 1650, three for the Curfew Tower of Windsor Castle, by that time occupied by Cromwell. Little more than a year after the execution of Charles I bells were were being cast for a former royal castle, albeit for a secular tower. Hard to believe, but true.

As he came to Hertfordshire in 1647, before the death of Robert Oldfield, the men may well have met and the very small amount of bell-metal recorded in the Oldfield inventory could be due to Whitmore taking over most of Oldfield's stock.

By 1653 he was on the move again, for he spent some months in the Chelmsford area, subcontracting for John Hodson of London, before returning to Watford in 1654 where he worked until about 1657. His major undertaking was the recasting of the four (or five) large bells at Waltham Abbey in 1656 at 'Wollford' (*sic*). This work was carried out on his own account and not for Hodson. One bell had been recast by Robert Oldfield in 1626; Whitmore's bells were to be recast in their turn by John Briant in 1806, a surprising example of local continuity with three Hertfordshire founders all working on them. Whitmore's last bell seems to have been the fifth at King's Langley, 1657, since recast.

John Hodson was not originally a bellfounder by training but began as a carpenter who specialised in bellhanging. He was also a change-ringer and was elected a member of the Society of College Youths in 1649, ringing being tolerated by the authorities as a secular, not religious, pastime. He set up his foundry in the parish of All Hallows, London Wall, in 1653 and employed Whitmore to cast for him. Hodson had a son named Christopher who, after 1669, became an important founder in his own right. Until Christopher was legally competent to run the foundry, a founder/manager had to be in charge and, from 1657, a man named William Hull filled the post for a number of years. Whitmore, although working for Hodson, sometimes used Hodson's lettering and sometimes his own and seems to have been an outside subcontractor rather than a regular member of the workforce.

His pattern of moulding wires when working for himself was normally four above and one below the inscription band, but the bell which he cast for Much Hadham in 1654 and which bears Hodson's initials has the pattern three and two. It appears therefore that he was working to Hodson's specification rather than his own, or using Hodson's strickles.

How old Whitmore was and when he died is not known. His bill for the recasting work at Waltham Abbey was not settled until 1659–60, so he was still alive then, although possibly retired from founding. Whether he made the long journey back to Gloucestershire or spent his last years in Watford is equally unknown.

He was sparing in the use of decoration on his bells, the most ambitious being a stylised oak leaf (*Fig. 20*) which is a good indication that a bell bearing Hodson's name was cast by Whitmore. He also used a plain lozenge as a stop between words and occasionally filled up spaces in the inscription band with dots and colons, with comical results at Hertingfordbury! (see No. 24) His own lettering was a very plain roman and his numerals were large and widely spaced, making his dated-only bells easily recognisable. When casting for Hodson, whichever lettering he used, he either put on his initials or the leaf stop, so again identification is not difficult. The standard of casting was consistently good, giving the impression of a man who knew what he was doing and did not indulge in superfluous fancy work; a down-to-earth craftsman.

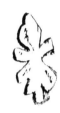

Fig.20

Chronological List of Bells

1.   1647 ALDENHAM, Herts.   St John the Baptist   Sanctus
      THOMAS ◆ WALLER ◆ RALPH HICKMAИ ◆ 1647
      Diameter 14¹³⁄₁₆"   Weight c.1 cwt
      ◆ – Lozenge   *Dodds, CB Herts.*

2.   1649 LANGLEY MARISH, Bucks. St Mary   5th, formerly 2nd of 5
      BENIAMIN x STILE x AGENT x FOR THE WORK OF THE BELLS 1649
      Diameter 35½"   Weight 7¼   cwt   Note A

3.   1649 LANGLEY MARISH   6th, formerly 3rd of 5
      W WHITMORE NOS FECIT MICHAEL TRENLEY AGENT x W W x
      1649 *(one line)*
      Diameter 38"   Weight 9 cwt   Note G#
      The 'agents' were presumably the men responsible for raising the necessary money.

4.   1649 LANGLEY MARISH   7th, formerly 4th of 5
      LET ARONS BELLS BE RVNG x W ITH PRAISES STIL AMONG W W
      I649 *(one line)*
      Diameter 42"   Weight 11 ½ cwt   Note F#
      x – Whitmore's oak leaf *Fig. 20*
      The treble and tenor of the old five were recast by Whitechapel at
      different dates, so these may have been the middle three of five.
                                                             CB Bucks.

5.   *1650 WINDSOR CASTLE, Berks. Clewer or Curfew Tower   Treble of 5*
      Recast by Thomas Lester 1741.

6.   1650 WINDSOR CASTLE   2nd of 8
      INCIPE DVLCE CEQVAR I650 W W HITMORE MADE MEE
      Diameter – ?   Weight 6 cwt 2 qr 0 lb   Note C#

7.   1650 WINDSOR CASTLE   2nd of 8
      I650 W W
      Diameter –?   Weight 7 cwt 2 qr 0 lb   Note B
      In *CB Berks.* p. 315, the late Fred Sharpe argued that Whitmore not only
      augmented the pre-existing six of 1612 by John Wallis of Salisbury, but
      also recast the 1612 treble, on the reasonable grounds that the present
      Whitmore bells are the 2nd and 3rd of the octave and that a ring of
      seven was unthinkable. However, on p. 301, he stated that the 3rd and
      the Whitechapel 5th have had their strike-notes *flattened*, while others,
      which would include the Whitmore 2nd, have been *sharpened* by skirt-
      ing. This implies that either the bells were wildly out of tune or that
      there could have been another bell between the 2nd and 3rd, which
      was removed, and the treble retuned to fill the gap. Whitmore almost
      certainly cast three bells, and any alteration was most likely done
      when Thomas Lester cast or recast the present treble in 1741.
                                                             CB Berks.

8.   *1650 EPPING, Essex St John the Baptist*   *Former single bell*
      WILLIAM LORD GRAYE OF WARKE I650
      Diameter c. 28"
      The Chapel of St John was in existance in the time of Henry VIII. The present
      church, designed by Bodley & Garner, was built in 1889, although the tower
      was not added until 1908-09. The bell from the old chapel was hung for chiming
      on the south-west corner of the new church but was recast in 1913 as the treble
      of the new octave installed 1910–13 by Mears & Stainbank. The inscription has
      been included on the new bell.
         Lord Graye of Warke became the first Major-General of the (Parliamentary)
      Eastern Association in 1643 and is known to have had his quarters in Watford
      for some weeks.   *CB Essex / David Hancock, Epping*

9.   1653 HARROLD, Beds. All Saints   5th, formerly 4th of 5
     JOHN :•: HODSON :•: OF :•: LANDON :•: MADE :•:
     ME :•: I6⊊ Ɛ
     Diameter 37½" Weight 9 cwt   Note G#
     This bell has not previously been noted as being by Whitmore. As John
     Hodson was not yet casting his own bells and before William Hull had
     joined him, it is logical to assume that Whitmore was the actual
     founder. The pattern of nail-heads between the words is very like that
     on the tenor at Hertingfordbury. The figures '53' are inverted giving a
     misleading impression that the bell was dated 1635!   *CB Beds.*

All the above bells were most likely cast at Watford. Numbers 10–17 were
cast in 1653 during the time when he moved temporarily to Essex. Chelmsford is near the geographical centre and it would be a reasonable place for
him to have worked, as did John Dier in the 1590s.

10.   1653 BOREHAM, Essex St Andrew   3rd, formerly treble of 6
11.   1653 BOREHAM   Tenor
12.   *1653 GOOD EASTER, Essex St Andrew   Old treble of 5*
13.   *1653 GOOD EASTER   Old tenor*
      The tower was severely damaged by fire on 22 March, 1885 and the bells
      melted. They were recast by John Warner & Sons, London in 1886.
14.   1653 SANDON, Essex St Andrew   2nd, formerly treble of 5
15.   1653 SANDON   3rd, formerly 2nd of 5
16.   1653 SPRINGFIELD, Essex All Saints   3rd of
                                                                  6
17.   1653 STEEPLE BUMPSTEAD, Essex St Mary   2nd of 6
     Details of all the above are taken from *CB Essex.* All were cast for John
Hodson.
     After this 'gap year', he returned to Watford where he seems to have
remained until the end of his career as a founder. Some of his later bells
were cast for Hodson but some were in his own name.

18.   1654 BOVINGDON, Herts. St Lawrence   2nd of 3
      IOHN GOLDE AND IOHN KNIGHT CHVRC   WARDENS   3
         I654 WW   *(below wires)*   4 / 1
      Diameter 28⅞" Weight 5 cwt   Note C   3
      Although the church and much of the tower were rebuilt   2
      in 1854 by Talbot Bury, the ancient short-headed, curved truss frame
      survives from the earlier tower. The bells are now hung dead and
      chimed by solenoid-operated hammers.   *Dodds, CB Herts.*

19. 1654 MUCH HADHAM, Herts. St Andrew   4th of 8
    x WM ◆ I H x CHVRCH ◆ W ◆ I H x MADE ◆ ME x 1654   2
    Diameter 28⅛ "   Weight 4 cwt 2 qr 0 lb   Note D   3 / 2
    ◆ – lozenge.   x – oakleaf. *Fig 20 p 113*   3
    This was a subcontract job for Hodson, although Whitmore   2
    did not put his own name on it. The fact that one churchwarden had
    the same initials as Hodson merely confuses matters. The presence of
    the leaf is, however, conclusive.   *Dodds, CB Herts.*

20. 1654 RICKMANSWORTH, Herts. St Mary the Virgin   Sanctus
    1654   2
    Diameter 18"   Weight 1 ½ cwt   Note B♭   3 / 2
    Identified by Whitmore's numerals. The moulding wires are   3
    very numerous for such a small bell.   2
                                                     Dodds, CB Herts.

21. *1656 EATON BRAY, Beds. St Mary*   *Old 2nd of 5*
    RB TH EB EC WW I656
    Diameter 34"
    No punctuation or stops recorded by North in CB Beds.
    Recast by Bond of Burford, 1913.   *R.I. Kendrick*

22. 1656 EATON BRAY   5th of 6
    W LM WHITMORE FOR RICHARD BURR ◆ AND ◆ THO ◆
    HAWARD ◆ E B ◆ E C ◆ 1656 *(one line)*
    Diameter 40" (?) Weight c. 8 cwt   Note B
    Again North gives no punctuation apart from dashes; lozenges are
    assumed.   *CB Beds.*

23. 1656 HERTINGFORDBURY, Herts. St Mary   5th of 6
    OPRAISE THE LORD FOR HIS GOODNES AND   3
    DECLARE HIS:W: • • : I656   4 / 1
    Diameter 33⅞ "   Weight 7 cwt   Note B ♭   3
    Whitmore ran out of space and yet filled up 3" with nail-heads! 2
    His intention appears to have been an abridged version of '*O that men
    would therefore praise the Lord for his goodness and declare the wonders that
    He doeth for the children of men!*', the refrain from Psalm 107
                                                     (*B.C.P. version*)

24. 1656 HERTINGFORDBURY   Tenor of 6
    ICEPE DVLCE SEQVAR: ⁞ • ⁞ ⁞ ⁞ W ⁞ WHITMORE ⁞ FOR • IOHN
    HVDSON ⁞ I656 ⁞   3
    Diam. 37½ "   Wt. 9¼ cwt   Note A♭   4 / 1
    The inscription suggests that Whitmore used Latin without   3
                                                                2

being aware of its meaning, as this belongs more properly to a treble rather than a tenor, ICEPE being a corrupt version of INCIPIO, (I BEGIN). The inscription on the treble, added in 1958 by Whitechapel, has the correct spelling, a charming touch.

Dodds, CB Herts.

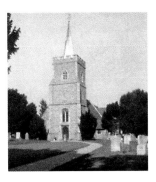

Hertingfordbury, St Mary.

25.   *1656 HARROW-ON-THE-HILL Middx. St Mary*

3rd of old 8

Recast by J. Taylor & Co. c. 1961.

26.   1656 NORTHOLT, Middx. St Mary   Treble of 3
     W ILLIAM KING AND THOMAS LEWES I656 x W   2
     Diameter 26 ¾ " Weight 4 cwt   4 / 1
     x – presumably oakleaf.   3
     This bell was inspected on 4 May 1897 and again on   2
26 May 1900 by H.B. Walters who described it as rather a rough casting with very flat letters. His incredibly neat notes do not make quite clear that what he drew as an x was the oakleaf, which does in fact vaguely resemble that letter. My grateful thanks to Valerie Payne, Hon. Librarian of the Middlesex County Association and London Diocesan Guild for making this information available before the publication of their researches.   *H.B. Walters*

27–   *1656–60 WALTHAM ABBEY, Essex   Holy Cross & St Lawrence*
32.   *There is a degree of confusion as to how many bells Whitmore actually cast for Waltham Abbey and at what date. At the time of the Accession of James I, there appear to have been four bells, which were known to have been rung in honour of his visit in 1625, shortly before his death. The following year one was recast by Robert Oldfield and the third 'subsequently suffered the same fate at the hands of "Ould" Whitmore the bellfounder.' By 1656 there appear to have been five bells, for not only was the great bell cast (or recast) at 'Wollford,' Hertfordshire, at the cost of the ratepayers but 'the Batchelors and Maidens of the Parish of Waltham Holy Cross did by Voluntary contribution purchase a new bell to the other five bells' thus raising the number to six. On balance, it seems possible that he cast a complete ring of six.*
The churchwarden's accounts record:

1654–5
The great bell was cast at Wollford Herts, there by Will[m] Whitmore, Sept, ye 4. 1656. The wayt of the bell to hym was 1836, paid more for tyme [tynne?] being 66 pound that hee put into the bell paid more for mettell that he put into the bell being 186 pound wayt which cost £10 11s. the wayt from hym back againe after he had cast his with the 66 pound wayt of Tyne and the 186 pound wayt of mettell which macke his wayt up compleet 2088 pound wayt and peyed him for Casting of his, fourteen pound.

It must have taken a great deal of patient explanation on the part of Whitmore before the churchwardens arrived at the above wording and even then they do not appear to be quite certain of the facts!

1659–60.
Paid to Ould Whitmore the bell founder for casting the third bell   £9. 5s. 0d.

From this it appears that the recasting was carried out in stages, probably as funds became available. Whitmore's bells were all recast in 1806 by John Briant of Hertford. (see p. 253)   *CB Essex*

33. *KING'S LANGLEY, Herts. All Saints*   *Old 5th of 8*
      THO ◆ *BIGG* ◆ *AND* ◆ *CHRIS* ◆ *BVCKOKE* ◆ *CHVRCH WAR* ◆ *I657*
      (below top wires)   ◆ *EDWARD* ◆ *DORINGTON*
                              : W W:
      Diameter 31"
      Recast by J. Taylor & Co. 1958; the 'W W' on the waist was not recorded by N & S.
                              Dodds, CB Herts.

After Whitmore there was a gap of about forty years during which no founder settled in the county, thus breaking the succession which had lasted almost continuously from John Clarke. This does not mean that no work was done; the Restoration brought about a great upsurge in bellfounding. Some bells came from the Whitechapel Foundry under Anthony and later, James, Bartlet, and some from the Hodsons, also of London, but no purely *local* bells were produced. The foundry in the tiny Buckinghamshire village of Drayton Parslow had been established in 1635 by Richard Chandler and his successor Anthony Chandler had cast bells for Northchurch in 1651. With no local founder working after 1660 the field was wide open and the Chandlers seized their opportunity. Apart from single bells they supplied complete rings of five bells to Great Gaddesden in 1662, Flamstead in 1664, St Paul's Walden in 1665, Datchworth and Tewin in 1673 and Essendon in 1681–5. There is no evidence that they ever set up a foundry within Hertfordshire. On the contrary, the churchwardens' accounts at St Peter's, St Albans, for 1678/9 state that one bell was taken to 'Drayton'.

Then, out of the blue, two completely independent founders appeared in north Hertfordshire at more or less the same time. (Rather like waiting for an hour then two buses turning up together!) One was a well-known, long-established Oxfordshire man named Richard Keene. The other man has not been identified, although many guesses have been made, so it is proposed to refer to him in the time-honoured way as 'X'.

PART III

HERTFORDSHIRE
1690–1703

TWO POOR FOUNDERS

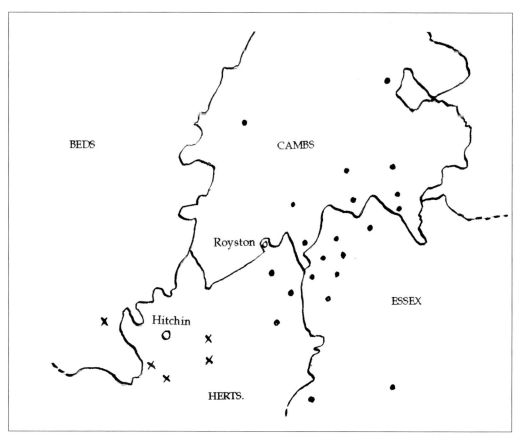

Map 6 'X' & Richard Keene
Distribution of Bells'   X' shown as x   Keene shown as •

11

'X' OF HITCHIN

B Y THE DISTRIBUTION of his bells, (*Map 6*) 'X' appears to have worked in the Hitchin area. All his bells are dated but only three were known to have had any other inscription. As none of the bells can be described as good castings, it may be that he preferred to remain anonymous! The dates themselves have caused innumerable problems, not only for researchers but for nineteenth and twentieth century bellfounders who had to recast many of these bells and wished (or were required) to reproduce the date. Earlier men, such as John Waylett, who recast them had no such scruples, merely putting on their usual name and inscription and wiping out any evidence of identification.

The identification problem is caused by the fact that each of the four digits in the date is mounted on a separate patera, roughly laid on so that it tends to stand proud at the lower edge and be flush with the surface at the upper edge. The 6 and the 9 are merely inversions of each other, both having the same noticeable flaw. When making a 'squeeze' for a plaster cast, this is

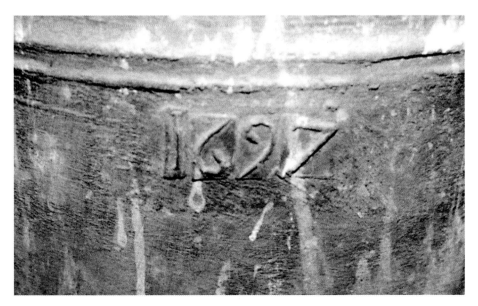

King's Walden, St Mary. The date 1697 on the 5th bell by an unknown founder, 'X'
[R. l. Kendrick]

very obvious and Geoffrey Dodds and the writer had no difficulty in deciding that the correct dates belonged to the 1690's. However, when taking a
rubbing, the protruding lower edge shows up as the horizontal stroke of a 2
and hence North assigned them to the 1620's. John Warner & Sons and
Mears & Stainbank fell into this trap when recasting.

Sir Henry Chauncy, change-ringer and past Master of the Society of College Youths, never failed to mention the bells in the parishes he wrote about
in 1700 and he is an invaluable guide to the to the casting dates of new rings,
such as Knebworth (see below). He probably rang on them all!

North and Stahlschmidt (N & S) claimed that the lettering was that used
by Samuel Knight, who was a notoriously untidy founder, as was 'X'. A man
named John Wood, also an untidy workman, fits the period, if little else. The
odd fact is that, poor castings or not, those few which have survived are
tonally quite good. It is kinder to ascribe them to an anonymous founder
rather than traduce some innocent person.

Chronological List of Bells by 'X'

1.   1696 BENINGTON, Herts. St Peter   7th of 8   o
     ☩ OHN ARCHER C W I696   2 / 2
     Diameter 36⅝"   Weight 9 cwt   Note G#   3
     This is a poor casting with a large area of slumping on the   2
     lower waist, yet the tone is good.   *Dodds, CB Herts.*

2–6. *1696 WALKERN, Herts. St Mary the Virgin*   *Old ring of 5*
      I696
      Treble diameter quoted by N & S as 24½" and inscription as 1626. In 1700
      Chauncy said that there were five bells, cast Anno 1697. (They may not not
      have been hung until that year) Only the treble can now be identified. Recasting
      of at least the back three was carried out as early as 1713 by John Waylett. In
      1909 John Taylor & Co. recast the treble and third, reproducing the dates only.
      They noted '1696' correctly.   *Dodds, CB Herts.*

7–11. *1697 KNEBWORTH, Herts. SS Mary and Thomas of Canterbury*   *Old 5*
      Chauncy, writing in 1700, gave the date of casting 'five small bells' as 1697.
      Again, as at Walkern, only the details of one bell can be identified. Recasting of
      the treble took place in 1716 by John Waylett, of the 2nd and 3rd in 1730–2 by
      Edward Hall of Drayton Parslow, Bucks., another notoriously bad founder, and
      the tenor by John Briant in 1812 (**see p. 268**). *Only the 4th survived of 'X's'*
      five to be recorded by N & S.

10. *1697 KNEBWORTH* Old 4th of 5
ŦOHN DARDS ᴄW Ŧ697
Diameter given as 35" by N & S who correctly, for once, quoted 1697.
This was recast by Warner's in 1889 and they plainly had difficulty with the date and reproduced it as 1627. Furthermore, there was no help to be got from the name John Dards, as several generations of that name served as churchwardens. Dodds, CB Herts.

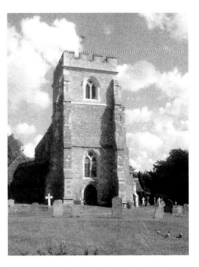

King's Walden, St Mary, has three bells by 'X'

1697 KING'S WALDEN, Herts. St Mary
6 bells (Nos. 12–17)
Chauncy recorded six bells, though he did not state 'new'. However, inscriptions on the three earlier bells given in the Edwardian Inventory of 1552 are scratched on the north side of the tower arch, probably noted on their being removed for recasting. The 2nd was either cast or recast in 1699 and the 3rd and tenor recast in 1865 by John Warner & Sons without reproduction of any inscription.

12. *1697 KING'S WALDEN* Old treble of 6
Ŧ627
Diameter quoted by N & S as 26½"
Recast by Mears & Stainbank 1929, with 1627 reproduced.

13. KING'S WALDEN 4th of 6 0
Ŧ697 2 / 2
Diameter 31⅞" Weight 6¼cwt Note A# 3
This is an appallingly poor casting 2
with the crown block actually recessed instead of standing proud or flush as on most bells.

14. KING'S WALDEN 5th of 6 0
Ŧ697 0 / 2
Diameter 35¼" Weight 7½cwt Note G# 3
This bell is so round-shouldered that 2
the inscription band had to be lowered and the upper wires omitted.

15.	1699 KING'S WALDEN	2nd of 6	0
	1699		2 / 2
	Diameter 28" Weight 4¾ cwt	Note C#	3
			2

16.	1697/9 KING'S WALDEN,	Old 3rd
	Recast by J. Warner & Sons 1866	N&S
		Dodds, CG Herts

17. BARTON-LE-CLEY, Beds. St Nicholas   Tenor
     IOHN HALE RI CHARD CROVCH C W I699
     Diameter 47"   Weight 16 cwt 1 qr 14 lb   Note E
     North gave the date , almost inevitably, as 1622.
     Rehung, tuned (and much improved!) by John Taylor & Co. 1990.

                                                              CJP

It will be noted from the above list that 'X' did not place any moulding wires on the crown and this odd characeristic is shared by the Hertfordshire examples of the next founder, Richard Keene. In most other respects, their bells are very dissimilar, especially in their numerals.

12

RICHARD KEENE
1699–1703

TRADITION ALONE SAYS that Richard Keene moved to Royston; there is no documentary proof whatsoever. All that can be said is that a very large number of bells was cast by him during this period in this area. Geographically, the centre of his activities would seem to have been Saffron Walden, as they are chiefly to be found in north-west Essex and the adjoining parts of south Cambridgeshire, with only two known in Hertfordshire. It must, however, be borne in mind that 'X' was producing his monstrosities in the Hitchin area in 1699, little more than twelve miles away, so a founder at Royston would face severe geographical restrictions for that reason. Hence it is perfectly understandable why so few of Keene's bells are to be found in Hertfordshire.

Richard was the son of James Keene, Robert Oldfield's contemporary, who had learned his trade at Bedford. James moved to Woodstock, Oxon., in 1631 and set up business in Oxford Street. As there is no record of any son being baptised at Woodstock, Richard must have been born while the family was still in Bedford. This is important because, at the time of his move to Royston, Richard would be about seventy, rather too old to be making a fresh start, one would have thought, but inevitable at that period; unless he had been able to make adequate provision for his old age, it was a case of work or starve.

James Keene died at Woodstock in 1654, being buried at Woodstock on 29 December of that year. Richard thereupon became the master founder and ran the business with reasonable success for over thirty years. On or about 24 December 1660 he married Mary Bignell and three children were born to them, James, baptised 14 December 1661, Elizabeth, baptised 29 November 1664: buried 3 June 1665 and Marie, baptised 28 February 1666, buried 30 May 1667. His wife died in 1670, being buried on 27 July. There is no evidence that young James followed his father and grandfather into bellfounding, although he lived until 1703, pre-deceasing Richard by eleven months.

During his years at Woodstock, Keene's output of bells was very large as he took advantage of the post-Restoration boom in bellfounding. His products can be found over Oxfordshire, Buckinghamshire and Warwickshire, as well as others in Berkshire and even a ring of six for Martley, in the far west of Worcestershire, where he cast them on the spot, as well as for Chipping Campden, Glos., and many other places. All this proves him to be a founder of major importance, although he was never reckoned to be the equal of his father in the quality of his work. His reputation was such that, during the restoration of Lichfield Cathedral after the damage it sustained in the Civil War, he received an order to cast a ring of six bells with a tenor weighing 37 cwt. These were completed and hung in 1670. They were not a success (a portent of things to come) and were recast into a ring of ten by Henry Bagley of Chacombe in 1686.

In 1678 Keene was commissioned to recast Great Tom of Christ Church, Oxford, which had been previously cast by Humphrey and James Keene (his grandfather and father) in 1625–6, probably at Woodstock, and again by Michael Darbie, an itinerant founder in 1654. Fred Sharpe, in *CB Oxon*. gives much-deserved credit to Darbie for casting so big a bell (2 tons 13 cwt 1 qr 9 lb was the quoted weight) without access to a proper foundry. His bells, although rough castings, were neither better nor worse than others of that time. For some reason, possibly damage, or the desire for a larger bell, it was decided to again recast Great Tom and an agreement was drawn up on 5 August 1678 with Keene, for a 93 cwt bell with the usual guarantees that it would last a year and a day, to be cast at the 'Workhouse' (i.e. Works' Department) on the north side of Tom Quad.

Keene was unlucky or incompetent, or both. He had three unsuccessful attempts, twice he ran short of metal and the third time the mould burst. Not unnaturally, the poor man was distraught, as anyone would have been. He was, after all, trying to cast a far larger bell than any which had been produced for many years, so was venturing into unknown territory. Fortunately for him, he was paid over £400 for his work and metal but the damage had been done to his reputation. It was all the more galling that the much younger Christopher Hodson was to succeed in recasting Great Tom at his first attempt the following year. (Christopher Hodson was the son of John Hodson, for whom William Whitmore had acted as sub-contractor in the 1650s)

During the 1680s Keene's output was fairly steady but a careful analysis of sources suggests that by 1690, trade was falling off badly, due partly to the Great Tom fiasco but more likely to the increasing competition from the Bagley foundry at Chacombe, Northants., established in 1631 and which continued working until 1746.

Although not every bell of these years has been listed, the figures speak for themselves in showing the downward trend.

1691	none found	1695	10 or 11
1692	2	1696	3
1693	4	1697	3
1694	7	1698	3

There were obviously others which have been missed or since recast but the picture is plain, he was not making a living, was possibly in debt and so, with the spectre of bankruptcy looming, it was time to move to a more profitable area. Why Royston? Nobody knows, but Keene must have done some research prior to moving and identified a need in that neighbourhood. As will appear, he was correct; there was a need but, with hindsight, was he really the right man to fill it? He was an old man. His reputation as a founder has not been enhanced by the number of mediocre rings of bells which he turned out in his last years. As Deedes and Walters in *CB Essex* so delicately put it – 'his work has not always stood the test of time; of six rings cast for Essex churches not one now remains intact'. Quantity rather than quality, in other words.

In January 1828, the aged John Briant wrote to the Surveyor to the Dean and Chapter of Lincoln, passionately trying to persuade them to entrust the recasting of *their* Great Tom to Mears of Whitechapel because 'I have no fear of a good article with a *proved* furnace; but the great uncertainty of effecting a cast with a new one is greatly decreasing the probability of success'. He was speaking from a lifetime of experience and specifically referred to the Great Tom of Oxford affair, blaming the trouble on an untried furnace. Perhaps Keene's Royston problems arose from the fact that his furnace was a new one. It would explain a great deal.

As there is only tradition to rely upon, the location of the foundry is, once again, unknown but at least fifty-two bells were produced there in five years. Keene maybe imported his work force as well as his equipment in order to achieve such a huge output; it was surely beyond the ability of one old man on his own, however hard working.

Chronological List of Bells by Richard Keene

As the list is a fairly long one and Keene's inscriptions were rarely inspiring, the writer proposes to list in detail only the more interesting examples, noting any changes which have occurred since they were cast. On his Royston bells he used no decorations whatsoever, in many cases putting on only the date. A blank bell at Reed, Herts., may also have been one of his.

1699 HEYDON,Cambs. formerly Essex	*St Peter or Holy Trinity.*
	Complete ring of five (Nos.1–5)

1. *1699*
2. *1699*
3. *SPIRITUS ALTA PETAT DAEMON PECCATA RESUMAT*
   (recast J.Taylor & Co. 1863)
4. *WILL MOVLE CW 1699*
5. *SR PETER SOAME BARNIT I699*
   Diameter 32 ½ "   Weight 5 cwt 0 qr 10 lb
   The inscription of the 3rd can be translated as [LET THE SPIRIT SEEK THE HEIGHTS, BUT THE DEVIL RESUMES HIS MISCHIEF].

H.B. Walters described the letters and numerals as being rough and careless. In 1940, the tower received a direct hit from a bomb which totally destroyed both it and the bells and severely damaged the church. Both have since been rebuilt and a new ring of five cast by Whitechapel was installed in 1962   *CB Essex*

6.   1699 HIGH EASTER, Essex   St Mary   5th of 6
         IOHN ARCHER HEZIKIAH WRIGHT CW ▌699
         Diameter 42 ½ " Weight 12 cwt   Note F#   *CB Essex*

7, 8.   RICKLING, Essex All Saints   Treble and 2nd of 5
         ▌699
         Both had date only. The 2nd was possibly recast by Bowell of Ipswich in 1927, according to a pencilled note in *CB Essex*.

9.   1699 DUXFORD, Cambs. St Peter   Tenor of 6
         GEORGE BARKER HE*V*RY WALLIS CW ▌699
         Diameter – ?   Weight 8 cwt 2 qr 6 lb   Note G
         This was the tenor of the former ring of five at St John, Duxford, which became redundant prior to 1949. In that year, the bells from St John's were combined with those of St Peter, with some recast, to form the present ring of six by Gillett & Johnston of Croydon. The largest bell from St Peter's is now the 5th and is heavier than this bell.
                                       Maureen Havil / R.F. Walker

10.   1699 HORSEHEATH, Cambs. All Saints   3rd of 4
         THO PVRKIS THO RVLE CW ▌699
         These bells have been unringable for many years. It is said that the tower was shaken (not damaged) in the Colchester earthquake of 1884, giving that as a reason for ceasing ringing.

11.   1699 SHUDY CAMPS, Cambs. St Mary   2nd of 5
         These bells have been unringable for many years.

12.   1700 ELMDON, Essex St Nicholas   3rd of
         6
         WIL KENT THO GRAVES CW ▌700
         Diameter 31 ½ " Weight 5 cwt   Note C
         Each letter is on a clearly marked patera.   *CB Essex*

         1700 HADSTOCK, Essex St Botolph Complete ring of 5   *(Nos.13–17)*
13.   *Treble recast by Thomas Gardiner of Sudbury, 1739.*
14.   *2nd, 1700*
15.   *3rd, recast by Pack & Chapman of London, 1774.*
16.   *4th, recast by John Thornton of Sudbury, 1719.*

17. *Tenor, RICH KEENE CAST THIS RING 1700*
This cannot be described as a success story! Within 75 years three had been
recast and the other two were both cracked, according to **CB Essex**. *The com-*
plete five were recast into a very light six by Mears & Stainbank in 1970. This
tower was also said to have been shaken by the 1884 earthquake.

18.   1700 RICKLING   Tenor of 5
      ROB LION CW   I ⅂ 00
      The 7 is reversed. (He may have cast a ring.)   *CB Essex*

      1700 WENDENS AMBO, Essex St Mary
      Complete ring of 5 (Nos.19–23)
      19–21. *I700, recast by Bowell of Ipswich, 1904.*

22.   I700

23.   ANDREW JAGGARD THOMAS BARKER CW I700
      Diameter 36"   Weight 8 cwt   Note G#
      The five were augmented to six by Bowell in 1904, the old 4th and
      tenor being quarter turned and becoming the 5th and tenor. To quote
      CB Essex – 'The old ring of 1700 was one of Richard Keene's poor per-
      formances. D. Raven in July 1861 noted it as "a wretched peal, Nos. 1–3
      cracked"; Stahlschmidt in September 1887 says "in no better order"'.
      CB Essex

24.   1700 HORSEHEATH.   Treble & 2nd of 4
      I700

25.   SR GILES ALINGTON GAVE THE TENOR I 606   I700
      Unringable, *see above No.* 10.
                                                       Raven, CB Cambs.

26.   1700 SHEPRETH, Cambs. All Saints   Treble of 3
      I700
                                                       Raven, CB Cambs.

27.   1700 ANSTEY, Herts. St George Treble of 6   0
      NICKLES BALDOCK WILLIAM GINN CW I700   2 / 2
                                                                   3
      Diameter 25 ¾"   Weight 3 ¾ cwt   Note D#   2
                                                       Dodds, CB Herts.

      1701 LITTLE SHELFORD, Cambs. All Saints
      2nd, 4th & 5th of 6 (Nos.28–30)

28. |70|

29.   CHRISTOFOR WOODGATE CW |70|

30. |70| *Raven, CB Cambs.*

31.   1701 ARKESDEN, Essex St Margaret   Treble of 6
        |70|
        Diameter 23″   Weight 2 ½ cwt   Note E

32.   *1701 ARKESDEN*   *2nd of 6*
        Recast by John Briant, 1814 (See No. 370, p.270). *The inscription may have*
        been RICH KEENE CAST THIS RING, as appears at Hadstock.

33.   1701 ARKESDEN   3rd of 6
        |70|
        Diameter 25″   Weight 3°cwt   Note C

34.   1701 ARKESDEN   4th of 6
        | ⅂0|
        Diameter 28″   Weight 4 cwt   Note B
        The numerals are particularly bad, the 7 being reversed and the final |
        misshapen.

35.   1701 ARKESDEN   5th of 6
        WILL MAYNARD ESQ[R] |70|
           Diameter 30″   Weight 4 ½ cwt   Note A

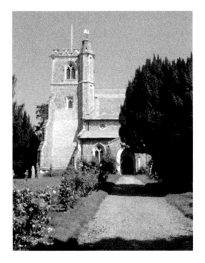

Arkesden, St Margaret has five Richard
Keene bells and one by John Briant

36. *1701 ARKESDEN*   *Tenor of 6*
NON CLAMOR SED AMOR CANTAT IN AVRE DEI
THO TRIGGE WILL MORRIS | ⅂ |0 (sic)   *(one upper line)*
CW (below)
Diameter 34″   Weight 5 cwt 3 qr 14 lb   *Note G*
NOT NOISE BUT LOVE SOUNDS IN THE EAR OF GOD. *This
reads as though the previous bell was cast by William
Haulsey of St Ives, who was fond of using this inscription.
For Keene, it was decidedly garrulous and is one of his most
ambitious efforts. The date was surely meant to be 1701.
The weight is very light for the note. Recast by Bowell of
Ipswich 1931.*   *CB Essex*
Following major restoration, a peal of 5040 changes
of Minor was rung by members of the Essex Associa-
tion on 10 June 2001, to commemorate the 300th
anniversary of the casting of the ring.

37.   1701 LITTLEBURY, Essex Holy Trinity   Tenor of 6
      WILL COW LIN THO PEARL CW | ꙅ0|
      Diameter 39"   Weight 8 cwt 1 qr 2 lb   Note F#
      The figure 7 is reversed. Again, this bell is very light for its note.

                                                                  CB Essex

38.   1701 GREAT HORMEAD, Herts. St Nicholas   Treble of 6
      WILLIAM BULL C :W: |70| 0
      Diameter 28¾" Weight 4¾ cwt   Note D   2 / 2
      The number 0 has points top and bottom, as though it had   3
      been cut out of a folded piece of thin leather. Keene certainly   2
      did not use stamped letters and numbers.
      Hormead bells were rehung by Mears & Stainbank in 1952.

                                                              Dodds, CB Herts.

      1702 LANGLEY, Essex St John the Evangelist
          Ring of 5, 2nd missing (Nos.39–43)

39. |702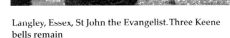
      Diameter 21"

40.   *Stolen (or cracked and sold)*

41.   *Recast by John Warner & Sons 1884.*

42. |702
      Diameter 27½ "

43.   WILL BANSO |702
      Diameter 31½ " Weight c.5 cwt   Langley, Essex, St John the Evangelist. Three Keene
      These form 1, 3, 4 and 5 of a five, the   bells remain
      second having apparently either been
      stolen at some unknown date or having become cracked and quietly
      sold. There is the usual hoary local tradition that these 'bells were
      interchanged with those of Heydon close by'; they were cast three
      years apart so it is not very likely.

                                                                  CB Essex

44.   1702 SHEERING, Essex St Mary   Tenor of 4
      PETER SALMON CW |702
      Diameter 35"   Weight 7½ cwt
      Recorded by Deedes and Walters as unringable. However, a major
      refurbishment and augmentation is in prospect. (*Essex Association
      Report 2000*)
                                                                  CB Essex

45.   *1702 WEST WRATTING, Cambs. St Andrew*   2nd of 5
       Recast by John Taylor 1958.

46–   1703 BURWELL, Cambs. St Mary the Blessed Virgin
49.   4th, 5th, 6th & 7th of 8
       |703
       These were Nos. 1–4 of what may have been a complete five, the tenor
       of which was recast by Thomas Newman in 1725. On 29 March 1793
       John Briant wrote to the churchwardens in an attempt to gain a com-
       mission for recasting these bells, but without success. His letter has
       been preserved (see *p. 172*). The bells were augmented by John Taylor
       & Co. in 1955, some bells having their cannons removed.
       Some remedial work was carried out in 2000.   *Dodds*

50–   1703 LOLWORTH, Cambs. All Saints   Set of 3
52.   (Cast) |703.

53.   1703 LITTLE SHELFORD   Treble of 6
       |703
       For Nos. 2, 4 & 5 see above Nos. 28–30.

54.   *Undated.   REED, Herts. St Mary*   *Old treble of 3*
       Blank.   Diameter 26 ½ "   Sold for scrap c. 1974.   N & S / RWMC

55.   Undated. REED   Single, formerly 2nd of 3
       Blank
       Diameter 30"   Weight 6 cwt
       Chauncy recorded three bells in 1700. These two bells are believed to
       have been cast in about that year.   *RWMC*

This was the last group of bells that Keene cast at Royston, as he moved
back home to Woodstock and proved that his old furnace was still use-
able by casting his last bell, the 7th for Ambrosden, Oxon. It was
inscribed

       THO HARRIS HEN COOPER OLIVER PANGBORN CW I703

and was recast by John Taylor & Co. in 1928.
    His return home to Woodstock must have been very unhappy as his son
James died and was buried on the 28 August 1703. Whether he reached
home in time to take his last leave of his son or whether he was called home
because of his death will never be known. The old man, and he must have
been well into his seventies, outlived James by less than a year, dying in July
1704 and being buried at Woodstock on the 17th. This brought to an end the
foundry which had existed in the town for over sixty years. The tragedy is

that Keene's reputation has suffered from the poor quality of much of his workmanship.

Before the simultaneous arrival of 'X' and Keene on to the Hertfordshire scene, there had been a gap of almost forty years; after the departure of Keene, there was no gap at all. His successor was an Essex man named John Waylett.

PART IV

HERTFORDSHIRE
1730–1742

AND
FROM BISHOP'S STORTFORD,
TO LONDON VIA SUSSEX

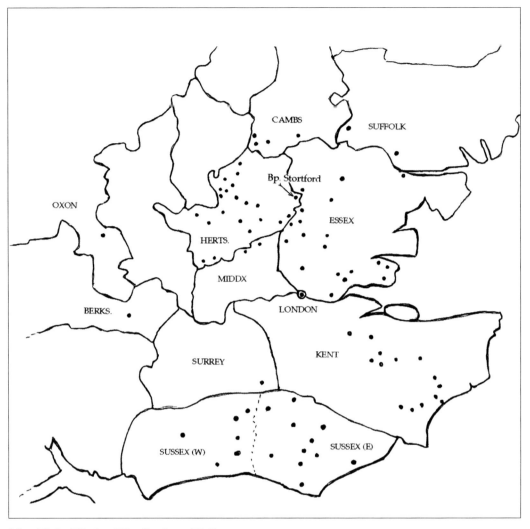

Map 7 John Waylett Distribution of Bells

13

JOHN WAYLETT

HIS LIFE AND FOUNDRIES

IN 1523 A BELL, the earliest dated example in Essex, was given to the church of Leaden Roding by one John Aylet. It was probably cast by Thomas Lawrence of London and is inscribed JOHN AYLET GAVE ME IN THE VORCHYP OF THE TRINITE A^O 1523. This indicates a man of substance able and willing to give generously to his parish church. At that date, spelling was fluid and Aylet and Waylett were variations of the same name.

It is not known exactly where Waylett the founder originated but there are clues. The Hertfordshire I.G.I. lists nobody at all of that name. Essex is more hopeful; the I.G.I. gives a son, John, to John and Ann Waylett of Chipping Ongar in 1670 and also to John and Lydia Waylett of Stock in 1673. Either of these could be the right man. Other people of the same name were to be found at North Weald, where Simon Waylett appears as churchwarden on the fifth bell, cast by Anthony Bartlet in 1673. More Wayletts lived at Doddinghurst. There is a Wayletts Farm by the A113, the Chigwell to Ongar road (*TQ* 525990) and also a hamlet marked Dunton Wayletts on the western outskirts of Basildon (*TQ* 657902) as well as an Aylett at Broomfield by the A130 (*TQ* 706113). All this suggests that an ancestor of the status of John Aylet, most likely a yeoman farmer, had a family of sons, the younger of whom, as they grew up and married, moved away from the centre and settled in outlying villages, while the eldest inherited the family home. The mere fact that two men with that surname became churchwardens proves that they were of good standing and reasonably literate. Certainly, most of the Wayletts were to be found within a radius of ten miles from Leaden Roding, mainly in the farming country in the upper reaches of the valley of the River Roding, although Stock was slightly further afield.

A century and a half later, several generations of the family were windmillers, first at Great Canfield Mill and then at Hockerill Mill, Bishop's Stortford; the road name 'Wayletts Drive' for the former uninspiring 'Urban Road' refers to the nineteenth century miller of Hockerill Mill, William James Waylett and not to John Waylett the founder. In the late seventeenth and eighteenth centuries, Essex had one of the highest concentrations of windmills in England, almost every parish having one, which makes it likely that John was brought up with some knowledge of the working of the local mill, thus awakening his interest in machinery. This makes it slightly less surprising that he did not follow family tradition and decided to become a

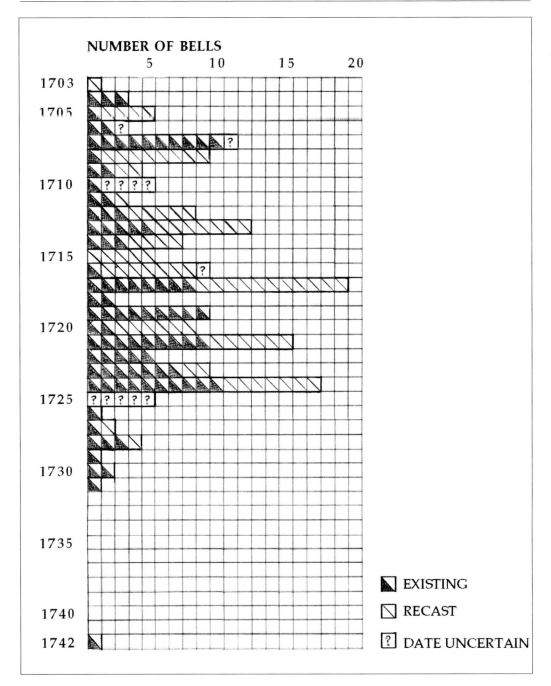

Fig. 21 John Waylett Annual production

bellfounder instead, unless, as in the later case of Islip Edmunds, economic circumstances within the family forced him to take up another trade. In view, however, of the life he led, it is obvious that the circumscribed existence of a farmer would not have satisfied him.

To whom he was apprenticed is uncertain, but Charles Newman seems the likeliest bet. Newman had worked for Christopher Graye at Haddenham, Cambs., in 1682 and his son, Thomas, was born there that year. Newman senior was something of a nomad, working all over East Anglia and dying in Bury St Edmunds in 1709. The Revd R.M.N. Owen, in *Church Bells of Huntingdonshire* (1899), considered that 'if business did not come to him he must go to the business.' This was the classic philosophy of the itinerant founder and it rubbed off onto John Waylett.

Studying his chronological list of bells, one point becomes plain. Having set up at Bishop's Stortford he stayed there for ten years, moved to Sussex to lead the life of an itinerant for about a year, moved back to Stortford for another year, followed by another spell in Sussex or Kent, and so on. These returns to Stortford suggest that he had a wife and family there and that he combined visits to them with the opportunity to cast a few bells in Essex or Hertfordshire, before setting off on his travels again. The mileage he covered was considerable.

Although the actual site of his foundry is not known, there is a street called Bells Hill, in itself suggestive, which runs down steeply from Windhill to Hadham Road. In a letter dated June 1994 to Geoffrey and Joyce Dodds, Doreen Wright of the Bishop's Stortford Museum wrote that J.L. Glasscock Jnr., a local historian who collected oral traditions and reminiscences in the 1890s, noted that in conversation with old inhabitants, they remembered their 'grandfathers' talking of the bells being recast on Bells Hill. As the bells were cast in 1713, the tradition must have been handed down from even earlier forebears. The street was probably named after the foundry as it does not appear in medieval churchwardens' records under that name.

A document of 1726, formerly in the church chest at Standon, is in existence showing that during Waylett's absence that year, his furnace was hired by Thomas Newman, then working in Cambridge, to recast two bells for Standon, neither of which survives. It reads :

> the Churchwardens … shall be reddy to bring the sd bells to the furnis of
> the sd Thomas Newman in Bishop Stortford.

Incidentally, by casting those bells, Newman qualified as a Hertfordshire founder – just! Whether or not Waylett carried out any more casting in Bishop's Stortford after that year cannot be certain but the evidence suggests that he did not. A study of his annual output shows that, like other founders before him, he went through periods of comparative prosperity alternating with lean times. Most of his bells over the preceding five or six years had been cast for Kent or Sussex and very few for Essex or Hertfordshire.

The reason is not far to seek. The Whitechapel Foundry had emerged from its seventeenth century doldrums and was being run from 1700 onwards by a capable and active man, Richard Phelps. He had cast a ring of six for Wheathampstead in 1717, during Waylett's absence in Kent and, as the latter's trade dwindled, Phelps established a near-monopoly in the Home Counties, gradually extending his range and, in the process, forcing Waylett to move ever further away from base. It is therefore not surprising that, in view of what must have been a serious drop in income, when Waylett was given the opportunity to move into a different field of founding, he took it.

By 1726 or 27, Waylett had settled in London, going into partnership with one Harrison, not a known bellfounder, but who appears from the evidence to have been more concerned with general casting for the up-and-coming business of engineering. Waylett, being an experienced bronze and brass founder, became involved with the early stages of the Industrial Revolution and came to meet one of its greatest pioneers. He still cast bells but in limited numbers and they include the word 'LONDON' in the inscription. It is considered that he remained there for his final years.

Evidence from parish accounts of St Mary's, Walthamstow, shows that in 1727, his foundry was at Windmill Hill, Clerkenwell. There had been a foundry on that site for a number of years, first in the hands of William snd Philip Wightman from 1680 to 1702 and then of Matthew Bagley III until his death in a tragic accident in 1716. Windmill Hill became known as Windmill Street and its present name is Leonard Street, partly in Hackney and partly in Finsbury. (*TQ* 329823)

In 1729 Thomas Newcomen, the first successful builder of steam engines, visited the foundry of Harrison & Waylett to enquire about casting bronze cylinders, something not too far removed from casting bells. Later, there was a letter from Waylett to a mine owner in the north of England apologising for the delay in delivery as 'he drove the horse too hard' and spoiled the cylinder which was being machined (E. Hughes, *North Country Life in the Eighteenth Century*. Vol. I. (1952), p. 153). Waylett was clearly using a horse gin as a vertical lathe. There is no evidence that he or any other founder of the period linked the idea of the horse- or donkey-gin to tuning bells, although the principle was already known in the Netherlands. During this time six bells were sent to Hertfordshire, including one for Bishop's Stortford in 1730, which confirms that by then he had given up his furnace there.

At some time in his life, maybe in his youth, he had become a bellringer and he was a sufficiently competent change-ringer to have been elected a member of the Society of College Youths in 1736, after he had given up full-time bellfounding.

The first recorder of Sussex bells, A.D. Tyssen, noted an Administration of John Waylett of St George's, Southwark, to Mary his widow, which was dated 1733. This could not have been the founder as he lived for several

more years, but it may have been the other man of similar age listed in the
I.G.I. They must have been related in some degree, probably cousins.

In 1740 Waylett was elected a 'Love Brother' or Honorary Member of the
Worshipful Company of Founders, presumably in his retirement. J.C.L.
Stahlschmidt, himself a member of the Company, notes on p. 107 of his
Church Bells of Kent, 1887, that in the minute book for 1740, 'it was ordered
that Mr. Waylett and Mr. Robert Cattilin, Founders, be admitted Love Brothers'. Robert Catlin was a skilled bellhanger and later founder who had
worked for Samuel Knight (for whom Waylett acted as a sub-contractor) and
became his successor in the business. Catlin and Waylett were well known
to each other both through work and bellringing.

Two years later, in 1742, a William Waylett, elsewhere described as 'a Citi-
zen and Vintner', was sworn in as a member of the Founders' Company. This
may have been a son or a nephew who possibly learned something of the
trade with his kinsman. The fact that there was another Waylett could
explain a 1742 bell with an inscription in Waylett's medium alphabet, and
bearing three digits identical to his (See No. 186).

It is not known whether the foundry of Harrison & Waylett still existed
after Waylett's retirement as it is not listed in either the Guildhall records or
those of the Worshipful Company of Founders. (Elphick, *Sussex Bells*, p.110)
The reason why the records are missing was explained to Geoffrey Dodds by
Mr A. Gillett, Librarian of the Founders' Company. It appears that
Stahlschmidt had borrowed the relevant volume in order to facilitate his
researches into London founders and it was in his possession at the time of
his death. Unhappily, it was never returned by his executors and its present
whereabouts is unknown.

Waylett used three different fonts, large, medium and small. The large
set was the first in which he used a 'U' as well as a 'V' when this was just
coming into fashion. The letters 'A' and 'Y' are very characteristic and
cannot be mistaken for anyone else's. His medium set used the 'V' but not
'U'. None of his fonts included a 'J'. His small set was very small indeed; his
monogram, found on the previously unidentified fifth bell at St Ippolyts
consists of an 'I' surmounted by a 'W' of this set; the total height is about an
inch. He seems to have stamped his inscriptions but his fleur-de-lys could
have been a cast wax figure, judging by the slight variations between different bells. He also appears to have welcomed the advent of the half-crown,
introduced in about 1704; he used the impres-
sion of two of these on Baldock tenor, his
largest bell, in 1711 as well as on the (recast)
6th at Monken Hadley. On the whole, he was
sparing with decoration, occasionally using
nailheads to fill up lacunae on inscription
bands.

His spelling was neither better nor worse

Fig 22

than average for the time; his Latin was phonetic; not all churchwardens' Christian names were spelled out in full but who can fail to appreciate ED CHANDLER RICH HILL at Monken Hadley, or GODFREY GARDINER RECTOR WALKON on the (recast) tenor at Walkern? There are others equally amusing, GORGE BAREY at Little Wakering for instance. We hope Mr Barey was lightly built – a portly man would have had just cause for complaint! And what *was* the correct name of WETHR IENNENS of Canewdon?

Some of his bells were slightly rough in finish and occasionally he was in too much of a hurry when stamping his inscriptions before the cope was sufficiently dry, causing parts of the cope to adhere to the stamp. His order of moulding wires above and below the inscription band was normally two over three, but in this he was not always consistent and he sometimes reversed the pattern.

The true number of bells cast by Waylett will probably never be known. Until the writer began compiling the chronological list, the sheer volume of his output had not been realised. After Briant, Waylett was easily the most prolific Hertfordshire founder. Many were cast without the benefit of a fully-equipped foundry which makes his achievement all the more amazing.

14

JOHN WAYLETT

CHRONOLOGICAL LIST OF BELLS

1. *1703 STANFORD-LE-HOPE, Essex   St Margaret.*   *Old tenor of 5*
   IERE • READ • CW ✤ IOHN WAYLET MAD ME 1703
   Diameter 39"
   Recast by Moore, Holmes and Mackenzie in 1884 and further recast when
   augmented to eight by J.Taylor in 1939.   *CB Essex*

2. 1704 ROMFORD, Essex   St Edward the Confessor   3rd of 8
   IOHN WAYLET MADE ME 1704 ✤   ✤   ✤
   Diameter 30"   ✤ – fleur de lys.
   These were probably made into an eight by 1756, although the 2nd is
   dated 1651.   *CB Essex*

3. 1704 OXHEY, Herts. St Matthew   Sanctus
   IOHN ·· WALKER ·:· 1704 :
   Diameter 16"   Weight 1 cwt   Note E
   see rubbing p. 159
   This bell came from the private Oxhey Chapel, in exchange for a late
   nineteenth century blank bell from St Matthew's. The name has
   caused some writers to ascribe the bell to John Walker, a mythical
   founder, but the date is in Waylett's numbers and the font is his
   medium set. John Walker was probably the chapelwarden.
   Dodds, CB Herts.

4. 1704 STANSTEAD ABBOTS, Herts. Clock House   Clock bell
   1704
   Diameter 17½"   Weight 1 cwt
   Identical numerals to Oxhey above.   *RS /CB Herts.*

5. *1705 GREAT BARDFIELD, Essex St Mary*   *Old 4th of 5*
   SR MARTIN LVMLEY CWI WAYLET FECT 1705
   Diameter 39"
   The old five were probably a recasting by Miles Graye I in 1602. This and the
   old 3rd were recast when J. Taylor added a treble in 1889.   *CB Essex*

6.   *1705 ROYDON, Essex St Peter*   *Old treble of 6*
      IOHN COWELL CHVRCH WARDEN I705
      Diameter 27"
      Recast as the 2nd of 6 by Mears & Stainbank in 1888.   *CB Essex*

7.   *1705 ROYDON*   *Old 3rd of 6*
      THO HILL TRVSTE EAST FROM MEE 1705
      Diameter 31"
      This was a very obscure inscription. TRVSTE was presumably meant for
      TRUSTEE, but the rest is not at all clear. Recast as the 4th of 6 by Mears &
      Stainbank in 1888.   *CB Essex*

8.   *1705 ROYDON*   *Old 4th of 6*
      IOHN WAYLET MADE ME I705
      Diameter 33"
      Recast as the 5th of 6 by Mears & Stainbank in 1888.   *CB Essex*

9.   1705 STANSTED MOUNTFICHET, Essex   St Mary   4th of 8
      MAT WODLEY IOHN SPELER CW]705
      Diameter 29½"   Weight 4 cwt   Note C#   *CB Essex*

10.   1706 HORNDON-ON-HILL, Essex   St Peter   3rd of 5
      ]706
      Diameter 24"   Weight 3 cwt 3 qr 6 lb
      These bells are hung dead for chiming only.   *CB Essex*

11.   1706 HERTINGFORDBURY, Herts.   *St Mary*   2nd of 6
      IOHANNES WAYLETT FECIT]706
      Diameter 27"   Weight 4¼ cwt   Note E♭   *Dodds, CB Herts.*

12.   1706? PAGLESHAM, Essex St Peter   Former tenor of 3, now single
      blank.
      '… supposed to have been cast by John Waylett about 1706 (Benton,
      Hist. of Rochford Hundred, ii. p. 423).'   *CB Essex*

13.   1707 CANEWDON, Essex St Nicholas   Tenor of 5
      RICHARD EDWARDS WETHR IENNENS CW   IW·]707
      Diameter 40"   Weight c.12 cwt
      Bells listed as unringable in *Dove's Guide*.   *CB Essex*

14.   1707 LITTLE WAKERING, Essex   St Mary   Treble of 3
      IOHANNES WAYLETT FESIT]707
      Diameter 26"   Weight c.3½ cwt   *CB Essex*

15.   1707 LITTLE WAKERING   2nd of 3
      GORGE BAREY CW 1707 ·♣·♣   (sic)
      Diameter 28″   Weight 4 cwt   CB Essex

16.   1707 LITTLE WAKERING   Tenor of 3
      IOHANNES WAYLETT FESIT 1707
      Diameter 32″   Weight 5 ½ cwt
      This was possibly his earliest complete ring.   CB Essex

17.   1707 EPPING UPLAND, Essex All Saints   2nd of 6
      MR IOHN SEARLE ANNO 1707
      Diameter 27″   Weight 3 ½ cwt   Note D
      This was a new bell to augment the earlier ring of 4.   CB Essex

18.   1707 EPPING UPLAND   3rd of 6
      IOHN WAYLETT MADE ME 1707
      Diameter 29″   Weight 4 cwt   Note C
      Recast treble of 4   CB Essex

19.   1707 EPPING UPLAND   4th of 6
      IOHN WAYLETT MADE ME 1707
      Diameter 32″   Weight 5 cwt   Note B
      Recast 2nd of 4.   CB Essex

20.   1707 EPPING UPLAND   5th of 6
      MR ANDREW SEARLE ANNO 1707
      Diameter 36″   Weight 7 ½ cwt   Note A
      Recast 3rd of 4.   The tenor, by Robert Oldfield, was the only bell not
      recast.   CB Essex

21.   1707 ROXWELL, Essex St Michael   2nd of 3
      IOHN WAYLETT MADE ME 1707
      Diameter 29 ½ ″ Weight 4 ¼ cwt   CB Essex

The distribution of Nos. 22–31 shows that they were all close to Royston.
Bearing in mind that Richard Keene had worked in that neighbourhood
until 1703 and that his furnace may not have been dismantled, it is possible
that Waylett temporarily worked from there in order to save the long haul to
and from Bishop's Stortford. This kind of arrangement was by no means
unique.

22.   1707 THERFIELD, Herts. St Mary the Virgin   Tenor of 6   3
      I.WAYLETTFECTI707 RALPH FFORDHⱯMED   2 / 3
      PEPPERCORN CW   *(one line)*   3
      Diameter 43"   Weight 14 cwt   Note G   2
      Recast tenor of 6.   *Dodds, CB Herts.*

23.   17xx SANDON, Herts. All Saints   2nd of 6   3
      IOHN WAYLETT   2 / 3
      Diameter 26⅜"   Weight 3 cwt 1 qr 21 lb   Note E♭   3
      This undated bell was probably cast sometime during   2
      Waylett's Stortford period, to augment the four bells.

                                                      Dodds, CB Herts.

24.   *1708 GUILDEN MORDEN, Cambs. St Mary   Old treble now 3rd of 6*
      IOHANIS WAYLETT ME FESIT 1708
      Diameter 28 ½"   Weight 4 cwt 3 qr 22 lb   Note B
      Recast by J.Taylor in 1992.

25.   *1708 GUILDEN MORDEN   Old 2nd now 4th of 6*
      IOHN WAYLET MADE ME 1708
      Diameter 30"   Weight 5 cwt 0 qr 8 lb   Note A#
      Recast by J.Taylor in 1992. The weights are for the recast bells.

26–   *1708 LITLINGTON, Cambs. St Katharine   The ring of five were recast*
30.   *and a treble added by A. Bowell in 1910. Inscriptions were not recorded by*
      Raven.

31.   1708 WHITTLESFORD, Cambs. SS Mary and Andrew   5th of 6
      IOHN WAYLETT MADE ME I708
      Diameter 38½"   Weight 9½ cwt   Note G
                                                      Jean Sanderson

The next group of bells was probably cast on a working visit to East Anglia
rather than at Bishop's Stortford. The Edwardstone bells will be dealt with
out of strict chronological order as they were originally part of the same
casting.

32.   *1708 LANGHAM, Essex St Mary   Old tenor of 5*
      IOHN WAYLET MADE ME 1708
      Diameter 39"   Weight 9 cwt
      A fire in the tower in the first decade of the nineteenth century necessitated this
      bell's recasting by T. Mears I in 1810. J. Taylor added a new treble in 1897 and
      recast the tenor in 1906.   *CB Essex*

33. 1709 EDWARDSTONE, Suffolk St Mary the Virgin   Treble of 6
     ✠ MR COOK AND NVTTING CW |709
     The subtle social distinction between the names should be noted.
     Nutting was presumably not quite a gentleman!

34. 1710 EDWARDSTONE   2nd of 6
     TVNED BY WM CVLPECK |710
     Waylett had the misfortune to offend Wm. Culpeck and had to recast
     the bell to suit him the following year. Culpeck, of course, did *not* tune
     the bell; it was Waylett's coded way of saying that Wm. C. was an inter-
     fering old busybody! Culpeck's status is not clear but whatever it was,
     he was obviously a tartar. In the present day, Diocesan authorities
     insist on strict rules and regulations before granting a faculty so it is
     doubtful whether the above untruthful inscription would comply with
     modern requirements. The tenor inscription below most certainly
     would not!

35. *c.1712 EDWARDSTONE*   *Tenor of 6*
     The tenor also offended Wm. Culpeck in some way and it appears that Waylett
     must have refused to recast it, unless he was given more beer to 'wet his whistle'
     if that is the meaning of the cryptic WANT-DWETT, so the work was given to
     Thomas Gardiner of Sudbury, later noted for his scurrilous inscriptions. He too
     fell foul of Culpeck and made his feelings abundantly plain on the bell. The 3½-
     line inscription read:
     ⛉ *ABOVT TY' SECOND CVLPECK IS WRETT = BECAVSE THE*
     ⛉ *FOVNDER WANT– DWETT = THAIR IVDGMENTS – WARE BVT*
     ⛉ ⛉ *BAD- AT LAST = OR ELCE THIS BELL I NEVER HAD CAST*
     THO GARDINER =
     thus damning both sides impartially. One is led to
     wonder if Culpeck actually READ the inscription and
     what was his reaction if he did. Altogether, this was
     not one of Waylett's more successful ventures!
     Recast by J. Taylor & Co 1986 with the inscription
     reproduced.   *RWMC*

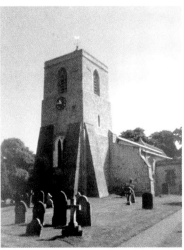

36. 1709 SANDON, Herts.   5th of 6   2
     IOHN *WAy*LETT MADE ME |709   2 / 2
     Diam. 33" Wt. 5 cwt 3 qr 22 lb   Note B♭   3
     This was a recasting of the old 3rd of 4.   2
                                    Dodds, CB Herts.

Sandon, All Saints has three Waylett bells
of different dates

37–   *c.1710 WESTMILL, Herts. St Mary the Virgin*   *Nos.1–4 of 8*
40.

*Chauncy recorded four bells in 1700, but about 1710 the old frame was
extended to accommodate four more, donated by William Auncell of Knight's
Hill, within the parish. By careful examination of the frame, it is clear that
these were very small bells indeed; the tenor weight is only 6½ cwt. Waylett
was certainly working in the area during this time and appears to have been
the only founder so doing. Thus, for lack of any contrary evidence, it is not
unreasonable to attribute these bells to him. They remained until 1838, when
two were sold to pay for repairs, the other two being recast by Thomas Mears
into a treble of five, which remains as the second of the present six. Local tradition says that two were sold to Benington and Benington tradition agrees with
this. Certainly, Squire Leonard Proctor augmented his bells in 1838; Henry
Symondson tuned and rehung them. (See Briant/ Henry Symondson p.
201). Benington bells are in the key of F#, while Westmill bells are in the key of
A. Westmill's two trebles, tuned to A and G# would obviously be unsuitable for
adding to Benington, but Westmill's third and fourth would give an octave with
a flat second which, while not very satisfactory to a musician's ear, would suf-
fice until more money was available. In 1853, Squire Proctor had them recast.
North, in N & S, gives a hint that this was because they were 'probably not
pleasing the correct ear of Mr. Leonard Proctor' which bears out this idea.*

41.   1711 BALDOCK, Herts. St Mary the Virgin   Tenor
LAUDO DEUM VERUM PLEBUM VOCO CONVOCO CLERUM ✤
IAM MANISON CH ○ ○ ✤   *(single top line)*
DEFUNCTOS PLORO NUPTOS COLO FESTA DECORO✤WM
           GOODWYN WARDS |7||✤ *(single lower line)*

Diameter 54"   Weight 26 cwt 2 qr 22 lb   Note D
The large lettering, especially W and Y,   3
combined with the fleur-de-lys (*Fig 22* p141)   3 / 1
identify this as being by   3
Waylett. Note the use of the letter 'U',   2
which is not found in the smaller alphabets.

    It is his biggest known bell. Note that the moulding
wires above and below the inscription band do not
conform to Waylett's usual pattern, because the two
lines of inscription are contained within a single
band. As this inscription is known to have been used
in medieval times, Waylett was probably recasting an
old bell bearing these words. (Translation – I PRAISE
THE TRUE GOD:
I SUMMON THE PEOPLE: I CALL TOGETHER THE CLERGY:
I MOURN THE DEAD: I HONOUR THE BRIDE AND
GROOM: I ADORN THE FESTIVALS)

Baldock, St Mary the Virgin

The cannons were removed, probably when John Taylor & Co. recast four of the other five bells and added two trebles in 1881/2.

Dodds, CB Herts.

42.   1711 COMBERTON, Cambs. St Mary   2nd of 4
IOHN WAYLETT MADE ME 1711
Raven, in *CB Cambs.* incorrectly listed this as the treble. After being unringable for many years the four were rehung in their old frame for swing-chiming only in 1999.   *R.F. Walker*

43.   *1711 MONKEN HADLEY, London   St Mary the Virgin*   *Old 6th of 8*
GOD · ⋮ · BLES · ⋮ · QVEEN · ⋮ · ANN · ⋮ · 1711 ·O·O·O·O·O·
CRIS COOPER
                    CHVRCH·WARDENS
ED CHANDLER
This was the recast of a James Bartlet bell of 1681; again recast by Mears and Stainbank in 1956. The coins were Queen Anne half-crowns. Dodds, CB Herts.

44.   *1712 AVELEY, Essex   St Michael*   *Treble of 5*
M^R · LAMBART C · W· M^R · PEAD VICAR · 1712 · ⋮ · ⋮ · ⋮ ·
Diameter 26"
Stated in CB Essex to be cracked.

45.   *1712 AVELEY*   *2nd of 5*
IOHN WAYLETT MADE ME 1712
Diameter 29"
1905 – cracked.   *CB Essex*
These bells were disposed of at some time between 1968 and 1988, according to **Dove's Guide**, *4th & 7th editions. This was confirmed by David Sloman, April '02.*

46.   *1712 NORTH WEALD, Essex St Andrew*   *Old treble of 5?*
IOHN WAYLETT MADE ME 1712
Recast by J.Warner in 1887.   *CB Essex*

47.   1712 NORTH WEALD   3rd
RICHARD WAYLETT CHVRCH WARDEN 1712
Diameter 30"   Weight 5 ½ cwt   Note B
Richard was surely a relative of the bellfounder. Medium alphabet.

CB Essex

48.   *1712 CHESHUNT, Herts.   St Mary the Virgin*   *7th of 8*
       IOHN WAYLETT MADE ME 1712
       This was a recast by Waylett and was again recast by Gillett & Johnston in
       1911. The inscription was reproduced but not in facsimile.

49.   *1712 CHESHUNT*   *Old tenor*
       WM WELCH ROB CARDEN IO FIELDING CH WNS IO WAYLET MAED
       MEE 1712 (not facsimile – one line)
       This was another recast by Waylett, again recast by Gillett & Johnston in 1911.
                                                                        Dodds, CB Herts.

50.   1712 LITTLE CORNARD, Suffolk All Saints   Treble of 5
       Cast in collaboration with John Thornton of Sudbury.

51.   1712 GREAT THURLOW, Suffolk All Saints   4th of 6
       Cast with John Thornton of Sudbury.

52.   *1713 GREAT HALLINGBURY, Essex St Giles*   *Old treble of 6*
       ✤ *HALLALUIAH* ✤ *1713*
       Diameter 29 ½ "
       The spelling is remarkable! Recast by Mears & Stainbank in 1896.

53.   1713 GREAT HALLINGBURY   4th of 5
       SIR EDWARD TVRNOVR AND PHILEM ROLFE CHVR W 1713
       Diameter 34 ½ "   *CB Essex*

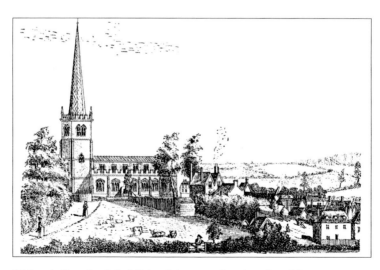

Bishop's Stortford, St Michael. in 1700 showing the old tower.
[Bishop's Stortford Museum]

54. *1713 BISHOP'S STORTFORD, Herts. St Michael*   (?) *3rd of 10*
     Probably recast in 1713 from part of the old tenor.
     Again recast in 1791 by Briant.

55. 1713 BISHOP'S STORTFORD 4th of 10   2
     IOHN♣WAYLETT ○ MADE♣ME♣ 1713 ♣♣   3 / 2
     Diameter 29"   Weight 6 cwt 0 qr 19 lb   Note D   3
     Probably recast from part of the old tenor.   2

56. 1713 BISHOP'S STORTFORD   5th of 10   3
     IOHN♣WAYLETT ○ MADE♣ ME♣ 1713 ♣♣   2 / 3
     Diameter 32½" Weight 7 cwt 0 qr 11 lb   Note C   3
     Probably recast from part of the old tenor,   2
     which was known to be very large.

57. 1713 BISHOP'S STORTFORD   6th of 10   3
     ○ THO CLAYTON ○ AND THO SCOTT ○ CH WAR 1713   2 / 3
                                                                     3
     Diameter 34½" Weight 8 cwt 0 qr 3 lb   Note B♭   2
     Probably recast from the old treble.

58. *1713 BISHOP'S STORTFORD   (?)*   *7th of 10*
     Probably recast in 1713 from the old 2nd and recast in 1791 by John Briant.

59. *1713 BISHOP'S STORTFORD   (?)*   *8 of 10*
     Probably recast in 1713 from the old 3rd and recast in 1792 by Briant.

60. *1713 BISHOP'S STORTFORD   (?)*   *9 of 10*
     *Probably recast in 1713 from the old 4th and recast in 1791 by Briant. When
     the above bells were recast, there were no charges for carriage, indicating that
     the foundry was local. C.W. accts*   *Dodds, CB Herts.*

61. *1713 WALKERN, Herts. St Mary the Virgin*   *4 of 6*
     1713   (no other inscription recorded)
     *Recast from the old 3rd of 5 of 1697 by 'X' of Hitchin. Recast in 1909 by J.
     Taylor.*

62. *1713 WALKERN*   *5 of 6*
     GODFREY GARDINER RECTOR WALKON 1713
     *Recast from the old 4th of 5 of 1697 by 'X' of Hitchin. Recast in 1932 by
     J. Taylor.*

63.   1713 WALKERN   Tenor   3
      EDWARD GREENE CHVRCH WARDEN 1713   3 / 3
      Diameter 35⅜"   Weight 6 cwt 2 qr 16 lb   Note A♭   3
      Recast from the old tenor of 1697 by 'X' of Hitchin.   2
      His bells had lasted no more than sixteen years.   *Dodds, CB Herts.*

64.   *1714 MONKEN HADLEY, London. St Mary the Virgin*   Tenor
      ED CHANDLER RICH HILL C W WAYLETT MADE ME 1714
      *This was a recast of a 1681 bell by James Bartlet, another short-term bell. The large
      alphabet was used. The bell was recast by Mears & Stainbank in 1956, with the inscrip-
      tion reproduced in facsimile.*   *Dodds, CB Herts.*

During the remainder of 1714, Waylett moved to Sussex, having temporarily
exhausted the possibilities in Hertfordshire. In Sussex, he cast ten known
bells, living the life of an itinerant. There is a delightful description of
Waylett in *Highways and Byways of Sussex*, by E. V. Lucas, (p. 399) referring to
Withyham.

> His method was to call on the Vicar and ask if anything were wanted; and if a
> bell was cracked, or if a new one was desired, he would dig a mould in a
> neighbouring field, collect his metal, and perform the task on the spot.
> Waylett's business might be called 'the higher tinkering.'

65   1714 BURWASH, Sussex St Bartholomew   The back five of the ring
–69. of Waylett's ring of five, the 2nd, 4th and 5th survive, as 5th, 7th and
      tenor of eight, the treble and 3rd being recast
70.   1714 ASHBURNHAM, Sussex St Peter   Tenor of 4
71.   *1714 HASTINGS, Sussex All Saints*   *Old ten or of 4, now 8*
72.   *1715 WITHYHAM, Sussex St Michael The 3rd, 4th, 5th and 6th of*
–75. *the present octave by J. Taylor & Co. of 1908 are recast Waylett bells.*

After this he paid a return visit to Bishop's Stortford which produced a small
crop of bells.

76.   *1715 MELDRETH, Cambs.*   2nd
      *This bell was sent to 'John Waylett of Bishop's Stortford' to be recast. The cost
      was £6 12s. 6d. (Churchwardens' accounts)*

77.   *1716 MELDRETH*   Treble
      This was also sent to Bishop's Stortford for recasting.
      *Both these bells were recast in 1855 by J. Taylor, or at some unrecorded earlier
      date.*   *John G. Gipson*

78. *1716 STANSTED MOUNTFICHET, Essex*   *Old treble of 5*
THO STOCK AND IOHN SANDERS C W 1716
Recast by J.Warner & Sons in 1867.   *CB Essex*

79. *1716 GREAT WYMONDLEY, Herts. St Mary the Virgin*   *Tenor*
Old tenor recast by Waylett and recast in 1903 by Mears & Stainbank.
      Dodds, CB Herts.

80. *1716 KNEBWORTH, Herts. SS Mary and Thomas of Canterbury*   *4th of*
        8

    Old treble of 5 by 'X' of Hitchin recast by Waylett after only 19 years.
Again recast in 1890 by Warner.   *Dodds, CB Herts.*

1716–21 Some sub-contracting for Samuel Knight.

81. *1716 REDBOURN, Herts.*   *St Mary*   *Treble*
PRAYSE THE LORD 1716 H. KNIGHT
This was almost certainly the recast of a treble of 161x by Oldfield, judging by
the spelling of PRAYSE. Note the 'H' instead of 'S' for Samuel Knight.
Waylett seemed unsure about his name and they may not have been well
acquainted. Recast (facsimile) in 1953 by J. Taylor & Co.

82. *1716 REDBOURN.*   *2nd of 6*
IOHN WAYLETT MADE ME 1716
This was a recast of the old 2nd. Recast, as above 1953.

83. *1716 REDBOURN.*   *3rd of 6*
IOHN WAYLETT MADE ME 1716
This was a recast of the old 3rd. Recast, as above 1953.   *Dodds, CB Herts.*

84. 1716 WESTON, Herts. Holy Trinity   2nd of 6
IOHN WAYLETT MADE ME 1716
Diameter 28¾"   Weight 4 cwt 0 qr 8 lb   Note C#
This was a recast of the old treble of 5.   *Clements/CB Herts.*

85. 1716 WESTON (probably)   3rd of 6
This was a blank bell until Gillett & Johnston inscribed 'MILONEM
GRAYE ME FECIT 1634' in 1927 to match the 4th, but by its shape,
R.W.M. Clouston considered it to be much more like a Waylett bell. A
close examination of the crown of the bell could show whether there is
a moulder's mark similar to that on the 5th at St Ippolyts.
      Dodds, CB Herts.

His next few months were spent in Kent and Sussex with a brief foray over the border into Surrey. Horne is close to the Sussex border.

86–88.	1717 ASH-BY-WROTHAM, Kent SS Peter and Paul	3, 4, 5 of 6

89.   1717 DITTON, Kent St Peter ad Vincula   2nd of 2
Stahlschmidt gives no founder's name, but the bell was cast in the same year as named ones for the neighbouring villages of Hunton and Linton.

90   *1717*   *HUNTON, Kent St Mary*   *A ring of six,*
–95. *all now recast by J. Taylor & Co. 1901.*

96–98. 1717 LINTON, Kent St Nicholas   1, 2, 3, of 6

99.   1717 EGERTON, Kent St James   5th of 6
No founder's name given, but dated the same year as those in the neighbouring villages of Hunton and Linton.   *CB Kent*

100   1717 RIPE, Sussex St John the Baptist   Anticlockwise ring of 5 of
–104. which only the treble and 2nd survive, *the back three being recast in 1887.*
                                              CB Sussex

105. *1718 HASTINGS, Sussex St Clement*   *Old 3rd of 6, now 8*
                                              CB Sussex

106. 1718 HORNE, Surrey St Mary   Tenor of 3
                                            CB Surrey

Waylett then seems to have returned home for another flying visit, before heading off on his travels again. It may be that once more there was not enough work to tempt him to stay in Bishop's Stortford and that there were better prospects elsewhere.

107. 1718 LITTLE BERKHAMSTED, Herts. St Andrew   Treble of 3   3
     IOHN : :WAYLETT : : MADE : ME : 1718 : : : : : : IOHN : · · :   2 / 3
     GODWARD : : CW : : : :   *(one line)*   3
     Diameter 28³⁄₁₆"   Weight 4 ½ cwt   Note – ?   2
     This was a recast of an old treble. Small numerals (*CB Essex*, p. 120
     footnote).   *RWMC / CB Herts.*

108.	1719 ARDINGLY, Sussex St Peter	Tenor of 6
109.	1719 ASHURST, Sussex St James	Treble of 3
110.	1719 NUTHURST, Sussex St Andrew	Treble of 3
111.	1719 NUTHURST	2nd
112.	1719 SHIPLEY, Sussex St Mary	2nd of 6
		CB Sussex

113   1719 EAST SUTTON, Kent SS Peter and Paul   2, 3, 4 and 5 of 6
-116.

There is some doubt as to whether Waylett cast the front five, leaving
the 1614 tenor intact, or the back five, with the treble being an afterthought. The second inscription reads:

THESE 5 BELLS WERE NEW CAST AT THE CHARGE OF YE PARISH BY JOHN
WAYLETT 1719
The tenor was 'new cast' by Samuel Knight in 1723. All very ambigu-
ous!

117.   1720 EAST SUTTON   Treble of 6

In 1720 Waylett moved to Hythe, where he seems to have spent a few
months. While there he cast several bells on behalf of Samuel Knight. Some
bear Knight's name, some his initials only and some are clearly stated to be
by Waylett. Any system appears to be lacking.

118-   *1720 HYTHE, Kent. St Leonard*   *Ring of 6*
123.   *These are known from documentary sources only, as the tower fell in 1750, the*
       treble being broken in the fall. Recast by Thomas Pack in 1752. Again recast by
       Thomas Mears I in 1802.   *CB Kent*

123.   1720 KENARDINGTON, Kent St Mary   Single
124   1721 RUCKINGE, Kent St Mary Magdalene   Treble, 2, 3 & 4 of 5
-127. The treble bears the name of Samuel Knight, with Waylett acting as
       sub-contractor, nos. 2 and 4 bear Waylett's name, the 3rd the date only.

129.   1721 STOWTING, Kent St Mary   Treble, 3rd and tenor of 4
-131. These were cast for Knight but the 3rd has the initials I W. Since
       augmented to 6.

132   *1721 WAREHORNE, Kent St Matthew*   *Old treble, 2, 3 and tenor of 5*
-135. *Recast by Bowell, 1912.*   *CB Kent*

Waylett then came home for some months and cast the following bells for
Hertfordshire and London.

136.   1721 BENINGTON, Herts. St Peter   Tenor of 8   2
       IOHN FISHER CHVRCH WARDEN IOHN WAYLETT   3 / 2
       FECIT [72]   *(one line)*   3
       Diameter 41 ½ " Weight 12 cwt   Note F#   2
       Waylett was here recasting the old tenor of a ring of five.
                                                     Dodds, CB Herts.

137.   1721 ST IPPOLYTS, Herts. St. Ippolyts   5 of 6
_W: BENEDICTVM NOMEN DOMINI: :GEO'LYLE' & IO¨
PATERNOSTER CW |72| .   (one line)

Diameter 36½ " Weight 8 cwt 2 qr 20 lb Note A	3
This was the recasting of the cracked 2nd of 3.	3 / 2
The monogram (p. 141) may be unique and is made	3
up from two letters from his smallest alphabet.	2

(See Bell 180, Latton) The rest of the inscription is in his medium font
and this was confirmed by comparison with the lettering on the tenor
at Benington, Herts., also of 1721. (See above)
This is altogether a most interesting bell and is the only old one in the
ring. The inscription is stamped and the indications are that the cope
was of the right consistency to take a good impression at the beginning
but, by the end the impressions were getting shallower and shallower,
showing that it was becoming too dry. There is also a moulder's mark
on the shoulder in the form of a cross, apparently made by a knife.
This same mark can be found on the blank 2nd at St Paul's Walden,
suggesting that it too is by Waylett.
Dodds, CB Herts.

138.   1721 SANDON, Herts.   3 of 6, formerly 2nd of 5   3
IOHN : WAYLETT : FECIT · : · |72| 2 / 3
Diameter 29⅝" Weight 4 cwt 1 qr 13 lb   Note D♭   3
Two sizes of letters, which is not common. (But see No. 113 above) 2
Chauncy recorded four bells in 1700, so this bell was an augmentation.
                                                        Dodds, CB Herts.

139,   1721 CITY OF LONDON St Stephen, Coleman Street
140.   Waylett cast two bells for this church; church, tower and ring of eight bells were
destroyed by bombing in 1940. The site was sold after the war.

141.   1722 SACOMBE, Herts. St Catherine   Treble of 3
:⸬TOH : :RICHARDSON C ⸬ W IOHN WAYLETT FECIT |722
Diameter 27⁵⁄₁₆"   Weight 3½ cwt   Note D
Recast treble of 3.   *RWMC/CB Herts.*

After this brief stay, he went back to Kent.

142	1722 SALTWOOD, Kent SS Peter and Paul	1–4 of 5
–146.	1723 SALTWOOD	tenor of 5
147.	1723 *WAREHORNE*	*4th of 5*
	Recast by Bowell, 1912.	*CB Kent*

148   1723 EAST HOATHLY, Sussex   Treble, 2, 3, 4 and 5 of 6
–152. A minor ring of 5, *of which the tenor was recast in 1876 and new tenor
       added.*

153.   1723 SOMPTING, Sussex St Mary the Virgin   Sanctus

154.   1723 WOOLAVINGTON, Sussex St Peter   Single   *CB Sussex*

This next bell must have been cast on one of his flying visits home.

155.   1724 FOBBING, Essex St Michael   Tenor of 5
       IOHN KNAPPING & VALENTINE GLASCOCK CW   1724 I W FECIT
       Diameter 38″   *CB Essex*

After this it was back to Sussex again, where he stayed for several months,
judging by the large number of bells recorded.

156.   *1724 BURWASH, Sussex*   *Old tenor of 5 (now 8)*

157   *1724 LAUGHTON, Sussex   All Saints*   *2, 3, 4, 5 of 6*

–161. *A ring of five, of which the 2nd and 3rd survive. The treble, 4th and
       tenor have been recast and a new treble added.*

162.   1724 LEWES, Sussex   St John de Castro   Treble of 3

163.   1724 LEWES   2nd

164.   *1724 LEWES*   *Old tenor, recast 1886*

165.   1724 MAYFIELD, Sussex   St Dunstan   3rd of 8

166.   1724 MAYFIELD   4th

167   *1724 STEYNING, Sussex   St Andrew*   *Complete ring of 6*
–171. *of which the 4th, (which may not have been Waylett's) was recast in 1775 and
       the rest recast in 1889 when Mears & Stainbank augmented to 8, except for the
       present 7th.*   *CB Sussex*

172.   *? SEAFORD, Sussex. St Leonard*   *Complete ring of 5, now 8*
–175. *The bells were recast into 8 by Thomas Mears of London 1811.*
                                                           CB Sussex

176.   1726 WATERSTOCK, Oxon. St Leonard   Sanctus
       I W   1726
       Diameter 12¼″
       Lever chimed, on its original headstock with some nailed straps. This is
       well away from Waylett's usual haunts and it may have come from
       elsewhere.   *CB Oxon.*

London – Harrison & Waylett 1727–31

178.   1727 BOUGHTON MONCHELSEA, Kent   St Peter   Tenor
       This inscription has the word London included and may be the first
       which he cast after settling there.

179.   *1727 TOTTERIDGE, London   St Andrew*   *Treble of 3*
       MR. JOSEPH DA COSTA C.W. JOHN WAYLETT LONDON FECIT 1727
       (not facsimile) Recast treble of 3, recast in 1952 by Mears & Stainbank. Prior to 1965
       Totteridge was in Hertfordshire.   *Dodds, CB Herts.*
       1727 Known from Parish records only (see p. 140). Some work either
       tendered for or carried out for St Mary's Walthamstow, probably recast
       by Chapman & Mears 1783.   *D. Sloman*

180.   1728 HIGH ONGAR, Essex St Mary   2nd of 6
       Plain cross used; unknown elsewhere.   *CB Essex*

181.   1728 LATTON, Essex St John the Baptist   Sanctus
       I W 1728
       Diameter 9½"   Very small alphabet, as used in the St Ippolyts
       monogram of 1721.   *CB Essex*
       Stated to have been transferred to a museum.   *D Sloman*

182.   1728 KIMPTON, Herts. SS Peter and Paul   4th of 8
       IOHN CARPENTER CHVRCH WARDEN 1728
       IOHN WAYLETT MADE ME LONDON H S   (below inscription band)
       Diameter 29"   Weight 4 cwt 2 qr 18 lb   Note D
       Recast of Oldfield 2nd of 6.   *Dodds, CB Herts.*

183.   *1728 SANDON, Herts.*   *4th of 6*
       IOHN∴WAYLETT∴LONDON FECIT 1728
       Present diameter 31" Weight 5 cwt 2 qr 13 lb   Note C
       The old 2nd of 4 was recast. Recast by John Taylor in 1908.
                                                             Dodds, CB Herts.

184.   1729 FLAMSTEAD, Herts.   St Leonard   Treble of 6   3
       IOHN WAYLETT LONDON FECIT 1729   2 / 3
       Diameter 30"   Weight 5 cwt 1 qr 12 lb   Note C#   3
       This augmented a complete five by Chandler of   2
       Drayton Parslow 1664.   *Dodds, CB Herts.*

185.   1730 SHINFIELD, Berks.   Treble of 6
       This is also well outside Waylett's normal range.   *CB Berks.*

186. 1730 BISHOP'S STORTFORD, Herts. St Michael   Tenor of 10
R̄O ::: BOVLTWOOD ::: WILLIAM ::: SPEARING ::: THO MOTT ::: **|**730
::: I. WAYLETT FACIT   *(one line)*   3
Diameter 47″   Weight 16 cwt 3 qr 15 lb   Note E\   2 / 3
Probably recast in 1713 from the old 5th and/or recast in   3
1730. This was Waylett's last bell for his old home town.   2

Dodds, CB Herts.

187. *1731 FELSTEAD, Essex   Holy Cross*   *6th, old 3rd of 5*
IOHN WAYLETT LONDON FECIT ☐ ○ ○ ○ *PETER .. ... VEY RICH^D S*
.. .. .. E .. C W **|**73**|**   *(one line)*
Diameter 38″
The decorations after FECIT were vague. The churchwardens were Peter Davey
and Richard Stacey. Recast by John Warner & Sons 1915.   *CB Essex*

(John and/or) William Waylett, his Son?

188. 1742 WELWYN GARDEN CITY, Herts., C. Miskin & Sons Ltd.
Disused bell

THO^S PEARSE ESQ^R **|**742
Diameter 20³⁄₁₆″   Weight c.2 cwt   Note F#

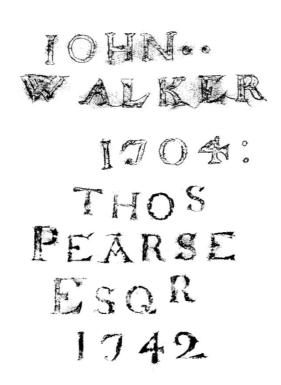

Miskins were long-established builders based in Romeland, St Albans. In 1870 they were called in by Sir Gilbert Scott to carry out emergency work to prevent the collapse of the tower of St. Albans Abbey. In 1985 they moved to Alban House, Brownfields, Welwyn Garden City taking their 'works bell' with them. According to H.V. Frost of St Peter's, St Albans, when at Romeland it was sounded at knocking-off time by a man known as 'Chalky' White. It had probably been acquired when working on a big house, maybe in the north London area, many years ago as it was clearly not a church bell, but the firm has no record of its provenance. The bell may have been cast either by John, two years after his retirement, or by William, which makes it of great interest. At some date it has fallen, breaking three of its six cannons.

The alphabet used appears to be Waylett's and is similar to that used on the Oxhey Chapel bell of 1704. The date figures '172' are identical with those on the St Ippolyts' bell of 1721, although the '4' belongs to a different set. Having last been used in 1724, it is possible that the figure had become lost or damaged in the interim.   *Dodds, CB Herts*

DISTRIBUTION OF JOHN WAYLETT BELLS BY COUNTIES

	Date	Ref.No.
BERKSHIRE		
Shinfield	1730	185
CAMBRIDGESHIRE		
Comberton	1711	42
Guilden Morden	1708	24
Litlington	1708	26
Meldreth	1715	76
Whittlesford	1708	31
ESSEX		
Aveley	1712	44
Canewdon	1707	13
Epping Upland	1707	17
Felstead	1731	187
Fobbing	1724	155
Great Bardfield	1705	5
Great Hallingbury	1713	52
High Ongar	1728	180
Horndon-on-Hill	1706	10
Langham	1708	32
Latton	1728	181
Little Wakering	1707	14
North Weald	1712	46
Paglesham	1706	12
Romford	1704	2
Roxwell	1707	21
Roydon	1705	6
Stanford-le-Hope	1703	1
Stansted M'ntfitchet	1705/16	9, 78
HERTFORDSHIRE		
Baldock	1711	41
Benington	1721	136
Bishop's Stortford	1713/30	54, 186
Cheshunt	1712	48
Flamstead	1729	184
Great Wymondley	1716	79
Hertingfordbury	1706	11
Kimpton	1728	182
Knebworth	1716	80
Little Berkhamsted	1718	107
Oxhey		3
Redbourn	1716	81

	Date	Ref.	No.
Sacombe	1722		141
Sandon	17xx/09		23, 36
	1721/28		138, 183
St Ippolyts	1721		137
Stanstead Abbots	1704		4
Therfield	1707		22
Walkern	1713		61
(Welwyn G. City	1742		188
Westmill	c. 1710		37
Weston	1716		84
KENT			
Ash-by-Wrotham	1717		86
Boughton M'nchelsea	1727		178
Ditton	1717		89
East Sutton	1719		113
Egerton	1717		99
Hunton	1717		90
Hythe	1720		118
Kenardington	1720		124
Linton	1717		96
Ruckinge	1721		125
Saltwood	1722		142
Stowting	1721		129
Warehorne	1721/23		132,147
LONDON/MIDDLESEX			
Coleman St, St Ste'n	1721		139
Monken Hadley	1711/4		43, 64
Totteridge	1727		179
Walthamstow?	1727		–
OXFORDSHIRE			
Waterstock	1726		177
SUFFOLK			
Edwardstone	1709/10		33
Great Thurlow	1712		51
Little Cornard	1712		50
SURREY			
Horne	1718		106
SUSSEX			
Ardingly	1719		108
Ashburnham	1714		70
Ashurst	1719		109

	Date Ref.	No.		Date Ref.	No.
Burwash	1714/24	65, 156	Ripe	1717	100
East Hoathly	1723	148	Seaford	1700	172
Hastings, All Saints	1714	71	Shipley	1719	112
" , St Clement	1718	105	Sompting	1723	153
Laughton	1724	157	Steyning	1724	167
Lewes, St John de C.	1724	162	Withyham	1715	72
Mayfield	1724	165	Woolavington	1723	154
Nuthurst	1719	110			

PART V

HERTFORDSHIRE
1779–1829

JOHN BRIANT OF HERTFORD

15

JOHN BRIANT OF HERTFORD

HIS BIOGRAPHY

JOHN BRYANT, son of John and Catherine Bryant, was christened at St Martin's Church, Exning, Suffolk, by Newmarket, on 8 June 1748. This spelling of the family surname is as given in the parish register, although John Junior always wrote it as Briant, both on his bells and in his voluminous correspondence. In order to distinguish between the two men, the writer proposes to adopt the same procedure, referring to the father as Bryant and the son as Briant.

Briant's obituary notice, published in the *Hertfordshire Mercury* on 7 March 1829, descibed him as the son of 'a respectable foreigner' i.e. somebody from outside the Borough! John Bryant's birthplace was probably also Exning, as there is a cluster of Bryant tombstones in the churchyard, showing that some part of the family was settled there, although all the legible ones date from the second quarter of the nineteenth century. At the same time, John Bryant had some connection with Hertfordshire and the Hatfield estate. Through the kindness of Robin H. Harcourt Williams, Librarian and Archivist at Hatfield House, many useful details from the Hatfield Manor Papers which shed some light on the matter, have been made available to the writer.

John Bryant, 'of Hatfield, Gentleman' (this statement in itself suggests residence but not necessarily origins), first acquired the following copyhold property on 5 June 1755:

> All those … customary or copyhold cottages or tenements with their appurtenances adjoining to the House Park and also all that piece of waste ground then made a garden lying near possessions to the south end of the town of Hatfield and abutting upon the King's highway there leading towards London on the west and upon the House Park aforesaid east containing in length about seven poles and in breadth one pole and a half as the same then were in the several possessions or occupations of Thomas Bray, William French, Thomas Smith and Robert Field their respective undertenants or assigns.

(For those readers brought up in the Metric Age, a pole, or rod, or perch, measured 5½ yards, one quarter of a chain, approximately 5 metres). Bryant was admitted tenant when the next court of Hatfield Manor was held on 23 April 1756. The person surrendering the property was Elizabeth Uncle, widow of Thomas Uncle, a watchmaker, which may be more than a coincidence.

In H.C. Andrews' study of John Briant, in the chapter on long-case clocks, p. 89, there is a reference to a long-case clock by John Bryant, London, which at his time of writing, 1929-30, was in the possession of the Starlin family of Maida Vale. John Briant is not known to have worked in London so it seems possible that the clock was by his father who, in his will, left a chest of tools (unspecified) to his son. This, and the link with the Uncle family, certainly makes this feasible.

The death of John Bryant was reported to the manor court held on 1 April 1785. The four cottages had by this time been converted into two and were in the occupation of the Reverend Samuel Bulkeley and Richard Edmonds of Hatfield, Gentleman. John Briant of Hertford, whitesmith, was admitted to the copyhold tenancy and also 'acknowledged to hold of the Lord of this Manor by the yearly rent of one shilling a freehold estate to him descended upon the death of his said father which was formerly the estate of (blank) Baker'.

The writer was told years ago by the late Stan Huckle of Hatfield, who did much research into Briant, that the Hatfield property had, in fact, descended from Catherine Bryant's family. If this were correct, then it is possible that her maiden name was Baker. In his will, dated 1779, while living at Clothall, near Baldock, probably in another house on the Salisburys' country estate of Quickswood, Bryant requested that he be interred with his wife's relations at Hatfield. This further reinforces the Hatfield connection.

In *Hatfield and its People* published by the W.E.A. (1959), it is stated that Bryant also owned the School House, now Church Cottage, at the corner of the churchyard, but as this is not mentioned in the Hatfield House material, it may not have been Salisbury property, but this seems unlikely.

At the time of the Bryant/Briant tenancies, the London road ran at the edge of Hatfield Park, passing very close to the House itself. This became inconvenient and the boundaries were moved to the west, more or less to the present line of the A1000, thus enclosing the cottages within the park, but with the old road still partly retained for access.

On 17 July 1788 John Briant surrendered to Richard Edmonds the tenancy of the cottage which he occupied and on 27 June 1791, surrendered the cottage occupied by the Revd Samuel Bulkeley to the Marquess of Salisbury.

John Briant's Early Years

John Bryant had decided ideas as to his only son's future career. He was to be thoroughly educated in classics and mathematics prior to a course at one of the senior universities with a view to entering the Church. Young John was duly sent to a school in Newmarket where he learned enough good Latin, if his bell inscriptions are anything to go by, sufficient maths to cope with the needs of clockmaking and bellfounding and an excellent grounding in English. He appears to have been an equable boy who made friends easily, as he did all his life. This was made apparent in later years with the casting of the treble at Gazeley, near Newmarket in 1808; of the ten donors listed in the triple inscription band, how many were old school friends? Probably several, if not most. His dealings with bell restoration committees and churchwardens show him always to have been held in considerable personal respect – 'Mr. Briant', hardly ever 'Briant'.

Another characteristic, not previously stressed, was his deep affection for Catherine, his mother. Of his four children, two were named after her. When she died is not known but it was certainly before 1779, when Bryant bequeathed his possessions to his son and it may be that the acquisition of the tenancy in 1755 by Bryant of the former Baker holdings came about through her death. If it were so, then the departure to school of young John, at the tender age of seven, could have also coincided with that event.

Whatever his father's wishes for his future, John had other ideas. He was more interested in using tools, which was probably hereditary – like father, like son. He therefore became an apprentice whitesmith, most likely at St Neots, one of the more progressive foundries of its period, where he would be able to learn other skills apart from clockmaking. However, no lists of apprentices have survived from the relevant years to either prove or disprove this, although added support comes from *A Book About Bells* by Revd G.S. Tyack (1898) where on p. 17 it is stated that '… An offshoot from this firm was established by John Briant, another of Arnold's apprentices …' The Victoria County History of Hertfordshire is of the same opinion.

The St Neots Foundry

Thomas Eayre of Kettering, a clockmaker, set up in business in or about 1710. He found, as other clockmakers were to find, that there was a need for bells for his clocks to strike on so his elder son, Thomas II, joined the firm in 1717 as clockmaker and bellfounder, remaining at Kettering until 1757, the year of his father's death. The younger son, Joseph, also became a bellfounder, moving to St Neots in 1735 where he was to remain until his death. The physical distance between Kettering and St Neots is only about twenty-five miles, but it ensured that the two brothers did not indulge in cut-throat competition with each other. This dispersal was normal good business practice. At St Neots, Joseph set up close to, but not actually in, the Priory area.

An article on the Eayre family, by Raymond M. Ayres, published in the *Ringing World*, 5 September 1975, p. 735, claimed that this building still exists which is sadly incorrect. No traces of the Priory remain standing. A photocopy of a section of an old map of St Neots in 1757 has recently been sent to the writer by a family member. It clearly shows a domed building on the site and labels it The Foundery (*sic*) and names the area between it and the river as 'Joseph Eayres LAND.' This engraving has also been mentioned by Trevor

Map 8. Site of St Neots Bellfoundry (1757). [*History of St Neots
for children by Rosa E. Young*]

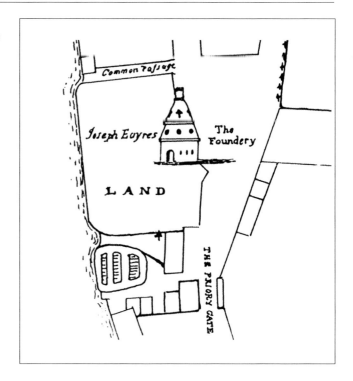

A. Bevis of March, who was shown it over forty years ago. (*Ringing World* 21
July, 2000, p. 731). As drawn, the 'Foundery' consisted of a tall, conical structure with what appears to have been a central flue, with air-holes or openings around the roof in two distinct levels, after the style of a medieval
monastic kitchen. It appears that it was actually built by Eayre and was not a
survival from the Priory. (Ref. *The History of St. Neots for Children* (1955) by
Rosa E. Young)

Apart from clockmaking and bellfounding, there was a steady trade in
weighing machines for turnpike roads, fire engines and what might fairly be
described as general engineering and brassfounding. All this was to stand
Briant in good stead in later years. At the time of the Great Tom of Lincoln
correspondence (see p. 191), Briant set to work and designed a complex
series of pulleys which could have been used to lower the bell from the
tower. That they were never used does not detract from his obvious ability as
an engineer.

One of Joseph Eayres' automatic chime barrels, which the writer well
remembers, still exists at St Mary's, Hemel Hempstead, although out of use
since 1951. It was installed in 1761 and played eight tunes. It may be no more
than a coincidence that the medieval tenor had to be recast in 1767! Another
chime barrel was installed at St Albans Abbey in 1765, the gift of Earl
Spencer. This also played eight tunes but has since been replaced.

While there is no written evidence that John Briant learned his trade under Joseph Eayre, circumstantial evidence can be found in a 'dagger' cross (*Fig 23e,* p. 205) and the type of lettering used on his bells, which is very similar to that used at St Neots, and in the fact that he and Robert Taylor, eleven years his junior, a known St Neots apprentice who later became the owner of the business, were closely acquainted and co-operated in several castings. They also both used a six-pointed star on their bells.

Exactly when Briant went to St Neots is obviously not known but the early 1760s would seem most likely, when he was in his mid teens. Because he had received a good education, he may have been slightly older than the average new apprentice. Apart from Joseph Eayre, two other experienced foremen/ founders are known from this period, Islip Edmunds and Thomas Osborn. Islip Edmunds was the eleventh and youngest child of William and Alice (née Islip) Edmunds of Melchbourne, Beds., baptised there on 27 November 1737. He was not a prolific founder under his own name but four bells at least are still extant, two in Bedfordshire, one each at Milton Ernest and Melchbourne and one at All Hallows', Wellingborough, Northants., dated between 1764 and 1765. Research by Chris Pickford has uncovered the fact that he also cast a bell for Bletsoe, Beds., in 1767, which had its inscription filed off by Robert Taylor in 1786 and was transferred to Great Gransden, Hunts., *as a new bell and charged for as such*, with Taylor's name incised as founder! Edmunds' Bedfordshire bells are inscribed ISLIP EDMUNDS LONDON. He possibly learned his trade in London and it is also said that in later years, he moved to Hertford and worked for a time with Briant but so far no evidence has been found to substantiate this.

Joseph Eayre died in 1771 and his business came into the hands of Edward Arnold, the son of Eayre's sister, a clockmaker but not then a founder, with Osborn becoming his partner and Edmunds presumably staying on as foreman. Osborn was also a relative of Eayre and believed to be cousin to Arnold. For the staff and apprentices, the change of ownership seems to have had little effect on their future prospects. Taylor certainly remained at St Neots and Briant probably did likewise, concentrating on clocks, for nothing is heard of him until 1779 when he was thirty or thirty-one years old.

In that year, while his father was living at Clothall, near Baldock, Briant cast his first known bell, for the ancient one-handed clock at Quickswood House, a Salisbury property within Clothall parish, where the 5th Earl of Salisbury lived with what might in this day and age be described as his alternative family, i.e. his mistress and children, while his legitimate heir lived at Hatfield. In 1780 the 5th Earl, who had become a recluse, died and in order to expunge the family disgrace, the 6th Earl had Quickswood, a vast seventeenth century mansion, razed to the ground. All that remains is the farm of that name and crop marks visible in dry weather. The clock, contemporary with the house, was transferred to the stables, where it remains.

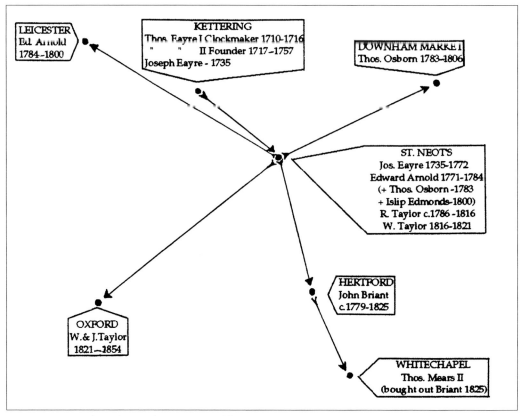

Map 9 St Neots foundry and migration of founders 1785–1825

Whether Briant's bell ever hung in the big house is uncertain; the dates are too close. What is possible is that John Bryant may have been involved with the transfer of the clock and then, having become homeless or unemployed with the destruction of the house, moved to Hertford with his son.

Briant's departure from St Neots was the first in what became an extraordinary migration of founders. (*Map* 9). It is said that there was a disagreement between Arnold and Osborn which led to the dissolution of their partnership. Thomas Osborn left in 1783 to set up a very successful foundry at Downham Market, his native town, where he was to remain, later in partnership with William Dobson, his grandson, until his death in 1806. In 1784 Edward Arnold left for Leicester where, for a time, he prospered, although he became bankrupt in 1793–4 and had to be virtually taken over by Benjamin Cort, who was later to become a business associate of Briant. Robert Taylor was thereby left in charge at St Neots, becoming the owner in 1786, with Islip Edmonds remaining with him for a least a short time before, it is said, joining Arnold in Leicester, possibly because of Taylor's sharp practice over the Bletsoe/Great Gransden affair. It is not known whether the mass exodus was fuelled in part by Taylor's abrasive personality but the suspicion remains. Through all these moves, the old etiquette held good; each man had moved far enough away to be no commercial threat to the others.

In 1789 Robert Taylor married Elizabeth Fowler of Eynsham, a relative of the Fowler family, the brewers who owned the Priory site, in the face of their disapproval, according to local tradition. She died in 1805. Taylor was joined in 1816 by William, his elder son. Two years later the brewers required the land for expansion of their business and forced Taylor out. The conical foundry building was demolished to make way for the expansion of the Brewery. After a short period working in Cambridge Street, either behind No. 14, on the south side or behind No. 23 on the opposite side, the Taylor family left St Neots for good and moved to Oxford and then to Loughborough, where the foundry remains. In that sense, therefore, the old St. Neots tradition survives.

Briant in Hertford

Briant had, through his father's Hatfield tenancy and links with Quickswood, become known to James Cecil, 6th Earl of Salisbury, and it was certainly by the same route of aristocratic patronage that he was able to set up in business in one of the Salisbury properties in Parliament Row, Hertford. This was a narrow street dating from sometime after Cromwell's visit in 1647 as it is not shown on Speed's map of 1611. It ran roughly north-south on the east side of the Castle walls. (*Map* 10). The buildings on the east side were pulled down in 1921 when the space was opened out and renamed Parliament Square, to form a suitable setting for the Great War Memorial. It is actually triangular. The buildings on the west side are much altered and that on the site of the bell foundry has a rather austere early nineteenth century frontage of five bays and three storeys. It now houses the Job Centre. The foundry was at the rear of the site, with the furnace backing on to the walls of the Castle. Two shallow alcoves still visible in the curtain wall are said to mark the remains of the furnace. This, and the site of Robert Oldfield's foundry in St Andrew's Street, are the only ones in the county that can be accurately pinpointed on a map, apart from a very minor one in St Albans (see p. 312). It is thought that John Bryant moved in at about the same time, as he was living in Hertford at the time of his death.

Once settled, Briant's reputation as a competent clockmaker and founder began to spread, at first slowly but later gathering momentum until he was running a very large business which could, and did, lead to occasional problems. Some of his commissions seem to have depended on links between members of the Upper Ten Thousand; commissions to cast bells for the Honorable Mary Leigh at Stoneleigh in 1792 and Ashow and Leek Wootton in 1793 almost certainly came via that route. In February 1825 at the end of his working life, he tendered, or was asked to tender, for rehanging work at

Cranborne, Dorset. (*The Bells and Belfries of Dorset*, Part I, by Christopher Dalton, p. 234). Cranborne was another Salisbury property, a hunting lodge acquired and altered by Robert Cecil at much same time as Hatfield House in the early seventeenth century and, as Briant was well known to the family through his former tenancies at Hatfield and his current tenancy in Hertford, his was the name which would naturally spring to mind. However, no action was taken at the time and if it had been, any work would certainly have been contracted out to one of his bellhanging associates.

Another way was to write to church authorities, in effect touting for business, as in the following letter, dated 29 March 1793 to Burwell, Cambs., which is now in the Cambridgeshire Record Office. (*R8/25/58*). The writer is indebted to Rob Walker for making it known. Burwell had one of Richard Keene's nondescript rings of five and is the next village to Exning, so Briant was plainly 'inform'd' by someone who knew the situation at Burwell and also knew him; probably one of his faithful old school friends or Exning relations.

> Sir!
> I am inform'd that you intend
> having an alteration in your church
> Bells ; if the Business is not particular-
> ly ingaged I wish to offer an estimate.
> If no more than Repair the Old Bells
> by new hanging them, – I will compleat-
> ly hang them for £ 23, – Recast
> them at 21s pr ct and add any
> (*quantity?*) of Metal that may be required
> (*at* £) 4 pr ct.   Yrs &c
>   John Briant
>   Hertford
>   29th Mar
> PS If you think it proper to give me   1793
> a line I can estimate the exact sum the
> Business will amount to, knowing the W^t
> of each of the Old Bells, and you mentioning
> what you wish to have done.
> (*The words in brackets are indecipherable*)

As in those days the recipient had to pay the cost of postage, that kind of 'junk mail' may not have been too popular and at Burwell as at Cranborne, nothing came of it, although the mere fact that the letter has been preserved proves that it must have been considered and put aside for future reference, rather than being thrown into the fire. However, once Briant gained a foothold in an area, other work came in quickly. Within Hertfordshire itself, he established a near-monopoly; his nearest rival, the Whitechapel Foundry, managing to provide only twenty-seven bells to Briant's 110-plus during his working life.

One other skill which was to prove useful in gaining contacts was that at

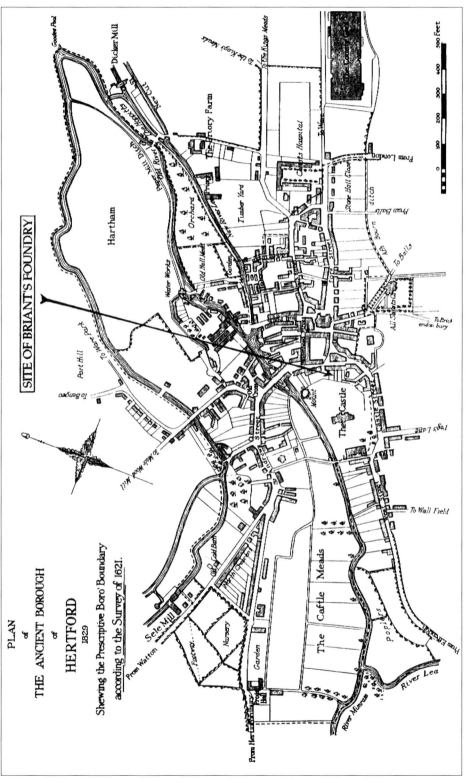

PLAN
of
THE ANCIENT BOROUGH
of
HERTFORD
1829
Shewing the Prescriptive Boro' Boundary
according to the Survey of 1621.

SITE OF BRIANT'S FOUNDRY

Map 10

some time, maybe during his years at St Neots, he had taken up bellringing and become very proficient at it. The ringing fraternity of that period had, as it still has, a most efficient grapevine and this must have been a vital factor when Bell Restoration Committees met to award contracts for work on their bells. The classic example of this was surely St Alkmund's, Shrewsbury, where Richard Wilding, a schoolmaster and a change ringer of great ability, was on the committee. A bellfounder who was also a practical ringer could be trusted to understand and rectify any problems which may have arisen in a new installation, as happened at St Alkmund's.

As well as being a practical ringer, Briant was interested in the theoretical aspects of ringing. In 1788 a new text book, the *Clavis Campanalogia*, which was to have a major influence on the future course of change ringing was published, somewhat unusually, by subscription. The list of subscribers contains the names of nine societies and 177 individuals. No fewer than five bellfounders are named: Edward Arnold, Leicester; John Briant, Hertford; George Hedderley, Nottingham; William Mears, Whitechapel and John Rudhall, Gloucester. This is proof that some, if not all, of the leading founders of the day were active change ringers.

The Hertford College Youths

The local ringing society, the Hertford College Youths, found in Briant a useful addition to their ranks. He must have joined them immediately after he arrived, because as their Peal Book records, on their annual Feast day, 9 August 1781, he was elected as a Steward of the Youths, which says a great deal for both his competence and his personal popularity, and possibly for the age-old system of voting a newcomer into office!

In 1782, he recast the front four bells at St Andrew's; the event was celebrated in the usual style by the ringing of a 'performance' on the bells by the Society of College Youths of London on 22 April 1782. This is recorded in the Peal Book of the Society but not numbered, so for some reason not now known, it could not be accepted as a true peal.

The details of this performance are:

Saint Andrew Hertford
On Monday April 22nd 1782
The Society celebrated the opening of the new bells
by ringing 5120 changes of
Treble Bob Major
in three hours and fifteen minutes

Performed by

Willm Scott	Treble	Josh Holdsworth	Fifth
James Darquit	Second	Willm Lyford	Sixth
Willm Wilds	Third	Edmd Sylvester	Seventh
John Povey	Fourth	Saml Muggeridge	Tenor

Conducted by Mr. John Povey

One must sympathise with the Londoners in their disappointment; the Hertford men saw it as an irresistible challenge to which they rose triumphantly! They scored *their* true peal on May 20 and, with what must have been unholy glee, rightly claimed it to be the first on the bells.

William Wilds was also a member of the Hertford College Youths, as he rang the same bell in both peals. Other H.C.Y. members who belonged to the London Society were Thomas North, elected 1764; William Randall and Robert Silversides, elected 1770; Mathew England and Thake Stallibrass, elected at the same time as William Wilds in 1774. Briant, elected 1782, was probably the youngest of the band, while Thomas North was the eldest.

The large and elaborate peal board still survives, having, like the bells, been moved from the old tower to the new when it was rebuilt in 1876. Three peals are recorded on the same board, in 1782, 1783 and 1784. The first reads:

The Society
of
HERTFORD COLLEGE YOUTHS:–
did ring the following PEALS, *viz;*

May 20th, 1782, 5280 Changes of Oxford Treble Bob;
in Three Hours Twenty four Minutes, being the first on these BELLS.

William Taylor	*Treble*	Thake Stallibrass	*Fifth*
Thomas North	*Second*	William Randall	*Sixth*
William Wilds	*Third*	Robert Silversides	*Seventh*
Mathew England	*Fourth*	John Briant	*Tenor*

The peal was called by R. Silversides

No modern type-setting can do anything like justice to the florid signwriting of the original. It is not easy to read and is even more difficult to photograph, due to lack of contrast between lettering and background. It was also slightly damaged when St Andrew's spire was struck by lightning and would greatly benefit from a judicious restoration.

Of the names on the board, Mathew England was the Treasurer of the Society while William Randall was a staymaker, highly respected in the community. Curiously, his name does not appear in the Hertford section of the *Universal British Directory of Trade, Commerce and Manufacture* published in 1794, in which Briant himself duly appears as clockmaker and bell-founder. Fortunately, details of Randall's funeral are recorded in the *Carrington Diaries* of November, 1801. (John Carrington was a farmer, Tax Assessor, Overseer of the Poor, Surveyor of Highways as well a District Chief Constable; his eagle eye missed nothing).

Carrington's account is quoted verbatim:

> Was Buried at All Saints' Church, Hartford, Mr. Wm. Randall, staymaker at Hartford. Lived above the Blackbirds Castle Street, next the Gate going into bayley hall, he was Sergant at Mace and used to take the toll of the Market, and Constable Money years, he belonged to the Association at Hartford,

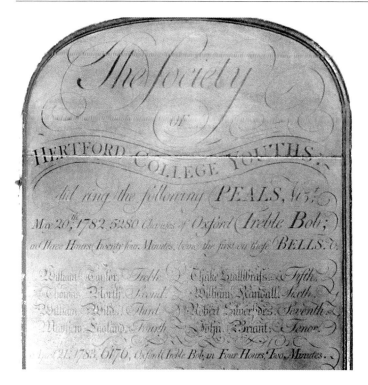

Peal board in the belfry of Hertford,
St Andrew, recording his ringing the tenor.
[*D. E. Hannaford*]

they marched the Dead March and fired over him, he was a Ringer and they muffeld the Bells. I was at the Buring, about 4 Clock, a Great Number of people aged 63.

The 'Association' referred to the local Militia or Volunteers.

Thomas North was probably a descendant of Hugh Northe or Oliver North, the lawyer and his clerk who were the signatories of Robert Oldfield's Inventory in 1650. It is clear that the then ringers were largely respectable tradesmen, contrary to the usual later nineteenth century picture of low-class drunkards. The Society had three types of member, Steeple ringers who were change ringers and who had to ring 1000 changes in order to qualify; non-ringing members of higher status who joined what was a social club in all but name and the tune ringers, handbell ringers who preferred to do their ringing in the comfort of the local pub. There was also another group of tower-bell ringers who did not practice change ringing and so did not qualify as Steeple ringers, although they did ring on numerous occasions. They were definitely of the lower orders.

It was possibly as a result of the unsuccessful peal attempt by the Society of College Youths that Briant was elected a member of that Society later the same year (1782). The name book records:

1782 John Briant. Hertford, Bell-founder.

The actual day and month are not specified, but A.J. Phillips, the present Librarian of the Ancient Society of College Youths, who kindly checked the reference, is of the opinion that, judging by the list of new members for that year, Briant's election took place in about July or August. This may be borne out by the record of a peal of Plain Bob Triples rung at St Mary's, Battersea, on 26 August, in which the tenor was rung by John Bryant (*sic*), no doubt a mis-spelling. This and the Hertford peal are the only ones known for certain in which Briant took part. The fact that he rang the tenor in both cases points to his being a competent heavy-bell ringer.

Briant's connection with the Hertford College Youths continued for many years, probably to the end of his life. In 1789 the Minute Book records the intention of augmenting the bells of All Saints' from eight to ten. The relevant entry reads:

> 1789. Jan. 8. 'At the Annual Christmas Meeting of the Steeple Ringing Members of this Society, it was unanimously Resolved and agreed to Subscribe one half part of the Money arising from Ringing until it became the sum of Twenty Pounds towards the Metal and all Expences attending the Erection of two new Tribbles in addition to the peal of eight Bells now in all Sts Steeple Hertford.

> *N.B.* It appears on the the statement of the auth. of this Society that there Now is the sum of £4 18s. 10d. resting in the Hands of Mr. Mathew England the Treasurer of this Society towards forwarding the business above mentioned.
> Witness M. England'.

Sixteen signatures are appended, including Briant's.

Two years later comes his receipt for the money:

> Recd 28th May, 1791 of Mr. Mathew England (Treasurer to the Society of Hertford College Youths) Twenty Pounds on Acct for the two new Trebles of All Sts being the noble subscription of the Society.

> £20 0s. 0d.   John Briant.

These bells were first rung in 1794 but were lost in the disastrous fire of 1891 which left only the outer walls of the church standing (*see* p. 219).

Old All Saints' bells had a chequered history. They were listed as five in 1552. In 1674 the old tenor bell was recast into four small bells to augment to eight and Chauncy in 1700 described them as a good ring of eight. In 1763, the church was severely damaged, to the cost of £ 3,000, by a 'fireball' which came through the roof. The tower was rebuilt into the classical structure which can be seen in pre-1891 photographs. The bells were rehung in the new tower and were rung again in 1767. (ref. *History of Hertford* p. 108). However, in 1771, they were recast by Pack & Chapman of Whitechapel. Briant's trebles were therefore being added to a modern ring of bells.

On 20 March 1798 Briant was one of sixteen members present at a meeting of the Society held at the Black Swan, Hertford, when

> … it was unanimously resolved that the sum of Ten Guineas be subscribed towards the exigencies of the State, and that sum of Ten Guineas be annually subscribed by the Ringing Society of Hertford College Youths, during the present War, and that the Treasurer do pay the same into the Bank of England accordingly.

The 'War' was, of course, what became known as the Napoleonic Wars which, as they dragged on until 1815, began to cause considerable hardship in the country, including 7d in the £ income tax. In this day and age, when

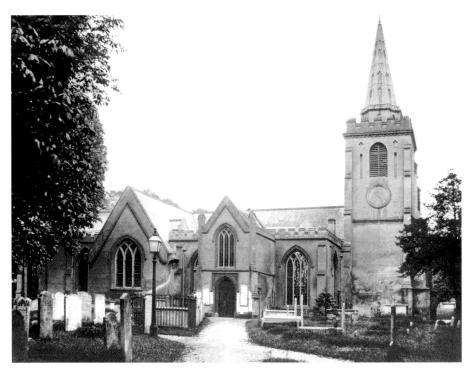

Hertford, All Saints as it was before the fire of 1891. John Briant was an active ringer here and cast two bells to augment the octave to ten bells in 1794. [HALS]

the main aim of most people seems to be to avoid paying tax, this voluntary contribution to the state is completely incomprehensible. It was then called Patriotism.

Much later, in 1821, another entry in the Peal Book shows that Briant was also supplying handbells. The entry reads:

Rec. 27th Decr, 1821, of Meſsrs. Worsley and Biggin, two Pound ten on Acct. for a Peal of 10 Hand Bells.
£2 10s. 0d.   John Briant.
£2   0s. 0d..
Recd. full 8th Apr. 1822.   John Briant.

These bells must also be assumed to have been destroyed in the fire at All Saints'. No sets of handbells by Briant are now known so the question is bound to arise as to whether he actually cast this set or whether they were made to his order by Henry Symondson, the London handbell specialist, who was also a good friend and with whom he had some working arrangement.

By this time, the Hertford Collage Youths was no longer the active change ringing group of twenty years earlier. It had sunk into a quiet decline and, although there was a succession of members, there is no evidence of any election of 'Steeple Ringers' and ringing had degenerated into rounds and call changes only. The inescapable conclusion must be that these handbells were to be used by the members to practise for their own entertainment, probably in whichever inn they patronised. Tower ringing practices were dropped altogether.

However, in *History and Art of Change Ringing* (1931) by Ernest Morris, there is an account of John Carr, a ringer from Waltham Holy Cross, being engaged to instruct a company of young men 'in the art' with such success that, after only six months, a peal of Grandsire Triples was rung at St Andrew's on 30 November 1822. They sang a song about it, of which the third verse runs:

> On November the 30th these lads they set to,
> In the year eighteen hundred and twenty and two;
> When Osborn and Skerman, Bill Farrow and South,
> Carr, Biggin, and Foster, with his brother so stout,
> Rang a Peal … etc.

Skerman was Briant's assistant 'clock and chime maker', who eventually continued that side of the business after Briant's retirement. His connection with the Hertford College Youths continued until at least 1847.

Family Affairs

John Bryant died in Hertford before 1 April 1785, the date on which his death was reported to the Hatfield Manor court. In his will, he left his possessions to his son. There were three boxes, labelled 1, 2 and 3, a bureau, his books and the earlier-mentioned chest of tools. These items form one of the most frustrating problems in writing a study of Briant. There are some indications of what kind of tools could have been in the chest but nobody will ever know just what was in those three mysterious boxes, so carefully numbered. Contrary to his wishes, Bryant was buried at Hertford instead of at Hatfield with Catherine's family.

The next year, Briant recast the bells at St Etheldreda's, Hatfield, and supplied a set of chimes, a major commission. It is not entirely clear whether he was recasting an existing octave or augmenting a ring of five. The Inn in Church Street was called the Five Bells and Sir Henry Chauncy recorded five in 1700, Chauncy being a reliable source. On the other hand, a letter of 1738 to Thomas Lester of Whitechapel is in the Hatfield House Archives, while the Five Bells had become the Eight Bells by 1756, which facts would seem to imply the existence of a ring of eight, but whether they were actually cast is not proven. The new Briant bells were dedicated on 5 June 1786. Two days later, on June 7, John Briant, at the age of thirty-eight, married Mary (Molly) Hanley at St Andrew's, Hertford.

The bride was aged twenty-six, having been born in 1760 and christened at All Saints, Hertford, on 18 April that year. She came from a long-established local family, the daughter of John Hanley and Mary Wetherall, married at All Saints on 12 May 1759. John Hanley's father, also John, had been a glazier by trade, so the family was well respected. Their name was occasionally spelled as Handley in the registers of both All Saints' and St Andrew's.

Briant's wedding was only just in time as Mary, daughter of John and Molly Briant was christened on 1 September 1786, having been born in August. By any reckoning, the bride must have been between six and seven months pregnant. Young Mary outlived both her parents, was intelligent and competent and a great help and comfort to John in his old age. A second daughter was born in July or August 1788. She was named Catherine after her dead grandmother, but lived only four months, dying on 3 November 1788 and was buried at All Saints, in the grave of one of her Hanley aunts who had died at the age of three in 1769.

The marriage seems to have been happy, although sadly short. Molly Briant died, aged thirty-three, on 22 November 1793 and was buried in her mother's grave in All Saints' churchyard five days later, where her husband was to be laid in his turn. It is possible that some member of the Hanley family helped Briant to bring up the motherless seven-year-old Mary.

Nine years later, at the age of fifty-four, the widower married again. This time his bride was less than half his age, being only twenty-four. Her name was Ann Fyson, spinster, and the ceremony took place at St Andrew's on 15 May 1802. Little is known about her origins but a hunt through the I.G.I. turns up two possible names; Ann Elizabeth Fison, daughter of Chalkley and Elizabeth Fison, *née* Lemon, christened at Royston, 20 February 1778 and, much more likely because of the spelling, Ann Fyson, daughter of William and Susan (Susanna), christened at Exning, Suffolk, on 28 October 1777. It may not be without significance that Briant had been working in Suffolk, at Great Waldingfield, in 1800. In 1808, on the treble at Gazeley, Suffolk, among the hugely amusing 'rhyming' list of donors, there appears the name Fyson, in the same spelling. Did Briant, by any chance, on his 1800 working visit to the county pay a social call on his old friends and relations at Exning and thus meet a young relative of Fyson's? Certainly the Exning connection makes this feasible.

There were two children from this tragically short marriage, the first a son, John, whose date of birth is unknown, both H.C. Andrews and the present writer having failed to find it, but which can be calculated to have been between February and June 1803. This child, the son to carry on the foundry, died in infancy and was buried at St Andrew's on 5 March 1804, two months before the birth of the second child. This was a daughter, another Catherine, baptised on 6 May 1804 and again named after her dead grandmother; such was Briant's devotion to his mother's memory. What effect the death of young John had on his mother and her unborn child must be left to the imagination. From later documentary evidence it appears that Catherine was either physically or mentally handicapped in some degree, which suggests that she had either suffered from a difficult birth or that a genetic factor was involved. Catherine did, however, outlive both parents. Less than a year later, Ann died at the age of twenty-seven from some unrecorded cause, maybe in premature childbirth, and was buried at St Andrew's on 3 March 1805, two days short of the anniversary of the burial of her baby son, bringing to an end a marriage which had seen more than its share of tragedy. The task of keeping house for her father fell back onto nineteen-year-old Mary's capable shoulders. It is highly unlikely that she was given the responsiblity for bringing up her half-sister; the baby was probably placed with fosterparents unless any of Ann's family were able to take care of her. Whether the very young stepmother and teenage stepdaughter had agreed or disagreed is impossible to know but the fact that Briant was buried with Molly rather than with Ann is not significant; it was at his own request.

At one time, a rumour was current that both Briant's daughters ended their days in extreme poverty in the Union Workhouse. This was not the case. It arose as a result of confusion with another Hertford family, that of a saddler and harness-maker variously called Bryan, Brian or Bryant, one of whose children was called John, another Ann and a third, Catherine. Small wonder that people became muddled. H.C. Andrews picked his way carefully through this minefield on page 4 of his book.

In fact, Mary Briant married Solomon George Shaw on 24 May 1810, at St Andrew's, Hertford. S.G. Shaw traded as 'Stationer, Bookseller and Binder at Market Place, St Albans'. He was also a printer with branches in Hertford, Ware and Hitchin and also called himself an Actuary, so he was obviously a man of parts. Through his branch in Hertford, he may well have been the printer of Briant's list of bells, published in about 1805, thus beginning his association with the Briant family. It is uncertain which shop he occupied but the Market Place was a small area, from Spencer Street to the Clock Tower on the west side and from what is now the alley behind the Town Hall on the east side as far as the High Street. (The Town Hall was not built until 1829-31). At that date the shops and houses would not necessarily have been numbered. It has been brought to the writer's notice that Shaw later moved from what was a very expensive site to much cheaper premises in St Peter's parish; whether because of financial difficulties or lack of trade is not clear. The business was known for a time as the Phoenix Press.

Andrews then added the following footnote, quoting from the St Albans Minute Book 1811:

> At a Court held at St Albans, on December 4th, Benjamin Agutter, tailor, was sworn a burgess by redemption. He, together with Samuel Avis, Solomon George Shaw and Henry Martin, was sworn an Assistant. Messrs. Shaw and Avis were chosen Wardens of the Innholders' Company and Agutter and Martin of the Mercers.

(Benjamin Agutter became a churchwarden at St Albans Abbey and his name appeared on the 1845 treble bell recast by C.& G. Mears of Whitechapel from the unlucky Briant treble bell of 1792 which cracked in

1829). Shaw, however, never rose above the status of Assistant to become a Burgess. This clearly rankled and may have been one of the reasons for his move to Hertford in later years.

S.G. Shaw has a minor claim to fame as in 1815 he produced a small book entitled

History of Verulam and St Albans

and of the

Present state of the Town

the

Abbey

(etc.)

with a title taking up most of the page, in the fashion of the time, which he printed and published himself. It was clearly intended as a pocket guide for visitors and would be on sale in his shop. Unfortunately for his own civic prospects, in its pages Shaw implied criticism of the St Albans Corporation. At that period, St Albans was what was rightly described as a 'rotten borough' and a very putrescent example of the species, so he was justified, but suffered for it.

Only a photocopy exists in St Albans City Library, where the above information was given by a member of the library staff with an exceptionally good memory for obscure items. Mary was therefore marrying a respected local tradesman and amateur historian who was to be a trusted aide to her father in his old age. It appears to have been a happy and stable marriage which lasted for about twenty-seven years.

The Years of Expansion

It must never be forgotten that, as Robert Oldfield worked in the shadow of the growing political unrest of the early seventeenth century, so also Briant's career was at its height during the Napoleonic Wars which were to bring considerable hardship to the country at large. Late payment of his bills could have been part of the cause of the financial difficulties he is said to have suffered in his old age. Some parishes were put to considerable trouble in trying to raise the cash.

The distribution of Briant's bells can best be seen from Map 11, p. 204 and shows the growth of clusters of his bells. Hertfordshire has the densest concentration, (giving the impression of a bad case of measles!) followed in descending order by Northamptonshire, Leicestershire, Essex, Buckinghamshire, Oxfordshire, Lincolnshire, Warwickshire, Cambridgeshire, Suffolk, Shropshire, Devon, Staffordshire and Kent. Certain features stand out; in Cambridgeshire, for example, he took care not to intrude onto the territory of his old friend, Thomas Osborn at Downham Market, while in Leicestershire only one Briant bell appeared before the retirement from founding of Edward Arnold in 1800, so once again the old 'gentlemens' agreement' held good.

By 1789 his fame had spread to Oxfordshire where he cast a new ring of eight for Adderbury, as well as a ring of five for Hanwell, six miles away. Also in his foundry at the same time were two bells for Littlebury, Essex, which led to a mix-up between these bells and those for Hanwell, Oxfordshire. (Details can be found under individual bells in the chronological list).

By this time, Briant must have been spending an increasingly large part of his working life in travelling the country in connection with his ever-expanding number of commissions and it may be that he was not able to give adequate personal supervision in the foundry. In an age when owning a carriage was a status symbol, Briant, essentially a modest man, never did so. His reason was that he was quite content as he was, as can be seen on the memorial plaque on the tower arch at All Saints, where his words are quoted verbatim (see photograph p. 198). He must therefore have travelled on horseback for short distances and by stage or mail coach for longer journeys and the 'Stage' was notorious for its lack of speed and comfort, although it afforded plenty of opportunities for meeting a wide variety of people. Under those conditions, his absences would necessarily have been prolonged, so his workforce must have been capable of carrying on while the 'Boss' was away. Just how many people were employed at the foundry cannot now be known but all the evidence points to it being a major concern.

A large part of Briant's time must have been taken up with paperwork; estimates, letters to restoration committees, bills, receipts – all the normal business correspondence. Some of these items have been preserved and they show the script of an educated, right-handed man, quickly written but legible, with a strong slope to the right. (e.g. Swaffham Prior, 16 April 1795). It must not be forgotten that, before the introduction of the Penny Post, the recipient had to pay the postage, unless the sender could obtain a frank from a Peer of the Realm or someone of similar status. This explains the reference in churchwardens' accounts to 'for a letter from Mr. Bryant 10d' at Condover, Salop, for 25 September 1813.

The Swaffham Prior receipt also proves another point; comparing his writing and signature with the manuscript additions to his published list of clocks, of about 1825/6, shows without doubt that these additions were not in Briant's hand. It must be assumed, therefore, that they were added for him, probably by Mary Shaw.

In 1790 Briant travelled to Chacombe, Northants., in connection with the recasting of the 5th bell. (Chacombe was the site of the famous bell-foundry of the Bagley family from 1631 to 1782, the foundry apparently lying just to the east of the churchyard). Thirty years later he added two trebles to the ring of six at St Mary's, Banbury, and appears to have called at Chacombe on his way home. While there, he saw that the tombstone to Henry Bagley

(1608–84) had become badly eroded and he thereupon paid for it to be recut and restored, with the addition of 'To the Memory of an ingenious Bell-Founder this stone was repaired' – a graceful tribute from one master crafts-man to another. H.C. Andrews claimed that the tombstone was in Banbury churchyard but in this he was in error. The Bagley stone is quite definitely at Chacombe, on the south side of the church, east of the path from the gate to the porch, where the writer has seen and photographed it. Since then it has been restored twice, the second time by the Peterborough Diocesan Guild of Church Bellringers, so continuing the good example set by Briant.

Briant was quick to seize the opportunity to transport his bells by canal, wherever feasible, thus cutting down on slow and tedious road journeys. Hertford was well placed on the River Lea for access to places which could be reached via the Thames. The bell for Ettington, Warwicks., (see No. 231) supplied to the order of J. Waters of King's Sutton in 1803, appears to have travelled down the Lea, up the Thames, via the Oxford Canal to Banbury, then by road to Ettington, near Stratford on Avon, as the Grand Junction link was not yet open. By 1806, when the ring of six for Padbury was cast, the Grand Junction system was used as far as Cosgrove and from thence via the Buckingham Arm which had recently been opened. To reach the Grand Junction Canal from Hertford, it was necessary to go across country to Hemel Hempstead and load on to boats at Boxmoor Wharf. This is exactly what happened, as the churchwardens' accounts make abundantly clear (See Nos. 262–7). The final leg of the journey, by road from Buckingham to Padbury was not much more than three miles. The story of Hanslope tenor is probably well-known; on unloading at Castlethorpe wharf, it fell into the canal and stayed there for a week, no doubt forming a serious obstacle to navigation (See No. 375). His bells for Old Wolverton, Newton Longville, Wavendon and Mursley could all have travelled much of the way by water. Had Briant lived a few years longer, he would have sent his products by rail! As it was, he just lived to see the dawn of the railway age.

The four commissions in Shropshire in 1812/13 were far outside his usual range, as was the 1814 bell for Montgomery. There is a clear statement in the churchwardens' accounts at St Alkmund's, Shrewsbury, of 'weighing' the bells and carriage to the quay. Transit could have been via the Severn to Stourport, up the Staffordshire & Worcestershire Canal to Birmingham and from there via the Grand Junction to Boxmoor; complicated but perfectly feasible. The recast bells, as well as those for Holy Cross Abbey, High Ercall and Condover, even Montgomery, would have travelled back by the same route.

Even further outside his territory, the bells for Barnstaple, Braunton and Tawstock were carried much of the way by sea, from Bideford, as the rele-vant accounts from Braunton and Tawstock plainly state. They could have gone up the Bristol Channel to Framilode Basin, been transhipped onto the Stroudwater Canal then the Thames-Severn Canal, through to the Thames itself and, finally, up the Lea to Hertford. The alternative route would have been around Land's End and along the English Channel by coastal shipping and up to the Port of London; not a route to be tackled in January and in wartime, certainly not before Nelson's victory at Trafalgar.

Clocks and Chimes

During most of his working life, Briant was heavily involved in clockmaking at which he was an acknowledged expert. In later life, he published a list of these (p. 290), describing them as 'Turret' clocks if they struck the hours only (two-train), or 'Quarter' clocks if they struck the quarters as well (three-train). The former type would have one bell, while the latter usually had three, two for the 'Ting-Tang' quarters and one for the hour. This list was usually said to have been published in or about 1825. It names not only churches but also private houses, as far afield as Scotland and Ireland. It was a formidable output, far beyond the capabilities of one man. In this side of the business, he was ably assisted by James Skerman, who lived in Water Lane, Hertford.

The last clock with which Briant was associated was that in the New Gatehouse at King's College, Cambridge. The Gatehouse was part of the new screen wall extending along King's Parade, designed by William Wilkins in 1823 and completed in 1827. The erection of the clock was actually supervised by Briant in January 1828, *after* his retirement to St Albans and in his eightieth year, as the Lincoln correspondence makes quite clear.

In connection with church clocks, Briant also produced sets of chimes, his earliest recorded being for St Etheldreda's, Hatfield, in 1786, where he supplied chimes for an existing clock at the same time as he recast the bells. Clock and chimes were replaced in about 1804 by the clock and chimes from St Peter's, St Albans, sold by the churchwardens towards defraying the cost of rebuilding their tower, which had partially collapsed in 1801. This transfer was probably done through the agency of Briant, who supplied a new clock for the rebuilt tower in 1805. Another clock with a set of chimes was supplied to the order of His Grace the Duke of Marlborough for the church at Woodstock in 1792. (Illustrated in *Clocks and Chimes* by Trevor Jennings, pub. 2000). In 1802, as well as a quarter clock with chimes, he added two bells to make a ring of ten bells at Melton Mowbray, thus increasing the number of tunes which could be played. Briant's last set of chimes, i.e. those ordered through him by name, were for All Saints', Northampton, dated 1829. As he had retired from bellfounding in 1825, it seems likely that he carried on with this side of the business assisted by James Skerman, who continued making turret and other clocks after Briant moved to St Albans, possibly in 1828, as the Lincoln correspondence implies.

At this point, it is worth looking at the later history of the foundry, after Briant sold out the bellfounding side to Thomas Mears II of Whitechapel.

James Skerman, said by the writer of Briant's obituary notice 'he has often been declared by his late master to be the most superior practical workman he had ever met with,' bought Briant's tools and machinery and carried on the business at Parliament Row and it was to his order that Mears supplied the recast 6th bell at Hatfield in 1841. Skerman reissued Briant's clock catalogue and added his own list. These he had printed on the back of his contracts to customers. An interesting fact is that he was an early advocate of the use of standard, or London, time for the convenience of rail travellers.

> To save the time, and to prevent the disappointment of so great a number of Persons as are continually travelling to the various Railway Termini, it is necessary that the Turret and Church Clocks should be well regulated, and kept to London Time, which cannot be done without a true Meridian Line; J.S. & Son have the advantage of one, and have the honor of keeping in order and regulating the Clocks at the under mentioned Gentlemens Residences and Parish Churches : – …
>
> *ex inf.* David Kingstone.

Skerman's son, William, became his father's partner and, after James Skerman's death at the age of eighty-five, continued the clock business. At some later date, he added iron and brass founding to his activities. The gates of St Andrew's Cemetery were cast by him in 1851 'at the Castle Foundry.'

Recent research by C.J. Pickford (Aug. 2001) into the archives of Thwaites & Reed of Clerkenwell in the Guildhall Library has shown that they supplied parts and, in some cases, complete clock movements to the Skermans and to Samuel Harry. He did not notice anything being supplied to Hertford before 1830, which gives the impression that either Briant had another source of supply or that he manufactured his own parts and movements, which is probable.

On William Skerman's retirement, his business was divided; Samuel Harry (who modified St Andrew's clock in 1876 for transfer into the new tower) took over the clockmaking, while the whitesmith's work was taken over by R.T. and W.F. Andrews on the condition that they paid Skerman an annuity for the rest of his life. William Skerman died in 1874, aged seventy-five. Samuel Harry had worked for Simson and Groombridge, jewellers and clock makers, in the Market Place. Harry Ilott Harry succeeded Samuel Harry and so was, at the time of H.C. Andrews' book, in direct line from Briant. Simson and Groombridge moved into Parliament Row, to the site of the old foundry, to be followed by Simson & Co. Printers and, more recently, by the Job Centre.

One lesser branch of Briant's clock business was the making of long-case clocks, of which two were extant in H.C. Andrews' day and were examined by him. Photographic reproduction in his book was not good but typical of its date; in spite of that, it is possible to make out sufficient detail to give a reasonable account of them. The present writer has not seen these clocks.

The first was supplied to Sir Geoffrey Church of Hatfield Woodside at some date between 1772, when the house was complete, and 1788, when the clock was included in the Inventory taken after his death. Briant had not moved to Hertford by 1772 and so a date of 1780 to 1788 is more likely. The clock is austere in its simplicity, almost like a regulator, having a single-sheet round dial probably of silvered brass, inscribed *John Briant Hartford*. There are two winding holes, for a two-train movement, i.e. going and striking. One of the holes seems to have a shutter, which would indicate that maintaining power was applied while the clock was being wound. No second hand is visible. The case is of London manufacture, judging by the shape of the trunk door, with a stepped-in half-round top, while the hood has its outline partly obscured by simple cresting and bears three ball-topped finials.

The second clock is very different and has an interesting history, involving a notorious local highwayman, Walter Clibbon. On Saturday, 28 December 1782, as Clibbon was attempting to rob Mr Benjamin Whittenbury on the road between Bramfield and Datchworth, he was shot dead by Shock North, Whittenbury's servant. (The gun which fired the fatal shot is preserved in Hertford Museum.) In gratitude for saving his life, his master gave him this clock as a wedding present. Benjamin Whittenbury died in 1801 and North moved to Watton-at-Stone to work as the doctor's man. He died before 1840 and the clock was purchased from Widow North by Charles Fletcher whose son owned it in 1930.

It is therefore possible to date this to within a few years after the attempted robbery, the mid-to-late 1780s. In style it could not be more different from the Hatfield Woodside clock. The case again is of London make, having the same stepped-in half-round top to the trunk door, but there the resemblance ends. This clock has an arch dial, with a brass chapter ring and cast brass spandrels in the corners and the arch. The centre of the dial appears to be matted, rather than engraved, although this may be due to the photographic reproduction. There are three dials, that in the arch having a strike/silent lever. Beneath the figure XII is a seconds dial and above the VI is a calendar disc, not a very common feature in this form, as usually the calender wheel was hidden behind the dial, with only a curved aperture to show the date. On either side of the VI is engraved *Jno Briant Hertford*. This was about the time when Briant was beginning to switch from 'Hartford' to 'Hertford' on his bells.

In its prime, this must have been a very tall clock, not much less than eight feet, as were many London clock cases. It has a pagoda top, which looks as though it has been slightly trimmed down to reduce the height and the plinth has been entirely removed, thus completely ruining the original appearance. Sadly, this happened to many clocks when they were moved from a large house to a smaller one.

The third clock, which the writer has seen, is in Hertford Museum and is in good going order. It was donated in September 1986. Not surprisingly, the

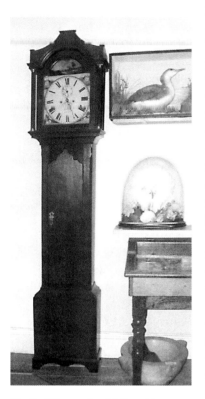

Hertford Museum has this Bryant long-
case clock. *[D. E. Hannaford]*

Museum is proud of it. It is a two-train clock standing 6′ 10″ high with a white dial by Osborne and Wilson of Birmingham, who probably included the name as part of the original painted design, spelling it as 'Bryant' and 'Hertford' and not Hartford, which Briant used at that time, raising a slight doubt as to whether it was his work or his father's. The case-work appears to be mahogany on the front and possibly oak on the sides, but has at some time been heavily stained, thus making identification difficult. Above the arch dial is a simple top with shallow concave slopes with flat sections which would originally have carried three finials. Fluted columns with brass pillar caps and bases flank the hood door and the hood itself is supported on elegant concave mouldings. In the main case, the door is of the long type, showing that the clock was probably made in the later years of the eighteenth century; the brass lock is original. The top of the door is of a complex shape with a stepped-in section, rising to a high centre point, again typical of the period. The plinth is complete and retains the original semi-French feet. Altogether, this is a most dignified and attractive clock case.

The white dial was unfortunately repainted about 1840 in a heavy-handed style by someone who perpetuated the spelling of the name. In the four corners and the arch are painted rustic cottages and a tower; they appear to be original. There is a calendar disk behind a curved aperture above the VI and a seconds dial below the XII.

Later Years and Retirement

The peak period for Briant's bells was between 1790 and 1816, with a slow falling-off from then on. (*See Production Chart. Fig. 206,* p. 24). This is not to be wondered at, as Briant was by then in his sixty-eighth or -ninth year. His last bells were cast for Boughton, Northants., Fenny Stratford, Bucks. and Hinxworth, Herts., not far from the home of his first church bell at Pirton. From about 1820, some of his dates were in roman numerals and it seems probable that, by this time, another person was stamping the inscriptions, someone less familiar with classical usage than Briant, who on two bells, Stanstead St Margaret, 1820 and Fenny Stratford, 1824, put a 'V' instead of 'D' for 500, unless Briant was beginning to suffer from failing eyesight, an explanation which has not hitherto been considered. The two bells at Boughton (now recast) bore the name of T. Briant; Fenny Stratford tenor inscription is in his small type, although there was adequate space for his larger letters. The most telling evidence is on the recently-discovered bell of unknown provenance at Croxley Green. This bell is inscribed J B J: B• MDC-CCXXII• around the lip, but the 'J's were put on upside down, even at a second attempt. At the first try, the 'J' was left in situ, while the first 'B' was hastily pulled away, leaving an imperfect impression. To the writer, this suggested an old man who had left his glasses at home! These are small clues as to why Briant decided to sell out the bellfounding business in 1825. Further evidence was to appear in his late correspondence.

Thomas Mears II of Whitechapel bought out the Aldbourne, Wiltshire, foundry in 1825 and was to buy out the ancient Rudhall foundry at Gloucester in 1830, so his acquisition of Briant's business was part of a wider pattern, rather than an isolated event. The sum of money involved in this transaction is not known as none of Briant's papers survive and Mears' archives were lost in a fire at Whitechapel in 1837. With the clock- and chimemaking in Skerman's safe hands, all that needed to be done was to clear out the lumber of years from the foundry. A small, undated bell had been presented to the National Boys' School, also in Parliament Row, in 1824; the broken remains are in Hertford Museum. (See. No. 438).

The money which Briant received from Thomas Mears was used to invest in some property at Datchworth. The Abel Smith papers in Hertfordshire Archives and Local Studies (*HALS*) record the sale of a lease to John Briant of a small area (3 rood) of ground which had been left in the will of 'William Brinkley, Shopkeeper', to John Brinkley, also 'Shopkeeper' who, with Polly his wife, was the seller. This parcel of land lay beside the highway leading from Bragbury End to Woolmer Green towards the north and from Pounds Green to Woolmer Green towards the south. This lies at approximately *O.S. ref. TL 263195*. At the time of purchase it was in use only as a garden and orchard but included in the sale were 'outhouses, buildings, barns and every part thereof to have and to hold' – items which appear not to have existed. The Indenture (*Ref. D/EAS 1423*) is dated 4 March 1826 and the Deed of Sale (*Ref.D/EAS 1421*) dated 10 March 1826. The sum involved was £140 and was witnessed by Joseph Hooper Squire, Elizabeth Squire and John Briant. A marginal sketch of the property gives the principal dimensions, but is obviously not to scale. One is led to wonder whether Briant was in this way making provision for a small regular income for his daughter Catherine's future support.

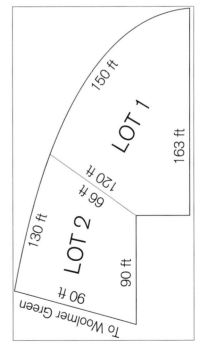

Sketch of Datchworth property bought by Briant as an investment. *[HALS]*

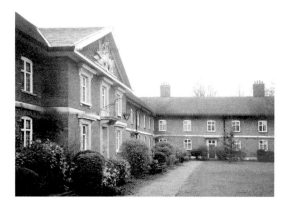

St Albans, Marlborough Almshouses, on Hatfield Road, St Albans. [W. A. Foster]

As with all legal affairs, nothing ran smoothly. *D/EAS 1424/1425* dated '15 days of Easter in the Seventh year of George IVth' records a Court plea by Briant v. Thomas Blindell, John Brinkley and Polly his wife for the sum of £60, in which Briant succeeded. The following year, on 25 October 1828, Briant released the property, now in the occupation of George Skeggs, to Philip Robins, carpenter, of Watton. (*Ref. D/EAS 1426*). He was apparently still capable of managing his monetary affairs; this is the last documentary evidence before his will.

For obvious reasons, Briant himself never occupied the Datchworth property. He moved into the Marlborough Almshouses in Hatfield Road, St Albans, a mere stone's throw away from St Peter's church at some date not specified but which, on the evidence of the Lincoln correspondence, may have been in 1826-7. These letters, which will be quoted in due course, were headed 'Hertford' in January 1828, but he also refers to his papers as being 'in St Albans' at that time, so he must have then still been doing some clock work, spending part of his time in Hertford and part in St Albans. It has always been said that the move was forced upon him by poverty; that by his generosity to impecunious churches he built up no reserves for his old age. Henry Symondson, his old friend, is on record as saying Briant would rather lose by a job than turn out a poor bell. This may have been so but possible physical disability due to age or failing sight has never fully been taken into account. He may have been in his late seventies but he had no need of charity. Sheltered accommodation, however, had probably become necessary, although it did not stop his travelling nor his continuing to act as a consultant, even as late as January 1828. He may also have preferred to retain his independence, rather than impose on Mary and Solomon.

The deciding factor in his move to St Albans must have been that Mary and her husband lived there, little more than ten minutes' walk away and Soloman Shaw, as an established businessman and burgess, knew the right strings to pull to find a suitable almshouse when it became available, rather than that George John, Second Earl Spencer, High Steward of St Albans gave him shelter, as said by Andrews. The truth, as usual, probably lies somewhere in between. It is unfortunate that research has failed to establish exactly which house was allotted to him.

The Marlborough Almshouses were founded by Sarah, Duchess of Marlborough in 1736. They consist of a large, two-storied block in dark red brick with a central pediment and wings of equal height at the east and west ends, the main facade facing on to a large lawn on the north side and there-fore mostly in shadow. The splendid mature cedar which was shown in the drawing facing p. 14 in H.C. Andrews' book has been felled in recent years and replaced by a deciduous tree.

Accommodation was for eighteen men and eighteen women, who were to live 'soberly and piously'. Each house had four rooms and a small garden . The present layout consists of a living room, bedroom, kitchen and bath-room, with internal lavatory and central heating, modern necessities unknown in Briant's day, when water, said to be exceptionally pure, was drawn from a well and lavatories were at the end of the gardens. Heating was by coal fires. Minor external alterations to the buildings have also been made, window frames are replacements and, most immediately noticeable, the chimney stacks are now much less top-heavy than they were when Andrews illustrated them.

As a sanctuary for a retired bellfounder and clockmaker it was ideal; he could hear 'his' clock of 1805 striking the hours at St. Peter's and also hear 'his' two trebles being rung there as well as being within sound of the Abbey bells where 'his' treble of 1792 was still intact – it cracked shortly after his death.

The Lincoln Correspondence

It says much for Briant's reputation that, when the Dean and Chapter of Lin-coln became seriously concerned about their bells, in particular Great Tom which was cracked, they should approach a man of seventy-nine for advice. The queries put to Briant through Edward Betham, the Surveyor, and Briant's replies have been preserved in the cathedral archives. This corre-spondence was quoted *in extenso* by North and Stahlschmidt in *Church Bells of Hertfordshire 1886* and also by Andrews, but is worth quoting again for the insight it gives into Briant's character and his amazingly lucid replies, as well as his use of English

31st December, 1827

Copy of queries put to Mr. John Briant, of Hertford, for many years a bell-founder (which he has lately declined) and church and turret-clock maker, aged nearly eighty years, by Edward Betham, surveyor to the Dean and Chapter, respecting the crack discovered in Great Tom o' Lincoln, which was particularly described to Briant.

First. Could such an accident occur by the accidental or intentional pres-sure, by any person, upon the bell at the time the clock was striking?

Second. It has been thought right to discontinue the striking of the clock, and tolling with the clapper for the present; but Mr. Briant is particularly requested to state, with as little delay as possible, whether any further injury would be occasioned by allowing the clock to strike, and the bell to be tolled with the clapper as heretofore?

Third. Whether any temporary improvement in the tone would be obtained by cutting a piece out of the bell as far or a little beyond the present crack?

Fourth. In case Mr. Briant should not think it safe to adopt any of the above plans, it is proposed to let the clock strike upon the tenor bell of the peal of eight in the opposite tower of St. Hugh. The quarters now strike upon the 4th and 7th of that peal. The treble bell is broken; therefore upon which two of the bells would Mr. Briant recommend the quarters to strike in the absence of the treble, the clock striking upon the tenor in the key of F? Would 2, 5 . . 8 do?

Fifth and Lastly. What would be the probable expense of recasting this stupendous bell, taking into consideration the getting down and up again, and having to pass through one groined stone ceiling?

And would it be more readily done at Lincoln or in London?

[The fact that this list is described as a copy would account for the use of the third person in referring to Briant. The original must have been included in Briant's personal papers, which are not known to have survived.]Briant's reply was as follows :

Hertford,

January 2nd, 1828

Dear Sir, Agreeable to your request contained in your favour of the 31st December, I do myself the pleasure to answer your enquiries.

First. I entertain no doubt that the fracture was not occasioned from either of the causes you have named.

Second. By continuing the clock to strike upon the bell, or tolling with the clapper, will probably extend the fracture.

Third. I am confident that cutting out a piece of the bell as you suggest would not produce any sensible improvement in the tone. Such an operation upon a bell in a peal, as at Peterboro', might not be so perceptible when rung with other bells; but upon a single bell, as at Lincoln, it would be exceedingly palpable. Any attempt that may be made will be attended with great trouble and expence, and be eventually abortive.

Fourth. As you are so unfortunately placed in respect to your peal of eight in having the treble cracked and thereby reduced to the necessity of having your quarters strike offensive to the musical ear, it is difficult to recommend which of the others would be best. I should rather that would be left to the musicians of your own neighbourhood. To my fancy the 4th and 7th would be the least objectionable.

I shall now take the liberty to offer you my opinion as to the cause that has produced the misfortune to your Lincoln bell. You state that the fracture is perceivable seven inches upwards from the extremity of the skirt (besides which there is probably a still further fracture that is not perceptible to the

eye), and which, in my opinion, has been occasioned by the line of the
momentum of the clock hammer being in too perpendicular a direction
with the bell, and striking on a thinner part than the extreme thickness of
the sound ball, (sic - sound bow?) instead of having its impetus inclined to a
more horizontal position. Most likely that part of the fracture above the
sound ball was done before it extended to the skirt, at which time the tone
was very little impaired.*

It is worthy of remark that during my late visits to Lincoln I felt a disappointment in the difference of the tone to what it was when I first heard it
about twenty years ago. I thought its vibrations of shorter duration, but
then I attributed it to the possibility of age having in some degree dulled
my ear. But now I believe my faculty of earing (sic) was not impaired, but
that the fracture then existed, and has since increased to its present fatal
termination.

I will, in the course of a short period give you the desired information as
to the expense of recasting, and also the fruits of my best experience as to
the place of founding it – they require more consideration than the time,
between this and the departure of our post allows. I trust you will rest
assured of receiving, and that you will command, my best advice and services, either as regards the clock or bells.

Mr. Shaw requests his respectful compliments and the acceptance of his
thanks for your kind attention while at Lincoln.

Vale,

JOHN BRIANT.

*A note from Edward Betham was appended by Andrews as a footnote:

These observations apply I conclude, to the presumed position of the old
clock hammer, which it appears struck upon that part of the bell which is
now cracked, and which was pointed out to Mr. Briant. The clock now, and
has done for upwards of fifty years, has struck upon the opposite side of the
bell.   (Signed) E.B.

Before continuing with this correspondence, it is necessary to note the
implications of the last sentence in Briant's letter. Mr Shaw was undoubtedly Solomon Shaw, his son-in-law, who either accompanied him to Lincoln
or acted as his representative there, probably the former.

Hertford, January 8th, 1828.

Dear Sir, –- I received your second letter duly, and now proceed to answer
it. It would be of no use whatsoever to drill any hole – rely on it, no more
good would result from such an experiment than making the excision you
mentioned in your first. It is in truth a cracked bell, and my experience of
now more than upwards of half a century has never seen any remedy
applied to one, although frequently attempted, nor do I entertain the least
prophetic knowledge I ever shall; and I should be extremely sorry that any
friend of mine should make an attempt to effect what I feel convinced is
impossible to be accomplished.

In reply to the material question, contained in your first letter, as to the
probable expence (sic), and the most eligible place to recast the bell at, I
offer the following as my opinion after the most mature deliberation. It is
now upwards of a century since a bell of this magnitude has been founded,

consequently no living experience derivable from founders concerned in them is now available to guide us. We must, therefore, place our confidence for success in the account that has been handed down to us by others, aided by our own, and this will concur in giving the most decided preference to London for this reason : – We know that there is a furnace of sufficient capacity that has been PROVED over and over again, and has at all times been capable of producing that heat to the metal which is the *desideratum* for ensuring a good bell; and allow me to remind you that heat is of all things what we have most to combat with for success.

I have no fear of a good article with a proved furnace; but the great uncertainty of effecting a cast with a new one is greatly decreasing the probability of success. Not that I think it wholly impossible; and did I myself feel equal, as I have so considerable experience in building furnaces both for myself and others, I should have had no repugnance to make an attempt; but the anxiety and care it would create upon my mind would be so great as to divest me of that equanimity I find necessary to retain at my advanced years.

Exclusive of the great risk of a good cast in a new furnace, there would also be a great additional expense in consequence. A proper furnace would cost about £60, besides which there would be many incidental and necessary expences in a new place of casting, all which would be avoided if founded in London; and the expense to be considered against this is the amount of carriage. Whether water carriage is available I cannot tell, probably not. If so, and land carriage is resorted to you can be supplied with a new bell before the old one is removed, and the same conveyance that brings the new one to Lincoln can carry the old one back to London. I have made some enquiry as to the probable amount of carriage, and, from the best information I can obtain, it would be less in proportion than one to two as to the erection of a furnace. But under every consideration London is the preferable place; nor is there another furnace *now* in England sufficient to contain the requisite quantity of metal.

In confirmation of my opinion upon the difference of a new and an old furnace, we have an elucidation of it at Oxford. The great bell there had a new furnace erected to cast it in, and after casting and recasting three times, produced the worst of all the great bells in England. St. Paul's, which was recast in 1709 in London, turned out a good one the first heat – the proved furnace in London being capable of producing the requisite intenseness of heat, but which the new furnace at Oxford could not effect after three attempts. And in a work of this magnitude I submit, with great deference, no experiment ought to be tried; yet, if the Dean and Chapter should desire to have it founded in their cathedral, so far as my best judgment and experience might be rendered useful, it would be one of my highest gratifications to promote their wishes.

It would be impossible, not having particularly noticed the groined roof where you propose to take this stupendous bell up and down, and also some other matters connected with it, to state anything like an accurate sum, but I think the operation of recasting will be from £200 to £250.

In undertakings of this nature, which so seldom occur, I am exceedingly happy that it is to be effected by so liberal and learned a body as the present Dean and Chapter of Lincoln, as upon their arrangements everything depends; and I entertain no doubt a proper regard will be had to obtain the greatest excellence, in preference to adopting a system that has of late been resorted to by inferior bodies, to induce persons contracting, to execute their orders at so low a price as to sacrifice all other considerations, of which there is a notable instance recently at Liverpool.

Having myself declined founding, I hope readily to receive your assent, as well as of those concerned, that I am not influenced by any other feelings in this affair, than a most ardent desire to be instrumental in producing as good a bell as the old one, which was the most superior great bell in England, and in the attainment of which object I hope I shall not be found to shrink from any exertions. On the subject of a new or old furnace, I have personally conferred with Mr. Mears, the London founder, whose opinion and mine are in unison in this respect. Should it be thought well, we shall be happy of an opportunity to examine the place, and to confer with you upon any further steps in this business, of which you will be pleased to let me know. Any communication for the succeeding three weeks will find me, if addressed to King's College, Cambridge, where I am going to fix a new turret clock.

I am, dear Sir, most respectfully your obdt. servant,

JOHN BRIANT.

Hertford, January 15th, 1828.

Dear Sir, – I have discovered since I wrote last that my Amanuensis has fallen into an error in stating the probable expence of recasting your great bell: the expence there stated is from £200 to £250, instead of which it should have been from £200 to £240, the latter being the extreme amount I conceived it could possibly come to; even if in recasting, the next bell should come heavier that the present one; and it would be quite impossible for any founder to cast it exactly the same wt. I much regret that such a mis-statement should have occurred, but be assured it was the accidental error of the writer, and not the individual who dictated it, which my rough calculations and copy of letter will evidence. But I have discovered an error of much greater consequence, and I congratulate you, and all those interested for a *new* bell, that it is one which will show that a bell of the same weight as the present one, can be recast for considerably less than even the lowest sum already named (£200).

The error alluded to, is in the accuracy of the weight, this has been variously stated, but none of them less than 95 cwt. On referring to some observations I made twenty years ago, and which I had no opportunity of referring to when I last wrote, on account of my books and papers being at St. Albans, from whence I have just returned, I find the true diameter is 6 feet 3 ½ inches. Now, we have a mode of ascertaining the weight of bells by their diamr. up to about 5 feet 6 inches to a great nicety, and although this, which is beyond all rule that we have on account of its great diameter, yet we can ascertain sufficiently to know it cannot be any such weight as 95 cwt. I believe 88 will be the actual weight, and in this I am confirmed by the opinion of Mr. Mears, the London founder, a man who has cast more *great* bells than all his competitors have *small* ones; and he lays it at rather less. Therefore, taking into consideration the reduction in the weight of metal to be cast, and the risk to the founders is thereby reduced, I think it may be recast in London for £165, taking the weight at 88.

I have at this instant such imperious claims on my time at Cambridge, that I cannot do all I wish, and I mean, as to ascertaining the *precise weight*; but when I return, which will be in about a fortnight, I will, by taking the cubic inches of metal it contains, which I can very well ascertain, knowing the exact thickness in every part.

I am, respectfully,
JOHN BRIANT.

Even after this, the cathedral authorities did not follow his advice; they tried to cut out a piece to stop the crack spreading, with the result that Thomas Mears had to recast it in 1835, proving Briant to have been correct all along. Briant had even designed a special set of pulleys for lifting the bell, a result of his excellent mechanical training in his youth.

It was a strange situation; an old man living in an almshouse, needing a secretary to write his letters, yet still spry enough to supervise the installation of the King's College clock. This suggests that eyesight, rather than immobility, was the real problem. For delicate adjustments to the clock, good hearing and sensitive fingers were more important than sight. There could be no doubt whatsoever about his mental capacity. The letters are slightly discursive, but his meaning is abundantly plain. Moreover, his poor Amanuensis, either Solomon or Mary, got the blame for the mistakes!

Death and Memorials

It can almost be said that the old man died in harness; in 1828 the Shillington churchwardens placed an order with Briant for the recasting of their Sanctus bell. Not surprisingly, the work was contracted out to Thomas Mears of Whitechapel, whose easily-recognisible numerals are on the bell. The bill was submitted by Briant's executrix, Mary Shaw, and the receipt was dated 1 September 1829, six months after her father's death.

After the Lincoln letters, apart from the correspondence over the Datchworth lease in October, there is silence. Briant was fading out quietly, living an increasingly circumscribed existence, becoming more frail and more blind. He wanted for nothing; he was solvent and Mary was close enough to keep an eye on him. How many times was she to be seen walking briskly along St Peter's Street with a covered basket on her arm, carrying a freshly-baked pie or other treat for the old man? Several times a week at a guess.

Towards the end of February 1829, the old man's health gave cause for alarm and on the 26th, too weak or too blind to write, he dictated his will, in the presence of two surgeons and a woman who may have been a nurse at the almshouse. The presence at the bedside of *two* surgeons suggests that he was not dying of mere old age. Had that been the case, a physician would have been called in, but two surgeons implies a sudden crisis requiring a second opinion, probably a serious fall. He was not far short of his eighty-first birthday and such accidents are common.

His will is a simple, lucid document, almost certainly drawn up in the presence of a lawyer. Through it some light is shed on his years of concern for the pathetic Catherine.

I hereby constitute and appoint my daughter Mary Shaw my Executrix to discharge my just debts and I bequeath the whole of my property of whatever nature it may consist as follows Namely two thirds to my said daughter Mary Shaw and the remaining one third to my daughter Catherine Briant and I hereby appoint George Jackson Upholsterer and James Nunn Ironmonger both of Hertford the guardians of my daughter Catherine Briant and desire my Executrix to pay to each of them Twenty pounds as follows Namely Ten Pounds each at the end of the first year after my decease and the other Ten pounds each at the termination of the second year if they shall have executed their Guardianship satisfactorily to my daughter Mary Shaw

In witness thereof I have unto fixed my hand and seal

his

John X Briant

mark

Dated at Saint Albans on the Twenty sixth day of ffebruary 1829 and signed in the presence of

Richard Webster Surgeon

George Robertson Baillie Surgeon

her

Martha X Denten

mark

The copy in HALS (Ref. *D/EAS 1429*) was extracted by F.C. Austen, Proctor, Doctors' Commons and has attached to it the Certificate of Probate granted to

Mary Shaw wife of Solomon George Shaw the Daughter of the said deceased the sole Executrix. on 10th March 1829.

A marginal note reads 'sworn under Three Hundred Pounds'.

John Briant died the following day, Friday, 27 February 1829, in his eighty-first year, greatly respected and deeply mourned. His obituary notice gave an oblique reference to his religious beliefs when it said that

… from some sentiments he was known to entertain, it might be supposed that Mr. Briant's mind was imbued with the principles of the Catholic Church; however, in his latter days, the principles of the Church of England predominated; and his last moments were such, that every Christian would wish to realise.

This hints at two things; he died peacefully and he was broadminded and tolerant in his beliefs.

As he had directed he was buried in All Saints' churchyard, in the grave of his first wife, Molly and her mother, on 10 March 1829, the service being conducted by the Curate, the Revd Thomas Lloyd. Under the entry in the register is written 'From St. Albans, late of this Town, an eminent bellfounder'. The Hertford College Youths rang half-muffled in respect the same day. Henry Symondson, his friend, related that Briant 'would have one gross

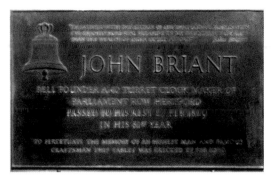

John Briant's memorial plaque in the base of the tower of All Saint's Hertford

of iron screws put into his coffin, which was done'.

The obituary notice gave a clear picture of Briant as a person.

Mr. Briant's life abounds with numerous anecdotes; he was a plain, blunt spoken man, there was never any ribaldry or foppery in his whole deportment. A reverend gentleman of this town, who had been a long admirer of his genius and industry, was expressing his regret to him a year or two ago, that he had not acquired a competency to run his carriage; when he bluntly replied, 'I don't want a carriage. I'm satisfied with the station of life that God has placed me in. I've enjoyed more real pleasure in my favourite pursuits than the wealth of India could afford.'

These words are on the bronze plaque in All Saint's, cast by the Warham Guild of London, and dedicated on the centenary of his death, on 27 February 1929, in a ceremony which consisted of a memorial service in the church in the presence of a large number of civic dignitaries, members of the East Herts Archeological Society, members of the Ancient Society of College Youths of London and members of the Hertford College Youths.

The tombstone still stands, on the north side of the churchyard, being one of the first to be passed by anyone entering from the direction of the pedestrian subway. With the building of the inner ring-road, Gascoyne Way, the increase in traffic fumes eroded the soft surface of the stone until, by 1999, it had become illegible and too friable to be moved. A new stone, laid horizontally at the foot of the original, was made as a replacement and dedicated on 13 May 2000.

The old stone read:

Mary Hanley
died December 21 ST 1790.
Aged 55 Years.
Mary Briant.Daughter of the above
died November 22 ND 1793.
Aged 33 Years.
John Briant.
Husband of the above
Mary Briant.
deceased Feb ^{RY} 27 TH 1829
in his 81 ST Year
He was a famous Bell founder,
and Clockmaker.

The last sentence was not part of the original inscription, but was added by Peck Brothers of Hertford when the stone was restored for the Centenary in 1929.

The new stone reads:

JOHN BRIANT
DECEASED 27th FEBRUARY
1829, IN HIS 81st YEAR

"HE WAS A FAMOUS
BELLFOUNDER
AND CLOCKMAKER"

The Datchworth property, then owned by Mary Shaw, is referred to in D/EAS 1430, dated 12 July 1834, when it was leased on a 500 year mortgage by Solomon George Shaw and Mary his wife (*née* Briant) and Catherine Briant, spinster, to Thomas Baron Dimsdale. It is signed by S.G. Shaw, Mary Shaw and 'The mark of Catherine + Briant', final proof if any were needed, of her incapacity. She was given as of the same address, so she appears to have settled with Mary and Solomon after the expiry of the two-year guardianship of George Jackson and James Nunn.

Either the Shaws were not so wealthy as they had been or else the small income from the lease had become insufficient to warrant the trouble of collecting it. Two or three years later, in 1837, Solomon died at his house in Cowbridge, Hertford, where he had moved after leaving St Albans.

The two respectable Hertford tradesmen appointed as guardians apparently carried out their duties satisfactorily. Little is known of George Jackson but James Nunn of Fore Street had set up shop in 1798 and was listed as churchwarden of All Saints' in 1833. One of his specialities was the hanging of small house bells which he either obtained from Briant, or may even have cast after suitable tuition from him. The Nunn family shop sign which now

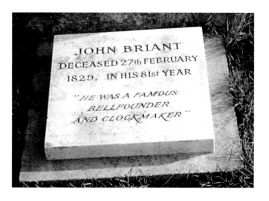

John Briant's new tombstone in Hertford, All Saints' churchyard Photo: David Harris

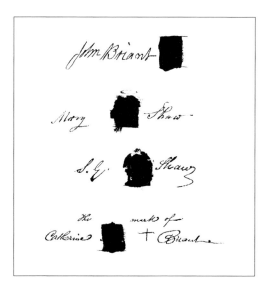

Late signature of John Briant and signatures of his family on a mortgage. Note the + for Catherine. [HALS]

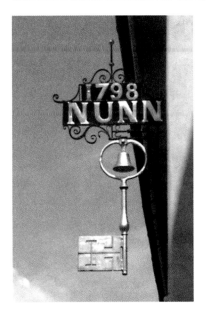

Hertford, James Nunn's shop sign

hangs outside the museum in Bull Plain consists of a key and a small bell with the date 1798.

Business Associates

H.C. Andrews included a section on people he described as 'Staff and Assistants', but who ought more properly to be described as business associates. They include bellhangers and clockmakers, including some whose role was less well-defined, although equally important. In some cases, they were the contractors for various works and Briant was the sub-contractor.

George Harman

Briant first worked with George Harman at St Mary's, Watford, in 1786, when he carried out various repairs to the frame and fittings and recast one ot the bells. At the same time Harman, of High Wycombe, a well-respected clock- and chimemaker, installed a new set of chimes. The bell-hanging did not go smoothly (*See Bell No. 21*) but that seems not to have affected the business relations between the two men as, when a new set of chimes was supplied to High Wycombe church in 1788, the work was again carried out by George Harman. This time, two new bells were required and these were cast by Briant to Harman's order. His name, and that of W. Ball, was cast on the bells, where they were called Assistants. This can be read to imply that they assisted Briant, although this is incorrect; Ball may have been Harman's assistant and they probably all helped with hanging the bells and any associated adjustments.

When in 1792, the Vestry of St Giles, Cripplegate, London, employed Harman to install a chiming machine to operate on twelve bells, Briant's name was not mentioned:

> Jan. 26, 1792. That a set of Chimes on 12 bells be put up in the steeple agreeable to the estimate now delivered by Mr. George Harman of High Wycombe in Bucks who proposes to re-cast the old Treble Bell (which is crackt) and to cast two new Bells at his own expense.
> That said Mr. Harman be employed to make the said sett of Chimes with a brass barrd barrel to play seven tunes such as the Gentlemen of the Vestry shall appoint and to re-cast the said old Bell and cast two new additional Bells agreeable to his Estimate and proposal for the sum of £400.

Harman was the contractor and Briant was plainly the sub-contractor. They appear to have worked together amicably; each knew good work when they saw it. Although at this time, Briant was busy with his own clockmaking, he did not turn down any opportunity which arose.

Henry Symondson

Symondson was a Londoner who, in a census of 1841, claimed to be sixty years old. This would have put his date of birth as 1781. As William Butler points out, however, in his recent book *Musical Handbells*, Symondson joined the Society of Cumberland Youths in 1793, the year when he rang a peal at St Sepulchre-without-Newgate. No child of twelve would have been capable of such a feat, neither would he have been admitted to the Society. It is more likely that he had been born several years earlier and that he either did not know the exact year, not uncommon before the days of compulsory registration of birth, or that he chose not to reveal it.

He married in 1800 and thereafter lived in the parish of St Giles-in-the-Fields, Holborn, for most of his life. He was a musician and specialised as a producer of musical handbells. At some time, he learned to tune tower bells and in later life carried out some bell-hanging, possibly under Briant. There is, however, no concrete evidence that he worked for Briant although they were friends and Symondson attended Briant's funeral. It is just possible that he may have done some work for Briant during Briant's final years and it is also possible that the handbells supplied to the Hertford College Youths in 1821 were cast for him by Pontifex & Wood of Shoe Lane, with whom he usually dealt, and were then tuned by him for Briant.

In 1838, long after Briant's death, Symondson supplied a set of thirty-two handbells for Benington, Herts. He discussed Briant's work with 'Squire' Leonard Proctor of Benington, a great ringer, while retuning and augmenting the tower bells there from six to eight, probably by the addition of the old third and fourth from Westmill. He is quoted as saying that 'no man took so much pains and trouble as his master in turning out superior bells in perfect tune' and that 'oftentimes he would rather lose by a job than have the reflection that he had sent out a bad bell'. The use of the word 'master' indicates that he must have worked for Briant, albeit possibly for a short time only.

It has been said that Symondson joined forces with Taylor to cast a bell for Redbourn, Herts., as the inscription read:

TAYLOR & SYMONDSON BELLFOUNDERS OXFORD LONDON & LOUGHBORO 1839.   *(one line)*

This was denied by John W. Taylor in the *Bell News* in 1900, who implied that it was cast by mutual arrangement. The bell was probably ordered through Symondson, who passed on the order to Loughborough. In his youth, Taylor had met Symondson, whom he described as 'the old gentleman', obviously a term of respect.

John Cabourn

John Cabourn, the Lincolnshire bell-hanger, whose home was at Sutterton, was also said to have been a change ringer, although his name has not been recorded in any local peals. Between 1795 and 1805 he and Briant collaborated on nine occasions, with Cabourn acting as agent for rehanging or augmenting rings of bells and with Briant again supplying bells as required on a sub-contract basis. Cabourn was born in 1738, being therefore ten years older than Briant; both being ringers, they had a great deal in common. As with Benjamin Cort and John Over, Briant included Cabourn's name on the bells, again wrongly implying that both worked at Hertford. He probably meant it as a compliment and acknowledgment for their help in obtaining these commissions. At Sutterton, Cabourn presented the treble bell, duly cast by Briant.

One thing the two men did not have in common was their attitude to money. Briant came from a reasonably well-to-do background, yet died in comparative poverty, while Cabourn began business in his early days with 'sixteen shillings gleaned in Christmas boxes' and worked up from there. He died 'after a severe and painful affliction which he suffered with patience and fortitude on 6 April 1813, aged sixty-three years', (*Gentleman's Magazine*, lxxxiv., p. 100) leaving property worth £20,000, a very tidy sum in those days. He was buried at Sutterton where his grave was marked by a plain headstone. It recorded that with much assiduity he 'carefully improved his talents'; that in him were united 'the skilful artist and scientific mechanic' and that he was 'celebrated and admired for his professional excellence as a church bellhanger.' (*H.C. Andrews*)

There are considerable discrepencies between the above account as cited by Andrews and that given by Dr J.R. Ketteringham in his newly published *Lincolnshire Bells & Bellfounders*, 2000, where Cabourn's age is more correctly given as seventy-five years and the reference to the *Gentleman's Magazine* as Volume xxxiv, p. 100, dated January 1814.

Since Andrews' day, however, the churchyard at Sutterton has been levelled and the headstone removed, hence the use of the past tense in the previous paragraph but one.

Benjamin Cort

Reference has already been made to Benjamin Cort, who is said to have given financial assistance to Edward Arnold. Andrews, following North, described him as probably a local ironmonger, while North, in the index to *C.B. Leics.*, lists him as 'Cort, B., not a bellfounder'. Both statements are correct, although they tend to give a negative image of someone who was to act as a local agent for several founders. In a trade directory of 1827, his address is given as 'Welford-place', Leicester. There is no evidence that he was in any way concerned with change ringing, but he must have had some interest in bells. To a student of industrial history, the name Cort suggests a family connection with Henry Cort who, in 1784, had successfully produced wrought iron by the puddling process. Before factory mass-production of tools and ironmongery, these items were made by local men for local use, so the term 'ironmonger' indicates someone who made as well as sold them.

The writer owes a debt of gratitude to the Leicester Record Office who so kindly provided the following information from their archives. In 1791, James Cort was listed as Ironmonger & Seedsman, Market Place, Leicester; by 1794, he had added Cutler to his list of trades. In 1805, Cort, Cort & Baston were listed as Furnishing Ironmongers, and by 1809, they had become Founders. By 1830, they had become Iron & Brass Founders. This shows a steady progression to a much broader range than the purely domestic goods with which they began. At no time did they cast bells, although several bear the name 'Cort & Co'. These can be found in both Leicestershire and Rutland.

Benjamin Cort's links with Edward Arnold led to his association with Briant. Arnold retired from founding in 1800 but continued as a bell-hanger until about 1802. The earliest Briant bells which bear Cort's name are dated 1803. If Cort were asked to supply bells, who better to approach than someone of whom Arnold had personal knowledge? This business link was of considerable benefit to Briant, who went on to cast twenty-nine bells for the county between 1803 and 1822. Previously, he had cast only one, for Shearsby in 1796. Those which he cast through Cort had Cort's name in the inscription, although Briant gave the wrong impression that he was in partnership with him, when he put JNO BRIANT AND B. CORT FECERUNT, as at Barkby. At Diseworth, he corrected this by saying JOHN BRIANT HERTFORD & B. CORT LEICESTER FECERUNT. The only other bell cast through Cort was the old 4th at Wigston Magna in 1804.

The sanctus bell at Cottesmore, Rutland, listed in the P. D. G. Dir., bears the name Cort & Co. Leicester 1831, after Briant's death, being cast by Thomas Mears of Whitechapel. No doubt Briant had recommended Mears to Cort, as Arnold appears to have done for Briant.

John Over

John Over was an established bell-hanger who lived in Rugby and whose work was to be found in Leicestershire as well as Warwickshire. Oddly for a bell-hanger, he was not a ringer. One of his contracts was for rehanging the (then) six bells at Monks Kirby, Warks., where the tenor headstock was noted by Revd H.T. Tilley as having the incised inscription 'John Over Rugby fecit 1795'. In all the cases where he and Briant collaborated, it appears to have been that Over was employed to rehang the bells, any that required recasting being subcontracted out to Briant. Their first joint work was at

Churchover, Warks., in 1803, where Briant wrongly implied that Over was working with him at Hertford, exactly the same mistake that he made with Benjamin Cort and John Cabourn. At Holy Sepulchre, Northampton, Over was the main contractor for rehanging the bells, as the Vestry Book makes plain:

On 15 April 1805, … it was ordered that a new bell [5th] be provided by the churchwardens, and that they have a levy for defraying the expenses'. On May 6th it was ordered that 'John Over of Rugby be employed for the fifth bell and also to rehang the other bells and repair the frame.' Only Briant's name appears on the bell. At Sapcote, Leics., Over's name is included, followed by the initials B.H., standing for Bell Hanger, as is the case at Nuneaton, Warks. He also hung the recast six at Stisted, Essex, in 1799. (*see Bell No.185*, note) This was well outside his normal working area.

John Waters

Waters was another respected bell-hanger whose home was at King's Sutton, Northants., where he was born in 1763. He was also a change ringer whose name appears on two peal boards in King's Sutton belfry. So far as is known, he and Briant collaborated on three occasions; at Ettington, Warks., in 1803 (*see No. 231*), where the complicated transfers from one tower to another are given in detail; at Shotteswell, 1808 (*see No. 288*) and Warmington, also Warks., in 1811 (*see No 333*). There is no ambiguity about the inscription which reads: J WATERS KING SUTTON BELL HANGER. In each case, Waters subcontracted the bell work to Briant. Waters died in 1836, aged seventy two.   *CJP* (*ref. RW9* August 2002, p. 815)

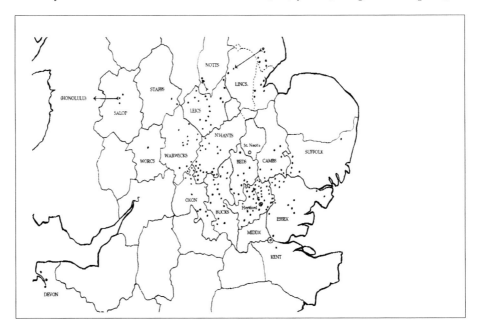

Map 11 Distribution of bells by John Briant pre-1965 counties

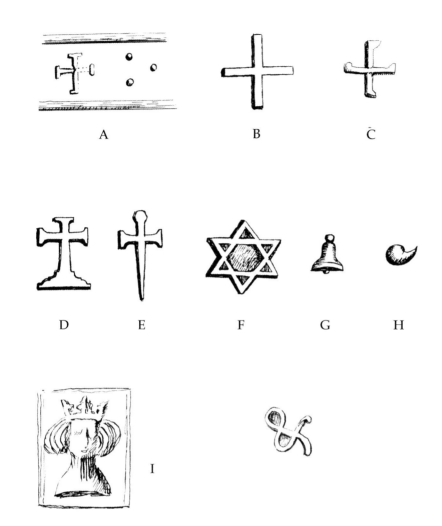

Fig. 23 John Briant Ornaments

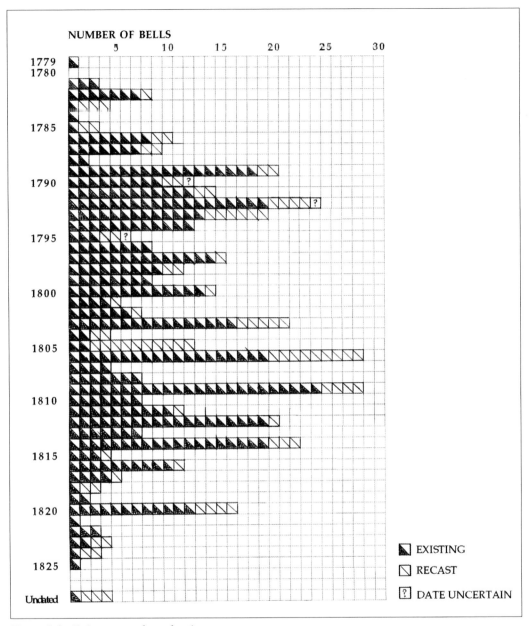

Fig. 24 John Briant annual production

16

JOHN BRIANT

CHRONOLOGICAL LIST OF BELLS

A summary of Briant's bells by counties is on p.285.

The standard ornaments are all shown on Fig. 21 and are as follows:

✝ – Fig.23$_D$ † – Fig.23$_E$ ✿ – Fig.23$_F$ ♠ – Fig.23$_G$ ➴ – Fig.23$_H$

1. 1779 CLOTHALL, Herts. Quickswood House Stables   Clock bell
   J : BRIANT HERTFORD FECIT I779. + : •
   Diameter 15″   Weight ¾ cwt   Note F#
   + – Fig.23$_A$. Not used elsewhere.
   This is Briant's earliest known bell. Quickswood House belonged to
   the Salisbury estate and was demolished in 1780 when the early 17th
   century one-handed clock was moved to the stables, where it remains.
   It is not known whether the bell ever hung in the House or was sup-
   plied direct to the stables. The bell is hung dead on a roof beam, high
   in a cupola on the steep ridge.   *Dodds, CB Herts.*

2. 1781 PIRTON, Herts. St Mary the Virgin   Treble of 5
   ABRAHAM BARBER. C: W. JOHN BRIANT HERTFORD FECIT I78I
   Diameter 29″   Weight 5 cwt   Note D
   This bell was a recast of a bell added in 1642 to make five.
            Dodds, CB Herts.

3. 1781 GREAT THURLOW, Suffolk All Saints   5th of 6
   A : GARDNER ✤ W: EAGLE C : W. JOHN BRIANT HERTFORD
   FECIT I78I.   *(one line)*
   Diameter 42¹⁄₁₆″   Weight 12 cwt 0 qr 2 lb   Note F♯
   Rehung by Mears & Stainbank in 1956, who also added a treble in
   1959.   *RWMC*

4. 1781 MUCH HADHAM, Herts. The Lordship   Clock bell
   J : BRIANT HERTFORD FECIT : SIR R^D CHASE HADHAM :
   (waist)   • : I78I : •
   Diameter 16½″   Weight 1 cwt
   The bell is hung dead in an elegant octagonal cupola over a Georgian
   stable block. A Richard Chase presented a treble to make a ring of six
   to the parish church in 1738.   *Dodds, CB Herts.*

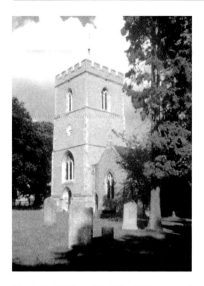

Codicote, St Giles, John Briant's first ring of bells

5. 1782 CODICOTE, Herts. St Giles   4th of 8
JOHN BRIANT HARTFORD FECIT I782
Diameter 28 ¾"   Weight 5 cwt   Note D

6. 1782 CODICOTE   5th of 8
JOHN BRIANT HARTFORD FECIT I782
Diameter 30"   Weight 5 ½ cwt   Note C

7. 1782 CODICOTE   6th of 8
JOHN BRIANT HARTFORD FECIT I782 : •
Diameter 31 ½"   Weight 6 ½ cwt   Note B

8. 1782 CODICOTE   7th of 8
JOHN BRIANT HARTFORD FECIT I782
Diameter 34"   Weight 8 cwt   Note A

9. 1782 HERTFORD, Herts. St Andrew   Treble of 8
JOHN BRIANT HARTFORD FECIT. I782 : •
Diameter 30 ¼"   Weight 6 cwt 1 qr 0 lb   Note F

10. 1782 HERTFORD   St Andrew   2nd of 8
JOHN BRIANT HARTFORD FECIT. I782 : •
Diameter 30"   Weight 5 cwt 2 qr 22 lb   Note E

11. *1782 HERTFORD St Andrew*   *Old 3rd of 8*
JOHN BRIANT HARTFORD FECIT I782 Recast by Mears & Stainbank,
Whitechapel 1876. The recsting took place at the time when the bells were trans-
ferred into the new tower, completed that year.

12. 1782 HERTFOR, St Andrew   4th of 8
JOHN BRIANT HARTFORD FECIT I782
Diameter 32"   Weight 5 cwt 3 qr 14 lb   Note C
Dodds / N & S / HCA

13. *1783 STEVENAGE Herts. St Nicholas*   *Old 3rd of 6*
JOHN BRIANT HARTFORD FECIT I783
Diameter 35"
Recast by J. Taylor & Co. 1950, inscription reproduced.

14. *1783 STEVENAGE*   *Old 5th of 6*
FULL THIRTY YEARS MY TONE I LOST.+ IN SHAPE SO NEAT I AM RECAST
BEEN BROKE AND TUMBLED DOWN. + BY BRIANT OF HARTFORD TOWN.   *AN: DOM: I783*
Diameter 41" Recast 1950, inscription reproduced.

15. *1783 STEVENAGE*   *Old tenor of 6*
JOHN BRIANT OF HARTFORD CAST ME I783 JAMES TITMUS &
W^M FIELD C : WARDENS THE REV^D MR HEN: BAKER RECTOR (one line)
Diameter 46" Recast 1950, inscription reproduced.   *Dodds, CB Herts.*

16. 1783 HATFIELD HOUSE, Herts.   Dinner bell
J: BRIANT HARTFORD FECIT I783
Diameter 22¼"   Weight 2½ cwt
This was the kitchen, or dinner bell, which used to hang in a wooden
frame in the NW turret. It is now in store in the Clerk of Works' yard.
Dodds, CB Herts.

17. 1784 DULLINGHAM, Cambs. St Mary the Virgin   Treble of 5
J: BRIANT HARTFORD FECIT I784, J : HAYLOCK & W: FROST. C:W:.
Diameter 28⅞"   Weight 5 cwt   Note D + .56 semitones.
These bells have long been unringable.   *RWMC*

18. *1785 STEVENAGE, Herts.*   *Old 4th of 6*
J : TITMUS & W : FIELD C : W. J : BRIANT : HARTFORD : FECIT : I795.
Diameter 37" Recast by J. Taylor & Co. in 1950. The inscription was
reproduced in facsimile.   *Dodds, CB Herts.*

19. 1785 SUTTON BONNINGTON, Notts. St Michael   Treble of 6
T: KIMPTON J: ROWLEY C:W. J: BRIANT HARTFORD FECIT I785
Diameter 30½"   Weight 4 cwt 3 qr 2 lb   Note C
This was the treble of the old six at Watton-at-Stone, Herts., which was
removed from Watton in 1977, when the octave from St Matthew's,
Upper Clapton, was installed in place of the old six. It was transferred
to Sutton Bonnington as a treble to augment their five to six.
Dodds, CB Herts./ CB Notts.

20. *1785 WATTON-AT-STONE*   *Old 4th of 6*
T: KIMPTON J: ROWLEY C:W. J: BRIANT HARTFORD FECIT I785
Diameter 37" This bell was removed in 1977 and sold to Whitechapel Bell
Foundry for scrap.   *Dodds, CB Herts.*

21. *1786 WATFORD, Herts. St Mary*   *Old 7th of 8*
JOHN SHACKELL & JOHN DUMMER C.W. JOHN BRIANT HARTFORD
FECIT I786   (one line)
Diameter 44¼"
Briant supplied this bell to replace one by Thomas Lester at the same time as he
was repairing the bellframe. With all the rest of the ring, it was recast by Gillett
& Johnston in 1919. The inscription was reproduced.
Extract from the Vestry Book:

November 1st . 1785. At a Vestry, holden this Day for the purpose of receiving the Proposals of such persons as shall offer, to repair the Bells, and the Frames, and also to receive an estimate of the proper repair of the Chimes – pursuant to the Order of the 4th Oct. last.

N.B. The Letter B (opposite the name of each person whose signature is appended) denotes that the person did vote in this Vestry that Jno. Briant should have the Repair of the Bells and Frame.

This was apparently carried unanimously.

Upon the Question being put whether to accept the Terms offer'd by Mr. Briant at eighty five pounds, or those offer'd by Mr. Patrick at ninety five pounds, the majority are for Mr. Briant, who engages to perform the whole business in a workmanlike manner, according to his proposals given us, together with a Model, and the principal Timber to be 12 inches by 8 inches, and the others in proportion. And to sign a proper Agreement on Stamped paper accordingly, for the sum of eighty six pounds and ten shillings.

For the work connected with the chimes, George Harman obtained the contract. From further entries in the Vestry Book it appears that all was not well with Briant's frame.

19th day of September 1786. There having been a great Fault found with the Bell Frame and the Hanging of the Bells, and several of the Parishioners objecting to Mr. Bryant's being paid unless it be altered forthwith to Satisfaction, and he being present acknowledges the Complaint to be just, and is willing to Rectify the same. It is therefore agreed to Referr the same on Behalf of the Parish to a Committee, who are Impowered to settle the same with Mr. Bryant accordingly. And Mr. Bryant agrees to Rectify what is amiss at his own Expence (sic), having allowed him sufficient Timber to raise the Frame and fixed by the Parish at their Expence for the purpose.

The 23rd October 1787. At a Vestry or Meeting this day for the purpose of considering what satisfaction ought to be made to the Bell Founder and Chime hanger for their Extra Trouble in making the Addition to the Bell Frame and Rehanging the Bells and replacing the Chimes it is ordered that: –

That Mr. Bryant be paid his bills amounting to £93 13s. 0d., vizt £86 10s. 0d. for his Contract, and £5 3s. 0d. for Additional metal to the Bell. And that if Mr. Bryant's further Charge of £3 for new   Hanging the Clock, Hammer Rods, &c., should be found reasonable, to be hereafter paid.   HCA

22.   1786 CROYDON, Cambs. All Saints   Single bell
      J : BRIANT HARTFORD FECIT I786
      Diameter 26¼"   Weight 4 cwt   Note E + .45 semitones.   RWMC

23.   1786 HATFIELD, Herts. St Etheldreda   3rd, formerly treble of 8
      JOHN BRIANT . HARTFORD FECIT. I786   *(one line)*
      Diameter 32½"   Weight 8 cwt 0 qr 10 lb   Note D

24. 1786 HATFIELD   4th, formerly 2nd
      JOHN BRIANT. HARTFORD. FEIT. I786
      Diameter 33½"   Weight 7 cwt 2 qr 7 lb   Note C#

25. 1786 HATFIELD 5th, was 3rd
JOHN BRIANT. HARTFORD. FECIT.
I786 + *(one line)*
Diam. 35" Wt.. 8 cwt 2 qr 9 lb   Note B

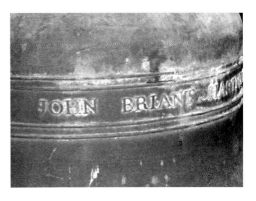

Hatfield, St Ethelreda. 4th bell. Briant cast an octave here and seven of his bells remain. *[D. E. Hannaford]*

26.   1786 HATFIELD 6th, formerly 4th
JOHN BRIANT. HARTFORD. FECIT.
I786 + *one line)*
Diam. 37" Wt. 9 cwt 0 qr 21 lb Note A
+ – Fig.23_B.

27. 1786 HATFIELD   7th, formerly 5th
JOHN BRIANT. HARTFORD. FECIT I786
Diameter 39"   Weight 10 cwt 2 qr 14 lb
Note G

28. *1786 HATFIELD*   *Old 8th, formerly 6th of 8*
Old inscription probably as above. This bell was recast by Thomas Mears of Whitechapel in 1841 and was supplied to the order of James Skerman.

29. 1786 HATFIELD   9th, formerly 7th of 8
CHARLES PRATCHETT ⅋ WILLIAM WOODWARDS. C:W. JOHN
BRIANT.HARTFORD.FECIT. I786.   *(one line)*
Diameter 46"   Weight 16 cwt 0 qr 22 lb   Note E

30. 1786 HATFIELD   Tenor
(CHARLES PRATCHETT). ⅋ WILLIAM WOODARDS. C:W. JOHN
BRIANT.HARTFORD.FECIT.I786+   *(one line)*
Diameter 52"   Weight 23 cwt 1 qr 20 lb   Note D
+ – Fig.23_B
The section of the inscription in brackets has been crudely chiselled off
for some obscure reason, probably a local feud. It is still perfectly legible, however. Charles Pratchett was the licensee of the Eight Bells, formerly the Five Bells, which had been 'augmented' by 1756, suggesting
that the ring may have been increased to eight by Thomas Lester in
1739. *(Letter in Hatfield House Archives, dated 1738; see p.179)*
                                          Dodds, CB Herts.

31. 1787 ASHWELL, Herts. St Mary the Virgin   4th of 6
T : HART ⅋ R : CHRISTY. C W. J: BRIANT. HARTFORD FECIT I787
Diameter 38"   Weight 9¾ cwt   Note G
Between the years 1787 and 1817, Briant recast four bells in this tower,
presumably as money became available. This was a recast of a bell by
Miles Graye 1610.   *Dodds, CB Herts.*

32. 1787 HUNSDON, Herts. St Dunstan   6th of 8
J LANGFILL C W THE REV ᴺᴰ W CΛLVERT RECTOR J BRIANT
HARTFORD FECIT 1787   *(one line)*
Diameter 36"   Weight 8 cwt 3 qr 8 lb   Note A
Briant must have picked up a V instead of an A in the name Calvert
and inverted it. The accurate weight was discovered in the *Herts.*
Express of 24/5/1884 by C.J. Pickford in the British Newspaper Library
in Colindale.   *CJP / Dodds, CB Herts.*

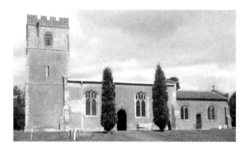

Rusheden, St Mary. A complete ring of five
by J. Briant, augmented 1976 by
Whitechapel

33. 1787 RUSHDEN, Herts. St Mary
                        2nd, formerly treble of 5
J : BRIANT. HARTFORD. FECIT. I787
Diam. 25 ¾ " Wt. 3 cwt 2 qr 20 lb   Note F

34. 1787 RUSHDEN   3rd, formerly 2nd
J : BRIANT. HARTFORD. FECIT. I787
Diam. 27"   Wt. 3 cwt 3 qr 17 lb Note E♭

35. 1787 RUSHDEN   4th, formerly 3rd
J : BRIANT. HARTFORD. FECIT. I787
Diam. 27⅝" Wt. 3 cwt 2 qr 18 lb Note D

36. 1787 RUSHDEN   5th, formerly 4th
J : BRIANT. HARTFORD FECIT. I787
Diameter 30⅜" Weight 4 cwt 2 qr 12 lb   Note C

37. 1787 RUSHDEN   Tenor
ADOLPHUS.MEETKIRK.ESQ ᴿ : BENEFACTOR.J: MALES.
CHURCHWARDEN.J: BRIANT.HARTFORD.FECIT I787   *(one line)*
Diameter 33 ½ " Weight 6 cwt 1 qr 15 lb   Note B♭
The complete Briant five were augmented to six by Whitechapel in
1976, with a treble cast from the tenor of the now-dispersed five from
Everton, Beds. *(See under Dier, p. 25)*   *Dodds, CB Herts.*

38. *1787 ST ALBANS, Herts. St Peter*   *Old treble*

RAISⅭ BY VOLUNTARY SUBSCRIPTIONS IN THE XXIIII YEAR
OF THE CHURCH WARⅭENSHIP OF CORNELIUS NICHOLLS J. BRIANT HARTFORD FECIT I787
Diameter 29⅛ "   Weight 6 cwt 0 qr 7 lb   *Note F#*

39.   *1787 ST ALBANS, St Peter*   *Old 2nd*
      CORNELIUS NICHOLLS C W J. BRIANT HARTFORD FECIT 1787
      Diameter 28 ⅞ "   Weight 5 cwt 2 qr 8 lb   Note E
      These bells were recast by Whitechapel Foundry in 1993.

                                                            Dodds, CB Herts.

40.   1788 HIGH WYCOMBE, Bucks. All Saints   3rd of 12
      JOHN BRIANT. HARTFORD. FECIT. 1788. { W. BALL. ... } ASSISTANTS.
                                          { G. HARMAN. }

      { THE GIFT OF THE EARL OF WYCOMB . . . . }
      { ELDEST SON OF THE MARQUIS OF LANSDOWN }   *(one line)*
      Diameter 30 ¼ "   Weight 6 cwt 0 qr 6 lb   Note E ♯
      John Henry, 2nd Marquis of Lansdowne was M.P. for Wycombe
      1786–90.

41.   1788 HIGH WYCOMBE   4th
      JOHN BRIANT. HARTFORD. FECIT 1788. { G. HARMAN } ASSISTANTS. ○
                                          { W. BALL ... }
      { THE GIFT OF LORD HENRY PETTY . . . . }
      { SECOND SON OF THE MARQUIS OF LANSDOWN }   *(one line)*
      Diameter 31 ½ "   Weight 6 cwt 2 qr 16 lb   Note D♯
      Lord Henry Petty became 3rd Marquis of Lansdowne in 1809. He was
      born in 1780 and was therefore only eight years old at the time of his
      'gift'.   *HCA / CB Bucks./ CJP*

42.   1789 MELBOURN, Cambs. All Saints   7th, formerly 4th of 5
      JOHN BRIANT, HERTFORD, FECIT 1789 JOHN HITCH, ESQ. C.W.
      Diameter 42"   Weight 12 cwt 2 qr 9 lb   Note F♯
      Augmented to 6 by Bowell 1913 and to 8 by Whitechapel 1987.
                                                J.G. Gipson / CB Cambs.

43.   1789 ASHWELL, Herts. St Mary the Virgin   Tenor
      W^M LEES & J^NO BALL. CHURCH WARDENS. JOHN BRIANT.
      HARTFORD. FECIT. 1789.   *(one line)*
      Diameter 47"   Weight 18 cwt 3 qr 10 lb   Note F
      This was the recast of a medieval bell inscribed ABEO NOMEN
      GABRIELIS MISSI DE COELIS.   *N & S / Dodds, CB Herts.*

44.   1789 ADDERBURY, Oxon. St Mary the Virgin   Treble of 8
      W^M BELLOW W^M GARDNER & JOHN GARDNER C WARDENS
      JOHN BRIANT HARTFORD FECIT AN DOM 1789
      Diameter 36"   Weight 8 cwt 2 qr 11 lb (?)   Note D
      Original weight 8–0–22 (sic)

45.   1789 ADDERBURY   2nd
       W : BELLOW. W : GARDNER & JOHN GARDNER C. WARDENS.
       JOHN BRIANT. HARTFORD. FECIT. 1789
       Diameter 37"   Weight 7 cwt 2 qr 23 lb   Note C#
       Original weight 9–0–1

46.   *1789 ADDERBURY*   *Old 3rd*
       Inscription probably a variant of 1 and 2 above. Original weight 9–2–22.
       Recast by G. Mears & Co. 1863.

47.   1789 ADDERBURY   4th
       W^M BELLOW W^M GARDNER & J^NO GARDNER
       CHURCHWARDENS.JOHN BRIANT HARTFORD FECIT I789
       Diameter 39"   Weight 9 cwt 3 qr 13 lb   Note A
       Original weight 10–1–25

48.   1789 ADDERBURY   5th
       W^M BELLOW. W^M GARDNER & JOHN GARDNER CHURCH
       WARDENS.JOHN BRIANT. HARTFORD. FECIT. A: D: I789
       Diameter 41"   Weight 11 cwt 0 qr 26 lb   Note G
       Original weight 11–2–21

49.   *1789 ADDERBURY*   *Old 6th*
       (Name filed off) *C WARDEN. JOHN BRIANT HARTFORD FECIT I789.*
       Original weight 13–0–18. Recast by J. Taylor & Co. in 1927.

50.   1789 ADDERBURY   7th
       W^M BELLOW W^M GARDNER & J GARDNER C WARDENS
       J BRIANT HARTFORD FECIT I789   *(one line)*
       Diameter 46"   Weight 16 cwt 3 qr 1 lb   Note E
       Original weight 17–1–26.

51.   1789 ADDERBURY   Tenor
       W^M BELLOW. W^M GARDNER. & J^No GARDNER. C: WARDENS.
       JOHN BRIANT. HARTFORD. FECIT. I789.
       VIVOS AD CAELUM MORTUOS AD SOLUM PULSATA VOCO H : B.
       Diameter 53"   Weight 24 cwt 0 qr 14 lb   Note D
       Original weight 25–3–10. Andrews, who obtained his data from H.B.
       Walters prior to 1929, quotes AN DOM on all bells. Sharpe, visiting in
       1947, agreed with this on the treble only and omitted it on 2, 4, 7 and
       tenor, but noted A: D: on the 5th. Sharpe's inscriptions are used above.
                                                   H.B.Walters / CB Oxon.

Northampton Mercury, Saturday 26 June 1790

On Monday Sen'night, a new peal of eight Bells, cast and hung by Mr. John Briant, of Hertford, were opened at Adderbury, in Oxfordshire, by the Oxford Society of Gentleman Change Ringers. They are allowed by unquestionable Judges to be a most excellent Ring of Bells. Weight of the Tenor 26 cwt. – The Fineness of the Day, and the Novelty of the Scene, brought a greater concourse of People to the Village than ever was known together by the oldest Inhabitants. – It may not be unworthy of Remark, that the Bells were rung round by eight Men, all Inhabitants of Adderbury, whose Ages together amounted to 657 Years. – On the following Day, a very pretty new Peal of five Bells, cast by the same Founder, was opened at Hanwell, a village in the same Neighbourhood. *CJP*

---

52. 1789 MOLLINGTON, Oxon.   All Saints   3rd, formerly 2nd of 5
JOHN BRIANT HARTFORD FECIT I789
Diameter c.26"   Weight 3½ cwt   Note F

53. 1789 LITTLEBURY, Essex   Holy Trinity   4th of 6
JOHN BRIANT HARTFORD FECIT I789 N PERRY
T TURNER C W. W GRETTON   COEXALTED HERE WE ARE ON HEGH
                                VI EMBLEMS OF PARISH HARMONY

Diameter 34"   Weight ?   Note A#
The parish registers of Littlebury contain the following memorandum:

> That in the month of June 1789 the inhabitants of this Parish voted unanimously the recasting of their fourth bell in the present peal and an additional Treble in commemoration of the above recorded happy event. (*i.e. the recovery of King George III*)   *CB Essex*

The word 'coexalted' does not exist. CO in the upper paired line and VI below it could stand for VICO as Bell No. 57 cast in the same year has 'W.GRETTON VIC^O' (vicar).

54. 1789 HANWELL, Oxon.   St Peter   Treble of 5
UNFEIGNED PRAISE TO HEAVENS ALMIGHTY KING.
FOR HEALTH RESTORED TO GEORGE THE THIRD WE SING. HÆC SEXTA ACCESSIT

A.D. I789. J. BRIANT. HART^D.FECIT   *(one line)*
Diameter 26"   Weight c.3 cwt   Note F
(See also No. 64)

55. 1789 HANWELL   2nd
JOHN BRIANT HARTFORD FECIT I789
Diameter 27½ " Weight c.3½ cwt   Note E♭

56.   1789 HANWELL   3rd
      JOHN BRIANT. HARTFORD. FECIT. I789.
      Diameter 28⅜"   Weight 4 cwt   Note D

57.   1789 HANWELL   4th
      EXALTED HERE WE ARE ON HIGH
      EMBLEMS OF PARISH HARMONY.   J. BRIANT. HARTFORD. FECIT I789.
      N. PERRY. T. TURNER. C.W. W. GRETTON VIC°.   (one line)
      Diameter 32½"   Weight c.5 cwt   Note C
      There is a curious similarity between these inscriptions and those of
      Littlebury. These bells were obviously in the foundry at the same time.
      Littlebury 2nd has been recast (see No. 65), but the old inscription was
      recorded and was almost the same as on this bell. Littlebury 4th (see
      above No 53) also bears the same vicar and churchwardens as this bell.
      These men had no connection whatever with Hanwell and properly
      belong to Littlebury.
      All cannons were removed by T. Bond of Burford c. 1938.
                                                          HCA / CB Oxon.
      (For the opening of these bells, on 15 June 1790, see No. 51 above)

58.   1789 OXFORD, St Ebbe's   3rd, formerly treble of 6
      J : BRIANT HARTFORD FECIT I789
      Diameter 24"   Weight 3 cwt 1 qr 12 lb   Note G

59.   1789 OXFORD, St Ebbe's   4th
      J : BRIANT HARTFORD FECIT I789
      Diameter 25"   Weight 3 cwt 2 qr 2 lb   Note F

60.   1789 OXFORD, St Ebbe's   7th
      J : BRIANT HARTFORD FECIT I789
      Diameter 28"   Weight 3 cwt 3 qr 23 lb   Note C

61.   1789 OXFORD, St Ebbe's   Tenor
      THIS PEAL WAS RAISD   BY VOLONTARY SUBSCRIPTION. H :
      RICHARDS, RECTOR. E. GOODYER, W. CLUFF C: W : J : BRIANT
      HARTFORD FECIT I789.   (one line?)
      Diameter 31"   Weight 4 cwt 3 qr 19 lb   Note B♭
      Sharpe gives J.W.CLUFF and CHURCHWARDENS in full.

62.   1790 OXFORD, St Ebbe's   5th
      J : BRIANT HARTFORD FECIT I790
      Diameter 26"   Weight 3 cwt 2 qr 24 lb   Note E♭

63. 1790 OXFORD, St Ebbe's 6th

UNFEIGNED PRAISE TO HEAVENS ALMIGHTY KING,
FOR HEALTH RESTORED TO GEORGE THE THIRD WE SING HÆC SEXTA ACCESSIT

A.D. I790. J : BRIANT. HARTFORD FECIT *(one line)*

Diameter 27" Weight 4 cwt 0 qr 12 lb Note D

64. 1790 HANWELL, Oxon. Tenor of 5

THOˢ DAVIS & SAMUEL GRANT C: WARDENS.JOHN BRIANT.
HERTFORD. FECIT. AN: DOM: I790. *(one line)*

Diameter 34⅝" Weight 7½ cwt Note B\

65. *1790 LITTLEBURY, Essex* *Old 2nd*

UNFEIGNED PRAISE TO HEAVENS ALMIGHTY KING,
FOR HEALTH RESTORED TO GEORGE THE THIRD WE SING } *HAEC SEXTA ACCESSIT.*

A.D. I790. Wᵒ GRETTON VICᵒ J :BRIANT } N.PERRY } *C.W.* *(one line)*
HARTFORD FECIT } T.TURNER }

Diameter 28" This bell was recast by John Warner & Sons, London, 1871.
A further entry in the Parish Registers (**see above** No. 53) *reads*
   '*That on the 19th March, 1790. the present peal of six bells was opened. The treble, a*
   new one, the fourth recast according to the above recorded vote. They were cast by J.
   Briant of Hartford. *HCA/ CB Essex*

66. *1790 EATON BRAY, Beds. St Mary* *Tenor of 5*

J : BRIANT HARTFORD FECIT I790 W. PEARSON MILLER. . .
R. GADSDEN SENᴿ R. ASHWELL C. WARDENS H. MORRISS
R. GADSDEN JUNᴿ OVERSEERS. *(one line)*

Diameter 43" *Height 33"* *Weight 9½ cwt* *Note A*

Recast 1913 when the ring was remodelled by Thomas Bond of Burford. The old
4th and 5th were recast into three trebles, to augment to 6. The inscription was
partially reproduced in Bond's lettering. Briant's name was omitted and the
order of names being altered to R. GADSDEN SENᴿ R. ASHWELL C.
WARDENS H. MORRISS R. GADSDEN JUNᴿ W. PEARSON MILLER
OVERSEERS. 1790 *HCA / CJP*

67. 1790 CHACOMBE, Northants. SS Peter and Paul 5th of 6

Wᴹ GIBBARD & J BENIT C.W. J.BRIANT HERTFORD FECIT I790

Diameter 38¾" Weight c.10 cwt Note G

Briant was probably recasting a bell by Henry Bagley 1694. While
working at Banbury in 1820 he had Bagley's tombstone in Chacombe
churchyard repaired at his own expense. *HCA / PDG Dir.*

68. 1790 THORPE MANDEVILLE, Northants. St John Baptist.   Treble of 3
J . BRIANT HERTFORD FECIT 1790
Diameter 26⅞ "   Weight 3 cwt 3 qr 16 lb   Note A
                                                                        HCA / PDG. Dir.

69. 1790 KELSHALL, Herts. St Faith   3rd of 5
W^M SHACKLETON. C. WARDEN . JOHN. BRIANT. HARTFORD.
FECIT. 1790
Diameter 34⅝ "   Weight 7 cwt 1 qr 6 lb   Note B
Originally, the inscription read C.WARDENS, but the S has been filed
off, leaving a gap. The tower was damaged by fire in c.1865, when two
other bells were cracked. John Taylor & Co. restored the bells in 1911,
when they gave the diameter as 32 ¾ ".   *Dodds, CB Herts.*

70. 1790 STANSTEAD ABBOTS, Herts. St James   Treble of 3
PHILIP. TRAYHERNE.C.WARDEN. JOHN.BRIANT.
HARTFORD.FECIT. 1790   *(one line)*
Diameter 30¾ "   Weight 5 cwt   Note C#
This was probably the recast of a bell by Robert Oldfield. The church is
now in the care of the Churches Conservation Trust.   *Dodds, CB Herts.*

71. *c. 1790 BAYFORD, Herts. St Mary*   *2nd of 3*
Briant's list includes an undated bell cast for Bayford. The tower contained 3
bells; the church was demolished in 1805, only a small blank bell being trans-
ferred to the new building, Briant's bell presumably being scrapped.
                                                                        HCA / Dodds.

72. 1791 ASHWELL, Herts.   Treble of 6
A HART W LILLY CW J BRIANT HERTFORD FECIT 1791
Diameter 32 ½ "   Weight 6 ½ cwt   Note D
This was a recast of a bell by Charles Newman of Haddenham, Cambs.
in 1694. That bell in its turn was probably cast, with the second, out of
the 'Great Bell' of 1599/1600, cast by Richard Holdfeld and tuned by
Robert Oldfield.   *Dodds, CB Herts.*

73. 1791 BISHOP'S STORTFORD, Herts. St Michael   3rd of 10
J BOULTWOOD & T SCOTT C W J BRIANT HERTFORD FECIT 1791
Diameter 29¾ "   Weight 6 cwt 1 qr 4 lb   Note E♭

74. 1791 BISHOP'S STORTFORD   7th of 10
J BOULTWOOD & T SCOTT C W J BRIANT HERTFORD FECIT 1791
Diameter 36¾ "   Weight 9 cwt 0 qr 18 lb   Note A♭

75. 1791 BISHOP'S STORTFORD 9th
JOHN BOULTWOOD & THOMAS SCOTT CHURCH WARDENS
JOHN BRIANT HERTFORD FECIT AN: DOM: I79I *(one line)*
Diameter 42 ½ " Weight 13 cwt 2 qr 2 lb Note F
None of the above 3 bells was new; all were recasts of bells by John
Waylett, or earlier.

Dodds, CB Herts.

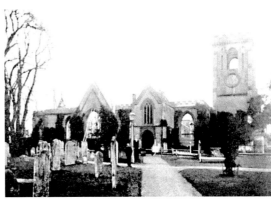

76. *1791 HERTFORD, All Saints*
Old treble of 10
JOHN BRIANT HERTFORD
FECIT AN. DOM. I79I *(one line)*
Diameter 29 ½ "

77. *1791 HERTFORD, All Saints Old 2*
RAISED BY VOLUNTARY SUB-
SCRIPTION BY HERTFORD
COLLEGE YOUTHS AN: DOM I79I

W : KIMPTON C · : · WARDENS
J : EVANS
JOHN BRIANT HERTFORD FECIT OO *(one line)*

All Saints, Hertord after fire (HALS)

These two bells augmented the eight by Pack & Chapman, 1771, to ten.
All the bells were lost in the disastrous fire of 1891. HCA / N & S

78. 1791 SWAFFHAM PRIOR, Cambs. SS Cyriac and Julietta Treble of 6
JOHN BRIANT OF HARTFORD FECIT I79I SAMUEL HART &
JOHN NUNN CHURCH WARDENS *(one line)*
Diameter 28 ⅞ " Weight 5 cwt Note E+ .08 semitones

79. 1791 SWAFFHAM PRIOR 2nd
JOHN BRIANT OF HARTFORD FECIT I79I
Diameter 30 ⅛ " Weight 5 ¼ cwt Note D+.16 semitones

80. 1791SWAFFHAM PRIOR 3rd
JOHN BRIANT HARTFORD FECIT I79I
Diameter 32 3/16 " Weight 6 cwt Note C+.16 semitones

81. 1791 SWAFFHAM PRIOR 4th
JOHN BRIANT HARTFORD FECIT I79I
Diameter 33 ⅜ " Weight 6 ¾ cwt Note B+.14 semitones

82. 1791 SWAFFHAM PRIOR 5th
JOHN BRIANT HARTFORD FECIT I79I
Diameter 35 ¼ " Weight 7 ¾ cwt Note A+.29 semitones

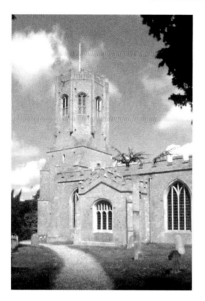

Swaffham Prior, SS Cyriac and Julietta, Cambs. Bells from adjacent ruined church tower of St Mary and here were recast by Briant into the present 6 bells

83. 1791 SWAFFHAM PRIOR   Tenor
JOHN BRIANT HARTFORD FECIT 1791. SAMUEL
HART & JOHN NUNN. CHURCH WARDENS.
(one line)

Diameter 39¼" Weight 10 cwt Note G exactly.
This was a major commission for Briant. The tower of
St Mary's church had been struck by lightning a few
years previously, the upper stages being ruined and
the bells being presumably damaged or destroyed.
These bells, and those from the adjacent church of St
Cyriac, were recast to form a new six which were
hung in the octagonal tower of the latter church, the
body of which was in poor condition and needed
rebuilding in 1809–11. It again fell into ruin in the
1960s, but the tower remained sound. St Mary's was
in use but, as its tower was still in ruins, the bells
were, and are, rung in one church for the other. St
Cyriac is now in the Churches Conservation Trust
and has been exquisitely restored for concerts and
exhibitions. The upper stages of the tower of St
Mary's have also been rebuilt, although it has no
bells. The two towers, side by side, form an unforgettable picture. The
bells, a fine six, were restored to their original condition by the Trust in
1989, with plain bearings and old-style fittings. There is also a clock
bell of 1798 (*see below No.*177)   *Dr M. Stanier / RWMC*
The following receipt was made known to the writer by the kindness
of Robert Walker of Histon. (*Ref. CRO Cambs. P*150/5/4)

> Rec^d, 16th April 1795 of
> Mr Samuel Hart Sixteen Pounds
> and three Pence being the Ballance
> in full of a Bill deliver'd for Recasting
> the Church Bells
>   £16 – 0^s – 3 Ent^d   John Briant   *R. Walker*

84.   1791 BYFIELD, Northants. Holy Cross   Tenor of 8
W^M COX & W^M THORNTON C.W. J. BROMLEY & J. SMITH
OVERSEERS J. BRIANT HARTFORD FECIT 1791.   *(one line)*
Diameter 43"   Weight 12 cwt 1 qr 17 lb   Note F#
H.C. Andrews records this as the tenor of five. Barwell augmented
these to six in 1905 and Whitechapel to eight in 1991.   *HCA / PDG. Dir.*

85. 1791 WARDINGTON, Oxon. St Mary Magdalen   2nd
W^M COLE & R^D GOODMAN C W J BRIANT HARTFORD FECIT 1791
Diameter 34⅛"   Weight 7½cwt   Note B
Briant lists this bell as No.2. These bells were rehung and retuned by J.
Taylor & Co. 1998/9 as a Millennium Project. (*see No. 143*)

HCA / CB Oxon.

86. 1792 HEADINGTON, Oxford   St Andrew   3rd, formerly treble
JOHN BRIANT HERTFORD FECIT 1792.
Diameter 27¼"   Weight 4 cwt 0 qr 5 lb   Note F
Canons removed. F. Sharpe on p. 159 of *CB Oxon.* noted in 1933 that
all the bells retained their cannons but that this bell had no argent, a
curious state of affairs. The ring has had several restorations and alterations since that date, in 1967 by F. White of Appleton when the cannons may have been removed; in 1974 when two trebles were added
by Whitechapel and again in 2000 when the 'new' trebles were recast,
the bells were tuned at Whitechapel and further rehanging was carried out by White's. The new weight as quoted in the *Ringing World*
2 February 2001, p. 106 is now 3 cwt 2 qr 22 lb.

87. 1792 HEADINGTON   5th, formerly 3rd
JOHN BRIANT HARTFORD FECIT 1792.
Diameter 29"   Weight 4 cwt 0 qr 2 lb   Note D♭
The weight is now stated to be 4 cwt 0 qr 0 lb. (*RW as above*)

HCA / CB Oxon.

88. 1792 CODICOTE, Herts   Tenor
J : ᗺRIANT HERTFORD FECIT 1792
Diameter 38¼"   Weight 10 cwt   Note G
Briant recast nos. 2, 3, 4 and 5 in 1782. Whether he cast this bell at the
same time and later found it to be unsatisfactory is not known. His list
merely says that he cast five bells but gives no dates. Since 1997, it has
been the tenor of eight. The B of Briant is inverted.

Dodds, CB Herts.

89. 1792 BENINGTON, Herts. St Peter   3rd of 8
JOHN:COCK:C:WARDEN:VOCE:TENUI:DULCE:CANO:1792:
JOHN:BRIANT:HERTFORD:FECIT:1792   (one line)
[THOUGH SMALL MY VOICE I SWEETLY SING]
Diameter 30"   Weight 5¼cwt   Note D#

Dodds, CB Herts.

90. 1792 BRENT PELHAM, Herts. St Mary the Virgin   5th of 6
     J : BRIANT HARTFORD FECIT : I792 J : WOODLEY C : WARDEN
     Diameter 33″   Weight 6 cwt 2 qr 15 lb   Note B
     Numbers 3 and 4 of the ring are by Miles Graye II, while the tenor is
     by Miles Graye I, suggesting that the 5th was also by one or other of
     the Grayes before recasting by Briant. The ring was augmented by J.
     Taylor & Co. in 1960 and 1964, hence the accurate weights.

     Dodds, CB Herts.

91. 1792 FURNEUX PELHAM, Herts. St Mary the Virgin   Tenor of 6
     J : BRIANT HARTFORD FECIT I792 J : PORTER C : WARDEN
     Diameter 39³⁄₁₆″ Weight 10 cwt 1 qr 10 lb   Note G
     This ring was rehung, tuned and weighed by J. Taylor in 1981.

     Dodds, CB Herts.

92. 1792 STANDON, Herts. St Mary   5th of 6
     J :BRIANT :HERTFORD :FECIT: I792 :W : BIGG : J : SNOW:C :
     WARDENS: *(one line)*
     Diameter 41⁷⁄₁₆″ Weight 11 cwt 3 qr 0 lb   Note F#
     The cannons were removed, all bells tuned and weighed by
     Whitechapel in 1994, before rehanging by Eayre & Smith.

     Whitechapel / E & S

93. 1792 WARE, Herts. St Mary the Virgin   3rd of 8
     J. PROCTOR J. EDWARDS C : W: J.BRIANT HARTFORD FECIT I792
     Diameter 34⅛″   Weight 8 cwt 0 qr 5 lb   Note C

94. 1792 WARE, Herts.   5th
     JOHN PROCTOR JAS. EDWARDS C:WARDENS JOHN BRIANT
     HERTFORD FECIT I792   *(one line)*
     Diameter 39½″   Weight 11 cwt 2 qr 6 lb   Note A♭
     Bells rehung by Whitechapel, 1977.   *Dodds, CB Herts.*

95. *1792 ST ALBANS, Cathedral and Abbey Church of St Alban   Old treble of 8*
     REVᴰ JOS SPOONER WILLM BENNIWORTH JAˢ WALLIS T PYGOTT
     CHURCHW ' J. BRIANT HERTFORD FECIT I792   (from a rough note)
     Weight 6 cwt. 1 lb.
     This bell was recast by Briant from a bell by Richard Phelps of 1730, which
     cracked in 1792. H.C. Andrews quotes its weight as 6 cwt 1 lb. The cannons
     were broken by bumping the stay during the ringing of the 7 o'clock peal on
     Sunday, 13 December 1829. Holes were drilled in the crown and the bell bolted
     to the headstock. It remained in this condition for a short while until the crown
     cracked. Ringing ceased for some years and the bell was sent to Whitechapel in
     1844, when the received weight was quoted as 5–2–14. It was recast by C.& G.

Mears in 1845. This unfortunate bell was again recast by Mears & Stainbank
in 1901.   *Bell News / St Albans Cathedral Archives*

96.   1792 CITY OF LONDON, St Giles, Cripplegate   Old Treble of 12
JOHN BRIANT HERTFORD FECIT 1792 THO^S WILLATS & THO^S SMITH
C. WARDENS   *(one line)*
Diameter 28"   *Weight c.6 cwt*

97.   1792 CRIPPLEGATE   Old 2nd
JOHN BRIANT HERTFORD FECIT 1792 THO^S WILLATS & THO^S SMITH
C. WARDENS RECAST 1908 VICAR : PREB. A BARFF
CHURCHWARDENS : STEPHEN ROGERS JOHN BADDELEY.
WARNER & SONS, LONDON, 1908
Diameter 29"   *Weight 6 cwt 0 qr 1 lb 14 oz*

98.   1792 CRIPPLEGATE   Old 3rd
This bell had the same inscription as the treble.
Diameter 30"   *Weight 6 cwt 0 qr 3 lb*
All three bells were destroyed by bombing in 1940.
This contract came to Briant rather than Whitechapel as a result the installation
of a new set of chimes by George Harman of High Wycombe. see p.000
                                        H.B. Walters / HCA

99.   1792 POTTERSPURY, Northants. St Nicholas   4th, formerly 3rd of 5
JOHN : BRIANT : HERTFORD : FECIT: 1792 : JOHN : ROPER : C.
WARDEN.   *(one line)*
Diameter 38"   Weight 9 cwt 3 qr 24 lb   Note G#
                                        HCA / PDG Dir.

100.   1792 DUNCHURCH, Warks. St Peter   Tenor of 6
I TO THE CHURCH THE LIVING CALL
AND TO THE GRAVE DO SUMMON ALL JOHN BRIANT HERTFORD FECIT AN :
DOM : 1792 W^M SMITH T: SUTTON J. & W^M BARNWELL C :
WARDENS. HENRY BROMFIELD VICAR.
Diameter 46¾"   Weight 17 cwt 0 qr 8 lb   Note E
Churchwardens' accounts record :
   1792 July 1 Mr. Briant of Heartford for Recasting the Tenor Bell per
   Contract £32 10s.

Weight of the Old Bell	16–3– 0	
New Metal added	1–1–10	
Weight of the Tenor	18–0–10	
To 1-1-10 New Metal at 13d per lb		8 : 2 : 6
		40 : 12 : 6

   April 21   My expences going to Hartford after the Bell £ 2 . 2 . 0
                                        CB Warks./ CJP

101. 1792 NEWBOLD-ON-AVON, Warks. St Botolph 5th, formerly treble of 6
      EX : DONO : REV : J : O • GLORY• TO • GOD • IN THE HIGHEST:
      J. BRIANT. HERTFORD : FECIT : 1792 ⚑
      Diameter 29½"   Weight 5cwt 0 qr 26 lb   Note D#
      This appears to be the earliest recorded use of the small bell decoration, *Fig.*23$_G$.

102. 1792 NEWBOLD   6th, formerly 2nd
      J : BRIANT : HERTFORD FECIT 1792
      Diameter 30⅞"   Weight 5 cwt 3 qr 4 lb   Note C#

103. 1792 NEWBOLD   7th, formerly 3rd
      JOHN BRIANT HERTFORD FECIT. 1792 :.
      Diameter 33½"   Weight 6 cwt 2 qr 9 lb   Note B
      The third figure of the date is an 8 which has been altered to make a crudely shaped 9, i.e. wrongly stamped as 1782 and altered to 1792.

                                                           CJP

104. 1792 NEWBOLD   8th, formerly 4th
      J : BRIANT : HERTFORD FECIT 1792
      Diameter 33⅞"   Weight 7cwt 0 qr 20 lb   Note A#

105. 1792 NEWBOLD   9th, formerly 5th
      J : BRIANT : HERTFORD . FECIT . 1792 . GLORIA : DEO IN .
      EXCELSIS   *(one line)*
      Diameter 37¾"   Weight 9 cwt 1 qr 6 lb   Note G#

106. 1792 NEWBOLD   Tenor
      J : PARKER : VICAR : T : COMPTON : J : NORMAN : ⅋ R : WEBB : C
      : WARDENS   *(first line)*
      VIVOS AD CÆLUM : MORTUOS : AD : SOLUM : PULSATA : VOCO : J : BRIANT :
      HERTFORD : FECIT . 1792 *(second line)*
      Diameter 41¼"   Weight 12 cwt 0 qr 1 lb   Note F#
      Prior to 1792, there were four bells, which Briant recast into six. The name of Rev. J.O. on the treble refers to the Revd J. Olney, a member of a family long connected with the parish. The weights are as given when the bells were retuned by J. Taylor in 1929. Two trebles cast from the metal of the dispersed ring from Everton, Cambs., were added to make eight in 1977 and two new bells added to make ten in 1992.

                                                CB Warks./ CJP

107. 1792 STONELEIGH, Warks. St Mary   5th, formerly 4th of 5
      J : JUDD ⚹ J : SIMPSON C : WARDENS J : BRIANT HARTFORD
      FECIT 1792   *(one line)*
      Diameter 35"   Weight 7 cwt 3 qr 2 lb   Note A
      Briant's list calls this No. 2. He was recasting a 14th century bell, possi-
      bly by John Rufford. Weight as retuned by J. Taylor 1956; augmented to
      6 in 1962, also by Taylor.   *CB Warks./ CJP*

108. 1793 ASHOW, Warks. Assumption of Our Lady   Treble of 4
      J BRIANT HARTFORD FECIT 1793
      Diameter 23¾"   Weight c.3 cwt   Note E

109. 1793 ASHOW   2nd
      J : BRIANT HARTFORD • FECIT 1793
      Diameter 23⅞"   Weight c.3¼ cwt   Note D#
      This bell has been heavily skirted to sharpen the pitch.

110. 1793 ASHOW   3rd
      J · BRIANT HARTFORD · FECIT : 1793 : W^M ·BADAMS · C · WARDEN :
      Diameter 28⅜"   Weight c.5½ cwt   Note C#

111. 1793 ASHOW   Tenor of 4
      JOHN BRIANT HARTFORD FECIT 1793 J HIORONS C WARDEN
      Diameter 31"   Weight c.7 cwt   Note B
      Casting fault in crown, cannons missing. Nos.1, 3 and 4 are maiden
      bells. Extensive rebuilding, including the South wall of the nave took
      place in this year, so the bell restoration was part of a larger pro-
      gramme of works.   *CJP*

112. 1793 LEEK WOOTTON, Warks.   All Saints   Treble
      THE GIFT OF THE HON^BLE MARY LEIGH. J. BRIANT HERTFORD
      FECIT 1793.   *(one line)*
      Diameter 26¼"   Weight 3 cwt 3 qr 24 lb   Note E

113. 1793   LEEK WOOTTON   2nd of 5
      THE GIFT OF THE HON^BLE MARY LEIGH. J. BRIANT HERTFORD
      FECIT 1793.   *(one line)*
      Diameter 27¾"   Weight 4 cwt 0 qr 18 lb   Note D
      Weights as supplied in 1793.
      Briant's bill survives among papers relating to the rebuilding of the
      church. It lists £49. 5. 10. for the bells, £10 for the hanging, plus carriage
      via London and Coventry £1. 4. 5. giving a total of £60. 10. 3.
          The Honble Mary Leigh, a noted benefactress to several local
      churches, was a member of the Leigh family from Stoneleigh Abbey.
      (*See No 114 overleaf*).   *CB Warks.*

114. 1793   WALLINGTON, Herts. St Mary   4th of 6
J•BRIANT•HARTFORD•FEIT•I793 :THE HON^{BLE}   MA...Y L... .. ...H
BENE...AC...RESS . W^M BADAMS :   ...WARD...N *(one line)*
Diameter 30⅛"   Weight 5 cwt 0 qr 17 lb   Note C
The first section of the inscription, from 'J' to '1793' is intact, but the
following part has been professionally filed off. A squeeze of the filed-
off section has revealed enough letters to reconstruct most of the miss-
ing words, with exception of the letters shown as dots. This showed
that the bell was not originally cast for Wallington, but for a church in
Warwickshire, as the Honble Mary Leigh appears on the treble at Leek

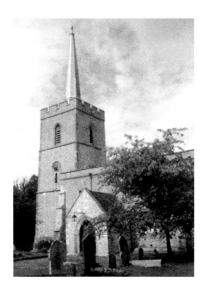

Wootton and Wm Badams on the third at Ashow.
Mary Leigh was benefactress at both places, but
Badams was named at Ashow and not Leek Wootton.
Furthermore, the use of Hartford, as at Ashow, rather
than Hertford, as at Leek Wootton, makes it safer to
assign this bell to Ashow. Briant had already had
trouble with the second there as it had required
heavy skirting, so it is possible that, rather than have
to tune thethird in the same way, he put it on one
side awaiting another suitable contract.

Dodds, CB Herts., amendment

115. 1793 COTTERED, Herts. St John the Baptist
Treble of 5
J • BRIANT HARTFORD FECIT I793 W^M •
GUTTERIDGE : C W: *(one line)*
Diam. 29¾"   Wt. 4 cwt 2 qr 24 lb   Note C#

Cottered, St John the Baptist; Briant recast
two treble bells

116.   *1793 COTTERED*   *Old 2nd*
*This bell was cast at the same time as the treble, but was
recast by Thomas Mears II of Whitechapel in 1841.*
Dodds, CB Herts.

117.   1793 HERTFORD, St Andrew   6th of 8
JOHN BRIANT HERTFORD FECIT I793
Diameter 36½"   Weight 8 cwt 3 qr 0 lb   Note A

118.   1793 HERTFORD, St Andrew   7th
JOHN BRIANT HERTFORD FECIT 1793
Diameter 39"   Weight 10 cwt 2 qr 7 lb   Note G
It is not clear whether Briant was recasting some of his own bells of
1782, or two of the 'four small bells' recorded by Sir Henry Chauncy in
1700.   *Dodds, CB Herts*

119.　*1793 WHITTLESFORD, Cambs. SS Mary and Andrew*　　　*Old tenor*
JOHN BRIANT HARTFORD FECIT. I793. R. WHISKIN S. BARNES C.
WARDENS　　*(one line)*
Recast by Mears & Stainbank 1905.
As an interesting sideline, the name 'Whiskin Close' has been given to a new
cul-de-sac of houses built on the land which the Churchwarden used to farm.
　　　　　　　　　　　　　　　　　　　　　　　　Jean Sanderson / I. Hinton

120.　*1793 CLAYPOLE, Lincs. St Peter*　　　　　　　　*3rd of 5*
PATMAN BRIGGS & W^{M} GRIMSHAW C : WARDENS JOHN BRIANT
HERTFORD ANNO DOM I793　　*(one line)*
Diameter 31"　　Weight 6 cwt 0 qr 27 lb　　　　*Note A#*
Recast by J. Taylor & Co. 1907.　　　　　　　　*GAD / CB Lincs.*

121.　*1793 KING'S SUTTON, Northants. SS Peter and Paul*　　*Treble of 8*
THE GIFT OF HENRY SMYTH ESQ. OF CHARLTON JOHN BRYANT
HERTFORD I793　　　　　　　　　　　　*(one line)*
Diameter 27"　　Weight 4 cwt 3 qr 23 lb　　　*Note G*

122.　*1793 KING'S SUTTON*　　　　　　　　　　　　*2nd*
THE GIFT OF HENRY SMYTH ESQ. OF CHARLTON JOHN BRYANT
HERTFORD I793　　　　　　*(one line)*
Diameter 27¾"　　　　　　*Weight 4 cwt 3 qr 14 lb*　　*Note F#*
Henry Smyth was a keen ringer. The King's Sutton ringers rang peals
in 1799 and 1802. H.C. Andrews, quoting from North's *CB Northants*,
states that the peal boards are in the belfry at Charlton, but there is no
place of that name in the locality which possesses a ring of bells. It
must be an error for King's Sutton.
HCA / PDG Dir.

123.　*1793 GODINGTON, Oxon. Holy Trinity*　　　　　*Sanctus*
J : B : (ornament) I793 :
Diameter 11"　　Weight c.40 lb
This very small bell hangs in an inaccessible position in the east
window of the tower. The inscription can only be felt with the finger-
tips.
　　　　　　　　　　　　　　　　　　　　　　　　HCA / CB Oxon.

124.　*1793 WHEATLEY, Oxon. St Mary*　　　　　　　*Tenor*
JOHN BRIANT. OF HERTFORD. FECIT. I793. GLORIA DEO IN
EXCELSIS ○○ ○ ○　　　　*(one line)*
Diameter 37½"　Weight c 9 cwt　　　　*Note A♭*
○ ○ ○ ○ – *four coins. This was a poor bell and was recast by Whitechapel in*
1996; present weight 9–3–10.

125.	*1793 TUAM, Galway	St Mary's Cathedral*
THE GIFT OF JOSEPH DEAN BOURKE LORD ARCHBISHOP OF
TUAM TO THE CATHEDRAL OF ST. MARY'S TUAM
EDMOND BURTON ARCHDEACON OF TUAM GLORIA IN EXCEL-
SIS
JOHN BRIANT OF HARTFORD IN ENGLAND. FECIT. AN DOM
1793
Weight quoted as 18 cwt.
The bell was 'irreparably injured' in 1892. Recorded on a board in the Dean's
Vestry.						*HCA p. 128.*

126.	*1793 BARKING, Essex St Margaret*				Old 6th
JOHN LAMBERT & JOHN HOMER C: WARDENS. JOHN BRIANT OF
HERTFORD FECIT 1793		*(one line)*
Diameter 40"
Recast, with others of the ring, by J. Warner & Sons in 1886.
CB Essex

(1794 BARKING.						*Nos. 2–5*
These bells appeared in Briant's list, but there is no evidence that they were ever
cast.)

127.	1794 GREAT HALLINGBURY, Essex St Giles			Tenor of 5
J . BRIANT HARTFORD . FECIT . 1794 . W^M BINCKS . C: W:
Diameter 39½"	Weight 10 cwt 2 qr 25 lb		Note G
								CB Essex

128.	1794 GREAT TEY, Essex St Barnabas				4th of 8
JOHN BRIANT HARTFORD FECIT 1794
Diameter 32"	Weight 6 cwt			Note C#

129.	1794 GREAT TEY						5th of 8
JOHN BRIANT HARTFORD FECIT 1794
Diameter 34"	Weight 7 cwt			Note B

130.	1794 GREAT TEY						6th of 8
J . HARRINGTON & J . COCK C WARDENS JOHN BRIANT
HARTFORD FECIT 1794		*(one line)*
Diameter 36"	Weight 8½ cwt			Note A#
All three bells have the 4 of the date lying on its back.	*CB Essex*

131.	1794 WALLINGTON, Herts. St Mary		2nd, formerly treble of 5
: JOHN • BRIANT • HARTFORD • FECIT • 1794
Diameter 28"	Weight 4 cwt 1 qr 20 lb		Note E♭

132. 1794 WALLINGTON   3rd, formerly 2nd
JOHN BRIANT HARTFORD FECIT
I794
Diam. 29⅝"Wt. 4 cwt 2 qr 21 lb Note D♭

133. 1794 WALLINGTON   5th, formerly 4th
: J · BRIANT HARTFORD FECIT I794
Diam. 33¹³⁄₁₆" Wt. 6 cwt 3 qr 14 lb Note B♭

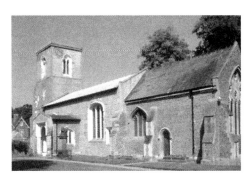

Wallington, St Mary. Briant recast four and
added a treble but the third was cast the
year before, originally for Ashow,
Warwickshire.

134. 1794 WALLINGTON   Tenor
T · SISSON RECTOR. W · DRAPER
C : WARDEN E : FOSSEY. J : FOSSEY. AND
J : SELL . BENEFACTORS • JOHN BRIANT
HARTFORD FECIT · I794   *(one line)*
Diameter 36⅝"   Weight 8 cwt 1 qr 25 lb   Note A♭
As with Great Tey, above, the 4 of the date on this bell is lying on its
back. These excellent bells were augmented to six by Mears &
Stainbank in 1932.   *Dodds, CB Herts.*

135. 1794 WHEATLEY, Oxon. St Mary   2nd
J. BRIANT HERTFORD. FECIT. I794 :
Diameter 28"   Weight 4 cwt 2 qr 25 lb   Note E♭

136. 1794 WHEATLEY   3rd
JOHN BRIANT HARTFORD. FECIT. I794 :
Diameter 29½"   Weight 5 cwt 1 qr 25 lb   Note D♭

137. 1794 WHEATLEY   4th
• J : BRIANT HERTFORD : FECIT : I794 :
Diameter 31½"   Weight 5 cwt 1 qr 0 lb   Note C

138. 1794 WHEATLEY   5th
: J : BRIANT HERTFORD. FECIT. I794 : GLORIA DEO IN EXCELSIS :
Diameter 33⅞"   Weight 6 cwt 3 qr 27 lb   Note B♭
                                                      CB Oxon.

139. *1795 KENILWORTH, Warks. St Nicholas*   *Old treble*
SAM BUTLER R RUSSELL C W JOHN BRIANT HERTFORD FECIT I793
This bell was recast by J. Taylor & Co. in 1875. Inscription not reproduced.
Briant's list refers to this place as Kilingworth. The date is as quoted in error by
H.T. Tilley in 1874. There are no entries in the churchwardens' accounts in
1793, but in 1796 is recorded:

1796 21 January paid to Mr Bryant for New Bell   £ 17 . 5 . 0
    Expences at the same time   8s. 4d
    John Over the bell hanger is not mentioned, but his list of works states.
    Kenilworth – the treble recast in 1795 and hung in 1796.   CJP

140. *1795 SAWBRIDGEWORTH, Herts. St Mary the Great*   *Old tenor*
    THE REV^D JOHN LANE VICAR. RICH^D ALGER & SAM GORROD C:W:
    JOHN BRIANT HERTFORD FECIT 1795 STATUTEM EST OMNIBUS
    SEMEL MORI   *(one line)*
    Diameter 52"   *Weight c.25 cwt*   *Note D*
    This bell was recast by J. Taylor & Co. in 1964. The inscription was reproduced
    in facsimile.   *Dodds, CB Herts.*

141. 1795 CLAYPOLE, Lincs.   Treble
    RAIS'D BY SUBSCRIPTION : J : BRIANT & : J : CABOURN
    HERTFORD FECERUNT 1795   *(one line)*
    Diameter 29⅝ " Weight 5 cwt 0 qr 25 lb   Note C#
                                    HCA / CB Lincs.

142. 1795 CUDDESDON, Oxon. St Peter.   Treble
    THE GIFT OF DR. E. SMALLWELL BPT OF OXFORD & c JOHN
    BRIANT HERTFORD FECIT AN : DOM : 1795.   *(one line)*
    Diameter 30″   Weight 5 cwt 2 qr 0 lb   Note D
                                   HCA / CB Oxon.

143. 1795 WARDINGTON, Oxon.   3rd of 6
    : J : BRIANT HERTFORD FECIT. 1795 :
    Diameter 37¼ "   Weight 8 cwt 2 qr 0 lb   Note A
    Wardington bells were retuned and rehung in 1969.
                            RW / HCA / CB Oxon.

144. *c.1795 KIRTON, Lincs.*
    Briant's list includes No. 4 of a peal of six at Kirton; but at neither Kirton-in-Holland nor Kirton-in-Lindsey, can any bell now be identified as his casting. At the former church the peal of eight was cast by T. Mears and hung by J. Cabourn in 1807, replacing a peal of five. It has been suggested that Briant assisted Cabourn in connection with No. 4, as they had already collaborated at Claypole, Coningsby, Frampton, Hagworthingham, Horbling, Moulton All Saints, Sibsey, Stickney and Sutterton. At Kirton-in-Lindsey the peal of six was cast by James Harrison of Burton (Barton-on-Humber) in 1798. The position of this item in Briant's list suggests a date about the year 1795.
    HCA, p. 61.

145. 1796 NETHER WINCHENDON, Bucks. St Nicholas   Treble of 5
JOHN BRIANT HERTFORD FECIT I796 THOMAS ROSE CHURCH
WARDEN   *(one line)*
Diameter 30 ¼ "   Weight 5 cwt 0 qr 18lb   Note G
This inscription is not in the inscription band, but on the sound bow.
Several of Briant's later small bells also have this feature. Tuned by
Whitechapel 1979, when the bells were rehung by White of Appleton.
CB Bucks./ CJP

146. 1796 GREAT CHESTERFORD, Essex All Saints   Treble of 6
JOHN BRIANT OF HERTFORD FECIT I796
Diameter 28"   Weight 5 cwt 0 qr 5 lb   Note E

147. 1796 GREAT CHESTERFORD   2nd
JOHN BRIANT OF HERTFORD FECIT I796
Diameter 28 ¾ "   Weight 5 cwt 0 qr 26 lb   Note D

148. 1796 GREAT CHESTERFORD   3rd
JOHN BRIANT OF HERTFORD FECIT I796
Diameter 31"   Weight 6 cwt 0 qr 25 lb   Note C

149. 1796 GREAT CHESTERFORD   4th
JOHN BRIANT OF HERTFORD FECIT I796
Diameter 32 ½ "   Weight 6 cwt 3 qr 10 lb   Note B

150. 1796 GREAT CHESTERFORD   5th
JOHN BRIANT OF HERTFORD FECIT T FISHER CURATE
Diameter 34 ¾ "   Weight 7 cwt 0 qr 16 lb   Note A

151. 1796 GREAT CHESTERFORD   Tenor
JOHN BRIANT OF HERTFORD FECIT I796 W^M KENT ⚒
J. WAKEFIELD C : W. J : PLUMPIN. VICAR. STATUTUM EST
OMNIBUS MORI   *(one line)*
Diam. 38"   Wt. 10 cwt 1 qr 10 lb   Note G
Rebuilding of the tower was begun in 1792,
so that recasting the bells was part of a
larger project. These are listed in *Dove's
Guide* as unringable, a situation that has
persisted for many years. Deedes and Walters describe the belfry as 'very dirty and
some of the timbers are shaky'. That was in
1909. In July 2001 the writer noted that an
Ellacombe chiming apparatus had been
installed at some date and that a lightweight

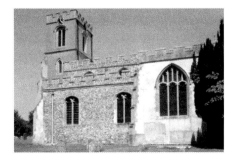

Great Chesterford, All Saints, Essex

chiming rope, probably for the Ting-Tang mentioned below, appeared
to be the only item in use.

A parish record says 'the new peal of bells came home 19 Nov. 1796'.
An item in the churchwardens' accounts referring to the recasting reads:

1790 March 16, paid for taking down of bells ...   £3   15   0
1793 Paid for hanging the Ting-Tang
1797 Feb. 25 paid Mr. Briant ....   £ 21   10   0
1798 April 9 paid for hanging the Ting-Tang and rope

HCA / CB Essex

152.   1796 SHEARSBY, Leics. St. Mary Magdalen   3rd of 4
JOHN BRIANT OF HERTFORD FECIT I796
Diameter 30½ "   Weight 5 cwt 1 qr 5 lb   Note – ?
Briant's list gives this bell as No. 2. North in *CB Leics.* quotes an old
tradition that the present treble formerly hung in the ruined church at
Knaptoft, which would explain the discrepency. It is also said that the
third bell was previously inscribed 'Maria', so that Briant was recasting
a medieval bell.   *CB Leics.*

153.   1797 BARKWAY, Herts. St Mary Magdalene   3rd
JOHN BRIANT HARTFORD FECIT I797
Diameter 31¾ "   Weight 6 cwt 3 qr 25 lb   Note D

154.   1797 BARKWAY   4th
JOHN BRIANT HARTFORD. FECIT . I797.
Diameter 33"   Weight 7 cwt 0 qr 1 lb   Note C

155.   1797 BARKWAY   5th
JOHN BRIANT HARTFORD FECIT I797
Diameter 35"   Weight 8 cwt 0 qr 1 lb   Note B♭

156.   1797 BARKWAY   6th
JOHN BRIANT HARTFORD FECIT AN:DOM:I797
Diameter 36½ "   Weight 8 cwt 3 qr 0 lb   Note A

157.   1797 BARKWAY   7th
JOHN BRIANT HARTFORD FECIT AN : DOM : I797
Diameter 39½ "   Weight 10 cwt 1 qr 5 lb   Note G

158.   1797 BARKWAY   Tenor of 8
THE REV^{ND} J STREET VICAR JOHN BRIANT HARTFORD FECIT AN:
DOM: I797.   *(first line)*
GLORIA DEO IN EXCELSIS. E• *MAZE* ⚹T: LEET • C : W.   *(2nd line)*
Diameter 44¼ "   Weight 14 cwt 2 qr 3 lb   Note F

Italic letters are incised. Obviously Briant did not receive sufficient details of names in time.

In 1700, Sir Henry Chauncy recorded 'Five bells and a clock bell'. The five were recast by Briant into the present back six, but the Bond, or guarantee, is dated 6 January 1798. They were augmented to eight by A. Bowell of Ipswich in 1914. The eight were tuned and rehung by Whitechapel in 1993, who supplied the weights.

R. Atkins / Dodds, CB Herts.

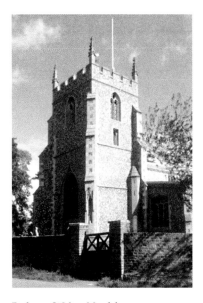

Barkway, St Mary Magdelene
Briant's ring of six is complete

159. 1797 HELMDON, Northants. St Mary
Magdalene   Treble of 6
J : ADKINS ᛆ L : FAIRBROTHER C : W : .
JOHN BRIANT HARTFORD FECIT 1797. *(one line)*
Diam. 28" Wt. 4 cwt 1 qr 14 lb   Note E
Briant appears to have added this bell to make six. The frame is contemporary and was re-used by Gillett & Johnston when they rehung the bells in 1951.   *CJP / PDG Dir.*

160. 1797 WHITCHURCH, Bucks. St John the Evangelist   2nd
JOHN BRIANT HARTFORD FECIT 1797 MAT : VARNEY ᛆ
W^M FINCHER C : WARDENS   *(one line)*
Diameter 32 ¼" Weight 5 ½ cwt   Note C
An odd fact about these bells is that the tenor was also cast in 1797 – by Thomas Mears I. Which came first?   *CB Bucks.*

161. 1797 HERTFORD, St Andrew   5th of 8
JOHN BRIANT HARTFORD FECIT 1797
Diameter 34 ¾" Weight 8 cwt 0 qr 7 lb   Note B♭

162. 1797 HERTFORD, St Andrew   Tenor
JOHN BRIANT HARTFORD FECIT 1797
     : :. GLORIA DEO IN EXCELSIS.
Diameter 44 ½"   Weight 15 cwt 1 qr 22 lb   Note F
These two bells completed Briant's 'modernisation' of St Andrew's bells. It is not clear whether he was recasting the last two of the 'four small bells' noted by Chauncy, or two of his own of 1782. The bells were rehung and retuned by Mears & Stainbank in 1948.   *Dodds, CB Herts.*

163.   1797 RIDGE, Tyttenhanger House   Clock bell
        J B I797
        Diameter 17⅛"   Weight 1 cwt   Note E
        This bell hangs in the cupola on the roof ridge, above the housing for
        the clock. It has cannons and has at some time been quarter-turned. It
        was also the bell for the private chapel on the second floor. The very
        beautiful seventeenth century house is now used as offices.   *CB Herts.*

164.   *1797 STEVENAGE, St Nicholas.*   *Old treble of 6*
        E : KITCHENER ⚹ T : CASS : C : W . JOHN BRIANT I797 HARTFORD
        Diameter 30"
        *There are considerable discrepencies between the inscription as given by North
        in 1886 and what is on the 1950 Taylor recast. The above version is that given
        by North; it has not been reproduced in facsimile.*   *HCA / N & S*

165.   1797 SUTTERTON, Lincs. St Mary the Virgin   Treble of 8
        THE GIFT OF JOHN CABOURN J : BRIANT ⚹ J CABOURN
        HARTFORD FECIT AN : DOM : I797   *(one line)*
        Diameter 29½"   Weight 6 cwt 8 lb.   Note F
        The above inscription is as given by North; *Lincs. K 2000* gives 'John
        Cabourn Hertford' with no punctuation.

166.   1797 SUTTERTON   2nd
        RAISD BY SUBSCRIPTION THE HON^BLE ⚹ REV^ND CH. LINDSEY
        VICAR A CASH ⚹ G : HARISON C : W : JOHN BRIANT ⚹ JOHN
        CABOURN OF HARTFORD FECERUNT AN : DOM : I797
        Diameter 29½"   Weight 5 cwt 1 qr 22 lb   Note E
        John Cabourn, the donor of the treble, was a noted bell hanger who
        died in 1813.
        Extract from 'Church Wardens' Accounts':
              1781. July 8. Bells finished half the estimate paid to
                        John Cabourn…………………….....………… 15 . 13 . 5
              1783   May 17. the last half of the money by
                        agreement for bells repairing …………………15 . 13 . 5
        Cabourn had obviously been doing necessary maintenance for some
        years, but more drastic work was needed, hence the calling in of Briant
        in 1797. The Honble and Rev^nd C. Lindsey was instituted in 1792; he
        later became Bishop of Kildare. The above inscription is as given by
        North; Ketteringham gives 'Harrison', 'Hertford' and again, no
        punctuation.   *CB Lincs.*

167.   1797 SAFFRON WALDEN, Essex St Mary 7th of 12, formerly 3rd of 8
        JOHN BRIANT HERTFORD FECIT I797
        Diam. 35"   Wt. c.7½ cwt   Note B

168. 1798 SAFFRON WALDEN   5th
JOHN BRIANT HERTFORD FECIT 1798.
JUSTICE PRUDENCE
Diam. 32″   Wt.6cwt   Note D

169. 1798 SAFFRON WALDEN   6th
JOHN BRIANT HERTFORD FECIT I798.
PRUDENCE JUSTICE   *(one line)*
Diam. 33″   Wt. 6 ½ cwt   Note C#

170. 1798 SAFFRON WALDEN   8th
JOHN BRIANT HERTFORD FECIT. I798
TEMPERANCE   *(one line)*
Diam. 38″   Wt. 9 cwt   Note A

171. 1798 SAFFRON WALDEN   9th
JOHN BRIANT HERTFORD FECIT I798.
FAITH
Diam. 40″   Wt. 10 ½ cwt   Note G

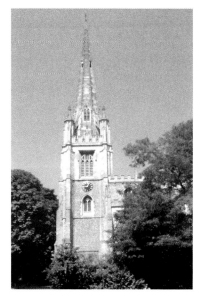

Saffron Walden, St Mary the Virgin. Briant provided an octave

172. *1798 SAFFRON WALDEN*   *Old 6th*
Recast by C.& G. Mears 1849.

173. *1798 SAFFRON WALDEN*   *Old 7th*
Recast by Thomas Mears II 1813.

174. 1798 SAFFRON WALDEN   Tenor
THIS PEAL WAS CAST AND HUNG BY JOHN BRIANT OF HERT-
FORD FROM A VOLUNTARY SUBSCRIPTION OF L[D] BRAYBROOKE
AND THE INHABITANTS. GLORIA DEO IN EXCELSIS   *(First line)*
THE LAW TEMPORAL. THE GOSPEL ETERNAL. THE REV[ND] W[M]
GRETTON VICAR R : LEVERETT ℣ J: BOWTELL C: WARDENS AN :
DOM : I798   *(Second line)*
Diameter 52″   Weight 22 cwt 2 qr 24 lb   Note D
Briant's octave was increased to twelve by the addtion of four trebles
in 1914. W[m] Gretton was also Vicar of Littlebury in 1789 and 1790 and
his name appears wrongly on the 4th at Hanwell, Oxon. (*see Nos.* 53, 57
and 65)   *HCA / CB Essex*

175. 1798 RADWINTER, Essex St Mary the Virgin   Tenor of 8
THOMAS GLASCOCK C : WARDEN. JOHN BRIANT HERTFORD
FECIT AN: DOM I798   *(one line)*
Diameter 41″   Weight 12 cwt 0 qr 22 lb   Note F
           CB Essex

176. 1798 MORTON, Lincs. St John the Baptist   4th of 6, formerly 3rd of 5
STATUTUM EST SEMEL OMNIBUS MORI EDWARD FRANKS C.W.
JOHN BRIANT HERTFORD FECIT 1798   *(one line)*
Diameter 39 ½ "   Weight 8 ½ cwt   Note A
The bells were augmented to 6 in 1892.   *CB Lincs.*

177. 1798 SWAFFHAM PRIOR, Cambs.   Clock bell
JOHN : BRIANT HARTFORD FECIT W: KILLINGBECK C : W • 1798
Diameter 21"   Weight 2 cwt   Note Bb– .04 semitones
The bell was supplied by Briant for an earlier clock by an unknown
maker, seven years later than the ring of 6. Andrews gives the date as
1793, quoting *CB Cambs. (See No. 83 above)* It was in use until 1989, when
much restoration was carried out on the tower by the Redundant
Churches Fund. At the time of writing, the bell is unhung, but is hoped
to be reinstated for the clock chime in the near future.
Dr M. Stanier / RWMC

178. 1798 WICKEN, Northants. St John the Evangelist   5th of 8
T. BRADBURY CHURCH WARDEN J. BRIANT FECIT HERTFORD
1798   *(one line)*
Diameter 34 ⅛ "   Weight 6 cwt 3 qr 22 lb   Note Bb
Briant recast a bell previously by Hugh Watts II.   *HCA / PDG. Dir.*

179. 1799 KISLINGBURY, Northants. St Luke   Treble of 5

JOHN BRIANT HERTFORD FECIT 1799. WM DUNKLEY }
                                  WM PAINE
CHURCHWARDENS   *(one line)*
Diameter 31 ½ "   Weight 6 cwt 0 qr 7 lb   Note C#
This bell was a recast of one by H. Bagley I of 1659.   *HCA / PDG Dir.*

180. 1799 STISTED, Essex All Saints   Treble of 6
JOHN BRIANT HERTFORD FECIT 1799
Diameter 27 ¾ "   Weight 4 cwt 3 qr 12 lb   Note F

181. 1799 STISTED   2nd
JOHN BRIANT HERTFORD FECIT 1799
Diameter 28 ⅜ "   Weight 5 cwt 0 qr 0 lb   Note E b

182. 1799 STISTED   3rd
JOHN BRIANT HERTFORD FECIT 1799
Diameter 30 ½ "   Weight 5 cwt 2 qr 14 lb   Note D b

183. 1799 STISTED   4th
JOHN BRIANT HERTFORD FECIT 1799
Diameter 31 ⅝ "   Weight 6 cwt 0 qr 0 lb   Note C

184. 1799 STISTED 5th
JOHN BRIANT HERTFORD FECIT 1799
Diameter 33 ¾ " Weight 7 cwt o qr olb Note B♭

185. 1799 STISTED Tenor
THE REV^ND JOHN BARLOW SEALE DD RECTOR : J : BAINES J :
SIBLEY C : WARDENS. JOHN BRIANT HERTFORD FECIT 1799 (one line)
Diameter 37 ¾ " Weight 9 cwt 1 qr 20 lb Note A♭
Prior to 1799, there were five bells, recast into a complete six by Briant.
Rehanging was carried out by Bowell of Ipswich in 1895 and by Gillett
& Johnston of Croydon in 1927, when the bells were tuned.
The Chelmsford Chronicle Friday 15 November 1799 :
      On Monday last a new peal of six bells was opened at Stisted, by the Bock-
ing company (and cast by Mr. Bryant, of Hertford,) there were several other
companies from adjacent parishes, who gave great satisfaction to the inhabitants.
      Ex. inf. John Illingworth (July 1993) – Stisted bells were 'recast and rehung
in 1799' by John Over of Rugby, a bellhanger who worked in association with
John Briant.
Churchwardens' accounts:
1799 11 Oct. Expence for Sibley and Self taking the Bell down   6d.
      26.   Expenses for meeting the Bellfounder   4s. 9d.
      Nov. 12 Expence for Ringers and Self   £ 1. 5. 4.
1801 18 June.   Payd Mr. Bryants Bill   £130. 0. 0.
      July 3   Payd two Letters from Mr. Bryant   1s. 0d.
                                          CJP / CB Essex

186. 1799 TEWIN, Herts. St Peter   2nd of 6, formerly treble of 5
JOHN BRIANT HERTFORD FECIT . 1799 T: DEAN C: WARDEN.
Diameter 26¹³⁄₁₆ " Weight 4 ¼ cwt   Note E♭
This was a recasting of the treble of a complete ring of five by Anthony
Chandler of Drayton Parslow, Bucks. in 1673.   *Dodds, CB Herts.*

187. 1800 NEWTON LONGVILLE, Bucks. St Faith 7th of 8, formerly 5th of 6
JOHN BRIANT HARTFORD FECIT 1800.
Diameter 37"   Weight 9 ½ cwt   Note A
This bell appears in Briant's list as No. 2. The name of this place is
given in *CB Bucks.* as Newnton Longville and by *H.C. Andrews* as
Newton Longueville.   *HCA / CB Bucks.*

188. 1800 COTTENHAM, Cambs. All Saints Treble   of 6
JOHN BRIANT HARTFORD FECIT AN: DOM :
1800 OMNES INCOLÆ AUDITE   (one line)
Diameter – ? Weight 6 cwt 3 qr 5 lb   Note D

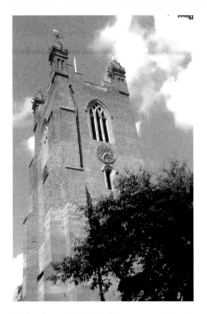

Cottenham, All Saints. These are an almost untouched ring of six by Briant

Note the use of Hartford, as on his earlier bells. By 1800, he was using the modern form of the name on most of his products. (*See however, Gt. Waldingfield, Nos.194–9*)

189. 1800 COTTENHAM   2nd
JOHN BRIANT HERTFORD FECIT I800
Diameter – ?   Weight 7 cwt 1 qr 6 lb   Note C

190. 1800 COTTENHAM   3rd
JOHN BRIANT HERTFORD FECIT I800
Diameter – ?   Weight 7 cwt 3 qr 14 lb   Note B♭

191. 1800 COTTENHAM   4th
JOHN BRIANT HERTFORD FEGIT I800
Diameter – ?   Weight 8 cwt 2 qr 14 lb   Note A
Note FEGIT instead of FECIT.

192. 1800 COTTENHAM   5th
JOHN BRIANT HERTFORD FECIT I800 W :
IVATT SENR W IVATT JUNR T : IVATT ℀ R : BACCHUS : FEOFFEES
FOR CHURCH AND CAUSEWAY   *(one line)*
Diameter – ?   Weight 11 cwt 0 qr 12 lb   Note G

193. 1800 COTTENHAM.   Tenor
JOHN BRIANT : HERTFORD FECIT I800 STATUTUM EST OMNIBUS
SEMEL MORI REV^ND PEPLOE WARD RECTOR. J : CALLENDER ℀T
: IVATT C : W :   *(one line)*
Diameter – ?   Weight 16 cwt 0 qr 22 lb   Note F
There are no inscriptions given by Raven in *CB Cambs.* so this may be the first published record. Weights are taken from the list in the belfry and are probably those supplied by Briant. The bells were opened on 15 December 1800 and to celebrate the 200th anniversary, a peal of Doubles in three methods was rung on 16 December 2000 by a local band, a splendid effort, as the bells have been difficult to ring for many years (*RW* 26/1/2001, p. 84). They were rehung in 2002.

Jean Sanderson / Peter Brown, Cottenham

194. 1800 GREAT WALDINGFIELD, Suffolk St Lawrence   Treble of 6
CANITE JOVAE LAUDES NOVO CARMINE. JOHN BRIANT
HARTFORD FECIT AN: DOM: I800   *(one line)*
Diameter 30⅜" Weight 5 cwt 1 qr 0 lb   Note D#+

195. 1800 GREAT WALDINGFIELD   2nd
OMNES INCOLAE AUDITE . JOHN BRIANT HARTFORD FECIT I800
Diameter 31⁹⁄₁₆"   Weight 5 cwt 2 qr 0 lb   Note C#+

196. 1800 GREAT WALDINGFIELD   3rd
SIT NOMEN DOMINI BENEDICTUM. JOHN BRIANT HARTFORD
FECIT AN: DOM : I800   *(one line)*
Diameter 33⅝"   Weight 6 cwt 3 qr 0 lb   Note B+

197. 1800 *GREAT WALDINGFIELD*   *4th*
LAUDATE DEUM (TYMPANIS ?) JOHN BRIANT HARTFORD
FECIT I800
Recast by John Warner & Sons, London in 1876.

198. 1800 GREAT WALDINGFIELD   5th
SUPREMIS LOCIS JOVAM LAUDATE. JOHN BRIANT HARTFORD
FECIT AN : DOM : I800   *(one line)*
Diameter 38¹⁄₁₆"   Weight 9 cwt 2 qr 0 lb   Note G#+
The E of Laudate is incised.

199. 1800 GREAT WALDINGFIELD   Tenor
ADESTE. REVᴺᴰ THOMAS BOYCE RECTOR . JOHN LOTT & Eᴰ
PRIOR C.W. ADESTE. JOHN BRIANT HARTFORD FECIT AN : DOM
: I800.   *(one line)*
Diameter 42¼"   Weight 13 cwt   Note F#+
Briant cast his ring of six out of five old ones. The inscription on the
third suggests that it was a medieval bell. These bells have been
unringable for many years; a chiming apparatus was installed by J.
Taylor in 1954.   *RWMC*

200. 1800 NEWBOTTLE, Northants. St James   Sanctus
J.B. I800 (?)
Diameter 12"   Weight 40 lb.
This bell appears only in the PDG Directory. It is not hung.   *PDG Dir.*

201. 1801 CONINGSBY, Lincs. St Michael   Treble of 6
J : BURCHAM C : WARDEN. J. BRIANT & J. CABOURN HERTFORD
FECERUNT I80I *(one line)*
Diameter 29⅝"   Weight 5 cwt 2 qr 19 lb   Note E
                             HCA / GAD

202. 1801 FRAMPTON, Lincs. SS Mary and Michael. 2nd, formerly treble of 5
REVND J WAITE VICAR J : ❦ T : TUNNARD C WS J : BRIANT ❦ J
CABOURN HERTFORD FECERUNT I80I   *(one line)*
Diameter 31¼"   Weight 5 cwt 2 qr 20 lb   Note C#
The inscriptions of the above two bells give the mistaken impression
that Cabourn was a bell founder.   *HCA / CB Lincs.*

203. *1801 HORBLING, Lincs. St Andrew   Old 2nd of five*
REV : J : LODDINGTON VICAR. T. KINSINGTON C : W . REV. J : SINGLAR CURA :
J. BRIANT ❦ J: CABOURN HERTFORD FECERUNT I80I.
Diameter 31½" Two sizes of letters, shown in Plate 7 of H.C. Andrews' book.
Recast by J. Taylor & Co. 1929 with the inscription reproduced.   *HCA*

204. 1801 SIBSEY, Lincs. St Margaret   4th
J : BRIANT AND J : CABOURN HERTFORD FECIT I80I.
W^M POCKLINGTON. C : W.   *(one line)*
Diameter 35¾"   Weight 8 cwt 2 qr 2 lb   Note B♭

205. 1801   SIBSEY   5th
J : BRIANT HERTFORD FECIT I80I. W : POCKLINGTON C : W : .
Diameter 37"   Weight 8 cwt 2 qr 1 lb   Note A♭
Briant uses the singular 'FECIT' thus correcting the error on previous
bells regarding the exact status of J. Cabourn.   *HCA / Lincs. K 2000*

206. 1802 WELBOURN, Lincs. St Chad   2nd
JOHN BRIANT ❦ J. CABOURN HERTFORD FECIT I802
Diameter 26⅜"   Weight 4 cwt 1 qr 6 lb   Note E#
(*CB Lincs.* diameter 27½"; weight 4–1–15).

207. 1802 WELBOURN   3rd
JOHN BRIANT ❦ J. CABOURN HERTFORD FECIT I802
Diameter 26¾"   Weight 4 cwt 0 qr 4 lb   Note D#
(*CB Lincs.* diameter 28"; weight 4-0-14).

208. 1802   WELBOURN   4th
J. WINGATE C : W: THREE BELLS ADDED BY SUBSCRIPTION.
JOHN BRIANT & J. CABOURN HERTFORD FECIT I802   *(one line)*
Diameter 29⅛"   Weight 4 cwt 1 qr 24 lb   Note C#
(*CB Lincs.* diameter as above; weight 4-2-6). *Lincs. K* 2000 gives no
punctuation.
These bells were originally cast for Holy Trinity, Hagworthingham,
Lincs., and were reputed to be the original of Tennyson's 'Wild Bells'.
After being unsafe for many years, the tower partially collapsed on 9
October 1972, the remains being demolished in 1981. The bells were

taken down and stored before being tuned and hung by J. Taylor & Co. at Welbourn in 1978/9, replacing a derelict ring of three.

GAD / Lincs. K 2000.

209. 1802 BISHOP'S STORTFORD, Herts.   8th, formerly 6th of 8
STATUTUM EST OMNIBUS EMEL MORI. J : BRIANT HERTFORD
FECIT I802   *(one line)*
Diameter 39"   Weight 10 cwt 2 qr 12 lb   Note G
The S in SEMEL is missing, and S in OMNIBUS and M in MORI are
damaged. There is also a casting fault on the shoulder.
Briant's Bill survives:

1802. May 21. To exchanging the old 6th bell for a new and fixing pr Contract	12	0	0
To the extra weight of the new bell weighing more than the old bell 0 cwt. 2 qrs. 0 lbs. at £7 per c.	3	10	0
To a new set of Bell ropes with worsted sallys	3	3	0
To a new top bolt one new bolt and keys to 4th Bell Clapper	0	5	0
	£18	18	0

The old 6th bell was presumably one by John Waylett.

Dodds/ HCA

210. *1802 ARDLEIGH, Essex St Mary   7th of 8*
J : BRIANT HERTFORD FECIT I802. P : BROMLEY ⅋ T : COOPER C :
WARDENS   (one line)
Diameter 39"   Weight 10 cwt   Note G#
Until 1892, this bell was the fifth of six. Recast by J. Taylor & Co. 1955.
CB Essex/ D Sloman

211. 1802 MELTON MOWBRAY, Leics. St Mary   3rd, formerly treble of 8
TWO BELLS WERE ADDED TO THE PEAL BY SUBSCRIPTION
ANNO DOMINI MDCCCII THOMAS FORD LL.D. VICAR VINCENT
WING ⅋ JOHN MOWBRAY C: WARDENS JOHN BRIANT OF
HERTFORD FECIT. GLORIA DEO IN EXCELSIS
Diameter 32"   Weight 7 cwt 0 qr 22 lb   Note F#

212. *1802 MELTON MOWBRAY   Old 4th*
OCTO CAMPANIS SACRA EXAUDIMUS IN ARCE. DULCES ALTI-
SONAS, O HILARES ! HILARES ! JOHN BRIANT HERTFORD FECIT
ANNO DOMINI MDCCCII STATUTUM EST OMNIBUS SEMEL MORI
Diameter 32½ "   Weight 6 cwt 3 qr 11 lb
This bell was recast by J. Taylor & Co. in 1994.   HCA / GAD
The setting dial of the former church clock is preserved in the ringing
chamber. It is inscribed 'John Briant, Hertford , 1804'.

Extract from the *Leicester Journal* No. 2608, Friday 26 November 1802:
We hear that the Bells, belonging to the parish church of Melton Mowbray, in
this county, have lately been re-hung, and two new trebles added thereto (by
Mr. Bryent, bellfounder, of Hertford) making a peal of Eight, are to be opened
on Thursday next. From the great professional abilities of Mr. B. as a Founder,
and the known scientific abilities of the Ringers who are expected to attend on
the occasion, we make no doubt it will prove a treat highly gratifying to the
Amateurs in the Art of Ringing.
Leicester Journal No. 2610. Friday 10 December 1802:
    On Thursday the 2d. inst. the new Peal of Eight Bells was opened at Melton
Mowbray, by the Leicester Society of Ringers, with two Peals of trebles and a
Bob-major Peal, which they executed in a masterly style; a society from
Grantham, and another from Stamford, attended on the occasion, each of which
gave convincing proof of their high abilities in the art of ringing.   *GAD/CJP*

213. 1803 BARKBY, Leics. St Mary   5th of 6
GLORIA DEO IN EXCELSIS J^{NO} ILLSON ⚬ TH^{OS} HENSON C :
WARDENS. J^{NO} BRIANT AND B. CORT HERTFORD FECERUNT :
I803   *(one line)*
Diameter 41 ⅜ "   Weight 11 cwt 0 qr 23 lb   Note F#
Briant gave a misleading inscription, as on some of his Lincolnshire
bells, by using the plural FECERUNT, thus giving the impression that
B. Cort was a bellfounder. Cort was a local Leicester ironmonger and
ironfounder through whom Briant did the casting, as sub-contractor.
                                                        HCA / GAD

214. *1803 DISEWORTH, Leics. St Michael*   *Old treble*
R. SOWTER ⚬ T. HASTINGS C.W. JOHN BRIANT HERTFORD ⚬
B. CORT LEICESTER FECERUNT I803
Diameter 32"   Weight 6 cwt 0 qr 8 lb
Briant corrected the inscription on this bell. (See above) Recast by J. Taylor &
Co. 1921.   *HCA / GAD*

215. 1803 OFFLEY, Herts. St Mary Magdalene   Tenor of 6
JOHN BRIANT HERTFORD FECIT I803 THOMAS BATES C :
WARDEN   *(one line)*
Diameter 44 ⅝ "   Weight 14 cwt 3 qr 20 lb   Note F
The weight is as given by Messrs. Eayre & Smith of Derby, who tuned
and rehung the bells during June and July 2000, the original (Briant)
weight being 15–1–0. A date of 1800 on a rainwater head (Pevsner, *Hertfordshire,* p. 264) seems to confirm the rebuilding date of the tower.
However, a church guide by Ron Pigram states that it was rebuilt in
1814, in which case the bells may have hung in the earlier tower. The
contemporary frame has been preserved and a new frame supplied.
                                          Dodds, CB Herts./ RW 25/8/00 p. 834

216. *1803 ST ALBANS, Herts Abbey Mill*
WOOLLAM HUGHES & WOOLLAM J. B. 1803
The Abbey Mill, originally a corn mill, later became a silk mill. The bell hung in
a cupola of c. 1800 on the roof-ridge. In the late 1980s, the mill was converted
for residential use and during the course of the work the bell was removed. If not
scrapped, its present whereabouts is unknown.   *HCA / Dodds*

217. 1803 BARNSTAPLE, Devon SS Peter & Mary Magdalene
                                        3rd, formerly treble of 6
IOHN BRIANT HERTFORD FECIT I803
Diameter 32 ½ "   Wt. 7 cwt 0 qr 24 lb   Note C

218. 1803 BARNSTAPLE   4th
IOHN BRIANT HERTFORD FECIT I803
Diameter 35"   Wt. 7 cwt 2 qr 6 lb   Note B♭

219. 1803 BARNSTAPLE   5th
IOHN BRIANT HERTFORD FECIT I803
Diameter 38"   Wt. 9 cwt 2 qr 11 lb   Note A♭

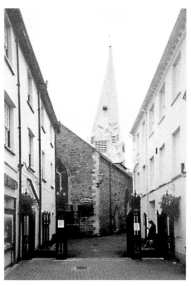

220. 1803 BARNSTAPLE   6th
IOHN BRIANT HERTFORD FECIT I803
Diameter 39"   Wt. 10 cwt 0 qr 23 lb   Note G

221. 1803 BARNSTAPLE   7th
GLORIA DEO IN EXCELSIS IOHN BRIANT
HERTFORD FECIT 1803   (one line)
Diameter 43"   Weight 13 cwt 3 qr 16 lb   Note F

Barnstable, St Peter and Mary Magdelene,
Devon. Briant's six bell are still complete

222. 1803 BARNSTAPLE   Tenor
JOHN BRIANT HERTFORD FECIT I803 THE
REV^D T. WILLIAM   MARSHALL VICAR
Diameter 49 ½ "   Weight 19 cwt 1 qr 0 lb   Note E♭
These were a complete six by Briant, well away from his normal area.
On 18 January 1803, a 'Licence was decreed by the Bishop to cast five
old bells into six' i.e. a Faculty. Ellacombe, in *CB Devon*, used I for J in
Briant's name on the front five, which was unusual, while noting a
normal J on the tenor.   *CB Devon / HCA*

223. *1803 BRAUNTON, Devon St Brannock*   *Old 5th*
Included in Briant's list. Cast c. 1803, recast by Taylor of Oxford, 1830.   HCA
The following extracts from the Churchwardens' accounts 1803–4 have kindly
been made available by the North Devon Record Office at Barnstaple: (ref. 3054
add 5/2)

1803
By going to Barum to Mr. Gribble about sending the Bell to be new cast, 2s. 6d.
By the Porters at Biddeford to unload the Bell, 3s.
By going to Biddeford with the Bell to deliver it to the Captain, 5s.
1804
By Quayage, etc. of the Bell, 4s.
By Mr. Briant as per Bill about the Bells, £57. 3s. 8d.   North Devon RO

224. *1803 TAWSTOCK, Devon   St Peter*   Old 4th
IOHN BRIANT HERTFORD FECIT I803
PROSPERITY TO THE PARISH OF TAWSTOCK.
Diameter 39"   Weight c.10 cwt   Briant's list calls it
No. 3. Recast 1867.

                                                        HCA / CB Devon
The following extracts from the churchwardens' accounts have also been made
*available by the North Devon Record Office : – (**ref.** 2288A/PW1).*
1803
The expense of drawing the Bell and Ceage (Quayage?) to Barnstaple, 6s. 6d.
1804
April 1st Paid to Mr John Briant Bellfounder for recasting the fourth Bell, £12. 18s. 3d.
May 29 For Drawing Home the Bell, 4s.
NB. The Bell cast this Last Year by John Briant of Hertford wieghed when sent off 10 wt.
2 qr. 17 lbs. to be recast at £1. 8s. per Hundred - it returned again 10 cwt. 0 qtr. 11 lbs
only for which Deficiency Mr. Briant allowed the Parish £2. 6s. 6d. June 6th 1804.
                                                        North Devon RO

225. 1803 KIRKBY-ON-BAIN, Lincs. St Mary   Single
F RENOLDS C WARDEN J BRIANT HERTFORD FECIT I803
Diameter 24"   Weight 3 cwt
The church was built in 1802. Incorrectly listed by HCA as Kirby-on-
Bain. Having become unsafe, the bell is now unhung.   *Lincs. K* 2000

226. 1803 STICKNEY, Lincs. St Luke   3rd of 8
REV^{ND} R : LOXHAM RECTOR W : MORTON C : W J : BRIANT &
J. CABOURN HERTFORD FECERUNT I803.   *(one line)*
Diameter 32 ½ " Weight 6 cwt 1qr   Note D♭

227. 1803 STICKNEY   4th
J : BRIANT & J : CABOURN HERTFORD 1803 FECERUNT
Diameter 32 ¾ " Weight 7 cwt   Note C
Cannons removed, J. Taylor 1907. The inscription and above diameters
are as given by Ketteringham. North gave the full treble inscription on
this bell also. Briant's list records only one bell here, the third of five.
Here again Briant gave a false impression of Cabourn as a founder.
                                                        Lincs. K 2000

228, *1803 OXFORD St Ebbe*   *Old treble & 2nd*
229. *Two bells, cast 1803, were added to Briant's ring, and were noted by W.C. Lukis*
   in **An Account of Church Bells** *1857, p. 91. They were sold in about 1845*
   and there is a tradition that they provided the metal for the two bells of Holy
   Trinity, Oxford, cast by William Taylor in that year. Two new trebles were
   installed in 1925.   *HCA / CB Oxon*

230. 1803 CHURCHOVER Warks. Holy Trinity   3rd of 4
   J. VOILE C : WARDEN J : BRIANT & J : OVER HERTFORD
   FECERUNT I803.   *(one line)*
   Diameter 29¾"   Weight c.5 cwt   Note C
   John Over was a bellhanger from Rugby, who acted as Briant's agent.
   A vestry minute dated 21 April 1802 records an agreement with John
   Over to recast the 3rd bell and provide a new frame and fittings for
   £49. This expenditure was recorded in the accounts for 1802–4.
                                     CB Warks./ CJP

231. 1803 ETTINGTON, Warks. Holy Trinity   Tenor of 4
   J : WATERS KING SUTTON BELL HANGER. W. HARRIS & E : ARCH
   C WARDENS JOHN BRIANT HERTFORD FECIT I803
   Diameter 38¾"   Weight c.10 cwt   Note G
   The old church of St Thomas-à-Becket which stood near Ettington Park
   had become ruinous, so a more conveniently sited church was built at
   Upper Ettington in 1803. The bells were also transferred, being hung
   by John Waters of King's Sutton, near Banbury. Another church was
   built as a replacement in 1902/3 and the bells again transferred. Briant
   was here recasting an old bell.
   The churchwardens' accounts include entries relating to the works of
   1803:

	£	s.	d.
1803 For Fetching the bells from the Old Church to the New ...	1	1	0
Pd Jno Walker for helping to lode the Bells		1	6
Pd Willm Baron for the Bel ropes	1	2	0
1804 Pd Willm Hall for fetching the Frames from Banbury	1	3	0
Recasting 10¼ cwt. of Bell-metal at 30s. pr hundred	15	7	6
Carriage of the old bell to Banbury	1	0	0
" " " from Banbury to London	1	1	0
Carriage of the new bell from London to Banbury........	2	11	7
" " " Banbury to Eatington ...	1	0	0

The route taken by the bell would be from Ettington by road to Banbury, from there via the Oxford Canal, the Thames and the River Lea
Navigation to Hertford and return.   *HCA / CB Warks.*

232. 1803 KELVEDON, Essex St Mary the Virgin   2nd of 6
JOHN BRIANT HERTFORD FECIT I803
Diameter 36"   Weight 8 cwt   Note B

233. 1803 KELVEDON
4th
J : MARTHAM & J : POOLEY C : WARDENS. THE REV^ND T : RIPLEY
VICAR. J : BRIANT HERTFORD FECIT I803   *(one line)*
Diameter 41"   Weight 11 cwt   Note G# *CB Essex*

234. 1804 CHRISHALL, Essex Holy Trinity   3rd, formerly treble of 4
JOHN BRIANT HERTFORD FECIT I804
Diameter 29"   Weight 4 cwt   Note D♭*CB Essex*

235. 1804 BURTON LAZARS, Leics. St James   Treble of 2
JOHN BRIANT HERTFORD FECIT I804
Diameter 23 ¼ "   Weight 2 cwt 1 qr 6 lb
Hung for chiming in a massive double bell-cote.   *HCA / GAD*

236. *1804 STREATLEY, Beds. St Margaret*   *Old treble*
W. SMITH & T. WELLS CHURCH WARDENS. J. HADDOW. VICAR.
JOHN BRIANT, HERTFORD, FECIT, I804
Diameter 24 "   Weight not recorded.
Diameter and inscription recorded in glebe terrier 1822.
Churchwardens' accounts :
      1804 Balance of Account of new Bells as per Bill of Bryant   £4 2s.
Recast or replaced by Thomas Mears 1832. Now treble of a chime of 4.   CJP

237. *1804 WIGSTON MAGNA, Leics.   All Saints.*   *Old 4th*
J. BRIANT CORT & CO. FECERUNT I804 HERTFORD. J. LANGHAM
AND J. HUNST C.W.
Churchwarden's accounts :
1805 20 Apr. Messrs. Cort's & Co. for the third bell   £25 . 4 . 0
Briant lists this as No. 3. The bell was recast by J. Taylor & Co. in 1922, only
the date 1804 being reproduced.   HCA / CJP

238. *1805 SHEPSHED, Leics. St Botolph*   *Old Treble of 6*
JOHN BRIANT HERTFORD FECIT AN. DOM I805
Diameter 31 ⅛ "   Weight 5 cwt 2 qr 24 lb

239. *1805 SHEPSHED*   *Old 2nd*
JOHN BRIANT HERTFORD FECIT AN. DOM. I805
Diameter 32 ½ "   Weight 6 cwt 0 qr 7 lb

240. *1805 SHEPSHED*　　　　　　　　　　　　　　　　　　　*Old 3rd*
JOHN BRIANT HERTFORD FECIT AN. DOM. I805
Diameter 34¾"　　Weight 7 cwt 1 qr 21 lb

241. *1805 SHEPSHED*　　　　　　　　　　　　　　　　　　　*Old 4th*
JOHN BRIANT HERTFORD FECIT AN. DOM. I805
Diameter 36"　　Weight 8 cwt 0 qr 0 lb

242. *1805 SHEPSHED*　　　　　　　　　　　　　　　　　　　*Old 5th*
JOHN BRIANT HERTFORD FECIT AN. DOM. I805
Diameter 39½"　　Weight 10 cwt 0 qr 0 lb

243. *1805 SHEPSHED*　　　　　　　　　　　　　　　　*Old tenor of 6*
JOHN BRIANT HERTFORD FECIT AN. DOM. I805. T. LUDLOW AND R.
THOMPSON CHURCHWARDENS. REV^D CHARLES ALLSOPP VICAR.
Diameter 46¾"　　Weight 13 cwt 2 qr 10 lb
Briant's complete six were opened on Friday, 27 December 1805, by the Leices-
ter ringers who rang 720 changes of Oxford Treble Bob Minor.
(H.C. Andrews received this information from Ernest Morris).
All six were recast and augmented to eight by J.Taylor & Co. in 1948. The above
appear to have been the old weights.　　　　　　　　　　*HCA / GAD*

244. *1805 MOULTON, Lincs. All Saints*　　　　　　　　　*Tenor of 6*
REV^ND MAURICE JOHNSON D. D. VICAR. VENITE CUM VOCO JOHN
BRIANT °⚭ JOHN CABOURN HERTFORD FECERUNT I805. R THORP⚭R KING C : W.
Diameter 46"　　Weight 15 cwt 1 qr 4 lb　　　　Note F
Lincs. K 2000 quotes the weight as 15 cwt 2 qr 25 lb, before removal of cannons.
　　　　　　　　　　　　　　　　　　　　　　　　　HCA / GAD

245. *1805 ST ALBANS, Herts. St Peter*　　　　　　　　　*Old 7th*
REV^ND ALFRED W: ROBERTS VICAR. J : READ.J : SANDERS.
J : BARNET .C: W: J : BRIANT HERTFORD FECIT. + THE TOWER
REBUILT I805　　　　*(one line)*
Diameter 39"　　Weight 10 cwt 1 qr 20 lb　　　　Note G
+ – Fig. 23_c. The cross was not known to have been used elsewhere. This bell was
recast with the other nine by Whitechapel in 1993. Full inscription not
reproduced.　　　　　　　　　　　　　　　　*Dodds, CB Herts.*

246. *1805 HAMSTALL RIDWARE, Staffs. St Michael*　　　*Treble of 4*
R. KNOWLES C.W. † J. BRIANT ⚭ B. CORT HEREFORD FECERUNT
I805　　　　*(one line)*
Diameter 27"　　Weight 4 cwt 0 qr 4 lb
Hereford is an obvious error for Hertford. The four bells were tuned
and rehung for chiming by J. Taylor in 1971-2.　　　　*HCA / CJP*

247. *1805 COVENTRY, St Michael now Cathedral*   *Old tenor*
STEPHEN CORBET ACT: C: WARDEN 1805. I AM AND HAVE BEEN
CALL'D THE COMMON BELL TO RING, WHEN FIRE BREAKS OUT TO
TELL † † † † † † JOHN BRIANT HERTFORD FECIT AN: DOM:
MDCCCV † GLORIA DEO IN EXCELSIS † † † † † † †
Diameter 56"   Weight 32 cwt 0 qr 9 lb
Recast in 1927 by Gillett & Johnston, Croydon.   CJP / HCA / CB Warks.

248. *1805 NORTHAMPTON Holy Sepulchre*   *Old 7th*
THE REV^D THOS WATTS VICAR THOS ARMFIELD ✠ J HARRIS C.
WARDENS. JOHN BRIANT HERTFORD FECIT 1805
Diameter 42 ½ "
Recast by Gillett & Johnston 1926.   HCA / PDG. Dir.

249. *1805 SYRESHAM, Northants. St James*   *Old tenor*
This bell, included in Briant's list, was apparently cast about 1805 and recast
by John Warner & Sons in 1867.   HCA

(1806   BIGGLESWADE, Beds.   *Old tenor of 5*
JOHN LANCASTER AND GEORGE COOPER CHURCHWARDENS. R :
TAYLOR ST. NEOTS FECIT 1806
Included in Briant's list, but obviously cast by Taylor.   CB Beds.

250. 1806 ASHBY ST LEDGERS, Northants. B.V.M. & St Leodegarius 3rd of 4
W : COLE ✠ W : BAWCUTT C : W. JOHN BRIANT HERTFORD
FECIT 1806 † † † †   *(one line)*
Diameter 37⅝"   Weight 8½ cwt   Note G
This was a recast of a bell by Matthew Bagley 1681.
                                                      HCA / PDG. Dir.

251. 1806 CULWORTH, Northants. St Mary the Virgin   3rd of 5
J. PAGE ✠ W UPSON C W JOHN BRIANT HERTFORD FECIT 1806
Diameter 36⅛"   Weight 7 cwt 3 qr 19 lb   Note G#
The churchwardens' accounts for 1806 contain a copy of an agreement
with Briant:

   I propose new hanging the Tenor bell with a new wheel, Gudgeons,
Braces, Repg the Clapper and turn the Bell to cause the clapper to strike on a
new place – and chip the edge of the 4th Bell to endeavour to make higher in
key for £ 10 0s. 0d.

        April 25th, 1806.   John Briant.
        Then follow these entries: £   s.   d.
        Paid Mr. Briant for recasting the third Bell   19   0   0
        Paid expences at the same time   11   6
        Paid Mr. Briant for new hanging the Tenor Bell, etc......   10   0   0
                                                      HCA / PDG Dir.

252. *1806 SULGRAVE, Northants. St James the Less*   *Old tenor*
      GLORIA : DEO : IN : EXCELSIS : W : MALSBURY ⚒ W : PAINTER C W:
      JOHN : BRIANT :HERTFORD : FECIT : 1806 W : BURCH : C W : T.
      CRICK RECTOR.
      Diameter 42"
      The names W. Burch and T. Crick also appear on the tenor at Little Thurlow,
      *Suffolk, (*see below No. 281*) so it appears that this was another example of*
      bells from two or more rings being in the foundry at the same time and their
      inscriptions becoming muddled. As there were already two churchwardens'
      names on this bell and only rector and one churchwarden on Little Thurlow
      tenor, it would seem that they more properly belonged to the latter place rather
      than Sulgrave. The ring of six was recast by Gillett & Johnston in 1928.
      HCA / J.D.

253. 1806 SULGRAVE   Sanctus
      J. Briant 1806 (Inscription not recorded).
      Diameter 13¼"
      H.C. Andrews does not mention this small bell, which was not recast
      in 1928 with the ring of six.   *PDG Dir.*

254. *1806 THENFORD, Northants. St Mary the Virgin*   *Former tenor of 5*
      E. STAFFORD VICAR C. EDWARDS AND J. LAW C.W. JOHN BRIANT
      HERTFORD FECIT 1806
      Diameter 33"
      *This bell was recorded by North, **CB Northants**, and by Andrews, so it did*
      *exist. Successive editions of **Dove's Guide**, 1962 and 1968 list Thenford as a*
      ring of five, but the later one recorded that the bells were not hung. The PDG
      Directory 1989 does not list this bell, there now being four only. It was presum-
      ably disposed of at some time post-1968, having become cracked.   *C. Dalton*

255. 1806 NORTH MYMMS, Herts. St Mary   3rd of 8
      JOHN BRIANT HERTFORD FECIT 1806 ☩ † ✿ ☩ ✿ † ☩ † ☩
      Diameter 30"   Weight 5 cwt 0 qr 23 lb   Note D#

256. 1806 NORTH MYMMS   4th
      JOHN BRIANT HERTFORD FECIT 1806 ☩♣ ♣ ♣ ☩ ♣ ♣ ♣ ✿ ☩
      Diameter 32"   Weight 6 cwt 0 qr 19 lb   Note C#

257. 1806 NORTH MYMMS   5th
      JOHN † BRIANT ✿ HERTFORD † FECIT † 1806   ✿ ✿ ☩ ✿ †
      ☩ † ♣ ☩ ✿ † ✿ ☩ ♣ † ☩ † (one line)
      Diameter 33½" Weight 6 cwt 1 qr 14 lb   Note B

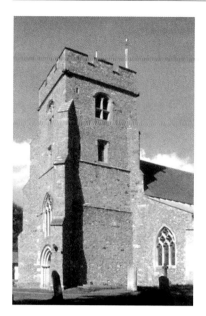

North Mymms, St Mary. Another complete
Briant six, this one richly decorated

258.   1806 NORTH MYMMS   6th
JOHN ♣ BRIANT ✡ HERTFORD ♣ † † FECIT
1806 † ✝ ✿ ✡ † † ✝ ⟟ ✿ † ✡ ♣ † ♣ ✿ ✝
(one line)
Diam. 34½ "   Wt. 6 cwt 3 qr 17   Note A#

259.   1806 NORTH MYMMS   7th of 8
JOHN BRIANT HERTFORD FECIT 1806 ✝   ✝
✝   ✝   ✝   ✝
Diam. 39"   Wt. 9 cwt 3 qr 0 lb   Note G#

260.   1806 NORTH MYMMS   Tenor of 8
JOHN BRIANT HERTFORD FECIT 1806 JOS :
SABINE AND RICHARD MASON C
WARDENS GLORIA DEO IN EXCELSIS ✝ ✿
✝ ✿ ✝ ♣ ✝ ✿ ♣ ✝ ♣ ✝ ⟟ ✿ ⟟ ✿ † *(one line)*
(Double inscription band; all the above in upper band, lower band blank)
Diam. 42½ "   Wt, 12 cwt 3 qr 0 lb   Note F#
This complete six was cast from an older ring
of five which was recorded by Sir Henry
Chauncy in 1700. According to the churchwar
dens' accounts, Briant was paid £146 for his
work, *(N & S* p. 200). Two trebles were added by Mears & Stainbank in
1920.   *Dodds, CB Herts.*

261.   *1806 MAIDS MORETON, Bucks. St Edmund*   *Tenor*
JOHN BRIANT HERTFORD FECIT 1806 J : LONG SUTTON RECTOR
J : SCOTT ⚭ R : HINSON C: WARDENS † ✿ † ✿ † ✿ †   *(one line)*
Cocks, **CB Bucks,** *recorded that the diameter had been reduced by about three-*
quarters of an inch by tuning. Briant's list gave the weight as 12 cwt. The name
of the rector should have been J.Long Hutton, not Sutton; a Freudian slip –
Briant had been working in Lincolnshire (!)
Recast by J.Taylor & Co. 1950.   *CB Bucks.*

262.   1806 PADBURY, Bucks.   St Mary the Virgin   Treble of 6
JOHN BRIANT HERTFORD FECIT 1806   ✿ ✝ ✿ ✡ ✿ ✝
Diameter 29"   Weight 4 cwt   Note F

263.   1806 PADBURY   2nd of 6
JOHN BRIANT HERTFORD FECIT   ✿ ✝ ✿ ✝ ✿ ✝
Diameter 30"   Weight 4½ cwt   Note E\

264. 1806 PADBURY   3rd of 6
JOHN BRIANT   HERTFORD
FECIT 1806 ✝ ✿ ✝
Diam.31 ¾ "   Wt. 5 ½ cwt   Note
D ♭

265. 1806 PADBURY   4th
JOHN BRIANT HERTFORD FECIT
1806 ✝ ✿ ✝ ✿ ✝ ✿ ✝ ✿
Diameter 33"   Weight 6 cwt
Note C

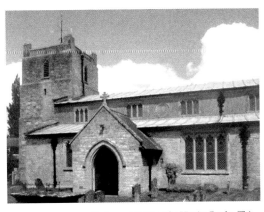

Padbury, St Mary the Virgin, Bucks. This
is another complete Briant ring of six

266. 1806 PADBURY   5th
JOHN BRIANT HERTFORD FECIT
1806 ✿ ✝ ✿ ✿ ✿ ✝ ✿ ✝ ✿ ✝
Diameter 35"   Weight 7 ½ cwt   Note B\

267. 1806 PADBURY   Tenor
JOHN BRIANT HERTFORD FECIT 1806 THE REV^D W^M : EYRE VICAR
: T : FLOWERS : ✾ W^M : HORWOOD : C WARDENS ✿ ✝ ✿ *(one line)*
Diameter 39"   Weight 10 ½ cwt   Note A\
The irregular spacing of the inscriptions is as shown by Cocks, who
was a meticulous observer. He also, *p. 546*, includes the following:
The bill for the present bells is pinned into the churchwardens' account book:

1806   } Mefsrs Horwood and Flowers
July 16

       Church Wardens of Padbury
       Dr to John Briant

	£	s.	d.
To a new Peal of 6 Bells, Frames and			
Hangings p Contract...........................	120	0	0
To carriage from Buckingham to Box More	2	5	6
Wharfage at Buckingham		4	6
Wharfage at Box More		7	4
Land Carriage 35^Ct at 1s/6d p Ct	2	12	6
Carriage of 1st Bell and Clapper sct 6Ct at 2s/6d		15	0
Carriage of new Bells &c from Hertford			
to Box More 45 ct at 1s/6d	3	7	6
Carriage of new Bells from Box More			
to Buckingham in same proportion			
as above	2	16	10
Wharfage at Box More		10	0
	£132	9	2

	C	Q	lb
Weight of old Bells	40	1	5 groß
Deduct 5 Crown Staples of Iron			20
	40	0	13 neat Wt
Weight of new Bells	38	3	13
Cr	1	1	0 at 15d

	8	15	0
£ 124	4	2	

Pinned in with the bill, on a piece of paper with embossed receipt stamp, is:
Receiv'd 24th July 1806 of Me ßrs Horwood &
Flowers, One Hundred and twenty four
Pounds, four Shillings and two Pence for
Casting a new Peal of 6 Bells &c as p Bill
anexed,

£	s.	d.	
-----	-----	-----	
124	4	2	JOHN BRIANT

(Box More is now known as Boxmoor, part of Hemel Hempstead. The
bells were carried on the Grand Junction Canal to Cosgrove, then
along the Buckingham Arm. J.D.)   *Cocks, CB Bucks.*

268. *1806 COGGESHALL, Essex St Peter*   Old 3rd of 8
      W : SWINBORNE T : ALLEKER C.W. JOHN BRIANT HERTFORD FECIT
      1806 ✿ † ⚏ † ✝   ✝ ⚏ ✝ ✿ † ✿
      Diameter 32"   Weight 5 ½ cwt   Note C#
      *Briant's bill for this bell was not settled until 10 September 1807, when the
      churchwardens' accounts record a payment of £17 10s to him.*   CB
      Essex
      Recast by Gillett & Johnston 1931. Inscription reproduced.   D. Sloman

269. *1806 WALTHAM ABBEY, Essex Holy Cross and St Lawrence*
      Old treble, formerly 3rd
      JOHN BRIANT HERTFORD FECIT 1806 ✿ ✝ ✿ † ✿ †
      Diameter 29"   Weight 5 ½ cwt   Note E
      Recast by J.W. & E.D. Taylor 1914.

270. *1806 WALTHAM ABBEY*   Old 2nd
      JOHN BRIANT HERTFORD FECIT 1806 ✿ K
      Diameter 30"   Weight 6 cwt   Note D#
      Recast as above, 1914.

271. *1806 WALTHAM ABBEY*   Old 3rd
      JOHN BRIANT HERTFORD FECIT 1806 ✿ † ✝
      Diameter 32"   Weight 6 ½ cwt   Note C#
      Recast as above, 1914.

272. 1806 WALTHAM ABBEY 6th of 12
JOHN BRIANT HERTFORD FECIT I806 ✡ K ☨
Diameter 34″ Weight 7½ cwt Note B
K – King's head. Fig. 23_1.

273. 1806 WALTHAM ABBEY 7th
JOHN BRIANT HERTFORD FECIT I806 ☨ †
✡ (the † is incomplete)
Diameter 36″ Weight 8 cwt Note A

274. 1806 WALTHAM ABBEY Old 6th, formerly 8th
JOHN BRIANT HERTFORD FECIT I806 † ❧ ✡
Diameter 38″ Weight 10½ cwt
Note G#
Recast by Taylor as above 1914.

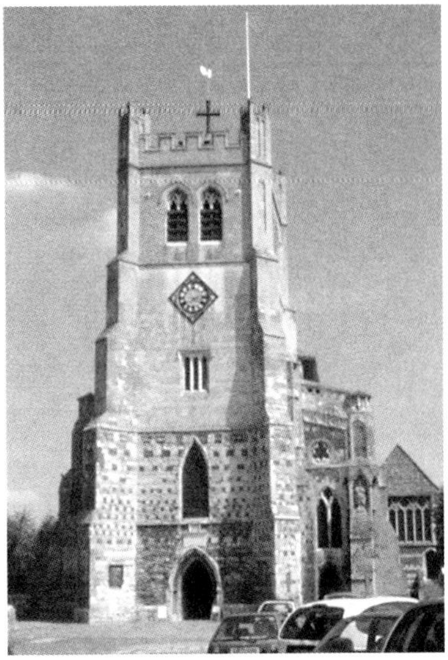

Waltham Abbey, Holy Cross and St Lawrence Essex. Briant cast an 18 cwt ring of eight

275. 1806 WALTHAM ABBEY Old 7th, formerly 9th
JOHN BRIANT HERTFORD FECIT I806 ❧ ✡ ❧
☨ ♟ ✡ ♟ † ♟ ✡ ❧ ☨ ✡ † *(one line)*
Diameter 42″ Weight 13 cwt Note F#
Recast as above 1914.

276. 1806 WALTHAM ABBEY 10th, formerly tenor
JOHN PAIN JOHN SMITH ❦ RICHARD BANKS C : WARDENS
JOHN BRIANT HERTFORD FECIT I806 ☨ ✡ † ☨ ❧ *(one line)*
Diameter 48″ Weight 18 cwt Note E
This was a major commission for Briant. His ring lasted until 1914 when it was augmented to twelve by the addition of two trebles and two tenors. Diameters and weights are as given in *CB Essex*.

277. 1806 LOCKINGTON, Leics. St Nicholas. 10th of 12
RV^ND. PHILLIP STORY VICAR T. PALMER C.W. JOHN BRIANT
HERTFORD FECIT I806 *(one line)*
Diameter 35″ Weight 7 cwt 1 qr 23 lb Note A
Briant's list calls this No. 1; by 1876 it was No. 3. Further augmentations have made it the 10th of 12. *HCA / GAD*

278. 1807 WALTON ON THE WOLDS, Leics. St Mary 4th of 5
JOHN BRIANT HERTFORD FECIT I807 REV^ND PHILLIP STORY
RECTOR J SHUTTLEWOOD C.W. *(one line)*
Diameter 34⅝″ Weight 7 cwt 1 qr 13 lb Note B♭
Note that the 'Revnd Phillip Story' appears on *No.* 277 above, where he is titled Vicar. The most likely explanation of this would be that he was holding the livings in plurality. North also incorrectly added the name

of J. Palmer to the inscription; the inference must be that his informant
was in error.   *HCA/GRD*

279. 1807 STANBRIDGE, Beds. St John the Baptist   3rd, formerly 2nd of 5
      F : ELLINGHAM C : W : JOHN BRIANT HERTFORD FECIT 1807
      Diameter 32″   Weight 5 cwt 2 qr 10 lb   Note B
      Weight as returned by Taylor 1951. This bell was the second prior to
      augmentation by J. Taylor in 1988.   *HCA / CJP*

280. 1807 BURROUGH GREEN, Cambs. St Augustine   4th of 5
      JOHN BRIANT HERTFORD FECIT 1807
      Diameter – ?   Weight – ?   Note D
      These bells have long been unringable, like many others in this
      neighbourhood.   *HCA*

281. 1807 LITTLE THURLOW, Suffolk St Peter   Tenor of 6
      T • CRICK RECTOR W : BURCH C : W• JOHN BRIANT HERTFORD
      FECIT 1807 ✿ ✝ ♟ ✝ ◯ (Bust in a wreath) ✝ ♟ ✿ ✝ ♟ ✝ ✿ ✝ *(one line)*
      Diameter 41½ ″ Weight 12 cwt 1 qr 0 lb   Note F# -
      Note that the names of the rector and churchwarden are the same as
      those on the tenor at Sulgrave, Northants. (*see above No 252*). The bells
      must have been in the foundry at the same time and, once again, a
      mix-up occurred.
      From 1965, the five bells were chimed only; they were augmented and
      rehung for ringing by Whitechapel Foundry in 1999 as a Millennium
      Project.   *RWMC*

282. 1808 SOHAM, Cambs. St Andrew   Treble of 10
      ✝ NEW BY SUBSCRIPTN. 1808, REV^ND H. FISHER VICAR, J.
      DOBEDE ⚭ R. TEBBET C.W. J. BRIANT HARTFORD FECIT.   *(one line)*
      Diameter 27¾ ″ Weight c.5 cwt   Note G#
      Cannons removed.

283. 1808 SOHAM   2nd
      NEW BY SUBSCRIPTION 1808. REV^ND H. FISHER VICAR. J. DOBEDE
      ⚭ R. TEBBET C.W. J. BRIANT. HARTFORD FECIT. *(one line)*
      Diameter 29″   Weight 5½ cwt   Note F#
      These two new bells augmented the ring from eight to ten.

284. 1808 SOHAM   3rd
      ✝ RECAST BY SUBSCRIPTION 1808. H. FISHER VICAR. J. DOBEDE
      ⚭ R. TEBBET C.W. JOHN BRIANT HARTFORD FECIT. *(one line)*
      Diameter 30¼ ″ Weight 6 cwt   Note E

285.   1808 SOHAM   4th
       ✝ RECAST BY SUBSCRIPTION 1808. H. FISHER VICAR. J. DOBEDE
       ⚵ R. TEBBET C.W. JOHN BRIANT. HARTFORD FECIT.   *(one line)*
       Diameter 31″   Weight 6¼ cwt   Note D
                                                       HCA / CB Cambs.

286.   1808 GAZELEY, Suffolk   All Saints   Treble of 6
       ✝ JOHN BRIANT ✝ A GRATEFULL STRAIN, BOYS, LET US SING ♠
                    TO PRAISE THE NAMES OF , MESS^RS KING   *(first line)*
       ✿ DE IXNING ✿ WEDGE, CORNELL, NORMAN, HYNES AND FYSON ♠
                    DEATH, BARNES, STAPLES, ALSO WILSON   *(second ine)*
       ✝ FECIT A.D.1808 ✝ BY WHOSE KIND AND GENEROUS AID ♠
                    I (LEADER OF THIS PEAL (WAS MADE ○   *(third ine)*
       Diameter 28⁷⁄₁₆″   Weight 4 cwt 2 qr 0 lb   Note E - ○ – coin
       Triple inscription band. This is Briant's acknowledgement to his Suf-
       folk origins, the IXNING being Exning, his birthplace. The bells have
       not been rung since the 1939–45 war, one bell only being chimed. The
       tower was rebuilt in 1884, possibly as a consequence of the Colchester
       earthquake, but there now appear to be structural problems with the
       north arcade of the nave.   *RWMC / J.D.*

287.   1808 GREAT PACKINGTON, Warks.   Single
       ✝ TRES OLIM CAMPANÆ E QUIBUS RUPT↑ QU↑DAM VICTO-
       RIAM AD TRAFALGAR RESONANDO A; D ☛ MDCCCV IN UNAM
       FUSAE A ; D ☛ MDCCCVIII ✿ ○   *(first line)*
       JOHN BRIANT HERTFORD FECIT 1808 ✿ GLORIA DEO IN EXCEL-
       SIS ✿ ♠ ✝ ☛ ♠ ✝ ☛ ✝ ♠ ✿ ○   *(second line)*
       Below: Two medallions.
       Diameter 44¼ “ Weight c.13 cwt   Note -?
       This bell records that there were formerly three bells and that one was
       broken in ringing to celebrate the Battle of Trafalgar. All three were
       recast to make this one.   *CB Warks.*

288.   1808 SHOTTESWELL, Warks. St Lawrence   2nd
       E : G : WALFORD VICAR. J. ABBATTS C W ✿ ♠ ♠ ♠ ✿ ♠ ♠ ♠ ✝
       JOHN BRIANT HERTFORD FECIT 1808.   *(one line)*
       Diameter 28⅝ “ Weight 4 cwt 1 qr 24 lb   Note C
       This was the treble of five until a new treble was added by J. Taylor & Co. in
       1995.
       The vicar and churchwardens are those during whose term of office
       the tower and spire were rebuilt. Until 1995, the frame and fittings
       dated largely from 1808. It seems likely that the work was carried out
       by John Waters of King's Sutton.   *CB Warks / CJP*

289.   1809 NUNEATON, Warks. St Nicholas   4th of 8
        J. HUSKINSON ⅋ J.GEARY C.W. J.BRIANT HERTFORD FECIT I809
        J.OVER B.H.   *(one line)*
        Diameter 34 ½ " Weight 6 ½ cwt   Note B
        Note B.H. stands for Bell Hanger; John Over came from Rugby and
        had previously worked with Briant at Churchover and several towers
        in Leicestershire. His practice was to contract for rehanging rings and/
        or providing new bells, which were cast under subcontract. Part of his
        frame survives.   *HCA / CB Warks.*

290.   1809 HADDENHAM, Bucks. St Mary   Treble of 8
        J : BRIANT HERTFORD FECIT I809. THO IM ALLOWD TO BE BUT
        SMALL, MY TONE IS HEARD ABOVE THEM AL   *(one line)*
        Diameter 30 ¼ " Weight 5 cwt 2 qr 10 lb   Note E

291.   1809 HADDENHAM   2nd
        JOHN BRIANT HERTFORD FECIT I809 ✿
        Diameter 30 ¼ "   Weight 5 cwt 1 qr 2 lb   Note D#

292.   1809 HADDENHAM   3
        ✝ JOHN BRIANT HERTFORD FECIT I809
        Diameter32 ¼ " Weight 6 cwt 0 qr 6 lb   Note C#

293.   1809 HADDENHAM   4th
        ✝ JOHN BRIANT HERTFORD FECIT I809 ✝
        Diameter 34" Weight 6 cwt 2 qr 16 lb   Note B

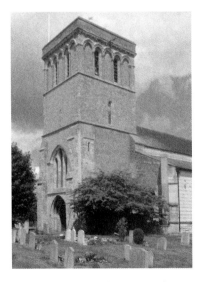

Haddenham, St Mary the Virgin, Bucks. A
full octave by Briant but 5th recast & 7th
replaced

294. *1809 HADDENHAM*   *5th of 8*
      JOHN BRIANT HERTFORD FECIT I809 ✝
      Diam. 35 ½ " Wt. 8 cwt 0 qr 14 lb   *Note A*
      Recast by J.Taylor 1986, after becoming cracked.

295. 1809 HADDENHAM   6th
      ✝ JOHN BRIANT HERTFORD FECIT I809 ✝ ✿
      Diameter 38 ½ " Weight 9 cwt 1 qr 22 lb Note G#

296. *1809 HADDENHAM*   *7th*
      ✝ *JOHN BRIANT HERTFORD FECIT I809*
      JOSEPH FRANCKLIN ESQ^R BENEFACTOR W
      RICHMOND SOLICITOR   *(one line)*
      Diameter 41 ½ "   Weight 11 cwt 3 qr 2 lb   Note F#
      This bell become cracked in 2001 and was replaced by
      a second-hand Gillett & Johnston bell.   *J.D.*

297. 1809 HADDENHAM   Tenor
✝ J TO THE CHURCH THE LIVING CALL ✝ AND TO THE GRAVE
DO SUMMON ALL ✝ ✠ † ✝ ✠ † ✠   *(first line)*
JOHN BRIANT HERTFORD FECIT I809 ✝ EDWARD HEDGES ✗
JOHN FRANCKLING CHURCH WARDENS   *(second line)*
Diameter 48 ¾ "   Weight 17 cwt 2 qr 14 lb   Note E
A complete ring all of one year, sadly no longer intact. W. Richmond
'solicitor' was not a lawyer; he was the man who wrote the begging letters and passed round the hat. Cocks clearly distinguishes between the
sizes of letters, and he also shows the erratic spacing of the words. The
bells were rehung by Webb & Bennett in 1902 and retuned and rehung
with new fittings by J. Taylor & Co. in 1978. Eayre & Smith replaced the
seventh.   *CB Bucks.*

298. 1809 BIERTON, Bucks. St James   Tenor of 6
✝ J : BRIANT HERTFORD FEICT *(sic)* I809 T = THORN ✗ H = WEBB C :
W ✝ ♣ † ♣ ✝ † ♣   *(one line)*
Diameter 42 ½ "   Weight 12 cwt 0 qr 27 lb   Note F#
= - two commas on their side, one above the other, not known to have
been used elsewhere.   *CB Bucks.*

299. 1809 ABBOTS LANGLEY, Herts. St Lawrence   Tenor of 6
JOHN BRIANT HERTFORD FECIT I809 L ᴰ RAYMOND BENEFAC-
TOR J.FILMER VICAR. J.REEVE J.RADWELL C : W ♣ ✝ ♣ ♣ ✝ ♣ ♣
♣ ✝   *(one line)*
Diameter 40"   Weight 9 cwt 2 qr 25 lb   Note G
All six bells were tuned by Whitechapel and rehung by White's of
Appleton, 1995.   *Dodds, CB Herts.*

300– *1809 HERTFORD Shire Hall*   *Quarter bells*
301. *No. 1 and No. 2 were cast with the hour bell in this year, for a clock earlier than*
      the present one. During the 1989–91 restoration of the building, which houses
      the magistrates' courts, these bells were stolen. The contractors had them
      replaced with new bells cast by J. Taylor, but bearing the name of Gillett &
      Johnston (Croydon) Ltd. Clockmakers. The clock dates from 1824. (**See Clock**
      No. 29)

                                                         Dodds, CB Herts.

302. 1809 HERTFORD Shire Hall   Hour bell
J BRIANT HERTFORD FECIT I809
Diameter 23 ¼ "   Weight 3 cwt   Note A
This bell retains its cannons and old hammer.   *Dodds, CB Herts.*

303. 1809 HERTFORD Museum
      JOHN BRIANT HERTFORD FECIT 1809 ✿ ❧ † ♟ ✝ ♟ † ❧
      This was the clock bell from Hallingbury House, Essex, near Bishop's
      Stortford. The large clock dial dated 1836 is also in the Museum.
      (Museum ref: HETFM 3319·2 DB 3/88 9/1933)

304. 1809 RAVENSTHORPE, Northants. St Denys   Treble of 5
      JOHN BRIANT HERTFORD FECIT 1809 † ♟ † ♟
      Diameter 26⅜ "   Weight 3 cwt 3 qr 3 lb   Note E

305. 1809 RAVENSTHORPE   2nd
      JOHN BRIANT HERTFORD FECIT 1809 OSTIN JOHNSON C. W. ♟
      Diameter 27⅞ "   Weight 3 cwt 3 qr 20 lb   Note D

306. 1809 RAVENSTHORPE   3rd
      JOHN BRIANT HERTFORD FECIT 1809 † ♟ † ♟
      Diameter 29¼ "   Weight 4 cwt 1 qr 21 lb   Note C#

307. 1809 RAVENSTHORPE   4th
      JOHN BRIANT HERTFORD FECIT 1809 † ♟ † ♟
      Diameter 31⁹⁄₁₆"   Weight 5 cwt 0 qr 10 lb   Note B

308. *1809 RAVENSTHORPE*   *Tenor*
      JOHN BRIANT HERTFORD FECIT 1809 J. HALL J ORLAND C. W. e
      Diameter 32¾ "   Weight 7 cwt 2 qr 0 lb   *Note A*
      This bell was recast by J. Taylor & Co. 1887.   *HCA / PDG. Dir.*

309. 1809 COWLINGE, Suffolk St Margaret   3rd of 5
      ✝ JOHN BRIANT HERTFORD FECIT 1809 ✝ ♟ ✿ ♟ ✝ ✿ ✝
      Diameter 32⅝ "   Weight 6 cwt   Note B+

310. 1809 COWLINGE   4th
      ✝ JOHN BRIANT HERTFORD FECIT 1809 ✝ † ♟ ✿ † ♟ ✝ ♟ † ✿
      ♟ †   *(one line)*
      Diameter 34½ "   Weight 10 cwt   Note A+
                                                                RWMC

311. 1809 ABINGTON, Northants. SS Peter and Paul   Treble of 3
      JOHN BRIANT HERTFORD FECIT 1809
      Diameter 28"   Weight 4¾ cwt   Note E♭
      This bell retains its 1809 fittings.   *PDG Dir.*

312. 1809 PRESTWOLD, Leics. St Andrew   7th of 8
JOHN BRIANT HERTFORD FECIT 1809
Diameter 36 ⅛ "   Weight 8 cwt 0 qr 16 lb   Note G#

313. 1809 PRESTWOLD   Tenor
JOHN BRIANT HERTFORD FECIT 1809. THE REV^D C J PACKE
RECTOR. E. GAMBLE AND T. SOMES C.W.   *(one line)*
Diameter 40 ⅛ "   Weight 10 cwt 3 qr 18 lb   Note F#
CB Leics./ GAD

314. 1809 SAPCOTE, Leics. All Saints   8th of 10, formerly 2nd of 4
J OVER B.H. † B PERKINS C W † J BRIANT HERTFORD FECIT
1809 †   *(one line)*
Diameter 33"   Weight 6 cwt 2 qr 7 lb   Note C
The † is probably Fig. 23$_E$. It was very rare for North to actually show
a cross in the text. Briant was recasting a bell by Thomas Newcombe of
Leicester 1611. There were four bells only in 1809. It was supplied
through John Over, the Rugby bellhanger, who was paid £45. 9. 0 in
1808-9 for 'Repairing the Bells'.   *CB Leics./ GAD / CJP*

315. 1809 WORMLEIGHTON, Warks. The Gatehouse   Clock bell
JOHN BRIANT HERTFORD FECIT 1809 ✝ ⚕ ✡ ⚕ ✝ ⚕ ✡ ⚕ ✝
Diameter 23"   Weight c.2 ¾ cwt   Note A+ (B♭ -)
Briant's published list of clocks and chimes includes a turret clock
made for R. Andrews Esq. of Harlston, Northampton in 1810. Transferred to Wormleighton c.1972. The bell has cannons and is sounded
by a clock hammer.   *CJP*

316. 1809 BOTTESFORD, Leics. St Mary   Tenor of 8
REV<u>ND</u> J THOROTON VICAR T. VINCENT AND T DERRY C.
WARDENS J BRIANT HERTFORD FECIT 1809   *(one line)*
Diameter 51 ½ "   Weight 22 cwt 1 qr 8 lb   Note E♭

317. 1810 BOTTESFORD   3rd
J. BRIANT HERTFORD 1810
Diameter 35 ¼ "   Weight 8 cwt 0 qr 18 lb   Note C
These two bells must have been cast either side of New Year. The
inscription on the third is shorter than usual, FECIT having been
omitted.   *HCA / GAD*

318. 1810 PRESTWOLD, Leics.   6th of 8
      JOHN BRIANT HERTFORD FECIT 1810
      Diameter 33¾"   Weight 6 cwt 3 qr 14 lb   Note A#
      In 1809–10, there were three bells only, which seem to have been recast
      on a piecemeal basis as money became available. In 1812, he added
      two trebles (*see below Nos. 350/351*).   *HCA / CB Leics.*

319. 1810 CLAYCOTON, Northants. All Saints   Treble of 3
      A JOHNSON C W : J : BRIANT HERTFORD FECIT 1810
      Diameter 28"   Weight 4¼ cwt   Note D?
      Briant lists this as No.3. It was probably a recast of a bell by H.Watts II.
                                                              HCA / PDG Dir.

320. 1810 MIDDLETON CHEYNEY, Northants. All Saints   Sanctus
      J. BRIANT HERTFORD 1810
      Diameter 16"   *HCA / PDG. Dir.*

321. 1810 ABINGTON, Northants.   Tenor of 3
      J. BRIANT HERTFORD FECIT 1810
      Diameter 34¼" Weight 7 cwt   Note C
      The fittings on this bell were renewed by J. Taylor & Co. in 1885.
                                                              HCA / PDG Dir.

322. 1810 ASTON, Herts. Clock House   Clock bell
      J BRIANT HERTFORD 1810
      Diameter 20¹⁄₁₆" Weight 1¾ cwt   Note A
      This, the former clock bell of Aston House, hangs in a cupola over the
      converted stables. The original one-handed dial remains but the pres-
      ent electric clock is by Smith of Derby. The 17th century clock mecha-
      nism is now in Stevenage Museum, in the undercroft of St George's
      church.   *Dodds, CB Herts.*

323. 1810 WELWYN GARDEN CITY, Panshanger Stables   Clock bell
      J BRIANT HERTFORD 1810
      Diameter 21¾" Weight 2¼ cwt
      Panshanger House was demolished in 1953/4; the stable block is now
      offices for Redland Aggregates Ltd. The empty cupola remains but the
      bell is on the floor inside the entrance.   *Dodds, CB Herts.*

324. 1811 ABINGTON, Northants.   2nd of 3
      JOHN BRIANT HERTFORD FECIT 1811   J.HARRIS. C: W:
      Diameter 31"   Weight 6 cwt   Note D –
      This bell completed Briant's work at Abington. The fittings date from
      1809 and the bells are classed as unringable. They are not in a major
      scale.   *RS / HCA / PDG Dir.*

325. *1811 AMPTHILL, Beds. St Andrew*   *Old 2nd of 5*
T: B: STONE & *KIRK C: WARDENS I: BRIANT HERTFORD FECIT 18II*
Diameter 31"   Weight 5 cwt 1 qr 20 lb
Weight quoted in Taylor's invoice, as received in part payment for new ring
1898.
Churchwardens' accounts:
> *1809 Novr. Pd for a Letter from Bryant Hertford.*   *7½ d*
> *1810 Feb. 17th Pd for a Letter from Bryant Hertford.*   *7½ d*
> *1811 April 29 Paid to Mr John Briant of Hertford as per Bill*
>   *for Recasting the Second Bell.*   *£12. 15. 0*
Recast by J.Taylor & Co. 1899 with the inscription not in facsimile.
                                                   HCA / CB Beds./ CJP

326. 1811 HOUGHTON REGIS, Beds. All Saints   4th of 6
J. BRIANT HERTFORD FECIT 18II + C: W. • ✝
Diameter 36"   Weight 7 cwt 2 qr 19 lb   Note A
+ – possibly Fig. 23$_E$.
The names of the churchwardens have been omitted or erased; it
would not be the first time that Briant did not receive all necessary
details of names to be included in inscriptions. On the other hand it
may have been like Ashow/Wallington and intended for somewhere
else.   HCA / CB Beds.

327. 1811   BRAUNSTON, Northants. All Saints   Treble of 6
JOHN BRIANT HERTFORD FECIT 18II
Diameter 32 ¼ "   Weight 6 cwt 2 qr 27 lb   Note D

328. 1811 BRAUNSTON   2nd
JOHN BRIANT HERTFORD FECIT 18II
Diameter 33 ⅝ "   Weight 6 cwt 3 qr 22 lb   Note C

329. 1811 BRAUNSTON   3rd
JOHN BRIANT HERTFORD FECIT 18II
Diameter 35 ⅞ "   Weight 8 cwt 0 qr 22 lb   Note B♭

330. 1811 BRAUNSTON   4th
JOHN BRIANT HERTFORD FECIT 18II
Diameter 37"   Weight 8 cwt 2 qr 16 lb   Note A

331. 1811 BRAUNSTON   5th of 6
JOHN BRIANT HERTFORD FECIT   18II
Diam. 40"   Wt. 10 cwt 0 qr 23 lb   Note G

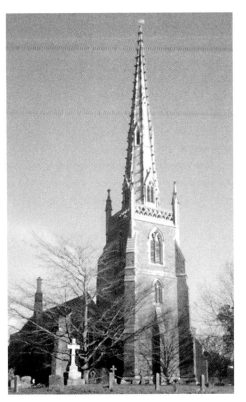

Braunston, All Saints, Northants.
A complete Briant ring of six.
[Elizabeth Gwynne, Braunston]

332. 1811 BRAUNSTON   Tenor of 6
J. EVANS VICAR : J: HALL ℞ W:
HARRIS C : W. JOHN BRIANT
HERTFORD FECIT I8II *(one line)*
Diam. 45 ⅜ " Wt. 15 cwt 1 qr 6 lb Note F
The diameters and weight quoted are
those from 1922 when the bells were
rehung and tuned by J. Taylor & Co. The
names of the church wardens on the
tenor are correct, but the incumbent of
the time was John Williams, Rector. A
possible explanation may be that, as
Braunston is in the gift of Jesus College,
Oxford, and both names are Welsh,
a J. Evans was here in 1811 as curate for a
non-resident rector, and that he was
described as 'Vicarius' or Vicar for short.
These bells were probably delivered via
the Grand Junction Canal.
The churchwardens' accounts record
that at a meeting held on 23 January
1812, a frame of good oak was ordered to
be made to receive the new ring at a cost
of £60. The following entries are of interest:

		cwt.	qrs.	lb.
April 8th, 1812 The weight of the new Bells, according to Mr John Briant's Bill :				
First bell		7	1	2
Second Do		7	2	20
Third Do		9	0	0
Fourth Do		9	2	0
Fifth Do		10	3	6
Sixth Do		17	2	13
Cwt.		61	3	13
1813 John Briants Bill.............. £ 237 15 6				

HCA / PDG Dir.

333. 1811 WARMINGTON, Warks. St Michael   Treble of 3
T: ROBINSON C: W: H: B: HARRISON VICAR ✝ J: BRIANT
HERTFORD FECIT 18II   *(one line)*
Diameter 34"   Weight c.6½ cwt
Revd R.B. Harrison was appointed Vicar in 1802. Churchwardens'
accounts record the provision of a new frame in 1809-11 by John
Waters of King's Sutton, whose work included 'new casting one bell'.
Briant's name is nowhere mentioned, so he was subcontacting for
Waters.   *CB Warks./ CJP*

334. 1811 HARDWICK, Bucks. St Mary   2nd, formerly treble of 5
J: BRIANT HERTFORD FECIT 18II W: FLOWERS C: W
Diameter 28"   Weight 4 cwt   Note C
This bell, as described by Cocks, was a recast and was hung using the
old headstock and clapper of its predecessor. These items have since
been replaced.   *CB Bucks.*

335. 1812 SHREWSBURY, Salop Holy Cross Abbey   4th of 8
✝ H BURTON VICAR R: BRATTON ✠ R: BETTON C: W: J: BRIANT
HERTFORD FECIT 18I2   *(one line)*
Diameter 34"   Weight 6½ cwt
Due to the weakness of the tower, the bells are chimed only.
                                              HCA / CB Salop

336. 1812 HONOLULU, St Andrew's Cathedral   Treble of 8
✝ IOHN BRIANT HERTFORD F CIT *(sic)* 18I2
(on waist, incised)   Queen Lili'uokalani
                        (1891–1893)
(On sound-bow) ✝ OUR LIFE IS CHANGEFUL, VIEW US NOW COMPLETE :
SEDATE WE ROSE IN SIX, WE'RE GAY IN EIGHT ✝   *(one line)*
Diameter 28½"   Weight 5 cwt 1 qr 7 lb   Note G

337. 1812   HONOLULU   2nd of 8
✝ IOHN BRIANT HERTFORD F CIT 18I2
(on waist, incised)   King Kalakaua
                        (1874–1891)
(on sound-bow) HEAR! HOLY ALKMONDS LONG FORGOTTEN SHADE : TO
THEE OUR NOTES WE RAISE, FOR THEE WERE MADE ✝ ♪ ✡ ♪ ✝ *(one line)*
Diameter 29"   Weight 5 cwt 1 qr 22 lb   Note F#

338. 1812 HONOLULU   3rd of 8
JOHN BRIANT HERTFORD FECIT 1812
(on waist, incised)   King Lunalilo
                                            (1873–1874)
(on sound-bow) THESE SACRED WALLS, THIS VENERABLE SPIRE, SHALL GIVE
OUR CHANGES SWEETNESS, RAISE THEM HIGHER   *(one line)*
Diameter 30″   Weight 5 cwt 2 qr 19 lb   Note E

339. 1812 HONOLULU   4th
✝ JOHN BRIANT HERTFORD FECIT 1812 ✝
(on waist, incised)   King Kamechameha V
                                            (1863–1872)
(on sound-bow) AND STILL AS SPORTIVE FANCY COUNTS THEM O'ER, SHALL
WAFT THEM FAR ON SEVERN'S FERTILE SHORE ✝ ✿   *(one line)*
Diameter 32″   Weight 6 cwt 0 qr 14 lb   Note D

340. 1812 HONOLULU   5th
✝ JOHN BRIANT HERTFORD FECIT 1812 ✝
(on waist, incised)   King Kamechameha IV
                                            (1855–1863)
(on sound-bow) ✝ HAIL! PATRIOT GEORGE FOR WHOM A NATION
PRAYS, THAT HEALTH AND PEACE MAY CROWN THY LATTER
DAYS ✝ ♟ ♟ ✿ ♟   *(one line)*
Diameter 33 ⅞ ″   Weight 6 cwt 3 qr 13 lb   Note C

341. 1812 HONOLULU   6th
✝ JOHN BRIANT HERTFORD FECIT 1812 ✝
(on waist, incised)   King Kamechameha III
                                            (1825–1854)
(on sound-bow) ✝ IN DEATHS WE MOURN, WITH HYMEN WE REJOICE: IN
PUBLIC GOOD WE JOIN THE PUBLIC VOICE ♟ ♟ ✿ ♟   *(one line)*
Diameter 34 ⅞ ″   Weight 7 cwt 1 qr 24 lb   Note B

342. 1812 HONOLULU   7th
JOHN BRIANT HERTFORD FECIT 1812 ✝
(on waist, incised)   King Kamechameha II
                                            (1819–1824)
(on sound-bow) ✝ HARK CURFEW TOLLS – NOW MATIN RITES PREPARE :
WHILST PIETY GIVES ALL HER SOUL TO PRAYER ✝ ♟ ✿ ♟ ♟   *(one line)*
Diameter 38″   Weight 9 cwt 1 qr 25 lb   Note A

343. 1812 HONOLULU   Tenor

✝ ED LINZEE VICAR ED BULL ⅋ J: BARNES
C: WARDENS ✝ JOHN BRIANT HERTFORD
FECIT 1812   *(one line)*

(on waist, incised)   King Kamechameha I
                                        (1795–1819)

(on sound-bow) FAITHFULL, I WATCH AND WARN
BOTH YOUNG AND OLD : TO ALL O GOD THY
LIGHT AND GRACE UNFOLD ✝ ✝ GLORIA DEO
IN EXCELSIS ✝   *(one line)*

Diam. 42"   Wt. 12 cwt 0 qr 26 lb Note G

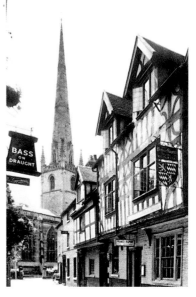

Shrewsbury, St Alkmund.
The only complete ring of eight cast in one
year by Briant in 1812. In 1972, they were
sold to Honolulu Cathedral.   [G. W. Pipe]

These bells were cast for St Alkmund's,
Shrewsbury, it is said at the same time as the
ring at Condover. The choice specimens of English Romantic verse were composed by the
school-master of High Ercall, Richard Wilding,
whose verses are also found on other bells in
the area, not only Briant's. Wilding had another
claim to fame; he was a change-ringer of great
ability, taking part in several peals at St Chad's
and St Mary's, Shrewsbury.

On 22 November 1810, the following letter was read to the vestry:

Gentlemen, At your request I have examined your bells and the whole
of it is in a very bad state the bells are badly worn with the clappers the
stocks are not safe to carry the bells, the gudgins are almost asunder,
and the brasses is almost worn through, and the wheels are very bad,
and the frame moves a great deal, a part of the frame is broke asunder,
which will be very injurious to the tower and spire in a short time if
proper care is not taken.

Gentlemen,

I remain your humble servant,
W. Ansell,

Church Bell Hanger

Not surprisingly, in view of this breathless report, ringing ceased
forthwith. After the catastrophic collapse of St Chad's in 1788, parish
authorities had become very nervous.

On 13 September 1811 it was ordered that the present peal of six
bells be taken down by

John Bryant of Hertford, Bell Caster, that the same be recast into a peal of
eight by the same person, and also rehung, and that the same be done under
the direction of the present Church Wardens Mr. Thomas Harris Mr. Richard

Wilding Mr. Charles Bigg and Mr. William Bull, and that the expense
thereof be paid and borne by this Parish.

1811–12	Messrs. Crowley, Hicklin & Co, for carriage of	£	s.	d.
	Bells..	22	18	0
	William Jones for do...........................		8	4
	Mr. Jarratt for ale for men taking bells down		4	8
1812–13	Mr. Blaney for drawing bells to Church.................	12		0
	Mr. Bryant on account of the bells	123	0	0
	Mr. Harris on account of the timber work to do ...	20	0	0
	At weighing the bells...........................		4	8
	For carriage of bells to the quay		5	0
1813–14	J. Bryant balance of account...........................	23	0	0
	Messrs. Beck & Co money borrowed for the bells			
	and interest	56	16	5

This work was duly carried out, but problems still arose:

June 11th, 1813. Mr. Bryant having examined the frame work of the bells done by Mr. Harris, which it was said had been the cause of injuring the steeple reports : – that in his opinion the same was not occasioned by any fault in the frame work, but Mr. Bryant having recommended that some bracing bits should be added to the frame to keep the trusses to the bearings so as to lessen the action of the frame, it was therefore resolved that the same be done under the direction of Mr. Bigg, Mr. Hand and Mr. Davies.

Throughout, the main weakness seems to have been in the structure of the steeple. The bells were rehung in 1909 and were rung regularly until 1925 when ringing ceased. In 1972, when the church was faced with the cost of urgent repairs, the bells were put up for sale. After several abortive attempts to find a home in this country, this fine octave was sold to St Andrew's Cathedral, Honolulu in 1989–90. The weights are as given by the Whitechapel Foundry in 1990. Before being transferred to their new home, each bell had an additional inscription incised on the waist, naming the Kings and Queens of Hawaii before annexation by the United States (*see Frontispiece*).

They are now the only surviving *complete octave cast in one year,* Condover being cast over two years and Haddenham and Hatfield each having had one bell recast.   *HCA/ CB Salop / CJP / RW 8/2/1991*

344. 1812 HIGH ERCALL, Salop St Michael   Treble of 8
✠ JOHN BRIANT HERTFORD FECIT 1812 ✠
(on sound-bow) TWIN SISTERS WE UNITE OUR TUNEFUL PO*WERS* WITH THIS
SWEET BAND TO CHARM THE VACANT HOURS :   *(first line)*
IN MAZY CHANGES CHEAR THE LANDSCAPE WIDE, AND COURT COY
ECHOES FROM YON MOUNTAIN'S SIDE   *(second line)*
Diameter 28″   Weight 4 cwt   Note F#
The last four letters of 'Powers' are incised. 'Yon mountain' is the Wrekin.

345. 1812   HIGH ERCALL   2nd
✠ JOHN BRIANT HERTFORD FECIT I8I2 ✠
(on sound-bow) WHERE MEANDERING RODEN GENTLY GLIDES OR
TURNES PROUD CURRENT FILLS ITS AMPLE SIDES :   *(first line)*
THENCE MEDITATION VIEWS OUR CALM ABODE : HEALS THE
SICK MIND AND YIELDS IT PURE TO GOD   *(second line)*
Diameter 29"   Weight 5 cwt   Note E#
More Romantic verse from Richard Wilding. 'Turne' is the River Tern.
These bells augmented the six of 1710-67 by Rudhall of Gloucester.

HCA / CB Salop

346. 1812 CODICOTE, Herts.   3rd, formerly treble of 6
JOHN BRIANT HERTFORD FECIT I8I2
(on sound-bow) THOMAS QUINT HE GAVE ME, WITH GOOD WILL
FRANK AND FREE; FOR TO RING MERRILEY   *(one line)*
Diameter 28"   Weight 4 ½ cwt   Note E
Two new trebles were added in 1998 as a Millennium Project, making
this the third.   *Dodds, C.B. Herts.*

347. 1812 KNEBWORTH, Herts. SS Mary and Thomas of Canterbury.
                                                          Tenor of 8

J. BRIANT HERTFORD FECIT I8I2
Diameter 38⅝"   Weight 12 cwt   Note F#
It is just possible that this bell may have been a belated recasting of
one by 'X' of Hitchin who cast a ring of five in 1697.   *Dodds, CB Herts.*

348. *1812 ST ALBANS St Peter*   *Old 4th*
J : BRIANT HERTFORD FECIT. RECAST BY SUBSCRIPTION. L:
BATTEN F: GOUGH ✠ J: WHITNEY, C: W: I8I2   *(one line)*
Diameter 35"   Weight 5 cwt 2 qr 13 lb   Note C#
Recast by Whitechapel 1993.   *Dodds, CB Herts.*

349. 1812 LUTTERWORTH, Leics. St. Mary   Tenor of 8
THE HON^BLE ✠ REV^ND HENRY RYDER RECTOR W. MASH ✠
J TILLY C.W. JOHN BRIANT HERTFORD FECIT I8I2 *(one line)*
Diameter 45 ¼ "   Weight 14 cwt 2 qr 1 lb   Note E
                                                CB Leics./ GAD

350. 1812 PRESTWOLD, Leics.   4th of 8, formerly treble of 5
THE GIFT OF CHARLES JAMES PACKE ESQ. JUNIOR
JOHN BRIANT HERTFORD FECIT I8I2   *(one line)*
Diameter 31 ⅜ "   Weight 6 cwt 0 qr 11 lb   Note C#

351. 1812 PRESTWOLD   5th formerly 2nd
JOHN BRIANT HERTFORD FECIT. THE GIFT OF C. J. PACKE ESQ.
JUNIOR 1812   *(one line)*
Diameter 33"   Weight 6 cwt 2 qr 11 lb   Note B
These two bells completed Briant's work on this ring, begun 1809/10.
Opened by the Sileby Ringers on Friday, 19 May 815 (?)

HCA / GAD / CJP

352. 1812 HARTLEBURY, Worcs. St James   3rd of 8
J : BRYANT OF HERTFORD FECIT 1812 J. STYLES ⚭ J WILLIAMS C :
W
Diameter 33 ½ " Weight 7 cwt 0 qr 17 lb   Note C
This is Briant's only bell in Worcestershire. Rehung and retuned by J.
Taylor & Co. 1959.   *Ex inform. H.B.*
Walters to HCA / CJP

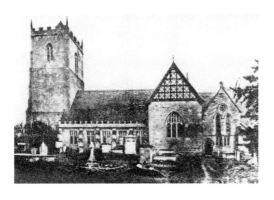

Condover, St Andrew, Salop. A complete
octave by Briant, C Dalton/Dean cranage

353. 1812 CONDOVER, Salop.
St Andrew   3rd of 8
JOHN BRIANT. HERTFORD. FECIT
1812   *(† on side)*
Diam. 30 ½ "   Wt. 4 ½ cwt   Note E

354. 1812 CONDOVER   Tenor
† JOHN GWILLIAMS. ⚭ JOHN
LEAKE. C : WARDENS • JOHN
BRIANT. HERTFORD. FECIT. 1812
† †   *(† on side)*
Diam. 42 ½ "   Wt. 13 cwt   Note G -
The cross after the date is on its side.
HCA / CB Salop

355. 1813 CONDOVER   Treble
✝ JOHN BRIANT HERTFORD FECIT   1813 + 🔔 ✡ 🔔
Diameter 28 ½ "   Weight 4 cwt   Note G

356. 1813 CONDOVER   2nd
✝ JOHN BRIANT HERTFORD FECIT. 1813. + 🔔 ✡ 🔔 *(one line)*
Diameter 28 ¾ " Weight. 4 cwt   Note F#
+ – Probably Fig. 202.

357. 1813 CONDOVER   4th of 8
JOHN BRIANT. HERTFORD. FECIT. 1813   *(one line)*
Diameter 32 ⅛ " Weight5 ¼ cwt   Note D

358. 1813 CONDOVER   5th
      JOHN BRIANT. HERTFORD. FECIT 1813 ♣ ♣   *(one line)*
      Diameter 32 ⅛ "   Weight c.6 cwt   Note C
      Diameter not given in *CB Salop*; given as above in *HCA*

359. 1813 CONDOVER   6th
      ✝ JOHN BRIANT. HERTFORD. FECIT. 1813   *(✝ on side)*
      Diameter 35 ¼ "   Weight 7 ½ cwt   Note B

360. 1813 CONDOVER   7th
      ✝ JOHN BRIANT. HERTFORD. FECIT. 1813 ✝ ✝
      Diameter 38"   Weight 9 cwt   Note A
      These bells retain their original chip tuning and are not in perfect tune
      with each other; all cannons were removed prior to rehanging in 1894
      by J. Taylor & Co.   *C. Dalton*
      The churchwardens' accounts contain the following entries: £   s.   d.
          1813. To takeing the Bells with two Teams to Shrewsbury
                          and Expences 1 11   6
          June 1. To assisting unloading & weighing   5   0
          June 11. Going to Mr Burley & Mr Bryant for
                          a Bond to compleat the Bells   2   0
          June 19 Mr. Burley for drawing Bond   1   1
          Sept. 25. For a letter from Mr Bryant   1   0
          Oct. 11. Ale at unloading the bells   4   0
          Oct. 27. Wm Roberts for Cuting Turffs & getting
                          them to the Bell Loft 2 day   5   0
          Oct. 29. For ale at the opening the Bells   5   0
          Oct. 30. Mr Bryant – see Bill   112   0   0
      Briant had added 6 cwt of metal to that from the old six. The cost of the
      work had to be defrayed by the sale of timber from 'Church Lands' and
      by a 'loan' or church rate of 6d in the pound. This is a good example of
      the shifts to which churchwardens were put in order to pay for such an
      expensive item as bells. This octave is now the only complete example
      by Briant in this country but, unlike St Alkmund's, Shrewsbury, and
      Haddenham, the bells were not all cast in the one year.
                                                    HCA / CB Salop

361. 1813 ORPINGTON, Kent All Saints   Single
      JOHN BRIANT HERTFORD FECIT 1813
      Diameter 29"   Weight 4 cwt
      All Saints is the ancient parish church of Orpington, from the time
      when it was a village, not a London suburb. Local tradition says that
      there was a peal of bells before the steeple was struck by lightning and
      burnt down about 1812, but they were then carried to St Mary Cray,
      (the next parish. J.D.). Hasted's *History of Kent* recorded two bells only,

and it seems likely that they were taken to London and sold to pay for repairs, Briant's single taking their place.   *HCA / CB Kent*

362. 1814 MONTGOMERY, Powys St Nicholas   3rd of 6
REV^{ND} M : E LLOYD RECTOR J : JONES ⚭ E : READ C :W
J · BRIANT HERTFORD FECIT 1814 ✝   *(one line)*
Diameter not known.   Weight c.5 cwt   Note D♭
This bell was a recast of one by Rudhall of Gloucester 1724.   *J.C.*
Eisel

363. 1814   ST. PAUL'S WALDEN, Herts. All Saints   5th of 6
✝ JOHN BRIANT HERTFORD FECIT I8I4 ✝
Diameter 37½" Weight 9 cwt 0 qr 16 lb   Note G
This was a recast of the fourth of a complete five by Chandler of
Drayton Parslow, 1665.   *Dodds, CB Herts.*

364. 1814 SOUTHILL, Beds. All Saints   Treble of 6
✝ JOHN BRIANT HERTFORD FECIT I8I4
Diameter 29"   Weight 5 cwt 2 qr 18 lb   Note D#

365. 1814 SOUTHILL   2nd
✝ JOHN BRIANT HERTFORD FECIT I8I4
Diameter 30"   Weight 6 cwt 0 qr 18 lb   Note C#

366. 1814 SOUTHILL   3rd
✝ JOHN BRIANT HERTFORD FECIT I8I4
Diameter 32"   Weight 7 cwt 0 qr 3 lb   Note B

367. 1814 SOUTHILL   4th
✝ JOHN BRIANT HERTFORD FECIT I8I4
Diameter 35"   Weight 7 cwt 1 qr 23 lb   Note A#

368. 1814 SOUTHILL   5th
✝ JOHN BRIANT HERTFORD FECIT I8I4
Diameter 37½" Weight 9 cwt 2 qr 2 lb   Note G#

369. *1814 SOUTHILL*   *Old tenor*
SOUTHILL CHURCH REPAIRED AND THE BELLS RECAST 1814.
GLORIA DEO IN EXCELSIS. JOHN BRIANT HERTFORD FECIT
Diameter 42"   Weight 12 cwt 3 qr 10 lb
The tenor was recast by Mears & Stainbank in 1867; neither **CB Beds.** *nor*
HCA make any mention of this bell, yet it is recorded in a church terrier of
1822. The weight is as received by the founders prior to recasting.   *HCA / C JP*

370. 1814 ARKESDEN, Essex St Margaret   2nd
J : WOLF ESQ. BENEFACTOR. J : BRIANT HERTFORD FECIT I8I4
Diameter 24"   Weight 3 cwt   Note C
This was a recast of the second of a complete six of 1701 by Richard
Keene who worked in the area from about 1699 to 1702 (*See above, p.
130, Bell 32*). Keene's Essex rings have 'not always stood the test of
time' (*CB Essex*, p.118) but at Arkesden only the 2nd needed recasting.
     The tenor weight is given in *Dove's Guide* as 5-3-14 in G, which is
extremely light for the note.   *CB Essex*

371. 1814 ASHBY-DE-LA-ZOUCH, Leics. St Helen   Treble of 8
THE TWO TREBLE BELLS WERE GIVEN BY VOLUNTARY SUB-
SCRIPTION IN COMMEMORATION OF THE PEACE OF I8I4 JOHN
BRIANT HERTFORD FECIT I8I4
Diameter 29"   Weight 6 cwt 0 qr 20 lb   Note E

372. 1814 ASHBY-DE-LA-ZOUCH   2nd
THE TWO TREBLE BELLS WERE GIVEN BY VOLUNTARY SUB-
SCRIPTION IN COMMEMORATION OF THE PEACE OF I8I4 JOHN
BRIANT HERTFORD FECIT I8I4
Diameter 31 ½ " Weight 6 cwt 1 qr 24 lb   Note D#
The parish must have acted speedily to order these two bells; the
'Peace of 1814' lasted only from April 1814 until Napoleon's escape
from Elba on 26 February 1815.   *H CA / GAD*

373. 1814 LUTTERWORTH   3rd of 8
JOHN BRIANT HERTFORD FECIT I8I4
Diameter 32 ¾ " Weight 7 cwt 0 qr 26 lb   Note C#
Andrews incorrectly described this bell as the 4th. Briant had also
recast the tenor in 1812 (*see above No. 349*).   *CB Leics.*

374. 1814 LONG BUCKBY, Northants. St Lawrence
                        4th of 8, formerly treble of 5
THE REV ᴰ T. COLE VICAR. J : BRIANT HERTFORD FECIT I8I4
T. WORSTER C : W   *(one line)*
Diameter 34 ½ " Weight 7 cwt 1 qr 24 lb   Note B
Briant recast the treble of a complete five by Hugh Watts II of 1624.
Augmented to eight in 2000.   *HCA / PDG Dir.*

375. 1814 HANSLOPE, Bucks. St James the Great   Tenor of 8
JOHN KITEL C : W ✿ ✿ JOHN BRIANT HERTFORD FECIT I8I4
Diameter 50"   Weight 22 cwt   Note E♭
This bell was carried by canal to Castlethorpe Wharf where, on unload-
ing, it fell into the water and remained there for a week.   *CB Bucks.*

376. 1814 MURSLEY, Bucks. St Mary Treble of 6
JOHN : BRIANT. HERTFORD. FECIT. I8I4
Diameter 28″ Weight 4 cwt 2 qr 24 lb Note E

377. *1814 MURSLEY* *2nd*
✝ *JOHN : BRIANT HERTFORD FECIT I8I4*
Diameter 29″ Weight 4 ½ cwt Note D
Cocks, CB Bucks., *records that all cannons were broken off (1897).*
Recast by A. Bowell of Ipswich 1933.

378. 1814 MURSLEY 3rd
† JOHN BRIANT HERTFORD. FECIT I8I4 †
Diameter 31″ Weight 5 cwt 1 qr 23 lb Note C
† – both on sides, the first pointing left, that after the date to the right.

379. 1814 MURSLEY 4th
JOHN : BRIANT. HERTFORD. FECIT I8I4
Diameter 32″ Weight 5 cwt 3 qr 7 lb Note B

380. *1814 MURSLEY* *5th*
JOHN BRIANT. HERTFORD. FECIT. I8I4
Diameter 34″ Weight 6 ½ cwt Note A
Recast by Bowell 1933.

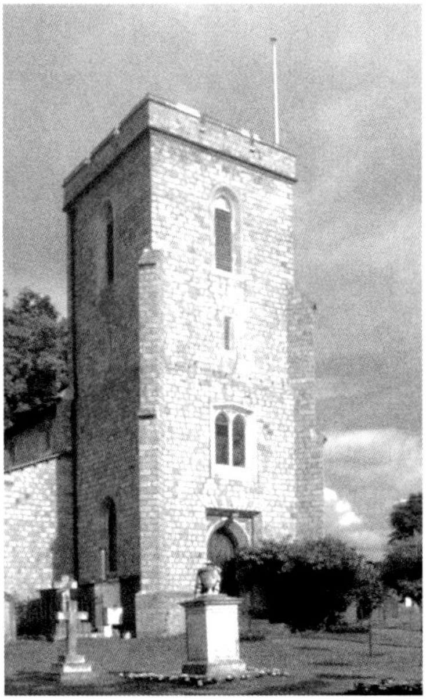
Halton, St Michael and All Angels, Bucks.
A rather odd four.

381. 1814 MURSLEY Tenor
✝ JOHN BRIANT. HERTFORD FECIT I8I4 ✝ T : DEVERELL. ❧ J : BRADBURY. C.W *(one line)*
Diam. 38″ Wt. 9 cwt 0 qr 20 lb Note G
The bells were rehung by A. Bowell of Ipswich in 1933. *CB Bucks./ CJP*

382. 1814 HALTON, Bucks. St Michael 2nd of 4
✝ J : BRIANT HERTFORD FECIT I8I4 ✝ ✡
Diam. 30 ¾″ Wt. 4 ¾ cwt Note D

383. 1814 HALTON 3rd
✝ J : BRIANT HERTFORD FECIT I8I4 ✝ ✡
Diam. 32 ¼″ Wt. 5 ¼ cwt Note D♭

384. 1814 HALTON   Tenor
✝ SIR JOHN DASHWOOD KING
BENEFACTOR. ✝ J : BRIANT HERTFORD FECIT 1814   *(one line)*
Diameter 35 ½ "   Weight 7 cwt   Note B♭
The old church was rebuilt by Sir John
Dashwood King, Bart., Patron of the Manor, in
1813. These three bells were recast from the
three which were in the old church. Briant
added a treble in 1815. *(See below)*

385. 1815 HALTON   Treble
✝   J : BRIANT HERTFORD FECIT 1815   ✝
Diameter 29 ¾ "   Weight 4 ½ cwt   Note E♭
This bell appears to have been an afterthought. The bells are in the
scale of E♭, D, D♭ B♭, which gives them a piquant quality all of their
own.   *CB Bucks.*

386. 1815 NORTON, Letchworth, Herts. St Nicholas
                                        6th of 8, formerly treble of 3
JOHN BRIANT HERTFORD FECIT 1815 ✝
Diameter 29 ⅞ "   Weight 4 cwt 2 qr 27 lb   Note C
This bell was the treble until 1946, when five new trebles were added
by J. Taylor & Co.   *Dodds, CB Herts.*

387. *1815 WAVENDON, Bucks. Assumption of B.V.M.*   *Old 4th of 5*
✝ JOHN BRIANT HERTFORD FECIT 1815
Diameter 35 ½ "
Lipscomb IV., p. 396: 'five small bells, the fourth is inscribed "Sancte Nicholas
ora pro nobis" '. Lipscomb was not the most accurate of copyists, but Browne
Willis mentioned two old bells, Sancte Nicholae and Sancta Maria. So Briant
was recasting a medieval bell. The five were all recast and augmented to six by
Mears & Stainbank in 1952.   *CB Bucks.*

388. 1815 HOUGHTON REGIS, Beds.   Treble of 6
JOHN BRIANT HERTFORD FECIT 1815 ✝
Diameter 31 ½ "   Weight 5 cwt 2 qr 26 lb   Note D
There were unsubstantiated rumours that the 4th from Wavendon and
this bell were in the foundry at the same time and that some mix-up
occurred, but the diameters were entirely different so, like many similar stories, it can probably be discounted.   *CB Beds.*

389. 1816 HOUGHTON REGIS   2nd
J : BRIANT HERTFORD FECIT I8I6 ✝ 🔔 🔔 🔔
Diameter 32"   Weight 5 cwt 3 qr 10 lb   Note C
Churchwardens' accounts:
   1817 Mr. Bryant, Hertford, as per Bill, for recasting and
                                    new Hanging 6 bells £121 . 13 . 0
(At back of volume) Vestry minute dated 17 July 1817 when
   Mr. Bryant of Hertford attended & reported that, agreeable to the directions of the Inhabitants assembled at the Easter Vestry 1814, he had taken
down the Framework of the Bells of the Church of this Parish, & upon examination found that no part of it could be advantageously made use of in the for-
mation of another Frame & that the fifth & second bells were not in Tune with
the other three. He therefore made the two following Proposals;
   1st. To make a new Frame of oak Timber, of sufficient strength to carry the
old Peal of 5 Bells, New hang the Peal with part new Stocks, new wheels, a new
sett of Gudgeons & Brasses, new Clappers, new Sally-pulleys, the whole to be
executed in a sound & workman-like manner, including carriage & every
other article & fixed in the Tower for the sum of £115. 0. 0.
   2nd. To make a Peal of 6 Bells by casting 3 new Bells, viz. 1st, 2nd & 4th &
retaining the 4th, 3rd & 1st old Bells, a new Frame & hangings, every article
new fixed in the Tower, compleat & fit for use, for the sum of £123. 0. 0.
Resolved
That the second proposal appearing to be the most eligible, Mr. Bryant be
employed to form a Peal of six Bells, & make a new Frame & fix them in the
Tower, as soon as he conveniently can.
That so much of the old Frame-work shall be made use of for repairing the
floor & Beams of the Tower, as shall be thought requisite, & that the remainder
shall be sold.
This does not agree with H.C. Andrews' statement that Briant recast
the 4th and added a treble and 2nd to augment to 6. There were previously five bells, with a tenor of 18 cwt of which the 4th, by Chandler
1673, became the tenor. The present frame is that supplied in 1816. The
weights are as given after restoration by Taylors in 1899.
                                                        R.I. Kendrick / CJP

390. 1816 MEPPERSHALL, Beds. St Mary   4th of 6, formerly the 2nd of 5
J : FOX C : W J : BRIANT HERTFORD FECIT I8I6.
Diameter 31⅝ "   Weight 5 cwt 0 qr 20 lb   Note A#
Prior to 1882 the present 3rd bell was the 2nd, and the then 3rd bell was an
ancient one, inscribed + CHRISTE : AVDI NOS. This old bell, being full of
flaws and of bad tone, was recast in that year for the 2nd bell (by J. Taylor) and
the old 2nd, cast in 1816, being much too flat for its position in the ring, was
adopted as the 3rd bell. (*CB Beds.*, p. 173)
This was one that Briant did not get right! (*J.D.*) The note had to be flat-
tened to bring it into tune with the rest. The five were augmented to six

with some retuning by Whitechapel in 1985. Weight as given by Whitechapel.

Churchwardens' accounts:

1814 Nov. 29th. Carriage of Second Bell to Hitchin.	5s.	(? Hertford)
1816 March 23d. Mr. Bryant a Bill	£17. 15. 0	
Men for assisting to get up the Bell	2s. 6d.	

H CA / CB Beds./ CJP

391. 1816 RISELEY, Beds. All Saints   4th of 6, formerly 3rd of 5
P : W : WHITE^{HEAD} ✠ S : RICHARDS C : W, R . TAYLOR ✠
J : BRIANT S^T NEOTS FECERUNT 1816 ♟ ✝ ♟   *(one line)*
Diameter 35 ½ "   Weight 7 cwt 1 qr 21 lb   Note A
Lettering and shape of bell are Briant's, not Taylor's. The letters in superscript in Whitehead are incised. North incorrectly gives Mr Whitehead's initials as F.W. This is corrected in the Hertford County Association of Change-Ringers' copy by the hand of L.H.Chambers, the book's first owner. No explanation has ever come to light as to why Briant was assisting his old friend and fellow St Neots apprentice in casting this bell. Taylor was born in Riseley and baptised there on New Year's Day 1760. His old birthplace is still there. He recast the tenor in 1814.

A vestry minute of 15 April 1816 'Agreed that the third bell, now broken, be recast and hung as soon as may be, and paid at Michaelmas'.

The cannons were removed either in 1891 or 1973. It became the 4th when a treble was added in 1987.

CB Beds./ CJP

392. 1816 BIERTON, Bucks. St James   Treble of 6
✝ ♟ J : BRIANT HERTFORD FECIT 1816 ♟ ✝
♟ ♟
Diam. 30"   Wt. 5 cwt 3 qr 16 lb   Note D#

393. 1816 BIERTON   2nd
✝ ♟ J : BRIANT HERTFORD FECIT 1816 ♟ ✝
♟ ♟   *(one line)*
Diam. 32 ¼ " Wt. 6 cwt 2 qr 4 lb   Note C#

394. 1816 BIERTON   3rd
✝ ♟ J : BRIANT HERTFORD FECIT 1816 ♟ ✝
♟ ♟   *(one line)*
Diam. 34 ½ " Wt. 7 cwt 0 qr 20 lb   Note B

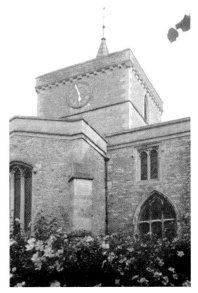

Bierton, St James, Bucks. Briant recast the tenor in 1809.

395.   1816 BIERTON   4th of 6
✠ J : BRIANT HERTFORD FECIT 1816 ✠ ♣ ✠ ♣
Diameter 35"   Weight 7 cwt 3 qr 3 lb   Note A#

396.   1816 BIERTON   5th
J : BADRICK, J : THORN, J : WHITE C : W :
J : BRIANT HERTFORD FECIT 1816. ♣ ✠ ♣ *(one line)*
Diameter 38¼"   Weight. 9 cwt 2 qr 13 lb   Note G#
This completed the recasting of the old six noted by Browne Willis in
1714. Briant recast the tenor in 1809 (*see No.298*).   CB Bucks.

397.   1816 LITTLE MUNDEN, Herts. All Saints   4th
R. PIKETT C : W. J.BRIANT HERTFORD FECIT 1816 +   *(one line)*
Diameter 32"   Weight 5 cwt 2 qr 5 lb   Note A#
+ – *Fig.23ᵦ.*
As well as the 4th being recast, a new frame was installed at the same
time.
In the churchwardens' accounts are the following entries:
      1817 Ap. 12 Recd. of Jas. Dixon, Thirty pounds on acct for
                          casting framing and hanging the Bells   £30
      John Briant.
      June 22 Recd. of James Dixon Fifty seven pounds 10 shillings
                          being the Ballance of the acct for Framing
                          and hanging the church Bells.   £57 10 0
                                                                  ─────────
                                                                  £87 10 0
                                                                        HCA

398.   1816 CLIFTON CAMPVILLE, Staffs. St Andrew   3rd of 6
J: COOPER C: W: THE REVɴ Ḍ I : WATKINS RECTOR J. BRIANT
HERTFORD FECIT 1816   *(one line)*
Diameter 30⅞" Weight 5 cwt 1 qr 14 lb   Note C
This bell was the 2nd of a ring of five, described in *Dove's Guide* 1968 as
unringable. In 1969 the bells were augmented to six and hung for
chiming only by J. Taylor & Co.   CB Staffs./ CJP

399.   *1816 COUNTESTHORPE, Leics. St Andrew*   *Old 2nd of 4*
J. HALL C : WARDEN. J. BRIANT HERTFORD FECIT 1816
Recast and augmented to six in 1925 by J.Taylor & Co. and since augmented to
eight.   *HCA / CB Leics.*

400.   1817 ASHBY-DE-LA-ZOUCH, Leics.   4th of 8
J. BRIANT HERTFORD FECIT 1817.
Diameter 34¾" Weight 8 cwt 0 qr 14 lb   Note B
(*See also Nos. 371/372 above*).   CB Leics./ GAD

401. *1817 ASHBY MAGNA, Leics.*　　　　　　　　　　　　*Old 2nd of 3*
JOHN BRIANT HERTFORD FECIT 1817 † † † † †
Diameter 31¾"　　Weight 5 cwt 3 qr 6 lb
Recast by J. Taylor & Co. 1925　　　　　　*CB Leics./ GAD*

402. 1817 ASHWELL, Herts.　　　　　　　　　　　　　　3rd of 6
✝ JOHN BRIANT HERTFORD FECIT 1817. ✝ ✿ ✝ ✿
Diameter 35⅜ " Weight 8 cwt　　　　　　Note B♭
This was Briant's final contribution to Ashwell.　　*Dodds, CB Herts.*

403. 1817 PASSENHAM, Northants. St Guthlac　　　　　　Tenor of 5
THIS BELL THE GIFT OF SIR ROBERT BANASTRE: AN: DOM: 1635 WAS
RECAST AT THE EXPENCE OF CHARLES VISCOUNT MAYNARD ✖ THE
PARISHIONERS AN: DOM: 1817:　*(first line)*
✝ THE REV^{ND} LORAIN SMITH RECTOR JAMES CLARE ✖ JOHN CLARK
C: W: JOHN BRIANT HERTFORD FECIT ✝ GLORIA DEO IN EXCELSIS ✿
✿ ✝　　　　　　*(second line)*
Diameter 45"　　Weight 17 cwt　　　　　　Note E
Diameter and weight are from the *PDG Directory*. *Dove's Guide* gives the
weight as 18 cwt.

　　Sir Robert Banastre 'raised and beautified' the chancel in 1626 to
High Church standards. It is believed that he may have been a Recusant. He was Comptroller of the Household to James I and made himself unpopular because of his grasping and high-handed ways, so that
in later years 'Bobby Banastre' became the local bogeyman who would
infallibly 'get' naughty children and he is also said to 'walk'. He was a
direct ancestor of Charles, Viscount Maynard who contributed to the
cost of the present bell.　　　　　　*Dodds / HCA / PDG Dir.*

404. 1817 BELVOIR CASTLE, Leics.　　　　　　　　　　Single bell
Inscription unknown.
Diameter 21¾" Weight 1 cwt 0 qr 14 lb
Rehung by J. Taylor & Co. 1938

405. *1818 BELVOIR CASTLE*　　　　　　　　　　　　*Clock bell 1*
*Inscription unknown. Recast J. Taylor 1890, replacing a bell by Briant weighing
2 cwt 2 qr.*

406. 1818 BELVOIR CASTLE　　　　　　　　　　　　Clock bell 2
Inscription unknown. Diameter 24"

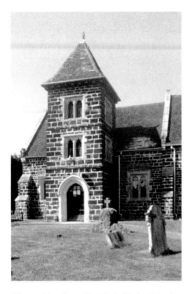

Upper Stondon, All Saints, Beds. Briant provided just one bell and in 1857 this was transferred to the south porch tower of the new church.

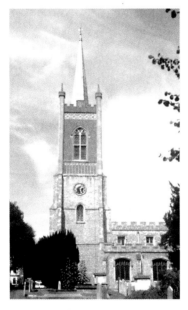

Bishop's Stortford, St Michael
The present tower and spire

407. 1818 BELVOIR CASTLE   Clock bell 3
Inscription unknown. Diameter 34 ½ "
These three bells are tuned as 1, 4 and 8 of an
octave.   *J. Taylor 1923 / GAD*

408. 1819 GREAT BENTLEY, Essex St Mary   4th of 8
† JOHN BRIANT HERTFORD FECIT I8I9.
Diam. 27"   Wt. 3 ¾ cwt   Note E♭
CB Essex gives the note as E and weight as 4 cwt;
the bells were not tuned to modern pitch.

409. 1819 UPPER STONDON, Beds. All Saints.   Single
J. BRIANT HERTFORD FECIT 1819
Diam. 20"   Wt. c.2 cwt
Hung in small south porch tower. North recorded
no inscription.   *CJP*

410. 1820. BISHOP'S STORTFORD, Herts.   Treble of 10
W : FRANCIS ⚥ J : FAIRMAN C : WARDENS.
J : BRIANT HERTFORD FECIT I820 ✝ *(one line)*
Diam. 27 ¾ "   Wt. 5 cwt 2 qr 3 lb   Note G

411. 1820 BISHOP'S STORTFORD   2nd
W : FRANCIS ⚥ J : FAIRMAN. C : WARDENS
J : BRIANT HERTFORD FECIT I820. ✝ ✿ *(one line)*
Diam. 28 ¾ "   Wt. 5 cwt 2 qr 7 lb   Note F
The upper stage of the tower was being rebuilt in
1820 but was still incomplete when George III
died and the Prince Regent became George IV.
The bell frame was hastily erected in the Market
Square and the bells hung so that they could be
sounded for the Accession. This fascinating item
was found by Mrs Doreen Wright of Bishop's
Stortford Museum, in a book of local memories,
'*For the Coronation*' recorded by J.L. Glasscock,
published in 1882. The Coronation took place the
following year, 1821; memories had probably
become hazy after more than sixty years.
       Dodds, CB Herts.

412. 1820 LITTLE GADDESDEN, Herts. SS Peter & Paul — Sanctus
J : BRIANT HERTFORD FECIT I820
Diameter 21¾" Weight 1 cwt 3 qr 23 lb — Note B♭ –
North in *N & S* gave the diameter as 18"
This was the treble of the old two, given by the 7th Earl of Bridgewater in 1820, and ordered by him as churchwarden. Chauncy recorded four small bells in 1700. These were sold to Briant for £74. He cast two out of them and charged £68, so the 7th Earl made a profit. It is now hung dead for chiming only. *Dodds, CB Herts.*

413. *1820 LITTLE GADDESDEN* — *Old 2nd*
✝ *J : BRIANT HERTFORD FECIT I820.*
Diameter quoted by North as 24".
Recast by J. Taylor in 1977 when two of the four bells from the redundant church at Chellington, Beds. were transferred intact and the other two as metal to form the present ring of six. The Briant bell was recast with facsimile inscription and is nominally the second of six. *Dodds, CB Herts.*

414. 1820 HINXWORTH, Herts. St Nicholas — 2nd of 6
J. BRIANT HERTFORD FECIT I820
Diameter 25⅞" Weight 3¾ cwt — Note E
This bell was the treble until 1908, when a new treble was added by Mears & Stainbank.

415. 1820 HINXWORTH — Tenor
E. SALE C : W : REV^ND G : COX RECTOR J. BRIANT HERTFORD
FECIT I820 *(one line)*
Diameter 34¾" Weight 8 cwt — Note A
Dodds, CB Herts.

416. 1820 STANSTEAD ST MARGARET, St Mary the Virgin — Single
J BRIANT HERTFORD MVCCCXX
Diameter 16⅛" Weight 1 cwt
The inscription is between single moulding wires above the soundbow. Note the error in the date : V instead of D for 500. There was never a church dedicated to St Margaret. The marshy area by the River Lea was owned by a lady of that name and became Margaret's Thele – Margaret's Isle. Later the name was corrupted to St Margaret's and took on the 'Stanstead' from the next village, Stanstead Abbots.
Dodds, CB Herts.

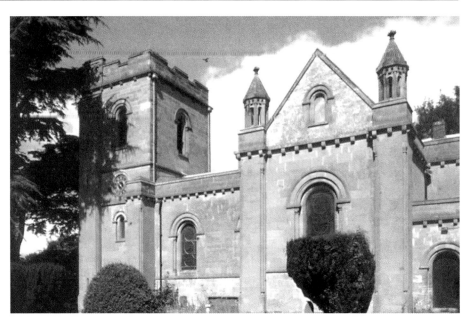

Old Wolverton, Holy Trinity, Bucks. There is
an almost untouched Briant ring.

417.   1820 OLD WOLVERTON, Bucks. Holy Trinity   Treble of 6
     ✝ JOHN BRIANT HERTFORD FECIT I820   *(one line)*
     Diameter 31"   Weight 5 ¼ cwt   Note E

418.   1820 OLD WOLVERTON   2nd of 6
     ✝ JOHN BRIANT HERTFORD FECIT I820 ✝   ✡ *(one line)*
     Diameter 33"   Weight 5 ¾ cwt   Note D
     The large gap between the cross and the star is as given in *CB Bucks*.

419.   1820 OLD WOLVERTON   3rd
     JOHN BRIANT HERTFORD FECIT I820
     Diameter 34 ¾ "   Weight 6 ½ cwt   Note C

420   1820 OLD WOLVERTON   4th
     JOHN BRIANT HERTFORD FECIT I820
     Diameter 35 ½ "   Weight 7 ¼ cwt   Note B

421.   1820 OLD WOLVERTON   5th
     ✝ JOHN BRIANT HERTFORD FECIT I820 ✝
     Diameter 38"   Weight 9 cwt   Note A

422. 1820 OLD WOLVERTON   Tenor of 6
✝ JOHN BRIANT HERTFORD FECIT I820 ✝
Diameter 42″   Weight 12 cwt   Note G
Dove's Guide gives the weight of the tenor as 14 cwt. The church was
rebuilt in the Norman style in 1815 by Henry Hakewill, replacing an
earlier one which had four bells in 1714. The anti-clockwise frame is
contemporary with the bells, making this a largely untouched ring. The
church stands close to the Grand Union Canal; the bells were probably
delivered by water. There is also a single-handed clock.   *CB Bucks.*

423. 1820 EASTON NESTON, *Northants.* *St Mary*   *Old 5th of 6*
✝ *JOHN BRIANT HERTFORD FECIT I820*
Diameter 32″
Recast by Gillett & Johnston 1910.

424. 1820 BANBURY, *Oxon. St Mary*   *Old treble*
THIS BELL WAS GIVEN BY FREDERICK EARL OF GUILDFORD TO THE
BOROUGH OF BANBURY. JOHN BRIANT HERTFORD FECIT I820 ✿
Diameter 31″   *Weight 6 cwt 1 qr 25 lb*

425. 1820 BANBURY   *Old 2nd*
JOHN PAIN JAMES HILL THOMAS NASBY C :WARDENS ✿
JOHN BRIANT HERTFORD FECIT I820
Diameter 32″   *Weight 6 cwt 2 qr 21 lb*
These two bells were recast by J. Taylor & Co. 1930.   *HCA / F. Sharpe*

426. 1821 EPWELL, *Oxon. St Anne*   Tenor of 2
(on sound-bow) J : BRIANT HERTFORD FECIT MDCCCXXI J : TURNER C.W.
Diameter 21¾″   Weight 2½ cwt
The bells are hung for ringing, but have neither stays nor sliders.
                                       CB Oxon.

427. 1822 ASHBY-DE-LA-ZOUCH   7th of 8
THE REV. Wᴹ MAC DOUALL VICAR : J. TOMPSON AND Wᴹ
DEVENPORT C. W. J. BRIANT HERTFORD FECIT I822.
Diameter 42½″   Weight 15 cwt 2 qr 7 lb   Note F#
This bell completed Briant's work in this tower (*See Nos. 371 and 372*).
                                    CB Leics./ GAD

428. 1822 EYDON, Northants. St Nicholas   3rd, formerly 2nd of 5
J. BRIANT HERTFORD FECIT 1822. W. LINES & I IVENS C.W.
Diameter 30½" Weight 4 cwt 3 qr 10 lb   Note C
This was a recast of a bell by Newcombe 1611. It was the 2nd until
1981, when the bells were rehung and augmented to six by J. Taylor &
Co.   *HCA/ PDG Dir.*

429. 1822 CROXLEY GREEN, Herts. St Oswald   Single, not hung
(above sound-bow) [B [: B MDCCCXXII
Diameter 16⅛" Weight 1 cwt   Note B♭
Briant had trouble with this inscription. He first stamped a J upside
down, then a B. The latter was quickly withdrawn, leaving a faulty
imprint. His second attempt was no more successful, so it was allowed
to stay (*see p. 189*). A plaster cast of this is included in the Dodds Hertfordshire collection in the Balfour Building of the Pitt-Rivers Museum,
Oxford. This bell was only noted in 1989 by G. & J. Dodds and its exact
origins and date of acquisition are uncertain. After retuning by
Whitechapel in 1963, the bell was hung on the chimney stack for solenoid chiming. When the stack became unsafe, the bell was taken down
and stored. The church was built in 1935.   *Dodds, CB Herts.*

430. *1823 EASTON NESTON, Northants.*   *Old 3rd of 6*
JOHN BRIANT HERTFORD FECIT 1823.
Diameter 32"

431. *1823 EASTON NESTON*   *Old tenor*
ISAAC MANNING THE TREASURER OF JOHN HULCOTE HIS CHAR-
ITY ADDED THIS BELL MVCCCXXIIJ JOHN BRIANT HERTFORD
FECIT.
Diameter 41"
Recast by Gillett & Johnston 1910. (See also No. 423 above)   HCA / PDG. Dir.

432. 1823 HERTINGFORDBURY, Herts. St Mary   4th of 6
JOHN BRIANT HERTFORD FECIT 1823 ✡ ✝ ✡ ✝
Diameter 31⅝" Weight 6¼ cwt   Note C
This could possibly have been a recast of a bell by William Whitmore
1656.   *Dodds, CB Herts.*

433. 1823 RUMBURGH, Suffolk SS Michael and Felix   Tenor of 5
THE REV[ND] LOMBE ALTHILLS PERP[T] CURATE. JOHN BRIANT
HERTFORD FECIT 1823. C : REYNOLDS C. W.   *(one line)*
Diameter 34⅝" Weight 7 cwt 2 qr 0 lb   Note A+ .23 semitones
This bell retains its contemporary T-headed clapper with a small flight.
Althills is an error for Atthills. (*HCA*)   *RWMC 1998*

434. 1824 FENNY STRATFORD, Bucks. St Martin   Tenor of 6
      JOHN · BRIANT HERTFORD FECIT MVCCCXXIV (sic)
      Diameter 34¾" Weight 8 cwt 0 qr 4 lb   Note A
      Cocks, in *CB Bucks*. particularly notes the very small, half-inch, letter-
      ing on this bell. The date again shows the use of V instead of D for 500.
                                                                CB Bucks.

435. *1824 BOUGHTON, Northants. St John the Baptist*   *Old treble of 3*
      T BRIANT HERTFORD I824 (sic)
      Diameter 23"

436. *1824 BOUGHTON*   *Old 3rd*
      T BRIANT HERTFORD FECIT I824 (sic)
      Diameter 36"
      HCA *lists these as 1 and 2. However, the* PDG. Dir. *shows that in 1907 J.*
      Barwell of Birmingham added a treble and tenor and recast a bell by T. Eayre of
      1749 to make five, leaving the Briant bells as Nos. 2 and 4. The diameters cer-
      tainly suggest that they were not adjacent. The complete ring was recast in
      1957 by J. Taylor & Co.   *HCA / PDG. Dir.*

437. 1825 HINXWORTH   5th of 6
      RVND J : LAFONT VICAR R : SALE C :W: J.BRIANT HERTFORD FECIT
      MDCCCXXV   *(one line)*
      Diameter 32¼" Weight 6½ cwt   Note B
      This appears to be his latest dated bell.   *Dodds, CB Herts.*

438. Undated. HERTFORD MUSUEM
      Diameter 11"
      John Briant gave this bell to the National School, Hertford in 1824. The
      school was also in Parliament Row, close to the foundry. The bell was
      later transferred to the Cowper Testimonial Boys School in London
      Road and hung under the stairs. (New book on the Cowper T. B. School
      just published) It fell while being chimed for the end of afternoon
      school at some time about 1945, breaking the crown, which was
      repaired with a double plate. This did not last long as parts of the
      shoulder broke off, so the pathetic remains were stored until the
      school was demolished before being given to the museum in 1992. The
      very neat surface and well-marked moulding wires are typical Briant
      workmanship.   *J.M. Kemp / Dodds, CB Herts.*

1827 CAMBRIDGE, King's College   Clock bell
JOHN BRIANT HERTFORD FECIT 1827
This is a hemispherical bell, 21″ diameter and was probably cast for Briant by
Thomas Mears II, who had bought out Briant in 1825. Briant was working on the
clock in 1828.   *HCA*

1828 SHILLINGTON, Beds. All Saints   Sanctus
1828
Diameter 14⅞″   Weight 2 qr 18 lb.
A receipted bill preserved among parish records reveals that it was obtained in
April 1828 from Mr Briant, the Hertford bellfounder, whose executrix (Mary
Shaw, *née* Briant) submitted the bill some time later, the receipt being dated 1
September 1829, i.e. after Briant's death. The cost of the bell was £6. 9s. 6d. plus
5s. for a clapper. The metal of the old bell, cast either 1626 (*CB Beds.*) or 1696 by 'X'
of Hitchin (?) of which this was a nominal recast, weighed 2 qr 16 lb, so £2. 14s
was deducted from the total, leaving the final bill as £4. 2s. 6d. As Briant at this
date was living in St Albans it could not have been cast by him. A close examination by G. Dodds, with a rubbing of the date (plus a 'squeeze'), shows that the
first numeral is not a capital I as used by Briant but the modern form of 1 as used
by T. Mears. The conclusion must therefore be that the bell was ordered from
Briant who sub-contracted the actual casting to Mears.   *CJP / Dodds*

Other Undated Bells

In addition to the dated examples in the previous section, H.C. Andrews includes
some Irish bells about which little or nothing is now known:

439. EDENDERRY, Tyrone
      One bell of two, weighing together 15 cwt.

440, LISBURN : Cathedral, Antrim and Down
441. Briant listed these as 1 and 2 of a peal of 3. The larger was recast in
      1861 by order of the Marquis of Hertford. The smaller was given in 1721, recast in
      1746. Whether Briant had again recast it, at some later date is not clear.

Tuam Cathedral bell of 1793 by Briant is listed above as No.125

DISTRIBUTION OF JOHN BRIANT BELLS
BY COUNTIES

	Date	Ref. No.		Date	Ref. No.
BEDFORDSHIRE			Swaffham Prior	1791/98	78, 177
Ampthill	1811	325	Whittlesford	1793	119
Eaton Bray	1790	66	**DEVON**		
Houghton Regis	1811	326	Barnstaple	1803	217
	1815/16	388	Braunton	1803	223
Meppershall	1816	390	Tawstock	1803	224
Riseley	1816	391	**ESSEX**		
Southill	1814	364	Ardleigh	1802	210
Stanbridge	1807	279	Arkesden	1814	370
Streatley	1804	236	Barking	1793	126
Upper Stondon	1819	409	Chrishall	1804	234
BUCKINGHAMSHIRE			Coggeshall	1806	268
Bierton	1809/16	298,392	Great Bentley	1819	408
Fenny Stratford	1824	434	Great Chesterford	1796	146
Haddenham	1809	290	Great Hallingbury	1794	127
Halton	1814/15	382	Great Tey	1794	128
Hanslope	1814	375	Kelvedon	1803	232
Hardwick	1811	334	Littlebury	1789/90	53, 65
High Wycombe	1788	40	Radwinter	1798	175
Maids Moreton	1806	261	Saffron Walden	1797/98	167, 168
Mursley	1814	376	Stisted	1799	180
Nether Winchendon	1796	145	Waltham Abbey	1806	269
Newton Longville	1800	187	**HERTFORDSHIRE**		
Old Wolverton	1820	417	Abbots Langley	1809	299
Padbury	1806	262	Ashwell	1787/89/	31, 43
Wavendon	1815	387		1791/1817	72,402
Whitchurch	1797	160	Aston Stables	1810	322
CAMBRIDGESHIRE			Barkway	1797	153
Burrough Green	1807	280	Bayford	N.D.	71
Cottenham	1800	188	Benington	1792	89
Croydon	1796	22	Bishop's Stortford	1791/	73
Dullingham	1784	17		1802/20	209,410
Melbourn	1789	42	Brent Pelham	1792	90
Soham	1808	282	Clothall, Quickswood	1779	1

	Date	Ref. No.		Date	Ref. No.
Codicote	1782/92/	5, 88	Watford	1786	21
	1812	346	Watton at Stone	1785	20
Cottered	1793	115	**KENT**		
Croxley Green	1822	429	Orpington	1813	361
Furneux Pelham	1792	91	**LEICESTERSHIRE**		
Hatfield	1786	23	Ashby-de-la-Zouch	1814/	371
Hatfield House	1783	16		1817/22	400,427
Hertford, All Saints	1791	76	Ashby Magna	1817	401
Hertford, St Andrew	1782/	9	Barkby	1803	213
	1793/7	117,161	Belvoir Castle	1817	404
Hertford, Shire Hall	1809	300	Bottesford	1809/10	316
Hertford Boys School	N.D.	438	Burton Lazars	1804	235
Hertford Museum	1809	303	Countesthorpe	1816	399
Hertingfordbury	1823	432	Diseworth	1803	214
Hinxworth	1820/5	414,437	Lockington	1806	277
Hunsdon	1787	32	Lutterworth	1812/14	349,373
Kelshall	1790	69	Melton Mowbray	1802	211
Knebworth	1812	347	Prestwold	1809/10/	312,318
Little Gaddesden	1820	412		1812	350
Little Munden	1816	397	Sapcote	1809	314
Much Hadham	1781	4	Shearsby	1796	152
North Mymms	1806	255	Shepshed	1805	238
Norton	1815	386	Walton-le-Wolds	1807	278
Offley	1803	215	Wigston Magna	1804	237
Panshanger Stables			**LINCOLNSHIRE**		
Welwyn G.C.,	1810	323	Claypole	1793/95	120,141
Pirton	1781	2	Coningsby	1801	201
Ridge, Tyttenhanger	1797	163	Frampton	1801	202
Rushden	1787	33	Horbling	1801	203
St Albans Abbey	1792	95	Kirkby-on-Bain	1803	225
St Albans, St Peter	1787/	38	Kirton	N.D.	144
	1805/12	245,348	Morton	1798	176
St Albans, Abbey Mill	1803	216	Moulton	1805	244
St Paul's Walden	1814	363	Sibsey	1801	204
Sawbridgeworth	1795	140	Stickney	1803	226
Standon	1792	92	Sutterton	1797	165
Stanstead Abbots	1790	70	Welbourn	1802	206
Stanstead St Margaret	1822	416	**LONDON**		
Stevenage	1783/85	13, 18	St Giles, Cripplegate	1792	96
	1797	164	**NORTHAMPTONSHIRE**		
Tewin	1799	186	Abington	1809/10/	311,321
Wallington	1793/94	114,131		1811	324
Ware	1792	93	Ashby St Ledgers	1806	250

17

JOHN BRIANT

INSCRIPTIONS, TURRET CLOCKS AND CHIMES

Inscriptions and Decorations

Nobody could possibly describe Briant's inscriptions as either inventive or inspiring. There are, of course, exceptions to every rule and the verses on his St Alkmund's, Shrewsbury (now Honolulu), are inventive but *un*inspiring! Usually, he kept to JOHN BRIANT HERTFORD (or HART-FORD) FECIT and the date. On the larger bells, he would add the names of incumbent and churchwardens because, the larger the bell, the more space there was for extra words. Andrews was of the opinion that, had the decision rested with Briant, nothing more would have been added. This habit of placing names only on the larger bells in a ring proved useful to the writer in the case of Southill, Bedfordshire, where the tenor is a later bell and there is nothing to indicate whether it was a recast or an addition. The lack of any names on the fifth suggested that Briant had indeed cast a tenor and this was proved when C.J. Pickford kindly provided the writer with the previous inscription which he found in a church terrier of 1822.

One delightful character was Briant's ampersand, ⅋, which conveys the impression of lying on its back and kicking its heels in the air. It was in fact very similar to that previously used by Thomas Lester and later by Lester & Pack of Whitechapel in the 1760s, and was a typical eighteenth century design.

GLORIA DEO IN EXCELSIS (*Glory to God in the Highest*) usually on the tenor of a ring, was his most common addition, used fifteen times.

STATUTUM EST OMNIBUS SEMEL MORI (*It is appointed to all men once to die*) was used five times, again normally on the tenor, being appropriate to the passing bell.

OCTO CAMPANAS SACRA EXAUDIMUS IN ARCE, DULCE ANTI-SONAS, O HILARES! HILARES! This appeared on the 2nd of the two cast for Melton Mowbray in 1802 and can be translated as *We hear eight bells in the sacred tower sound soft and loud, O joyful, joyful!* It was not used elsewhere.

Many of his special inscriptions like that above were used once only and can be found under individual bells. The thanksgiving inscriptions for the recovery of King George III were obviously in use for a very short period only.

Another one-off inscription was that on the 1808 treble at Gazeley,

Suffolk, (*No. 286,* p. 255). This can in no way be described as a serious effort! Judging by the laboured rhyme, it was composed amid roars of laughter and gallons of ale in the local inn. As quoted by H.C. Andrews, one vital phrase was omitted – JOHN BRIANT *DE IXNING FECIT*. Briant was a Suffolk man and proud of it. This was one bell where the use of decorative cross and star stops was an essential part of the punctuation, due to the close spacing of the words in the three line inscription band.

Until 1805, Briant was very sparing in his use of decorations. His earliest bell, cast for Quickswood House, was said to have borne the Salisbury Crest but no trace of it was found, the only unusual item being a simple Greek cross (*Fig.23$_a$*). He later used a plain cross (+) at Hatfield in 1786 (*Fig.23$_b$*) and a curious asymmetrical cross at St Peter's, St Albans, in 1805 (*Fig.23$_c$*, p.248). His large tenor (*No. 247*) for St Michael's, Coventry, in 1805 bore a series of crosses which may have been either the Calvary Cross or the 'dagger' cross. In 1806 a neat set of decorations came into regular use, consisting of a Calvary Cross on a stepped base (*Fig.23$_d$*), a cross like a dagger (*Fig.23$_e$*), a six-pointed Star of David (*Fig.23$_f$*) a minute but exquisitely-modelled bell (*Fig.23$_g$*) and an inverted comma lying on its back (*Fig.23$_h$*) which resembles a tadpole! All of these were used in great profusion on the ring of six cast for North Mymms that year. After this exuberent outburst, the decorations were used with more circumspection and most later bells bear one or two items only. One which appeared once only was a bust in a wreath, as found by R.W.M. Clouston on the tenor at Little Thurlow, Suffolk.

A survival from the Middle Ages is on the sixth at Waltham Abbey, Essex, where the head of King Edward III (*Fig. 23$_i$*) was originally on the eighth as well. This stop was known to have been used by John Rufford in the fourteenth century. It is also known that the old bells of Waltham Abbey were recast from four into six by William Whitmore in 1656 (*see above p. 117*), thus raising the interesting question as to whether Whitmore found it on one of the bells, liked it and reused it, with the same recurring in 1806, or whether Briant came by it in some other way.

During his early years at Hertford, Briant used the old version of the name Hartford, which was still current at the time but even then going out of fashion. Over a number of years he adopted the modern spelling so that by 1800 the new form predominated. It was a haphazard process and he seems to have had no real system. Similarly, his punctuation varied from bell to bell, even within a complete ring, ranging from none at all to meticulous placing of colons and stops between words. Unfortunately, many of the older county histories are incomplete in this detail so that, while the Hertfordshire bells are correct and Buckinghamshire and Essex can be assumed to be so, Cocks and Walters both being highly reputable observers, in other cases there can be a matter of doubt. Wherever there is conflict, the writer has used the most up-to-date source.

JOHN BRIANT,
Church and Turret Clock, and Chime Maker,
HARTFORD;

Respectfully submits the following list of Clock and Chimes, which he has had the honor to make for the undermentioned Noblemen and Gentlemen, to the attention of those who may have occasion for similar Articles, and solicits their Orders.

OOO

His Grace the Duke of Marlborough,...	*Woodstock, Oxon,*............	Church Clock and Chimes,
——————————— Rutland,...	*Belvoir Castle, Lincolnshire,*.........	Quarter Clock,
——————————— Grafton,...	*Wakefield Lodge, Northampton,*...	Turret Clock,
The Most Noble the Marquess of Salisbury,	*Hatfield House, Harts*............	Turret Clock,
——————————— Hartford, ...	*Lisburn, Ireland,*....................	Quarter Clock,
The Right Honorable Lord Mansfield,...	*Scone Palace, Scotland,*............	Turret Clock,
——————————— Cowper,...	*Panshanger, Harts*..................	Turret Clock,
——————————— Montague,...	*Ditton Park, Bucks*.................	Turret Clock,
——————————— Breadalbane,	*Taymouth Castle, Scotland,*	Turret Clock,
——————————— Hardwick, ...	*Wimpole,*.............................	Turret Clock,
Sir Thomas Rumbold,.......................	*Watton Wood Hall, Harts*............	Turret Clock,
R. Andrews, Esq............................	*Harlston, Northampton,*............	Turret Clock,
R. Perry, Esq.................................	*Moore Hall, Essex,*.................	Turret Clock,
R. Burnisconie, Esq.........................	*Harrow Weal Priory, Middlesex,*...	Turret Clock,

(Manuscript additions)

Countess De Grey............................	*Wrest Park, Bedfordshire,*	Dº
JamesYoung Esqre, ...	*Kingerby Green, Market Rasen*.........	Dº
Earl Mulgrave,...............................	*Mulgrave Castle, near Whitby,*...	Quarter Clock
Earl De La Warre, ——————	*Bourne, Cambridgeshire*............	Turret Clock
Charles Chaplin Esqre M.P., ————	*Blankney House, Lincolnshire,*.........	Dº

OOO

ALSO FOR THE FOLLOWING CITIES AND TOWNS.

St. Ives, Hunts................................	*At the Market House,*	Turret Clock,
Shrewsbury, {	*St. Chad's Church,*	Quarter Clock,
....	*St. Julian's Church,*..................	Quarter Clock,
....	*The Grammar School,*	Turret Clock,
Melton Mowbray, Leicestershire,.........	*Church,*...............................	Quarter Clock & Chimes,
Coventry, Warwickshire, ...	*St. Michael's Church,*...............	Quarter Clock,
Aylesbury, Bucks................................		Church Clock,
Seven Oaks, Kent, ...		Church Clock,
Kelvedon, Essex, ...		Church Clock,
Royston, Harts.–...............................		Church Clock,
St. Alban's, Harts.............................	*St. Peter's Church,*	Clock,
Northampton,................................	*All Saints,*.............................	Set of Chimes,
Hatfield, Harts.		Set of Chimes,
Barkway, Harts................................		Church Clock,
Bishop's Stortford, Harts.		Church Clock.
Hartford,......................................	*Town Hall,*	Quarter Clock,
Barking, Essex,...............................		Church Clock,
Bassingbourn, Cambridgeshire,.............		Church Clock,
Hartford,......................................	*St. Andrew's,*	Church Clock.

(Manuscript additions)

Sleaford, Church, Lincolnshire, ...	Quarter Clock
King's College, New Gate House, Cambridge,..	Turret Clock

Catalogue of Turret Clocks and Chimes

An important part of John Briant's work was the design and maufacture of turret clocks, which skill he had acquired in his training at the St Neots foundry. The printed catalogue opposite was issued in or about 1825. This is borne out by the inclusion of the clock for Kingerby Hall, Lincs., dated 1826, in the manuscript additions, suggesting that the list was compiled before the clock was ordered. As Briant was most likely dictating the list from memory, it may be incomplete. The handwriting of the additions is definitely not Briant's; it most resembles that of Mary Shaw, his daughter, his 'Amanuensis'. The original printing would have been done by Solomon Shaw who had the facilities and probably did not charge for the work.

The list contains no dates when the various works were actually done. Some data can be found in churchwardens' accounts and some from personal observation. It is, as H.C. Andrews remarked on p. 83, no easy task listing up all the turret clocks, as many were installed in private mansions as far afield as Scotland. However, it is possible to give approximate dates from other sources, such as known building dates and Pevsner's *Buildings of England* series which, although not infallible, gives a reasonable period during which the clock could have been set in place.

1. 1782 HATFIELD HOUSE, Herts. Turret clock
    The seventeenth century clock, with bell dated 1604, was repaired by Briant to the order of James Cecil, 1st Marquis of Salisbury and is his earliest dated work. The setting dial is inscribed

    REPAIR'D BY
    John ○ *Briant*
    HARTFORD
    1782

2. *1782 WATTON-AT-STONE, Herts. Wood Hall* *Turret clock*
    Setting dial inscribed JOHN BRIANT HERTFORD FECIT 1782
    Removed at unknown date.

3. 1786 HATFIELD, Herts. St Etheldreda Set of chimes
    These were added to an existing clock at the same time as Briant recast and augmented the bells to a ring of eight.

    (1786 WATFORD, Herts. St Mary, Briant tendered for repairing the clock but the contract was given to George Harman of High Wycombe.)

4. 1790 HERTFORD, Balls Park Turret clock
    The clock is contemporary with the house built for Sir John Harrison c.1640. It was repaired and restored by Briant.

5. 1790 BASSINGBOURN, Cambs.   Church clock
    This was an earlier clock repaired by Briant.

6. 1792 WOODSTOCK, Oxon. St Mary Magdalene
                                          Church clock and chimes
    Made to the order of His Grace the Duke of Marlborough.
    The brass dial is inscribed

    > *John Briant*
    > HERTFORD
    > GEORGE COLES, MAYOR.
    >
    > O
    >
    > Jos^Ph^. Brookes } CHURCH
    > Wm Lewington   } WARDENS
    > 1792

    There was also (*1930 H.C.A.*) a chime barrel still in use but which is
    now removed. (Illustrated in *British and Irish Chime Barrel Mechanisms
    their music and the Community Response 1550–1930* by Trevor Jennings) It
    was a large machine, incorporating an ingenious tune-change mecha-
    nism of Briant's design. Seven tunes were played: Hanover; Marriage
    Vow; Happy Clown; Marlbrouck s'en va-t-en guerre (a nice touch,
    that!); Highland Laddie; Marionette; Haunted Tower.
        (Interestingly, the chimes made by Eayre for Hemel Hempstead in
    1761/3 also included Hanover and Highland Laddie, so Briant had
    used his old master's pinning plan.)
        It seems possible that this commission may have been one small
    factor in Briant's obtaining shelter in the Marlborough Almshouses, St
    Albans, in his extreme old age.

7. 1793. ROYSTON, Herts. St John the Baptist.   Church clock
    This work was the repair and restoration of an existing clock and,
    judging by the money involved, was extensive.
    Churchwardens' accounts:
        1793 28 Dec. Paid on Acct. for Church Clock........................... £30
        1794 2 May Paid Jno. Briant Hertford the
                    Remainder of the Money for the Clock ....£15   *CJP*

8. 1796. LISBURN, Ireland. Cathedral.   Quarter clock
    Two bells, stated to be 15½" and 18½" diameter and a clock with dial
    plate inscribed
    THE GIFT OF THE MOST NOBLE MARQUESS OF HARTFORD.
        JOHN BRIANT, HARTFORD, ENGLAND FECIT 1796
    Exact layout unknown.   *HCA*

9.   1797. ST ALBANS, Herts.

Tyttenhanger House   Turret clock
Provided to the order of Philip Yorke,
3rd Earl of Hardwick. The clock and
associated bell were disused when
seen by G. and J. Dodds in April
1990. The bell had been quarter-
turned and the crown staple cut
away at some unknown date. In
1992/3 a fire caused minor damage
to the cupola and clock-room but the
clock and bell survived and have
since been restored to working order
by Smith of Derby. As it is impossi-
ble to see the external dial when setting the clock,
a painted dial with *reversed Roman numerals* was
added on the back wall. The brass dial-plate bears only quarter-hour
markings.   *HCA / Dodds, 2001 / Dodds, CB Herts.*

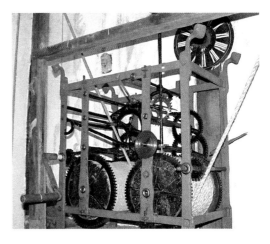

St Albans, Tyttenhanger House. Turret clock by Briant [D.E.Hannaford]

10.   1798 SWAFFHAM PRIOR, Cambs. SS Cyriac & Julietta   Clock
Briant cast a clock bell and may have added a striking train to an existing clock by an anonymous maker. This work was probably part of the
alterations necessary when transferring the clock from the ruined
tower of St Mary's. H.C. Andrews, quoting J. J. Raven, gave the date as
1793, but both R.W.M. Clouston and Dr Peggy Stanier of Swaffham
Prior confirm 1798 as being correct. At the time of writing (2000), the
bell is not hung.

11.   1798 WALTHAM ABBEY, Essex   Church clock
The clock, 'which was in use for 291 years, is now preserved in the
Lady Chapel. Briant repaired it in 1798 and placed a circular brass
plate on it inscribed
          REPAIRED BY JOHN BRIANT HERTFORD 1798.
   ROB^T. DENTON, RICH. PHILLIPS, WILL^M HASTER, C. WARDENS'
                                                      HCA
This was eight years before Briant's major work in recasting and augmenting the ring of bells from six to eight. His repair gave this ancient
clock another eighty-nine years of active life – not bad value! It was
replaced in 1887 by a new one from Gillett & Bland of Croydon.

   According to information kindly supplied by Barry Fisher of
Waltham Abbey, the clock was supplied to the order of the Earl of
Carlisle in 1637 at a cost of £15 3s. 8d. For security, it is no longer kept
in the Lady Chapel but is stored high above the nave on a windowsill,
accessible only by ladder. The brass plate described by H.C. Andrews

has disappeared and this may have been the reason for relocation. The clock has a birdcage frame of early form with two winding drums, one large and one small.   *B. Fisher*

12. *1802 MELTON MOWBRAY, Leics.*   *Quarter clock and chimes*
    This work was in addition to the two new bells cast by Briant the same year. It
    replaced an earlier clock which was moved to St Swithin's, Great Dalby, Leics.,
    where it still remains. Referring to the Briant clock, Andrews quotes a letter from
    the Revd Dr Thomas Ford, Vicar of Melton Mowbray 1773–1822, dated Jan
    18th, 1803 '… a new set of chimes, and a most excellent clock … all made by Mr.
    John Briant, a bell-founder at Hertford, and which do him great credit'.   HCA
    The clock was removed from Melton Mowbray at some unrecorded date.   GAD

13. *1804 HATFIELD, Herts. St Etheldreda*   *Church clock*
    In 1804 the churchwardens of St Peter's, St Albans, sold their clock to Hatfield
    in order to raise funds for rebuilding their tower which had fallen in 1801. Briant
    was probably involved in the repairs necessary before re-erecting it at Hatfield.
    This clock lasted until 1873 when Messrs Dent supplied a new one.   HCA

14. 1805 ST ALBANS, St Peter   Church clock
    Having sold their old clock to Hatfield the previous year (*see above*), the
    churchwardens obtained a replacement from Briant, who was at the
    time recasting the 7th bell and providing a new frame for twelve bells.
    In about 1888, Godman of St Albans altered the clock to take the
    Grimthorpe escapement. It is still an excellent timekeeper.

15. 1810 HERTFORD, All Saints   Turret clock
    This clock is in its third home. It was supplied new in 1810 to St Mary
    the Virgin, Ware, where it remained until 1886–7, when the church
    acquired a new clock and chimes. The clock was then transferred to the
    King's Mead Schools, a boarding school for boys with learning difficulties, which had been built in 1835 as the Union Workhouse and rebuilt in 1869. In about 1970, the Schools, dour buildings with a tall tower in Ware Road, were demolished and a new police station erected on the site. The clock was then transferred to All Saints church, where it remains. It has a birdcage frame and is two-train, striking the hours only. The setting dial is not original and is uninscribed. Automatic winding equipment was added on transfer to All Saints'.

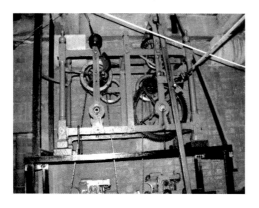

Hertford, All Saints' church clock by Briant.
[*D.E.Hannaford*]

                                                                    J. M. Kemp

16. *1810 PANSHANGER, Herts.*   *Turret clock*
Supplied to the order of the Right Honourable Lord Cowper. The clock and bell
were installed over the main door of the stables and the position of the dial can be
seen in the brickwork. Panshanger House was begun in 1806 and demolished
1953/4, the stables being converted into offices for Redlands Aggregates Ltd. At
some date between 1968 and 1973, the clock disappeared; its present whereabouts
is unknown. (Letter, **Hertfordshire Countryside**, *Dec 1978). The bell, dated*
1810, survives, unhung (see No. 323).

17. 1810 WORMLEIGHTON, Warks.   Turret clock
Originally supplied to the order of R. Andrews Esq. of Harlston, (sic)
Northampton. Harlestone lies close to the edge of the Althorp estate.
The house was remodelled between 1809–11 by John Adey Repton and
demolished in 1939. From then until c.1972 the clock and bell (*see No.
315*) were stored at Althorp before being re-erected at Wormleighton,
another Spencer property. The clock has no external face and the movement is said to have replaced an earlier disused clock. The setting dial is
inscribed

JNO. BRIANT

HERTFORD ◯ FECIT

1810

CJP

(1811 BEDFORD, St Paul
An estimate dated 11 February 1811 was submitted for a new clock. It
was not accepted.   *CJP*)

18. 1812 SEVENOAKS, Kent St Nicholas   Church clock
In 1811 a committee was appointed to deal with the repair of the church,
and on 9 September the following year it was ordered that 'a new clock
with a proper dial plate' should be put up. The record continues:
'Mr. Briant, of Hertford, was selected to put in a new clock at a cost of
£100.' (From J. Rooker: *Notes on the Parish Church of St. Nicholas, Sevenoaks,*
1910' quoted by H.C. Andrews.)

19. 1812 SHREWSBURY, St Julian   Church clock
On 22 October 1812 John Briant wrote to the churchwardens of St
Julian's:
  'Sir, I received your order for a new T'r clock for St. Julians Church &c, …
  Be pleased to give my duty to the Rev: Hugh Owen' – Vicar of the neigh-
  bouring St Alkmund's, for whom he had cast the ring of eight; Briant
  seems to have made friends wherever he went.
Mr Byolin, who contributed this letter to *Shropshire Notes and Queries* in
1897 adds that
  … the present clock at St Julian's, which is admirably made and is said to be

the best timekeeper in the town, is a specimen of Briant's work as a clockmaker.   *HCA*

20. 1814 SHREWSBURY, former Grammar school   Turret clock
This building stands in Castle Gates and dates from c.1590–1630 with
later additions. The staircase tower contains the clock, supplied in 1814.
The school moved to a new site in 1882 and the building now contains
the Library and museum.

21. 1816 AYLESBURY, Bucks.   Church clock
The old ring of six bells was recast into the present eight in 1773 by Pack
& Chapman, a new set of eight-bell chimes not being added until 1798,
supplied by George Harman of High Wycombe and costing £60. The old
clock was replaced by Briant at a cost of £125 10s in 1816. He bought the
old one for £10. The clock and chimes were renewed by John Moore,
clockmaker, of Clerkenwell in 1828 at a cost of £200. A further renewal
took place in 1854 when the contractor was Thwaites & Reed of
Clerkenwell.   `   *CJP*

(1816 WILLIAN, Letchworth, Herts. All Saints   Clock
Briant submitted an estimate for repairs to the clock and bells.
(*HALS, ref. D/P* 125/6/2)   *CJP*

22. 1817 BELVOIR CASTLE, Leics.   Quarter clock
This clock was designed to strike the quarters and was supplied with
three bells, two for the Ting Tang quarters and one as an hour bell. (*See
above Bell Nos. 405–7*)

23. 1820 BISHOP'S STORTFORD, Herts. St Michael   Church clock
Following the rebuilding of the church tower, this clock was installed at
the same time as two treble bells were added by Briant. (As an interesting historical note a clock was made by one Bukberd in or about 1431
and may have been destroyed in the fire of 1440. Bukberd died before
he was paid; the money was finally settled with his executors about
1439. Ref. *Early Churchwardens' Accounts of Bishops Stortford 1431–1558.*
pub. Hertfordshire Record Society, 1994.)
    On the front of the frame of Briant's clock there is a circular brass
plate, probably added in 1840 on which is incribed
                 JOHN BRIANT HERTFORD FECIT 1820.
        NORTH, SOUTH AND WEST DIALS THEY WERE ADDED TO THIS CLOCK
            BY VOLUNTARY SUBSCRIPTION, CONSTRUCTED AND ERECTED BY
                 JAMES YARDLEY BISHOP'S STORTFORD 1840
This implies that the original dial was, unusually, on the east side of the
tower but facing the town.   *HCA*

24. 1820 WATTON-AT-STONE, SS Andrew and Mary   Turret clock
This struck on the tenor of the old six, which were superseded in 1978
by the eight from Upper Clapton. It no longer strikes the hours.

E. Shippin

25. 1821 STANDON, Herts. St Mary   Turret clock
Briant carried out repairs to this clock in 1821.   *CJP*

26. 1823 HERTFORD, St Andrew   Church clock
St Andrew's church was rebuilt in
1861, the tower in 1874, the clock and
bells from the old church being
installed in the new tower. The clock is
on the north side and strikes on a bell
cast by Mears & Stainbank in 1948,
hung half way up inside the spire. The
clock frame is less ornate than that at
All Saints but, like it is two-train only.
The dial plate is hidden behind a
moveable panel. The pendulum shaft
is within the north wall of the tower
and the pendulum bob is at the level
of the ringing chamber behind a
hinged peal board which swings out
to provide access. The dial plate is inscribed

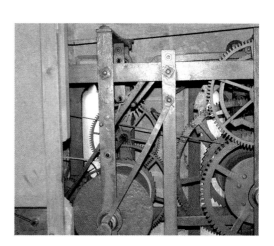

Hertford, St Andrew's church clock by
Briant, AS RESTORED BY S. HARRY
[D.E. Hannaford]

JOHN BRIANT HERTFORD FECIT 1823.
RESTORED AND REFITTED BY S. HARRY HERTFORD 1876.

The work carried out by Samuel Harry was made necessary by the
transfer of both clock and bells from the old tower to the new, the
dimensions of which appear to have been completely different. Samuel
Harry was in business in Castle Street as a clockmaker and jeweller and
had acquired the Skermans' clock making business.

27. 1823 SHREWSBURY, St Chad   Quarter clock
Thomas Mears of Whitechapel installed a new ring of twelve bells in
New St Chad's in 1798, ten years after the collapse of the old church.
Briant was well-known in Shrewsbury for his works at St Alkmund's
and St Julian's, therefore it was hardly surprising that the St Chad's
commission for a quarter clock came to him. By about 1825 there were
complaints that the new tenor was ineffective both for ringing and striking the hours, therefore it was recast with additional metal. There
appear to have been no complaints about the clock.

28. 1824 HERTFORD, Shire Hall, formerly Town Hall   Quarter clock
This important clock superseded one which had been on the corner of
No. 1 Market Place, and was erected by public subscription. It is a three-
train clock with a double-sided dial projecting at roof level on the south
side of what is now the magistrates' court. The hour dial plate has the
following inscription

THIS PUBLIC CLOCK WAS ERECTED ANNO DOMINI 1824, DURING THE MAY-
ORALTY OF THOMAS COLBECK, ESQ., AND WAS PAID FOR BY A VOLUNTARY
SUBSCRIPTION, TO WHICH THE MEMBERS OF THE CORPORATION COLLEC-
TIVELY AND INDIVIDUALLY, WITH MANY OF THE NOBLEMEN AND GENTLE-
MEN OF THE COUNTY AND TOWN LIBERALLY CONTRIBUTED. – JOHN BRIANT,
HERTFORD FECIT 1824.

The minute dial plate is inscribed

JOHN BRIANT, HERTFORD FECIT 1824.

There were originally three very small bells by Briant, cast in 1809, (*See
Nos. 300–302*) which raises the question as to whether they were cast for
the old Market Place clock and had been re-used. During restoration
work on the roof in 1989–91, the two quarter bells, said to have been
very poor-sounding, were stolen, leaving behind the old levers and bar
headstocks. The stolen bells were replaced with newly-cast ones in 1991
and fitted with new hammers while the hour bell retains its old
hammer.   *HCA / Dodds*

An undated cutting from a local paper in Hertford museum has a
letter by W.F. Andrews giving an account of work carried out on the
clock over the years. It contains the following details:

A new dial was substituted for the old copper one in 1871, and was an illu-
minated one, and the clock was first lighted with gas on the 5th December in
that year. The cost was about £30 and was
raised by subscription, the result being an
immense improvement upon the former
style, and has been found to be so until the
present time. On November 23, 1886, this
dial was destroyed during the process of its
removal, when extensive alterations were
being carried out at the Town Hall, which
necessitated taking the works of the clock
away from the building. A rope which was
being used for the purpose of lowering the
dial (which weighed 7 tons) to the ground
gave way, with the result that it was dashed
to pieces, and in the fall a workman was
caught by the rope and dragged to the
pavement below and killed instantly.

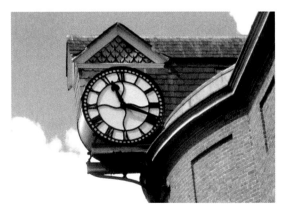

Hertford Shire Hall clock by Briant 1824.
The present external dials are modern.

Another dial was afterwards placed in position, and the clock was lighted with gas as before. In 1907 an installation of electric light was provided to the building, but this was not extended to the the clock.

(7 tons sounds rather excessive. J.D.)

29. 1824 WIMPOLE HALL, Cambs.   Turret clock
Made to the order of the Right Honourable Lord Hardwicke.

30. 1825 WREST PARK, Beds.   Turret clock
Made to the order of Countess De Grey. The clock is still extant, but
most of the mechanism has been removed.   *CJP*

31. 1825 SLEAFORD, Lincs. St Denys   Quarter clock
This appears in the manuscript additions to Briant's list of clocks.

32. 1826   KINGERBY GREEN (sic), Lincs.   Turret clock
To the order of James Young Esq. Kingerby Hall, near Market Rasen, was
built in 1812, but the clock was not supplied until 1826. The setting dial
is inscribed:

JOHN BRIANT
HERTFORD FECIT
1826.

There is a single uninscribed hour bell possibly by Thomas Mears, so
the clock is two-train only. It is noted among the manuscript additions
to the printed list. The clock is in a square turret with a cupola above the
stables.   *GAD / Lincs. K 2000*

33. 1827 CAMBRIDGE, King's College, New Gate House   Turret clock
Briant was actively working on this clock while he was corresponding
about the recasting of Great Tom of Lincoln. For a man in his 79th year
this was quite remarkable. The New Gate House was part of the screen
wall facing on to King's Parade, designed by William Wilkins after winning
an architectural competition in 1823. Inside the rather bulbous
cupola there is a hemispherical bell on which the clock strikes,
inscribed JOHN BRIANT HERTFORD FECIT 1827, but almost certainly
cast by Thomas Mears of Whitechapel.   *HCA / Pevsner*

1829 NORTHAMPTON, All Saints   Set of chimes
This appears in Briant's printed list of 1825, not as a manuscript addition
so the original order was to Briant. The long delay in completion
could have been caused by a variety of factors; the sale of the clock business
to James Skerman, Briant's move to St Albans and possibly the forgetfulness
of old age. It is also included in Skerman's own trade list.
  Of the seven tunes for these chimes listed by Jennings, Hanover,

Highland Laddie and The Happy Clown had been set at Woodstock in
1792 and the first two by Eayre in 1761.

British and Irish Chime Barrel Mechanisms Jennings, 2000.

Undated Clocks

Briant's published list did not give dates for clocks or chimes supplied, so it
is necessary to use other means to give at least an approximate period
during which work was most likely to have been carried out. C.J. Pickford
has dated many of those listed above but there remains a number for which
no firm dates exist.

The writer's approach has been to consult the various county surveys in
Pevsner's *Buildings of England* series, in order to discover whether any building work was being carried out within the period concerned, i.e. from 1779,
the date of Briant's earliest bell, to the time of his death in 1829. The degree
of correlation is too high to be mere coincidence; new clocks were being
provided for new buildings, especially private houses. Church clocks are
less likely to conform to this pattern. Also, a satisfactory bell or ring of bells
could lead to a commission for either a clock or a set of chimes, occasionally
several years later.

34. (Before 1788) HATFIELD, Woodside   Turret clock
    The clock above the stables can only be assigned to the years 1772-88.
    House building commenced in the former year for John Church Esq.
    and the erection of the stables probably followed immediately after-
    wards. John Church died in 1788. 1772 is too early for Briant and there-
    fore c.1782 is more likely.

35. 1788+ HARROW WEAL (sic) PRIORY, Middx.   Turret clock
    Now known as Bentley Priory. H.Q. Fighter Command during the
    Second World War. Building began 1788.   *Pevsner*

36. 1792+ WAKEFIELD LODGE, Northants.   Turret clock
    Made to the order of His Grace the Duke of Grafton.
    The house, which is in the parish of Potterspury, was built by Kent for
    the second Duke in 1745 but Briant cast a bell for the church there in
    1792 which may have led to this commission.

37. 1797 BARKWAY, Herts.   Church clock
    There was a clock in the tower in the 15th century, prior to the present
    undated one, which strikes on the 'Angelus' bell, cast by Reignold
    Chirche of Bury St Edmunds c.1450. It therefore seems likely that Briant
    repaired an existing clock, probably after recasting the old ring of five
    bells into six in 1797.

38. 1801+ TAYMOUTH CASTLE, Scotland   Turret clock
To the order of the Right Honourable Lord Breadalbane. Building work
on the castle began in 1801. It is now a school.

Shell Guide to Scotland

39. 1803–8 SCONE PALACE, Scotland   Turret clock
To the order of the Right Honourable Lord Mansfield. The new Palace
was begun in 1803 and completed in 1808.

Shell Guide to Scotland

40. 1805+ COVENTRY, St Michael   Quarter clock
There was a clock and chimes by Worton of Birmingham 1778 which
played at least seven tunes. A different set of tunes is recorded in 1818.
Whether or not Briant carried out repairs or alterations in 1818, or
whether he did work in 1805 after recasting the tenor, is not clear. The
earlier date seems more likely, as the removal and replacement of such
a large bell would necessitate much dismantling and refitting of clock
hammers and other gear.   *CB Warks.*

41. 1814+ MULGRAVE CASTLE, N. Yorks.   Quarter clock
To the order of Earl Mulgrave. The 18th century castle, near Sandsend,
was altered and extended at various dates from 1786 to 1805, with
towers added on east and west sides in 1814.

42. 1825+ BLANKNEY HOUSE, Lincs.   Turret clock
To the order of Charles Chaplin Esq. The ruins of the grand Palladian
Blankney Hall were being demolished, according to Pevsner in 1964. The
stable block remained at that date, having been built in 1825, a possible
date for Briant's clock.

No firm dates can be ascertained for the following:
BARKING, Essex   Church clock   Bell recast 1793
KELVEDON, Essex   Church clock   Two bells recast
1803
ST. IVES, Hunts.   *Turret clock at the Market House*
The market clock, originally of 1728, was in a turret above Kiddle's shop in
Bridge Street. It was demolished in 1922.   (*Norris Museum*)

CONDOVER, Salop.   *? Clock and/or chimes.*
In Part 6 of his 9-part opus on Shropshire churches, Dean Cranage implies that
the clock here was 17th century, therefore Briant was possibly repairing or mod-
ernising an older clock and installing chimes rather than supplying a new one in
1812–13. All evidence has gone as the present clock is modern.   *C. Dalton*

PART VI

HERTFORDSHIRE
1850–1920

EIGHTEENTH CENTURY AND
MODERN BELLFOUNDING
JOHN WARNER OF HODDESDON
AND
GEORGE NEWMAN OF ST ALBANS
(IRONFOUNDER)

18

EIGHTEENTH CENTURY AND MODERN
BELL FOUNDING

THE CHIEF DIFFERENCES between the techniques of Robert Oldfield's time (see *Fig. 25*) and those of John Briant were in details, the
main principles being similar. Most obvious to the eye is in the lettering; the
irregularites of laid-on wax figures had given way to stamped letters and
numerals. This had in fact been used as early as 1616 by Thomas Pennington
I of Exeter, although the London founders did not follow suit until the late
seventeenth century in the case of John Hodson, and the Whitechapel
founders not until about 1763 when they adopted a completely new font.
There is ample evidence that John Briant followed the techniques of Joseph
Eayre and the St Neots' foundry, where stamped inscriptions were standard
from the start, and the Croxley Green bell of 1822 clearly shows where an
incorrectly-placed stamp was pulled away, leaving a partial impression.

The old technique of core, model bell and cope was still used by semi-
itinerant founders like John Waylett, for the simple reason that it was easier
to use when setting up a temporary furnace, rather than carrying around
heavy equipment such as cope cases. Just exactly when the custom-made
cope case came into use is not known (see *Fig. 26*). It was not until 1853 that
John Warner patented the ventilated cast-iron cope case that is in use today.
(*The Warner Family*, p. 310). This was suitable only for an established foundry
with ample storage space, as they are heavy and bulky objects and many
sizes are needed. There was, however, a half-way stage which survived in use
until as late as the outbreak of the 1939–45 war, and which is shown on p. 473
of *Church Bells of Oxfordshire* by Fred Sharpe. Thomas Bond, the very last rural
church bellfounder in this country, who died in 1947, is pictured standing
behind several cope moulding cases of a pattern which could go back to the
eighteenth century. They consist of a lattice of metal strips formed into the
rough shape of a bell with strengthening hoops around the outside. Any
competent blacksmith could have made them, and since all founders needed
a blacksmith for forging clappers and other iron-work, it was likely that each
founder designed and made his own on the premises, as required.

A more sophisticated version is shown on p. 10 of *Bellfounding* (*Shire
Album* 212) by Trevor Jennings which was in use at Taylors' Loughborough
foundry until the advent of the solid cope case. As the firm is the lineal
descendant of the St Neot's foundry, the design probably derives from there
and would be familiar to Briant.

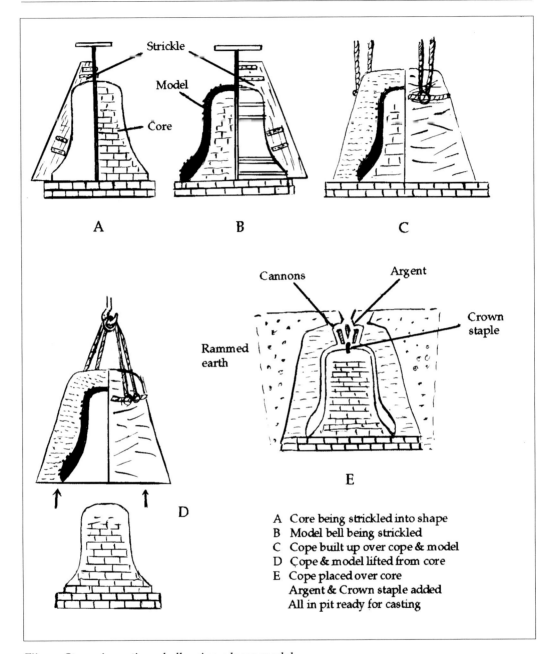

A Core being strickled into shape
B Model bell being strickled
C Cope built up over cope & model
D Cope & model lifted from core
E Cope placed over core
   Argent & Crown staple added
   All in pit ready for casting

Fiig. 25 Stages in casting a bell: using a loam model

Another device in use today on the continent consists of a series of cast rings in a graduated range of diameters which are used to strengthen the outside of the clay cope. This technique is of considerable antiquity and was known in the Middle Ages. It still requires making a model bell and was the system in use at the Whitechapel foundry in the nineteenth century. Exactly which method Briant used cannot now be known.

Using a cope case (*Fig. 26*) did away with the necessity for making a clay model bell and was a saving both of time and material. The modern cope case is first lined with thin curved bricks, then a layer of loam is built up on this and strickled into shape. Lettering and decorations, if any, can then be stamped on to the inside of the cope, which is then dried before assembly with the core.

Looking at a comparatively complete ring such as Hatfield, one is struck by the care which Briant took over the proportions of his bells. The lighter bells are much higher in the crown than the heavier ones, the tenor being surprisingly flat-topped, with a sharp angle at the shoulder. This was normal good practice and allowed the lighter bells to turn more slowly. His usual pattern of moulding wires was 3 on the crown, 2/2 on the inscription band, 3 on the soundbow and 2 on the lip, which is now the standard pattern at Whitechapel. There were exceptions, such as a 2- or 3-line inscription which would need a variation.

Briant used the same chip-tuning method that had been used at Ashwell in 1602/3. Lathe tuning as practised by founders in the Netherlands had made little headway in England, although the Rudhalls of Gloucester were using this method from about 1790 with a speeding-up of the process but indifferent results. It is therefore not altogether surprising that a technically-minded man like Briant may not have been sufficiently convinced of the advantages compared with the cost of the lathe. He would not reject it out of hand, but only after mature consideration. Despite Henry Symondson's statement that 'Briant never knowingly sent out a bad bell', one is forced to admit that not all his bells were perfect. Some were very good and with modern tuning are even better, e.g. Barkway and Hatfield, but it is only necessary to hear an untouched ring like Halton, Bucks., in no known scale, to realise that Briant had his lapses. Abington, Northants., is another example. Condover, now the only complete Briant octave in the country, is not tuneful; neither were the two trebles of 1805 at St Peter's, St Albans, while his bell at Meppershall was much too flat for its original position in the ring. At the other end of the scale there are the superb tenors at Passenham and Hanslope and the octave at Hatfield. The fact remains that, for his time, he was a good founder, better than many if not most of his contemporaries.

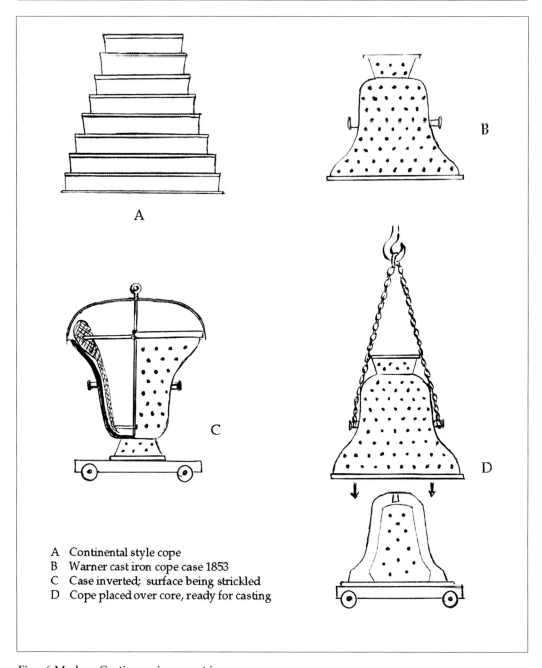

A   Continental style cope
B   Warner cast iron cope case 1853
C   Case inverted; surface being strickled
D   Cope placed over core, ready for casting

Fig. 26 Modern Casting: using a cast iron cope case

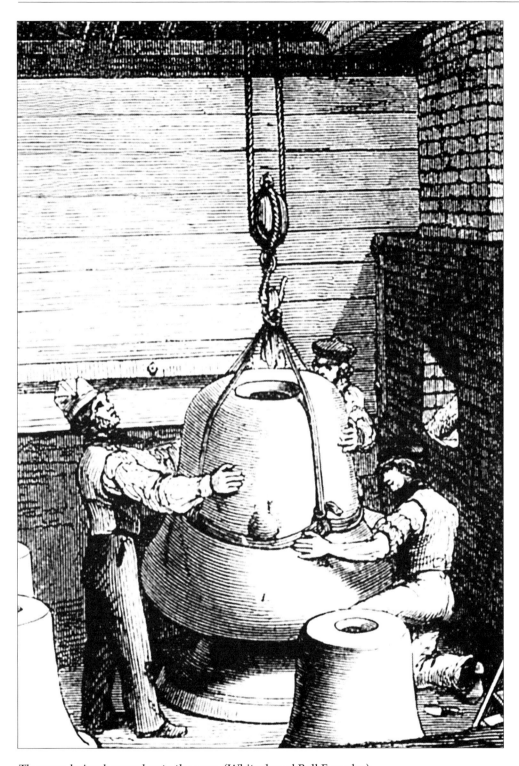

The cope being lowered onto the core. (Whitechapel Bell Foundry)

19

THE WARNER FAMILY OF HODDESDON
AND
GEORGE NEWMAN OF ST ALBANS

A T NO TIME DID THE WARNER family cast any bells in Hertford-shire but, as innovators who were also respected and influential members of the Hoddesdon community, they deserve a brief section to themselves.

Their connection with founding began with Jacob Warner, 1701-62, a Quaker whose grandfather and father came from Waltham Abbey. Jacob became a tinplate worker in St Albans and while there married Ruth Tomson, a local woman. In about 1739 the Warners moved to Wood Street, London, where, to the annoyance of the Founders' Company who maintained a monopoly in founding in the City, he set up as a brassfounder. When ordered to desist, he took no notice and went his own way, eventually overcoming their opposition and being elected a 'Love Brother' or Honorary Member. His two sons, John and Tomson, were both admitted to the Company.

Jacob died in 1762 and was buried in the Society of Friends' burial ground in what was then Sweetbriar Lane but is now Victoria Street, St Albans; it lies in front of the police station.

Jacob's elder son, John, served for a time as churchwarden of St Giles, Cripplegate, (a civic, rather than religious obligation) and, during his term of office, the bells were repaired by Robert Patrick who had worked for William Mears at Whitechapel. Warner's name appeared on the tenor bell as 'contractor'. The late George Elphick, in *Sussex Bells and Belfries*, thought it possible that Warner had cast the bell under Patrick's direction. Whatever the facts, it led to the first stage of bellfounding by John Warner which began about 1789 and lasted until his death in 1820. Their foundry was in Jewin Crescent, Cripplegate.

The younger brother, Tomson, had two sons, John II and Robert. John married twice; first Esther Borham and after her death, her sister Sarah, by whom he had eleven children. At that period it was considered normal for a businessman to 'live over the shop' but with so large a family it became necessary to find more space, so John bought what was then a country estate at Hoddesdon. In the grounds of Lowewood, a tall Georgian-fronted house on the west side of High Street, he built Woodlands, a large house with extensive stabling and outbuildings. An important factor in the choice of Hoddesdon must have been the opening of the Northern & Eastern Railway as far as Broxbourne in 1840 which allowed for commuting to Shoreditch. Another factor may have been the existence of a Friends' Meeting House in Lord Street, Hoddesdon. To John, already a prosperous brassfounder, is due the second phase of bellfounding, which led to the firm becoming one of the Big Three nineteenth century bellfounders along with Mears of Whitechapel and Taylor's of Loughborough. A portrait of John, reproduced on p.164 of Elphick's *Sussex*, shows a striking figure, bald, with piercing eyes and clad in sober black. As a devout Quaker, he addressed all men as 'Friend'.

John died in 1852 and his eldest son, Charles Borham Warner, took over the business as well as making his home at Woodlands. Charles was an innovator and what was perhaps the greatest advance in bellfounding techniques occurred during his time. In December 1853, Patent No. 2319 was taken out under the names of Frederick Warner and John Shotton. This, the introduction of the cast-iron ventilated cope case, revolutionised the whole process and was slowly and reluctantly adopted by the other founders. At that date Whitechapel bellfoundry was using the continental type of cope strengthened with iron hoops. Prior to then bellfounding had been more of a craft than an industrial process and in essentials had not altered significantly over 200 years. (*See Fig. 25* p. 306). The invention of the perforated cope case changed all that. (*Fig. 26* p. 308). There were some disadvantages with the new system; cope cases took up a large amount of storage space and were weighty items. Warner also modified the core by introducing a ventilated iron structure on a metal base-plate instead of bricks. This, however, was not universally adopted at the time by the other foundries. These innovations effectively abolished the old three-stage sequence of core, model bell and cope, and reduced it to two only, core and cope.

In 1856 Charles Warner had the misfortune to cross swords with the mighty Edmond Becket Denison over the casting of Big Ben. Much acrimonious correspondence emanated from Denison, later Lord Grimthorpe, but, however sorely provoked, Warner kept his temper and always addressed his letters to 'Respected Friend' which probably inflamed Denison still further! (Ref. *Lord Grimthorpe*, by Peter Ferriday, p. 45. Published by John Murray 1957).

Like most Quakers, Charles Warner was interested in social conditions and even started a temperance insurance company (*Elphick*, p. 165). This social conscience was a family characteristic which persisted into the twentieth century. They were connected with Woodlands until about 1920 when the three surviving sisters, the Misses Warner, were living at Lowewood, the original house. Miss Cecily, who outlived her sisters, left Lowewood to the town of Hoddesdon to form a museum, which it still is. Family photographs displayed there show the three elderly sisters, tall, slender, white-haired, black-gowned charming Quaker ladies. A few papers connected with the casting of Big Ben are also preserved as are two small bells, one of which may have been a trade sample and the other a clock bell. There is also a blank 9" servants' or gardeners' bell on the parapet.

Woodlands House has gone and Broxbourne Civic Hall now stands on the site although the extensive grounds remain. Woodlands Close runs behind the museum. The stables, complete with clock and bell, are now a house known as Little Woodlands. The Warner connection has not been forgotten; the name of John Warner was given to a local school and a road to the west of his grounds is called Warners Avenue. In the whole county, he is the only bellfounder to be so honoured.

The members of the far-flung Warner clan still meet annually in Hoddesdon.

George Newman of St Albans – 1863

Every county has a hard core of small blank, anonymous bells, usually in lesser nineteenth century churches. Hertfordshire is no exception; three specimens of brassfounders' work can be found at St Bede's R.C. church at Croxley Green; a smaller one in Watford Museum and the bell at St Barnabas, Adeyfield, Hemel Hempstead, this latter transferred from elsewhere. It therefore comes as a complete surprise that information has been received from Anne Willis of Bradford on Avon, Wilts., that at least two and possibly four bells are said to have actually been cast in St Albans, at an easily identifiable site.

A notebook in Devizes Museum library gives details of two bells of unknown size which were apparently commissioned by John Harris C.E., a bell and bell-frame enthusiast. Both bells bore the inscription

HABEO NOMEN MICHAELIS
IOHN HARRIS HAD ME CAST AD 1863
GEORGE NEWMAN FOUNDER ⊠
OLD COLLEGE WORKS SAINT ALBANS
H LEWIS AND E HARRIS M C S

(⊠ Henry Lewis, son of a former Mayor, was a prominent ringer at St Peter's, St Albans)

One of these bells was cast for the Clock Tower, St Albans, although no record of it appears in published Corporation Records. The tower was undergoing extensive restoration at that time. It seems that this bell was something of an embarassment, as a further reference says that it 'was hung in a closet'. It's whereabouts is not known.

The other bell was cast for the Chapel-of-Ease of All Saints at Newtown, near Tisbury, Wilts., which is now a house. This bell has recently been seen and photographed by Anne Willis. In 1871 John Harris commissioned two more bells from Thomas Bamford, Newman's successor. Nothing is known.

The Old College Iron Works was on the site of the Collegium Insanorum, a private asylum run by a Dr Cotton. A map of 1881 shows the works at

TL 144073 with an entrance in Lower Dagnall Street. Kelly's Directory of 1860 and 1862 lists George Newman as ironfounder, smith and agricultural implement maker. In 1870 the business was run by Thomas Bamford.

John Harris described himself at various times as 'Architect' and 'Surveyor' and seems to have been something of a nomad, his work taking him about the country. Noting his addresses at various dates shows a correlation with railway projects and he may have been employed on some ancilliary work with railway connections.

He claimed to have surveyed and drawn over 500 bell frames, even including some American ones, and, in an acrimonious correspondence with N.N. Hills, Ringing Master of St Albans Abbey, conducted in the pages of *Church Bells* between April and November 1883 (Article by H.V. Frost, *Ringing World*, 19 August 1988 pp. 798–800), he claimed to have amassed between one and two hundredweight of paperwork on the subject. One small notebook has come to light; if more can be found, bell archeologists will have a field-day.

GLOSSARY

1 hundredweight (cwt) – 50.8 kg	1 penny (d)	– 0.5 p (approx.)
1 quarter (qr) – 12.7 kg	1 shilling (s) = 12d	– 5p
1 pound (lb) – 0.564 kg	1 pound (£) = 20s	– 100p
1 inch (") – 2.54 cm		

Parts of a bell – Fig. 1, p. xv

Argent – strong suspension loop, cast as part of the bell; old hanging.

Cannons – cast suspension loops, usually six; two on each face of the argent and one on each side of the argent, in the same plane. The argent and cannons are often removed on rehanging to assist in accurate engineering. Modern bells usually have a flat crown and are bolted to a flat machined face on the headstock.

Crown staple – Suspension loop from which the clapper swings.
(1) Iron loop or staple cast centrally inside the crown. Differential expansion of the bronze bell and iron (and rust) has often led to cracking in the crown.
(2) If the bell has been **quarter-turned** to present a fresh part of the soundbow for the clapper to strike, the crown staple is replaced by a **false crown staple**, as the original is in the wrong plane.
(3) A modern bell has a machined flat crown, with no cannons, and an **independent crown staple** bolted through the full height of the headstock.

Inscription band – an inscription is usually placed here, just below the shoulder, although inscriptions are often placed on the waist or round the soundbow.

Long-waisted – Early bells have much longer waists (*see Fig. 1*) than modern bells. English change ringing demanded bells with a smaller Moment of Inertia able to respond to small changes of timing of swings.

Moulding wires – decorative ridges formed circumferentially on the outer surface. On a modern bell there are two on the crown just above the shoulder, two each above and below the inscription band, three above the soundbow and two just above the lip.

Soundbow – the thickest part, where the clapper ball strikes.

Bell fittings.

Clapper – a device suspended from the crown staple to strike the soundbow
and is constrained to swing in the same plane as the bell. The main
body is made of wrought iron or, nowadays, cast spheroidal graphite
steel.
Ball – where most of the mass is concentrated, to strike the centre of the
soundbow.
Flight – an extension beyond the ball, to aid the throw of the clapper
and to place the centre of inertia in the ball.
Stem – the rod linking the clapper bearing and the ball, made thin for
lightness, yet strong to withstand shock.
Deadstock – A headstock without gudgeons, so the bell is rigid and is usually struck externally on the soundbow.
Gudgeon pins – Iron or steel rods accurately aligned at each end of the
headstock and rotating in bearings on the bellframe. With cast iron or
steel headstocks, the gudgeon pins are machined integral with the
stock.
Headstock – The block of elm, cast iron or steel from which the bell is hung
by iron straps from the cannons or through-bolts from the top of the
headstock to the inside of the bell, and on which a lever or wheel and
gudgeon pins are fitted.
Lever – A bar of wood or steel fitted horizontally to the headstock with a
rope attached to the outer end for small angle chiming. The clapper
strikes one side only; that nearest the rope.
Stay – A length of carefully seasoned ash bolted to the headstock, near the
opposite end to the wheel. It engages with the –
Slider – A wooden bar, pivoted to the cill under the wheel, with the other
end free to slide between stops on the slider board attached to the
opposite cill. This system prevents the bell from flying much beyond the
balance yet allows the bell to rest there, which is called 'set'. In this position it is very dangerous for non-ringers to touch the rope.
Wheel – to guide the rope which is attached to a spoke and with a special
arrangement of spokes to take the variable loads. Quarter and half
wheels are modifications of the lever to enable the bell to swing
through a larger angle and strike at both ends of the clapper swing.

Bellfounding – See Figs. 25 and 26.

False bell – Before mid-nineteenth century, the required bell shape was
made in loam over the core before the cope was formed over it. After
baking, the three parts were separated (*Fig. 25$_d$*) and the false bell
broken up. After reassembly of core and cope, bellmetal was cast to fill
the void.

Loam – A carefully blended wet mixture of sand and clay with a binding of horse hair, goat hair, hay or other organic material, used in moulds for bell casting.

Strickle board – 'A board used for sweeping off excess material … a template used for shaping a mould.' (*Collins*)

Bellframe – made to support the bearings and to resist the thrust of the swinging bell. For full-circle ringing, each bell hangs in a pit of sufficient length and depth to clear the wheel and clapper flight. The frame heads and cills are linked by strong timber or cast iron struts in line with the bearings, two on each side, and vertical, cross-braced posts at each corner. For four of more bells, the bells are usually arranged so that horizontal stresses are balanced for the tower and ropes made to fall in the ringing chamber, so that, when ringing Rounds and viewed from above, the sequence is clockwise. However, there are a number of rings where the order is reversed – anticlockwise.

Inscriptions.

Black letter – Gothic font, e.g. 𝔟𝔩𝔞𝔠𝔨 𝔩𝔢𝔱𝔱𝔢𝔯. Gothic capitals are sometimes called 'Old English'.

Cross cercelée – A cross with the ends divided and curled back.

Cross patée – A cross with the ends of the arms much wider than the roots.

Incised – Inscription chiselled into the bell's surface. Usually used when an addition was required after the bell was cast.

Lombardic – Pre-Black letter capitals used on bells and in stone carving, simpler than the script of 'Old English'

Lozenge – A rhombus or (Heraldry) diamond-shaped charge. (*Collins*)

Patera – the block on which a character or word is formed. For an old style bell, it is the impression produced by the wax sheet in the mould after it has been stuck on the 'false or model bell' (*Fig. 25*) or, new style, the rectangular hollow produced by too strong a blow to the stamp, which is very like a letter press printer's type, on the cope.

Rebus – 'A heraldic emblem or device that is a pictorial representation of or pun on the name of the bearer.' (*Collins*)

Roman – Latin characters.

Squeeze – A technical term for squeezing Plasticine over a raised or incised inscription and using this to make a plaster cast.

Stop – A cross, fleur-de-lys or other decoration to separate words or to indicate the start or end of a sentence.

Ringing.

Chime barrel – Mechanical tune player, a musical box drum on a large scale.

Clocking – The rope is tied round the clapper flight and the clapper is
pulled to strike the soundbow without the bell moving. The momentary
holding of the clapper against the soundbow has cracked many a bell.
Safe clocking is where the rope is tied to a loop welded high on the
clapper stem and a pull produces an impulse to the clapper sufficient to
strike the soundbow and swing back.

Full-circle – For English change ringing bells rotate ±180° from mouth
downwards position.

Hammer chiming – Clock and tune chimes lift blocks of hardwood and
release them to strike the outside of the soundbow, being then lifted
clear by a firm spring.

Solenoid chiming – A short electric current is passed through a solenoid
which throws a bolt against the soundbow before a spring returns it to
the solenoid.

Swing chiming – The bell is made to swing through a small angle and strike
by checking the rope at the top of its swing to force the clapper to meet
the soundbow.

Ellacombe chimes – A chiming arrangement devised by the Revd. T. Ellacombe whereby rings of bells can by sounded by one man. A lever is
placed in the bell pit, with an iron ball on one end, which lifts to strike
the inside of the soundbow when a rope fixed to the other end is pulled
down. Ropes from the bells are drawn to a chiming cabinet in a floor
below, past pulleys in the top of the cabinet to adjusting reels below. The
ropes are plucked horizontally to chime tunes or changes.

Tuning

Chip-tuning – The early method of tuning a bell, by chipping the inside of
the bell with a chisel-ended hammer to flatten it, or chipping the lip to
sharpen it (skirting) – a very noisy process.

Lathe-tuning – All bells are now tuned in a vertical lathe. The earliest were
driven by a horse gin (see Harrison and Waylett, p. 140) although first
used for bells by Rudhall's of Gloucester in early 1800s. (Their original
lathe is in the Whitechapel bellfoundry)

INDEX

References in italic type are to illustrations; those in Roman figures refer to the preliminary pages. The index is divided into three sections: General, People and Places. The General section includes the location of all clocks which can then be found under Places. The People section includes bellfoundries, bellfounders and clockmakers, but excludes founders within their own chapters: these can then be found under their individual names.

GENERAL

a, two types 9,11
Acorn stops 53,75, 77, 88-9, 96
Argent xiv, 37

Bell, The 51, 55
Bell, The One 59
Bell and Punchbowl, The 59
Bell and Shears, The 59
Bellmakers' Guild 4
Bell Mould, The 54–6
Bells scrapped, *see* Scrapped bells
Bells stolen, *see* Stolen bells
Bells transferred, *see* Transferred bells
Benefactors *see* People index
Big Ben 311
Bocking company of ringers 237
Briant's list of clocks 290

Canal transport 184, 246, 251–2, 262, 271, 281
Cannons xiv, 37
Canvas, cope reinforcement 38
Casting, bell 3, 37, 305–9, 311
Chimes, *see* Places
    Hatfield, Hemel Hempstead, High Wycombe, London, Cripplegate, Melton Mowbray, Northampton, All Saints, St Albans Abbey, St Peter, Watford
Chip-tuning 38, 307
Chip-tuning hammer 38
Churches Conservation Trust 218, 220
Churches, fire damage to, *see*

Fire damage
Civil War, The 56–7, 111–2, 114, 126
Clavis Campanalogia 174
Clocks, *see* Places
    Aylesbury, Barking, Barkway, Bassingbourn, Bedford, Belvoir Castle, Bishop's Stortford, Blankney Castle, Cambridge, King's College, Clothall-Quickswood House, Condover, Coventry, Great Dalby, Harlston, Harrow Weald Priory, Hatfield, -House, --Woodside, -Hertford All Saints, -Balls Park, -King's Mead Schools, -St Andrew, -Shire Hall, Kelvedon, Kingerby Hall, Lisburn Cathedral, Melton Mowbray, Mulgrave Castle, Northampton, All Saints, Royston, St Albans, St Peter, Ridge Tyttenhanger House, St Ives, Scone Palace, Sevenoaks, Shrewsbury, -Grammar school, -St Chad, -St Julian, Sleaford, Standon, Swaffham Prior, Taymouth Castle, Wakefield Lodge, Waltham Abbey, Ware, Watford, Watton-at-Stone, Welwyn Garden City Panshanger, Willian, Wimpole

Hall, Woodstock, Wormleighton, Wrest Park
College Youths, Society of 112, 122, 140, 176, 198
Cope 3, 38, 305–9
    cage 305
    case 305, 307
Core 3, 37, 305–9
    ventilated, iron 305
Cross crosslet design 75
Crown staple xiv, 37
Cumberland Youths, Society of 201
Cylinders for steam engines 140

Dates 70
Distribution of founder's bells 17, 82, 120, 136, 204

Earthenware letter moulds 37
East Herts Archeological Society 198

Facsimile inscription, early 63, 69, 71
False bell 37–8, 72
Fire damage to churches
    Langham 146
    Good Easter 115
    Hertford, All Saints 177–8, 219
    Kelshall 218
    Orpington? 269
    Shenley 79
    Stapleford Tawney 80, 99
Founders, Worshipful Company of 141, 310

319

PEOPLE

PLACES

HERTFORDSHIRE PUBLICATIONS

Hertfordshire Publications began 40 years ago and was re-launched as an imprint of the University of Hertfordshire Press in February 2001. It is published by the Press on behalf of the Hertfordshire Association for Local History (HALH) whose membership includes both individuals and local history societies in Hertfordshire. Members receive a discount on the retail price of books published in the series.

Tracing your Family History in Hertfordshire
Hertfordshire Archives and Local Studies (HALS)
ISBN 0 9542189 2 2 Paperback, 152 pages, £9.99

This practical and comprehensive guide provides an introduction to everything family historians need to know in order to trace their ancestors in Hertfordshire. Every aspect of our ancestors' lives has been considered, from their birth and baptism to their death and burial. Examples of source material, together with photographs and drawings illustrate the text. All major sources are covered irrespective of location and web addresses allow preliminary searching to be done online.

"This book will be of enormous help to all those who attempt to trace their ancestors in the county". **Anthony Camp**, President of the Hertfordshire Family History Society and Former Director, Society of Genealogists

Cinemas of Hertfordshire
Allen Eyles with Keith Skone
ISBN 0 9542189 0 6 Paperback, 172 pp. £9.99.

Almost all of these buildings in Hertfordshire have disappeared or been altered out of all recognition but this book recalls and describes each of them and also records the triumphant arrival of the county's newer multiplex cinemas. This is a book that will intrigue and entertain film buffs, local historians, and anyone who has ever had a liking for "going to the pictures". It contains some 149 black and white photographs and includes every cinema in Hertfordshire since the first opened its doors in 1908 is arranged by town for ease of reference.

The Common People are not for nothing: conflict in religion and politics in Hertfordshire, 1575 to 1780
Lionel M. Munby
ISBN 0 901354 80 5 paperback, 178 pages, £9.95

The theme of this book is the reverse side of traditional history, a turning upside down of what has been a conventional viewpoint. The existence of a continuing under current of social opposition to the established society and the way this found religious forms of expression are the underlying themes linking the separate chapters. The studies are all local to Hertfordshire but provide a rich source of new material and insights for the study of local history in all parts of the country.

Hertfordshire Brasses
Mary Rensten
ISBN 0 901354 20 1 paperback, 103 pages, £5.95

This popular guide to the figure brasses in the churches of Hertfordshire, with 76 illustrations and a detailed index of names and places, is the first complete guide to the brasses of Hertfordshire to be published since1903. Includes a short introduction to brass rubbing, a glossary and guide to further reading.

So that was Hertfordshire: Travellers' jottings 1322 to 1887
Malcolm Tomkins
ISBN 0 901354 87 2 paperback, 91 pages, £6.95

Hertfordshire history seen through the books, diaries, journals and letters of those who visited the county or merely passed through it. The 'innocent eye' of the visitor, from foreign kings and princes to humble travellers on foot, provide a colourful, informative and occasionally funny insight into Hertfordshire people, agriculture and industry. Arranged chronologically with an index of travellers, places and houses.

Garden Cities and New Towns
ISBN 0 901354 58 9 hardback, 115 pages, £14.95

As well as describing the growth of the two original Garden Cities in Herfordshire, Letchworth and Welwyn Garden City, and four of the post-war New Towns. from original concept to the present day this book looks at their influence on the new towns which followed.

Hertfordshire Inns and Public Houses, an historical gazatteer
Graham Jollife and Arthur Jones
ISBN 0 901354 58 9 paperback, 177 pages, £12.95

An attractive new edition of Branch Johnson's pioneering work, *Hertfordshire Inns,* first published in 1962 in two volumes. Mostly consisting of 'pubs' predating 1900 it is arranged alphabetically by parish and gives former names and a brief history of each house. Extensively illustrated.

Bedrooms, Chimneys and Lavatories: the development of Hertfordshire houses from shelters to homes
Arthur Jones
ISBN 0 901354 29 5 paperback, 32 pages, £4.95

An attractively illustrated booklet with many plans, drawings and photographs of buildings from Iron Age huts to modern tower blocks but mainly focussing on the development of the timber and brick buildings which are so treasured by their present day owners and occupiers and so characteristic of the county.

Hertfordshire 1731 to 1800 as recorded in the *Gentleman's Magazine*
Edited by Arthur Jones
ISBN 0 901354 73 2 hardback, 266 pages, £18

This book containing all Hertfordshire material of any importance published in *The Gentlemans Magazine* from 1731 to 1800 is a rich resource for research: history, news items of every kind, reports of robberies, court proceedings, executions, fires and, of course, the obituaries for which G.M. was particularly famous. Arranged chronologically with a detailed index of names and places and with supplementary listings for births, marriages, bankruptcies and deaths

Hertfordshire in History
Edited by Dr Doris Jones-Baker
ISBN 0 901354 63 5 hardback, 311pages, £18

A collection of eighteen papers from the thirteenth to the latter part of the twntieth century compiled in honour of Lionel Munby, one of Hertfordshire's leading historians of the twentieth century.

The following title has been accepted for publication

St Albans 1650-1700: a thoroughfare town and its people
J.T. Smith and M.A. North (eds) for the St Albans 17th century Research Group
ISBN 0 9542189 3 0 paperback, approximately 320 pages, price tba.
Publication: September 2003

UNIVERSITY OF HERTFORDSHIRE PRESS

The University of Hertfordshire Press also publishes the following academic books on regional and local history under our own imprint:

Population, economy and family structure in Hertfordshire in 1851
Volume 1: The Berkhamsted region; *Nigel Goose*
ISBN 0900458-73-9, 416 pages, paperback, £14.95
Volume 2: St Albans and its region; *Nigel Goose*
ISBN 0 900458 83 6, paper back, 704 pages £19.95
ISBN 0 900458 84 4, hard back, 704 pages £35

Studies in Regional and Local History
Volume 1: A Hertfordshire demesne of Westminster Abbey: profits, productivity and weather; *Dr Derek Vincent Stern; edited and with an introduction by Christopher Thornton.*
ISBN 0 900458 92 5, 320 pp, hard back, £29.99
Volume 2: From Hellgill to Bridge End: aspects of economic and social change in the Upper Eden Valley circa 1840-1895; *Margaret Shepherd.* ISBN 1-902806-27-1, hard back, #35. *Forthcoming.*

The University of Hertfordshire Press
University of Hertfordshire, College Lane, Hatfield, Hertfordshire AL10 9AD, UK
Tel: + 44 707 284681 Fax: + 44 707-284666 Internet: UHPress@herts.ac.uk
Web address: http://www.herts.ac.uk/ UHPress/